Smart, Eric

Community Builders Handbook Series

RECREATIONAL DEVELOPMENT HANDBOOK

Sponsored by the
Executive Group
of the
Recreational Development Council
of
ULI–the Urban Land Institute
1981

ULI–the Urban Land Institute, Washington, D.C.

About ULI–the Urban Land Institute

ULI–the Urban Land Institute is an independent, nonprofit research and educational organization incorporated in 1936 to improve the quality and standards of land use and development.

The Institute is committed to conducting practical research in the various fields of real estate knowledge; identifying and interpreting land use trends in relation to the changing economic, social, and civic needs of the people; and disseminating pertinent information leading to the orderly and more efficient use and development of land.

ULI receives its financial support from membership dues, sale of publications, and contributions for research and panel services.

Ronald R. Rumbaugh
Executive Vice President

ULI Staff for Recreational Development Handbook

Senior Director, Publications	Frank H. Spink, Jr.
Managing Editor	J. Eric Smart
Manuscript Editor	Nancy H. Stewart
Production Manager	Robert L. Helms
Production Assistant	Regina P. Agricola
Artist	Silvia de Uribe
Graphic Consultant	Ken Fuller
Administrative Assistant	Jane Lynas

Fifth book in a new series of publications based on the philosophy of The Community Builders Handbook
First Edition and First Printing 1947
Revised Printing 1948
Second or J. C. Nichols Memorial Edition and Second Revised Printing 1950
Third or The Members Edition and Third Revised Printing 1954
Fourth Revised Printing 1956
Fourth or The Executive Edition and Fifth Revised Printing 1960
Sixth Printing 1965
Fifth or Anniversary Edition and Seventh Revised Printing 1968

Other books in the series:
Industrial Development Handbook, 1975
Shopping Center Development Handbook, 1977
Residential Development Handbook, 1978
Downtown Development Handbook, 1980
Recommended bibliographic listing:
Urban Land Institute, *Recreational Development Handbook*.
Washington: Urban Land Institute, 1981.
ULI Catalog Number R-13

1090 Vermont Avenue, N.W.
Washington, D.C. 20005

Second Printing, 1989

International Standard Book Number 0-87420-599-9
Library of Congress Card Catalog Number 81-51294

Printed in the United States of America

Author

J. Eric Smart, associate, publications division, Urban Land Institute

Contributing Authors

John A. Casazza, associate, publications division, Urban Land Institute
Joseph D. Steller, Jr., senior associate for education, Urban Land Institute
Douglas M. Wrenn, associate, publications division, Urban Land Institute
Nancy Nye, 1979 summer intern, Urban Land Institute

with
The Recreational Development Council
of the
Urban Land Institute

Acknowledgments

This book resulted from a long process of gathering materials from a variety of experienced persons under the guidance of ULI's Recreational Development Council. These acknowledgments properly begin with past council Chairmen Ronald Campbell and Richard Miller and present Chairman Erling Speer, who over their terms of office coordinated the focus of the council from early conceptualizing, to putting thoughts down on paper, to reviewing the produced manuscripts. More particularly, it was Phil Stukin, Chairman of the Council's Handbook Steering Committee, and committee members Colin Cameron, Jack Mathis, Dick McElyea, and David Pearson, who actually got the job done.

Individual contributors of special note include council members John Adams, Joe Brooke, Wendell Brooks, David Brown, Patty Doyle, Ron Duplanty, Rollie Herberg, Tom Morrish, Kingsbury Pitcher, William Reilly, and James Rester. Also essential at various stages was the involvement of staff from Amfac, Economic Research Associates, Gus Novotny Associates, Laventhol and Horwath, Sasaki Associates, Inc., and Vail Associates, to mention only a few.

Finally, credit must be given ULI staff: Joe Steller for initially overseeing the project and for his case study work; Nancy Nye for her research regarding the introduction and the chapter on commercial recreation; John Casazza and Doug Wrenn for case study contributions; Libby Howland for identifying references; and Nadine Huff, Paul O'Mara, and Karen Rice for their support along the way.

To the many people who helped, thank you.

Eric Smart

About ULI Councils

Within the Urban Land Institute there are nine councils: Urban Development/Mixed-Use, Commercial and Retail Development, Industrial and Office Park Development, New Communities and Large-Scale Development, Residential Development, Recreational Development, Federal Policy, Development Policies and Regulations, and Development Systems and Services Councils. Each council is composed of 50 active members drawn from the ULI Membership. Council appointment is based on knowledge, experience, and a willingness to share. Developers, consultants, public officials, and academicians are included on each of the councils to provide a broad perspective and to encourage interaction among various disciplines.

Executive Group of the Recreational Development Council 1978–1981

Chairmen:

Erling D. Speer (1980–81)
President
Environmental Ventures, Inc.
Stuart, Florida

Richard W. Miller (1978–80)
Senior Vice President
The Penn Central Corporation
New York

Ronald L. Campbell (1977–78)
Executive Vice President
David D. Bohannon Organization
San Mateo, California

Vice Chairmen:

Colin C. Cameron
Chairman and Chief Executive Officer
Kapalua Land Company, Ltd.
Kahului, Maui, Hawaii

Neil Crawford
President
Neil Crawford Associates
Weston, Connecticut

William E. Finley
President
The Bankers Land Company
Palm Beach Gardens, Florida

Reverdy Johnson, Esq.
Vice Chairman
Pettit & Martin
San Francisco

Adam Krivatsy
President
HKS Associates
San Francisco

J. Richard McElyea
Senior Vice President
Economics Research Associates
San Francisco

David H. Pearson
President
Pearson, Sandor Associates
Coral Gables, Florida

Nelson Schwab III
Vice President
Taft Broadcasting Company
Cincinnati

Edward D. Stone, Jr.
President
Edward D. Stone, Jr., & Associates
Fort Lauderdale, Florida

Philip S. Stukin
President
Urban Projects, Inc.
Los Angeles

John M. Adams	President Blue Ridge Real Estate Company Blakeslee, Pennsylvania
Thomas M. Bailey, Jr.	Director Community Development (1979) City of Kissimmee Kissimmee, Florida
Richard M. Bauer	Director of Planning New Castle County Department of Planning Newark, Delaware
Fredric A. Benedict	President Benedict-Mularz Associates Aspen, Colorado
Joseph A. Brooke, Jr.	President Treasure Lake Companies/Urban Systems Development Company Coral Springs, Florida
Wendell F. Brooks, Jr.	Managing Director Chaney Brooks & Company Honolulu
Brent W. Brown	Director of Community Relations Arizona State University Tempe, Arizona
David L. Brown	President Recreation Consultants Incorporated Santa Clara, California
Carl Burlingame	Editor and Publisher The CHB Company Los Altos, California
Steven L. Charlton	President A-T-O Properties, Inc. Willoughby, Ohio
William L. Cohill	Project Manager Florida Land Company (1979) Smyrna Beach, Florida
Robert H. Dedman	Chairman of the Board Club Corporation of America Dallas
Patricia E. Doyle	Owner Patty Doyle Public Relations Fort Lauderdale, Florida
Franklin G. Drake	President Donald M. Drake Company Portland, Oregon
Ronald K. Duplanty	President Lakeway Company Austin
Scott Durdan	Professor Portland State University Portland, Oregon
William R. Eager	President TDA, Inc. Seattle
E. Llwyd Ecclestone, Jr.	President National Investment Company West Palm Beach, Florida
Stanley A. Eisner	Director of Planning City of Oxnard Oxnard, California
David G. Ellsworth	Partner Memel, Jacobs, Pierno & Gersh Los Angeles
Grover G. Ericksen	President Caldwell Lee Development Company Ft. Myers Beach, Florida
Charles E. Fraser	Chairman Sea Pines Plantation Company Hilton Head Island, South Carolina
C. W. Frye, Jr.	Associate Rockefeller Family & Associates New York
Allen Gerstenberger	Owner Gerstenberger Associates Vail, Colorado
Samuel L. Hall	Chief, Division of Urban Programs Heritage, Conservation and Recreation Service U.S. Department of the Interior Washington, D.C.
Lee E. Ham	President Wilsey & Ham Foster City, California

Byron R. Hanke
President
Bryon R. Hanke Associates
Chevy Chase, Maryland

Emil A. Hanslin
Chairman
Emil Hanslin Associates, Inc.
Grantham, New Hampshire

Erik L. Hansen
Manager
Peat, Marwick, Mitchell & Company
Los Angeles

R. L. Herberg
President
Hawaiiana Investment Company, Inc.
Honolulu

Cyril C. Herrmann
Vice President
Arthur D. Little, Inc.
San Francisco

Sheridan C. F. Ing
President
Sheridan Ing Corporation
Honolulu

Morris Janowitz*
Distinguished Service Professor
University of Chicago
Chicago

Robert Trent Jones, Jr.
President
Robert Trent Jones II
Palo Alto, California

Ryland Kelley
President
Hare, Brewer, & Kelley, Inc.
Palo Alto, California

John W. Kessler
President
John W. Kessler Company
Columbus, Ohio

Arthur M. King
President
King Investment Company
Kansas City, Missouri

Terrill Knight
Director
Department of Community Development
Eagle County
Eagle, Colorado

Walter A. Koelbel
President
Koelbel and Company
Denver

Fred P. Kuentz
Del E. Webb Corporation
Phoenix

Benjamin T. Lake II
President
Olin-American, Inc.
Pleasant Hill, California

Benjamin V. Lambert
President and CEO
Eastdil Realty, Inc.
New York

John B. Matheney
Director
City-County Planning Commission of Warren County
Bowling Green, Kentucky

John H. Mathis, Jr.
President
Team Plan, Inc.
Palm Beach, Florida

John W. McGrath
Vice President, Development
Associated Inns & Restaurants Company of America
Denver

Brian A. McLaughlin
Executive Vice President
Brian A. McLaughlin Company, Inc.
Hilton Head Island, South Carolina

William A. Mettler
Planning Director
City of Williamsburg
Williamsburg, Virginia

Charles B. Moffett
Vice President
The First National Bank of Chicago
Chicago

John W. Morgan
Director
The Development Group
Columbia, South Carolina

Thomas M. Morrish
President
Village Resorts, Inc.
Lafayette, California

Hunter Moss**
Board Chairman
The Moss/Fleming Company
Boca Raton, Florida

Richard Norman
President
All-American Realty Company, Inc.
Wayne, New Jersey

Charles E. O'Keefe
Architect
Williams & Works, Inc.
Grand Rapids, Michigan

Lewis F. Payne, Jr.
President
Wintergreen
Wintergreen, Virginia

Kingsbury Pitcher
President
Lake Peak Corporation
Santa Fe

George W. Reeve
Executive Vice President
Del E. Webb Corporation
Phoenix

William K. Reilly***
President
The Conservation Foundation
Washington. D.C.

James M. Rester
President and General Manager
Amelia Plantation Company
Amelia Island, Florida

William B. Rick
President
Rick Engineering Company
San Diego

Eugene I. Ross
Senior Vice President
Berger Realty Group
Chicago

Peter M. Ryan
Vice President
The Chase Manhattan Bank
New York

Peter A. Sanborn
Executive Vice President
Michael-Sellers Advertising
San Francisco

Federico F. Sanchez
President
Federico F. Sanchez & Company
Hato Rey, Puerto Rico

Thomas L. Sandor
Director, Hotels and Tourism
Peat, Marwick, Mitchell & Company
Philadelphia

Don J. Saylor
Deputy City Manager
City of Las Vegas
Las Vegas

Peter W. Seibert
General Partner
Snow Basin, Ltd.
Huntsville, Utah

Jack A. Shaffer
Senior Vice President
Sonnenblick-Goldman Corp.
New York

Robert C. Speicher
President
Crow-Terwilliger & Speicher
West Palm Beach, Florida

Frank P. Stanek
Vice President
Tokyo Disneyland Administration
WED Enterprises
Glendale, California

Willard J. Stluka
Director, Planning and Development
The Estate of James Campbell
Honolulu

Lovick P. Suddath
President
Foxfire Inn & Country Club
Pinehurst, North Carolina

Dudley S. Taft
President
Taft Broadcasting Company
Cincinnati

Ronald J. Terwilliger
President
Crow-Terwilliger Company
Atlanta

Peter Walker
Chairman
Department of Landscape Architecture
Harvard University
Cambridge, Massachusetts

Neal G. Walton
Assistant City Manager, Community Development
South Lake Tahoe, California

David C. Wheatley
Vice President, Planning and Design
Centex Homes Corporation
Dallas

Wayne R. Williams
Chairman of the Board
Smith & Welhams
South Pasadena, California

Pete Wilson***
Mayor
City of San Diego
San Diego

*ULI Fellow **Past President of ULI ***ULI Advisory Member

Contents

1. Introduction 1

Recreational Development Types 1
- Resort/Residential Communities 1
- Theme Parks 3
- Commercial Recreation 3
- Supplemental Recreation 3

Recreational Demand 4
- Economic Forces 4
- Psychological Elements 8

Historic Patterns 10
- Land Sales and Government Control 13
- Recent Trends 15

General Issues 18
- High Risk 18
- Seasonal Effects 19
- Community Impacts 19
- Lot Sales 20
- Regulation 21
- Specialized Markets 22
- Opportunities by Income 22

2. Resort/Residential Communities 25

General Characteristics 25
- Commercial Versus Resort Hotel 25
- Second Homes 27
- Characteristics 28
- Recreational Vehicle Sites 29
- Types of Consumer Ownership 30
- Location 32

Development Process 33
- Predevelopment Planning 33
- Development Strategy 40
- Development Team 41
- Feasibility and Planning 42
- Financing 45
- Approval Process 48
- Overall Plan 50
- Marketing 54
- Management and Operation 57

Considerations by Special Type 60
- The Retirement Community 60
- Recreational Vehicle Parks 62
- Conference Centers and Recreational Development 65
- Contingencies and Workouts 68
- Rehabilitation 69

Coastal Projects 70
- Amelia Island Plantation, Amelia Island, Florida 70
- The Homestead, Glen Arbor, Michigan 76
- Sea Pines Plantation, Hilton Head Island, South Carolina 80
- Kiawah Island, South Carolina 82

Hawaiian Island Projects: Maui 87
Kaanapali Beach Resort 88
Whalers Village, Kaanapali Beach 92
The Whaler, Kaanapali Beach 93
Kapalua 95
Wailea 98
Mountain Projects 101
Sunriver, Sunriver, Oregon 101
Lakeridge, Torrington, Connecticut 111
Snowmass, Colorado 115
Beaver Creek, Colorado 117
Jack Frost Mountain, Poconos, Pennsylvania 120
Created Amenity Projects 123
Boca West, Palm Beach County, Florida 123
The Pointe, Bloomington, Indiana 129
Lake Arrowhead, Georgia 133
Treasure Lake, Clearfield County, Pennsylvania 135
Foxcross, Mariner Sands, Florida 137
Recreational Vehicle Project 140
Marina Village Campground, Trinity County, Texas 140
Workouts 145
The Lakeland Village Workout, South Lake Tahoe, California 145
A Workout Strategy 147
The Mariner Sands Turnaround, Stuart, Florida 148
The Wintergreen Turnaround, Wintergreen, Virginia 149

3. Theme Parks 153

Form and Use 154
Types and Locations 155
Mini-Theme Parks 155
Major Park Sites 156
Sites for Smaller Attractions 157
Special Issues 158
Design Constraints 158
Local Impact 160
Marketing Strategy 160
Financial Aspects 161
The Bottom Line 162
Projects 164
Kings Island, Cincinnati, Ohio 164
The Old Country, Virginia 168
Wet 'n Wild, Orlando, Florida 172

4. Commercial Recreation 175

Locational Characteristics 176
Special Issues 176
Risks 176
The Business Cycle 177
Conservative Forecasting 177
Management 178
Competition 178
Development Types: Facts and Strategies 179
Bowling 180

Roller Skating Rinks ... 182
Racquetball Courts ... 184
Health Clubs ... 187
Dinner Theaters ... 188
Golf Driving Ranges ... 190
Miniature Golf ... 192
Arcades ... 194
Family Recreational Centers ... 194
Scale Grand Prix Tracks ... 194
Go-Cart Tracks ... 195

5. Supplemental Recreation ... 197
Primary Residential ... 198
Heritage Hills, Somers, New York ... 200
The Rotonda, McLean, Virginia ... 202
Sunpointe, Tucson, Arizona ... 204
Commercial/Retail ... 205
Specialty Shopping Centers ... 205
The Cascades, Ocala, Florida ... 207
Trolley Square, Salt Lake City, Utah ... 210
Industrial/Business Parks ... 211
Inverness, Englewood, Colorado ... 212
Mixed-Use Development ... 215
The Galleria, Houston, Texas ... 215

6. Emerging Trends ... 217
Demand ... 218
Location ... 219
Energy and Mobility ... 220
Finance and Management ... 222
Marketing ... 223
Environment ... 224
Government's Role ... 224
The Recreational Development Industry ... 226

Appendices ... 229
A. Selected References and Information Sources ... 231
B. Lakeridge Regulations ... 233
C. Sunriver Design Committee Rules ... 235
D. Bylaws for Amelia Island Plantation Club ... 238
E. Master Deed, Loggers Run Condominium Project, The Homestead ... 239
F. Lakeridge, Inc., Purchase Agreement ... 241
G. Amelia Island Plantation, Villa Owner's Rental Agreement ... 242
H. Model Timeshare Ownership Act ... 244
I. Rules and Regulations, Marina Village Camping Club, Inc. ... 248
J. Preparing a Property Report ... 250
K. Sample Questions in a Second-Home Property Buyers' Guide ... 250
L. Town of Snowmass: Village Master Plan ... 251
M. Example of Facility Standards Per Participant ... 253
N. Recommendations for Developing a Major Ski Project in the Rocky Mountains ... 253

Index ... 254

List of Illustrations

		Page
1- 1	Second home on rural lot	2
1- 2	Facilities adjacent to ski slope	2
1- 3	Dwelling units and amenity orientation	2
1- 4	Water attraction	3
1- 5	Wave pool	3
1- 6	Atrium in office building	4
1- 7	Amenities in residential project	4
1- 8	Destination resort, Walt Disney World	5
1- 9	Table—participation in outdoor recreation	6
1- 10	Road travel	7
1- 11	Air travel	7
1- 12	Retirement communities as country clubs	8
1- 13	Escape to isolated, natural settings	9
1- 14	Urban diversions at resort areas	9
1- 15	Golf and the vacation environment	9
1- 16	Modern conveniences and leisure living	10
1- 17	Highlighting activities in advertising	10
1- 18	Railroad company hotel, Banff Springs	11
1- 19	Historic landmark, Hotel Del Coronado	12
1- 20	Scenic highway travel	13
1- 21	Open space and lot sales	14
1- 22	Beachfront high-rise condominiums	15
1- 23	Fuel pumps, Lakeridge	15
1- 24	Alai Kai II timeshare units	16
1- 25	Spanish theme, Kings Island	17
1- 26	Thrill rides at theme parks	17
1- 27	Site plan, Northstar at Tahoe	18
1- 28	Encouraging year-long facility use	19
1- 29	Competing land uses, Lake Tahoe	20
1- 30	Map of conservation and development values	21
1- 31	Beachfront lots, Sea Pines Plantation	21
1- 32	Miami Beach	22
1- 33	Campground	22
1- 34	Motel	22
1- 35	The experience of fishing	23
2- 1	Resort and convention hotel	26
2- 2	Do-it-yourself vacation retreat	27
2- 3	Attached units	28
2- 4	Custom built home	28
2- 5	Campground advertisement	29
2- 6	Capri-by-the-Sea	30
2- 7	Interval ownership, Shell Island Beach Club	31
2- 8	Water-based destination, Sea Pines	32
2- 9	Hawaiian view, Kapalua Bay Hotel	34
2- 10	Natural and manmade amenities	35
2- 11	Security as principal buyer concern	36
2- 12	Simultaneous construction for economy	37
2- 13	Land uses adapted to landscape	38
2- 14	Views in resort residential planning	39
2- 15	Site plan, The Wilderness	40
2- 16	Operating facilities for profit	41
2- 17	Experienced development team	42
2- 18	Owner age, Hilton Head Island	43
2- 19	Assessing highest land use, beachfront	43
2- 20	Clarifying development concepts	44
2- 21	Marketing a plan	45
2- 22	Facilities, poorly understood economics	47
2- 23	Determining amenity value	47
2- 24	Provision for resort maintenance	47
2- 25	Development process flow chart, Beaver Creek	48
2- 26	Protecting projects with dune preservation	49
2- 27	Employee housing integrated into resort	49
2- 28	Phased development, Moss Creek Plantation	51
2- 29	Housing type plan study	51
2- 30	Narrow street maximizes lot area	52
2- 31	"Hammerhead" street layout, The Landings	52
2- 32	"Double T" road system, Sea Pines	53
2- 33	The Hammocks	53
2- 34	New construction, Sea Pines	54
2- 35	Utility building	54
2- 36	Resort logo, Kapalua	54
2- 37	Signage	55
2- 38	Sales and reception center	55
2- 39	Lodging, resort/residential community	56
2- 40	Recreational community activity	56
2- 41	Tennis tournament, Amelia Island Plantation	57
2- 42	Facility maintenance	58
2- 43	Security, Rossmoor Leisure World	61
2- 44	Rossmoor promotion	61
2- 45	Recreational vehicle park	62
2- 46	Destination park amenity	63
2- 47	Recreational vehicle storage	64
2- 48	Resort and conference hotel, The Broadmoor	65
2- 49	Golf clubhouse, Silverado	67
2- 50	Conference facilities, Silverado	67
2- 51	Site plan, Mountain Bell Training and Education Center	68
2- 52	Renovated resort hotel, The Ahwahnee	69
2- 53	Landscaped entrance, Amelia Island Plantation	70
2- 54	Water and open space for visual effect	70
2- 55	Beach and dunes, Amelia Island	71
2- 56	Central lodging, Amelia Island Inn	72
2- 57	Condominiums and private pool	72
2- 58	Townhouses, Amelia Island Plantation	72
2- 59	Site plan, Amelia Island Plantation	73
2- 60	Park overlooking marsh	74
2- 61	Beach club with pool	74
2- 62	Lakeshore and escarpment, The Homestead	76
2- 63	Site plan, The Homestead	77
2- 64	Units on steep slopes	78
2- 65	Trail network	78
2- 66	Harbour Town	80
2- 67	Natural style of architecture	80
2- 68	Treehouse design solution	81
2- 69	South Beach, Sea Pines	81
2- 70	Nature preserve	81
2- 71	Resort/residential development, Kiawah Island	82
2- 72	Coastal sea islands	83
2- 73	Site plan, Kiawah Island first phase	84
2- 74	Tennis as major attraction	85
2- 75	Resort specialty shops, Kiawah Island	86
2- 76	Map of Hawaii	87
2- 77	Sheraton Maui Hotel, Kaanapali Beach Resort	88
2- 78	Oceanfront, Kaanapali Beach	89
2- 79	Water-oriented activities	90
2- 80	Internal transportation	90
2- 81	Site plan, Kaanapali Beach Resort	90
2- 82	Whaling industry theme at shopping complex	92
2- 83	Site plan, Whalers Village	92
2- 84	Whalers Village Museum and Shopping Complex	92
2- 85	Twin towers of The Whaler	93
2- 86	Oceanfront and golf condominiums, Kapalua	95
2- 87	Development following natural contours	96
2- 88	Ocean, slope, and fairways for dramatic vistas	96
2- 89	Kapalua Bay Hotel	96
2- 90	Site plan, Kapalua	97
2- 91	Wailea Beach Hotel	98
2- 92	Resort tennis club with tournament court	99
2- 93	Landscaping, Wailea	99
2- 94	Tennis clubhouse	100
2- 95	National forest as neighbor, Sunriver	101
2- 96	Aerial view, Sunriver	102

2- 97 Lodge focus of activities 103
2- 98 Site plan, Sunriver 105
2- 99 Unit appearance reviewed by design committee 106
2-100 Recreational activity near lodge 106
2-101 Condominiums in rental program 109
2-102 Clustered development 110
2-103 Shopping complex, Sunriver 110
2-104 Preserving vegetation 111
2-105 Site plan, Lakeridge 112
2-106 Activity center 113
2-107 Signage, Lakeridge 114
2-108 Villas under construction at Snowmass 115
2-109 Site plan for The Snowmass Club 115
2-110 Site plan, hillside townhouses, Snowmass 116
2-111 Access to amenity gives premium value 117
2-112 Ski runs and golf course, Beaver Creek 118
2-113 Blended architectural style, Beaver Creek 119
2-114 Aerial view, Jack Frost Mountain 120
2-115 Helicopter in lift construction 121
2-116 Lodge, Jack Frost Mountain 122
2-117 Manmade snow 122
2-118 Fairways and lakes 123
2-119 Map locating Boca West 123
2-120 Site plan, residential cluster, Boca West 124
2-121 Tennis courts and pools as amenities 125
2-122 Townhouses around courtyard 125
2-123 Site plan, mid-rise units, Boca West 126
2-124 Real estate promotion, Boca West 126
2-125 Construction of mid-rise units 127
2-126 Main entrance, Boca West 128
2-127 Clustered units with open space 129
2-128 Site plan, The Pointe 130
2-129 Lake or golf views from units 131
2-130 Natural wood exteriors 131
2-131 Gatehouse for security, The Pointe 132
2-132 Manmade lake, clubhouse, Lake Arrowhead 133
2-133 Golf course through mountainous terrain 134
2-134 Condominiums for resort rental 134
2-135 Map of Treasure Lake 135
2-136 Site plan, Mariner Sands 137
2-137 Attached units, Foxcross 138
2-138 Site plan, Foxcross 138
2-139 Marketing of project within community 139
2-140 Campsites, Marina Village 140
2-141 Location map, Marina Village 141
2-142 Security at campground entrance 141
2-143 Site plan, Marina Village 141
2-144 Community center 142
2-145 Separate youth center 143
2-146 Comfort station for campsites 143
2-143 View from lake, Lakeland Village 145
2-148 Townhouse units, Lakeland Village 146
2-149 Country club and cottages, Mariner Sands 148
2-150 Single-family home, Mariner Sands 148
2-151 Development near ski slopes, Wintergreen 149
2-152 Use of natural materials 150
2-153 Mountain top setting for summer activities 151
3- 1 Theme areas, Walt Disney World 154
3- 2 Theme park rides 155
3- 3 Sketches of theme park activities 156
3- 4 Prime park site, Great America 157
3- 5 Water theme 158
3- 6 Specialty play park, Sesame Place 159
3- 7 Creating interesting amusements 161
3- 8 International Street, Canada's Wonderland 162
3- 9 Early landscaping for established appearance 163
3- 10 Multiple facilities, Kings Island 164
3- 11 Nighttime at a theme park 165
3- 12 Adding new dimensions to older rides 165
3- 13 Adventurous rides as main attraction 165
3- 14 Large rides use substantial space 166
3- 15 Sports attractions to promote theme park 166
3- 16 Theme architecture, The Old Country 168
3- 17 Site plan, The Old Country 169
3- 18 Replica train, transportation at theme park 170
3- 19 Site plan, German Village, The Old Country 171
3- 20 Aquatic facilities and food service 172
3- 21 Cleanliness at park, River Country 172
3- 22 Aerial view, Wet 'n Wild 173
3- 23 Water slide, Wet 'n Wild 174
4- 1 Baseball stadium 176
4- 2 Roller skating 176
4- 3 Commercial locations for recreation 176
4- 4 Skateboard park 177
4- 5 Municipal facility urban recreation center 178
4- 6 Management post at entrance to sports club 178
4- 7 Players in bowling league 179
4- 8 Plan of bowling center 180
4- 9 Lounge area at sports facility 184
4- 10 Racquetball instruction 185
4- 11 Parking at urban sports facility 187
4- 12 Chanhassen Dinner Theaters 189
4- 13 All-season golf driving range 191
4- 14 Miniature golf course 192
4- 15 Scale Grand Prix Track 195
5- 1 Site plan, recreation center 198
5- 2 Amenities used for view orientations 198
5- 3 Open space, Portola Valley 199
5- 4 Tennis shelter and play lot 199
5- 5 Indoor lounge at residential project 199
5- 6 Multipurpose clubhouse, Heritage Hills 200
5- 7 Homes along walkways 201
5- 8 Homes grouped around paved court 201
5- 9 Site plan, The Rotonda 202
5- 10 Swimming pool complex 203
5- 11 Site plan, Sunpointe 204
5- 12 Interior view, Eaton Centre 205
5- 13 Window shopping and pedestrian comforts 206
5- 14 Food service at specialty center 206
5- 15 Floor plans, The Cascades 207
5- 16 Floral garden at specialty complex 208
5- 17 Waterfall as part of setting 208
5- 18 Section elevation, The Cascades 209
5- 19 Artifacts related to theme, Trolley Square 210
5- 20 Golf, Arvida Park of Commerce 211
5- 21 Preservation of natural features, Inverness 212
5- 22 Golf course as private open space 212
5- 23 Site plan, Inverness 213
5- 24 Stormwater retention ponds 214
5- 25 Signage as part of overall development plan 214
5- 26 Mixed-use complex, The Galleria 215
5- 27 Skating rink in shopping mall 215
6- 1 Retirement market 218
6- 2 Family entertainment center, Pyramid Place 219
6- 3 San Diego 220
6- 4 Destination resort—Waikiki Beach 221
6- 5 Typical second home convenient to urban area 221
6- 6 Cruise ship 222
6- 7 Quality amenity equals consumer value 223
6- 8 Merchandising a full lifestyle 224
6- 9 Preserving a unique environment 225
6- 10 Scale Grand Prix car 226
6- 11 Timeshare conversion, Jackson Court 226
6- 12 Rendering of Epcot Center, Walt Disney World 226

A Brief History of the Community Builders Handbook Series

The Community Builders Handbook Series came into being when the *Industrial Development Handbook* was published in 1975. This new series expands and replaces *The Community Builders Handbook*, first published in 1947.

The objective of the original handbook was to share the experience and knowledge of developers and to encourage the improvement of land use and development practices. The handbook was sponsored by the Community Builders Council (now the Residential Council), which had been formed in 1944. The first edition contained 205 pages and was sparsely illustrated, but it was a major accomplishment since, for the first time, a book was made available which described the development of residential communities and shopping centers.

The second edition, the J. C. Nichols Memorial Edition, was published in 1950. It incorporated a modest revision and updating of the original text. In 1954, the third or Members Edition, with 315 pages, significantly expanded the scope of the work. The fourth or Executive Edition of 1960 continued this expansion in response to the increasing complexity of development practices. By this time, the handbook had grown to 476 pages, but it continued to focus on residential and shopping center development. The fifth or Anniversary Edition was published in 1968. The handbook had now grown to 526 pages and had been broadened once more in coverage. In addition to sections on residential and shopping center development, new material discussing a variety of special types of land development was included. Also added was a section on industrial development, drawing on the experience of ULI's Industrial Council, which had been formed in 1951. The Industrial Council had sponsored other ULI publications but was now represented for the first time in the handbook.

The Community Builders Handbook became widely recognized as a major reference source and textbook on land use and development practice based on the practical experience and accumulated knowledge of leading practitioners in the field. In 1965, as work on the 1968 edition was beginning, ULI was growing rapidly in membership and in areas of interest. The development industry was maturing and new directions for the Institute were being examined. By 1970, a decision had been made to publish future editions of *The Community Builders Handbook* in separate volumes, in order to provide the expanded and more comprehensive coverage not possible in a single text.

In 1972, the three original councils of the Institute—the Community Builders, Central City, and Industrial Councils—were reorganized into six councils in order to accommodate the new diversity in development activities and ULI's membership. Several members of the Community Builders Council who were active in residential development, primarily second homes, formed the nucleus of the Recreational Development Council under whose aegis this volume has been developed. When the ULI council structure was modified again in 1979, expanding it into nine councils, the Recreational Development Council's focus was enlarged to include resort development, retirement communities, all types of commercial recreational facilities, theme parks, mobile home/recreational vehicle parks, and campgrounds. The handbook reflects this variety of perspectives on recreational development.

The *Recreational Development Handbook* is the fifth volume of the new series, following the *Industrial Development Handbook* (1975), the *Shopping Center Development Handbook* (1977), the *Residential Development Handbook* (1978), and the *Downtown Development Handbook* (1980). Other volumes, each focusing on a specific land use type, will be added to the series in the future.

Frank H. Spink, Jr.
Managing Editor
Community Builders Handbook Series

Foreword

The *Recreational Development Handbook* clearly demonstrates the expanded focus of ULI through its nine councils. Until the Recreational Development Council was established, resort, second-home, and retirement communities were treated only as specialized forms of residential development. Recreational amenities were largely thought of as adjuncts to other forms of development and not as development types in and of themselves. The majority of the members on the Community Builders Council, under whose umbrella of interests recreational development was included, were essentially suburban residential developers and builders, a few of whom began to expand into recreational development as markets for this kind of development grew rapidly in the late 1950s and 1960s. When the Recreational Development Council was formed in 1972, it had few members with any experience outside of second-home development. In 1978, after several years of building council membership and leadership, the council was prepared to undertake the task of producing a handbook on recreational development for the Community Builders Handbook Series.

The term "recreational development" is used in this handbook in its broadest context, that is, as it relates to real estate activity. The objective of the handbook is to provide information on development practices for a diversity of recreational developments—major destination resorts, second-home projects built around natural or manmade amenities, and commercial recreational facilities ranging from those on the grand scale of a major theme park down to the small freestanding racquet club or miniature golf course. As a result, the book's structure is somewhat different from its predecessors in the series. Variations in both concept and development practice of different types of recreational projects have made it impossible to discuss recreational development as a single topic divided into various specialized types, as has been the format of other books in the series. Therefore, broad groupings of recreational types have been treated somewhat independently of each other.

Defining the objectives of the handbook, preparing an outline, and producing the final volume required a substantial commitment of time and effort over 3 years from the Recreational Development Council; this included the inspired attention of past council chairmen, David Sawyer, Ronald L. Campbell, and Richard W. Miller. An initial outline was considered by the council in the spring of 1978. By the fall of 1978, a steering committee composed of J. Richard McElyea, Colin C. Cameron, John H. Mathis, Jr., and David H. Pearson, and chaired by Philip S. Stukin, had been formed within the council to establish a program of work that would develop materials needed for the handbook. By the spring of 1978, a much expanded outline had been organized and ULI staff members had been assigned.

The council developed a series of work papers to be used by staff authors on the draft manuscript. Most of the case studies needed for the book had been researched when the Institute held its meeting in Hawaii in the spring of 1980. Members of the Recreational Development Council were asked to review pieces of the handbook as they were developed, and the full draft manuscript was submitted to the handbook steering committee in August 1980 for detailed review and comment. This was followed by the final rewriting, editing, and production.

Thus, many members of the council contributed in varying degrees to the development of the manuscript. It draws heavily on the knowledge and experience of individual council members as well as on their access to others outside the council when further specialized information was needed.

The long lead time required to complete the handbook could have been shortened had we relied on the skills and judgment of fewer individuals. However, this volume, as does each book in the ULI Community Builders Handbook Series, draws its strength from the breadth of experience, ideas, and judgment offered by a large and highly diversified group of developers, consultants, public officials, and others who constitute the council. We of the Recreational Development Council offer this volume of the Community Builders Handbook Series in the hope that it will provide insights into and an understanding of the nature and scope of recreational development activities. In a nation as affluent as the United States, recreation is desired and pursued by the majority of the population and is an integral part of the changing economy. Because recreational development occurs to a great extent in areas of natural beauty and fragile environments, it requires sensitive and skillful direction if it is to enhance rather than damage the very features that attract development. We believe this handbook provides guidance for development which is responsive to increasingly specialized markets, and in doing so, sets a standard by which future development activity can be measured.

Erling D. Speer
Chairman
Recreational Development Council
1980–1981

1.
Introduction

Recreational Development Types

This handbook focuses on real estate development which is distinguished by recreational elements that provide income and add value to associated real estate. It is designed to be a how-to guide for those interested in one or more of the many aspects of this type of development.

The subject is discussed both in a general sense and by specific development type. In many respects, it is difficult to formulate a precise and definite typology for recreational development because of countless regional, socioeconomic, consumer, and developer variations affecting the nature and specific elements of such development. Nevertheless, the following development types have been identified in organizing the handbook.

Resort/Residential Communities

Resorts are short-term destinations which provide an assortment of recreational activities, as well as lodging, dining, and entertainment services, in settings ranging from opulent to primitive. They are aimed at supplying an infinite variety of recreational experiences and include a host of vacation/business destinations, varying from waterside hotels and motels to mountain ranches and health spas. Whether large or small in scale, comprehensively planned or haphazardly built, resorts are established around a primary and usually natural recreational attraction, a factor which has traditionally made them seasonal in their popularity. More successful resorts enjoy substantial year-long operation and often have real estate sales programs associated with them, eventually becoming combined resort, second-home communities.

1-1 Individually built second homes on lots in rural areas formed the most common types of recreational communities developed in the 1960s and early 1970s.

1-2 Proximity to a specific recreational opportunity, such as skiing facilities, gives premium value to lodgings and services developed in more dense arrangements.

1-3 Resort/residential communities may include a combination of dwelling unit types oriented toward natural and manmade recreational amenities.

Recreational residential communities are planned second-home developments which exhibit many of the characteristics and much of the appeal of primary-home planned unit developments (PUDs), such as high standards of land use planning, architectural design, and private community amenities. In fact, an often standard trend of a successful second-home development is for its impermanent residents to become increasingly permanent until it has evolved into a retirement or other primary, year-round community after 15 to 20 years.

The birth and growth of a recreational community are based on a distinctive recreational attraction, whether it be a natural amenity such as water, topography, or climate; a manmade attraction such as a golf course or ski lift; a subdivision of rural plots of land developed for second-home use; or, as often is the case, a combination of various amenities. One amenity may cause the outgrowth of another. For example, second-home developments frequently spring up close to an existing recreational resort area.

Theme Parks

The theme park is a manmade recreational attraction whose emphasis on fantasy creates special design considerations and the need for a variety of capital investments. The classic example is the large-scale amusement park of which Disneyworld is the grandest illustration. However, small-scale specialty centers (such as a water activity park) may also qualify as thematic attractions in which a special environment and atmosphere have been created.

Commercial Recreation

Commercial recreation is urban in nature. It is not a destination in itself, but rather an attraction within an already existing market area. Commercial recreation relates directly to an already established market population, either permanent or transient, and abounds in popular resort areas. It can have a passive (spectator) or active (participant) orientation. Many types can be included, from health clubs to arcades to dinner theaters, some of which are documented in this handbook.

Supplemental Recreation

Supplemental recreation pertains to recreational facilities which are subsidiary to the main function of a real estate development, whether it be for residential, commercial, or industrial/business purposes. A supplemental attraction, such as a swimming pool or golf course, can be an important complement to the primary land use.

1-4 A wave pool is a type of commercial recreational attraction; in combination with other water-related facilities, it projects a strong water theme.

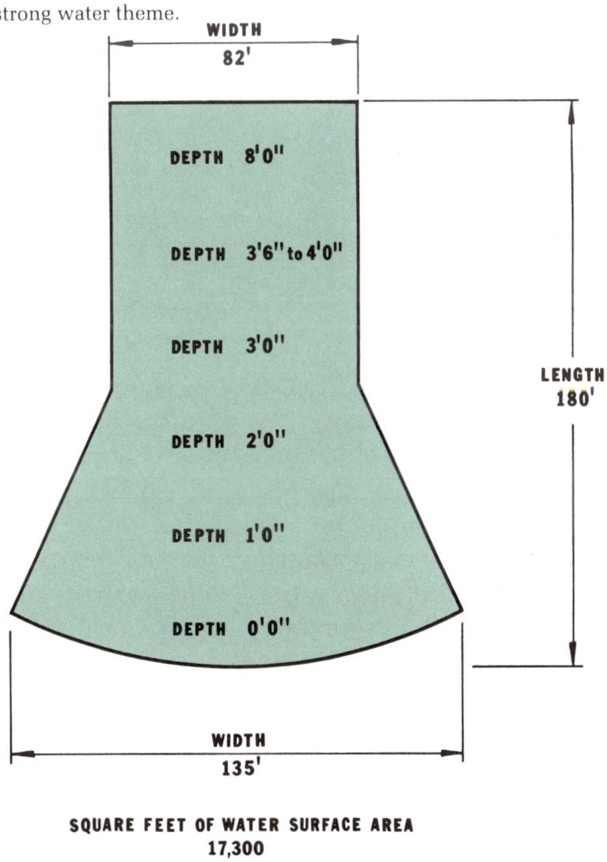

1-5 Typical wave pool plan. Waves are normally generated in intervals between periods of calm water.

1-6 Relaxing environments conducive to leisure time enjoyment are popular supplements within business settings.

1-7 Major and minor amenities in residential projects can be significant, often essential attractions.

Recreational Demand

The myriad opportunities offered by the recreational development industry are in direct response to the increasing public demand for leisure activity. Many factors influence this demand, and understanding them may help give a perspective to the current and future trends of the recreational development industry.

Economic Forces

Three primary factors have contributed to the demand for recreational development and are inseparably joined in determining the public's ability to support such development. The factors are income, leisure time, and mobility.

Income levels have grown substantially for most sectors of society since World War II. Annual family income in the United States increased by 100 percent from 1950 to 1970. While the decade of the 1970s was more severely affected by inflation and slower economic growth, real or constant dollar increases in income have continued, allowing more discretionary spending for recreational activities. The rise in disposable income has been particularly noticeable in dual-income households.

Along with greater affluence, the increase in free time has been an equally important factor in recreational development. The 40-hour work week was established in 1938, setting a standard that remains fairly constant. Since World War II, the institution of paid vacations, which now average over 2 weeks per year for most employees, has allowed people to enjoy many more recreational opportunities. The standardization of certain paid national holidays which established 3-day weekends has created additional periods of free time.

The 4-day work week has been much discussed, its 3-day weekends heralding great promise for recreational community development. The 10-hour day, 4-day week was instituted by some companies but has not received the general acceptance once predicted. A shift has been predicted toward a commuter society with more people making their homes in rural recreational communities. The trend, however, now seems to be toward greater flexibility of daily working hours—popularly known as "flextime"—and more part-time work which could have an increasing effect on urban demand for recreational facilities.

The third primary factor which has influenced recreational demand and facilitated development is greater mobility, through the use of both the automobile and the airplane. Between 1960 and 1980, the United States interstate highway system was essentially completed. This interconnecting system of approximately 40,000 miles makes once remote areas more accessible and allows travelers to reach distant destinations conveniently and efficiently, provided fuel is reasonably available.

Air travel has become increasingly important to recreational development. Since 1960, air travel has increased in exponential leaps and bounds. Many new airports serve resort and recreational areas and the number of international gateways has multiplied, facilitating travel for foreign visitors. Attractive foreign exchange rates and domestic political stability have further enhanced foreign travel in the United States and Canada.

1-8 The Contemporary Resort Hotel, part of the Walt Disney World complex near Orlando, Florida. Planned as a total destination resort, including hotels, campground, and a multitude of recreational facilities, Walt Disney World was host to more than 14 million visitors in 1979. (Walt Disney Productions photograph.)

Activity	Participating At Least Four Times Annually 12–17	18–24	25–34	35–44	45–54	55–64	65–Up	Total Participating At Least One Time Annually
Camping in a Developed Area	14%	18%	13%	15%	11%	11%	3%	30%
Camping in a Primitive Area	13%	13%	10%	11%	6%	4%	4%	21%
Canoeing, Kayaking, River-Running	10%	6%	5%	7%	8%	1%	1%	16%
Sailing	9%	7%	5%	4%	3%	2%	1%	11%
Waterskiing	9%	17%	10%	8%	4%	1%	0%	16%
Fishing	51%	40%	36%	38%	36%	34%	21%	53%
Boating	28%	24%	23%	21%	19%	13%	11%	34%
Outdoor Pool Swimming	75%	67%	62%	57%	37%	27%	11%	63%
Beach Swimming	53%	48%	46%	39%	28%	16%	6%	46%
Nature Walks	37%	34%	42%	43%	39%	34%	23%	50%
Hiking or Backpacking	19%	23%	23%	21%	11%	10%	6%	28%
Walking or Jogging	74%	67%	67%	54%	46%	41%	40%	68%
Bicycling	80%	56%	47%	38%	26%	11%	9%	47%
Horseback Riding	17%	13%	10%	7%	4%	2%	*	15%
Hunting	17%	19%	13%	20%	14%	13%	6%	19%
Picnicking	48%	52%	62%	58%	52%	42%	25%	72%
Golf	10%	11%	11%	12%	12%	15%	5%	16%
Outdoor Tennis	46%	38%	34%	25%	13%	4%	1%	33%
Cross-Country Skiing	2%	1%	2%	2%	1%	1%	0%	2%
Downhill Skiing	9%	10%	5%	3%	1%	*	*	7%
Outdoor Ice-Skating	21%	13%	12%	10%	5%	2%	*	16%
Snowmobiling	6%	9%	5%	4%	4%	2%	1%	8%
Outdoor Sports or Games	76%	60%	54%	48%	30%	17%	8%	56%
Sightseeing	30%	39%	41%	42%	42%	32%	24%	62%
Driving for Pleasure	43%	72%	65%	66%	57%	53%	40%	69%
Visiting Zoos, Amusement Parks	47%	51%	52%	42%	31%	28%	13%	73%
Attending Outdoor Sports Events	66%	57%	52%	42%	31%	28%	13%	61%
Attending Dances or Concerts	34%	38%	24%	18%	18%	13%	8%	41%

1-9 Table showing percentages of surveyed U.S population participating in selected outdoor recreational activities. Data from *1977 Nationwide Outdoor Recreation Survey* by the Heritage Conservation and Recreation Service, U.S. Department of the Interior. An asterisk indicates percentages greater than zero but less than 0.5 percent.

All these factors are significant requirements for growth in the recreational industry. For two decades, recreational planning has relied on the assumption that affluence, leisure time, and unrestricted travel will continue to increase. However, the specter of energy shortages and economic stagnation threatens the future growth of recreational development. Energy-driven inflation increases the percent of income which must be spent on basic necessities, and fuel shortages and prices may severely limit transportation for would-be travelers.

Although these are potential limitations for recreational development, other factors contribute to the rising demand for recreational opportunities. The increase of planned retirement due to the increase in human longevity means that growing numbers of people are looking for residences suitable for their retirement years. Improved pensions, retirement plans, and appreciated home values have provided additional resources with which retired persons can pursue leisure living. Retired people today are more active and mobile and demand a variety of recreational amenities in many locations. Moreover, the retirement market is one of the fastest growing segments of the population.

The desire to own property is also a factor in the demand for recreation. As with any form of residential development, many see the appreciation of property as a hedge against inflation. For city residents, owning property elsewhere gives a sense of independence in addition to the recreational benefits. Property ownership conveys the symbolic quality of having control over a part of the land. Recreational lot developments have provided this opportunity to many people who do not own urban or suburban land.

Travel in the United States

In the United States the automobile is overwhelmingly the preferred mode of transportation. According to the 1980 National Travel Survey, over 80 percent of "person-trips" (a term used by the survey to describe one person on one trip) were made by private automobile or truck, as compared with 12 percent by air, 1 percent by rail, 3 percent by bus, and the remaining 2 percent by a combination of modes.

The reasons people travel are also reflected in the National Travel Survey results:

- Visit friends or relatives — 37 percent
- Business or convention — 20 percent
- Personal/family affairs and medical reasons — 13 percent
- Outdoor recreation — 13 percent
- Entertainment — 8 percent
- Sightseeing — 5 percent
- All other — 4 percent

These figures relate to the primary purpose of the trip. Many people, of course, will go sightseeing while visiting friends and relatives or seek entertainment while attending a convention.

Destination areas, which benefit only marginally from transportation expenditures, gain most if visitors stay overnight in commercial accommodations. Very little is spent by day trippers and tourists who stay with friends and relatives; their expenditures are principally for amusement and recreation, occasional meals and snacks, and souvenirs and gifts. The highest spenders are convention attendees and businessmen traveling on expense accounts.

The convention/business visitor staying in commercial lodgings in the Wilmington, Delaware, vicinity, for example, spent about $56 a day in 1980; other visitors in commercial lodgings, about $46; those staying with friends and relatives, $17; and day visitors about $10.

One of the greatest benefits of tourism lies in the potential creation of employment. During 1979, the travel industry provided over 6.5 million jobs in an average month, up about 5 percent from the 1978 level of 6.25 million jobs. The food service industry alone provided about 4.5 million jobs, or over two-thirds of all jobs in the tourism industry. About 1 million jobs are in the transportation sector and about 1 million in commercial lodging places.

In 1980, between $27,000 and $30,000 in receipts were required to support a job in the travel industry. The ratio is high because the transportation industry has heavy capital equipment and fuel costs. In the lodging industry, a job may be created by $20,000 to $23,000 in receipts; the food service industry requires between $16,000 and $18,000. In both of these sectors, large numbers of unskilled workers are employed at the minimum wage.

Another characteristic of the tourism industry is that small business dominates. According to the U.S. Census Bureau, 99 percent of the 1.4 million travel-related business firms in the country are classified as small businesses.

1-10 Travel, via road . . .

1-11 . . . and air, has flourished since 1950, determining in great measure the nature of recreational development.

1-12 As increasing numbers of the population go into retirement, recreation, often provided in a country club setting, plays a key role in the popularity of retirement communities.

Psychological Elements

Recreation has been defined as any activity undertaken because one wants to do it. For example, one possibly unlikely activity which is becoming increasingly popular as a form of recreation is leisure shopping: modern retail markets are filled with attractions for the leisure time shopper. It is one's own subjective evaluation of an activity which determines whether that activity is recreational or not. In other words, recreation depends on the attitude of the participant. Thus, it is important for recreational developments to project and maintain a particular image. Recreational development deals with fantasy and image to a much greater degree than other types of development. It is this element of fantasy which contributes to the sizable risk of a project as well as to the potential for gain.

A variety of motivational factors—primarily related to the need for relaxation and a change from daily tasks—influences the demand for recreation. One of the strongest motivations for recreation is the desire for outdoor activities. Whether it indicates an instinctive pull to return to nature or an adventurous spirit of pioneering the wilderness, the desire for open space and untamed nature is an essential part of the North American psyche. The "frontier" spirit for some means encountering physical challenge, for others, appreciating the natural environment.

Modern society seems dominated by metropolitan areas and urban dwellers. The rural out-of-doors offers an escape from the problems of crime, pollution, and crowding, which are associated with urban living. Recent studies have reported a shift in year-round population from urban to rural areas for the first time in many years. But for many, a vacation home in a rural area combines the best of both worlds.

The appeal of outdoor recreation is further stimulated by the sedentary work life of our increasingly service-oriented society. When one works in a controlled environment in a high-rise office building and lacks regular exercise and visual and sensory stimulation, the demand for active recreation, open space, and travel is heightened. Perhaps the chief purpose of recreation is to provide relaxation—which can be in the form of an "escape" from the pressures and fast pace of jobs and modern daily life or in the form of a diversion from the monotony of everyday routine. In practice, recreation should be fun, offering people the chance to seek fantasies, excitement, or a variety of diversions to refresh their spirits. Theme parks, theaters, exotic travel resorts, and even specialty shopping and dining facilities provide avenues for new experiences. Highly urbanized beach resorts, while not offering solitude, offer intense diversions from the entrenched patterns of daily life.

Personal health and physical fitness have become top priorities as evidenced by the huge surge in active sports participation, jogging, diet and weight consciousness, and the increased demand for facilities to provide these activities. The pursuit of health and fitness in the United States generated revenues of $15 billion in 1978, and projections are for continued growth in the future.

At one time affordable only to the very wealthy, a greater variety of leisure activities is now available to the average person. However, certain activities still retain a more affluent image than others. Thus, striving for social status can create the demand to participate in a special activity, belong to a certain club, or visit a well-known resort. Tennis, although popular among many sectors of society, continues to attract some people as a sport of status and glamor. Country clubs have generally retained an exclusive, elitist image, and many recreational developments attempt to capture that image to attract the socially conscious.

Although it is important for recreational development projects to offer a variety of opportunities, it is also necessary to provide for the property maintenance and security needs of the owners, thus satisfying the demand for problem-free environments. Urbanites and suburbanites who seek recreational diversions in the country are accustomed to convenience and amenities. Thus, their demands for recreational development usually include certain conveniences of city life. More often than not, it is the appearance of rusticity which is attractive—not the actuality. The idyllic cabin in the woods, therefore, must have electricity and plumbing and more probably will be one of a group of condominium units, each with a dishwasher and microwave oven. The lack of community services in rural areas can come as a disconcerting surprise.

Having a "family experience" has become another major factor in recreational demand. A vacation home can provide the opportunity to participate as a family in activities which appeal to all age groups. On the other hand, rapidly increasing numbers of single persons and dual-career couples without children have created a demand for sophisticated, adult-oriented resorts emphasizing active sports and nightlife.

1-13 Dramatic, isolated natural settings offer urban residents contrasts to the routine of daily life.

1-14 Higher-density resort areas provide urban-oriented diversions.

1-15 Activities like golf are an important part of recreation in many vacation environments, particularly for the more affluent, mature vacationer.

1-16 Conveniences such as those found in the modern kitchen can be significant to marketing leisure living.

1-17 Recreational activities are primary highlights in advertising second-home communities.

Images of leisure lifestyles are projected and reinforced by media advertising. Increased advertising and mass marketing of recreational projects have expanded the public's awareness of recreational opportunities and therefore enhanced the demand.

Finally, recreational products have increased in supply, variety, price range, and amenities. Substantial amounts of agricultural, forest, and other land have been converted to recreational uses. In some cases, local communities have promoted recreational development to increase the tax base and stimulate the local economy. Until the mid-1970s, rural areas were fairly easily developed due to the lack of regulations, standards, and controls. The number of recreational projects multiplied rapidly. Low down payments or other low-cost mechanisms, facilitated the purchase of recreational sites, making them affordable to greater numbers of people.

In sum, the demand for recreational opportunities grew dramatically during the post–World War II period. Current estimates project continued growth. The decade of the 1980s is expected to be one of transition from the established pattern of freely expanding opportunities and rapid development to a new order of controlled and managed growth. This transition will be forced by conflicts between the continued pursuit of life's rewards and an enligntened appreciation of strained natural resources.

Historic Patterns

Throughout history, there has been a demand for real estate for recreational purposes. Before the 19th century, travel and leisure were generally available only to the rich. Recreational homes were designed exclusively for the gentry.

In ancient times, wealthy Romans maintained rural villas near the sea and in the mountains to escape Rome's summer heat. The village of Ostia at the mouth of the Tiber River was a popular vacation spot from the 4th century B.C. to the 3rd century A.D. Hadrian's villa at Tivoli, built in 124 A.D., epitomized the elaborate leisure home with its theaters, gardens, and baths occupying extensive grounds.

In later centuries, the summer palaces of European royalty became the seasonal centers for the nobility. But as in modern times, conveniences were not forsaken in the search for a rustic, recreational experience. In France, Germany, Spain, England, and Russia, castles dotted the countryside with their splendor and served as sites for the rustic diversions of the wealthy who could then observe and imitate the picturesque elements of peasant life while preserving the convenience and elegance of the court. The Palais de Versailles is the ostentatious extreme of such rural mansions with its hugely scaled, monumental architecture and elaborate gardens. In the 1700s, Louis XVI built for Marie Antoinette the Petit Trianon on the grounds of Versailles. There, she could act out her bucolic fantasies playing shepherdess and milkmaid in silk costumes with perfumed animals.

Leisure colonies and grand tourist hotels were built to accommodate the traveling aristocracy. Popular watering spots such as Lake Lucerne in Switzerland, the Riviera, and health spas like Germany's Baden-Baden and England's Bath developed elaborate leisure cultures.

Rural peasants had to satisfy their desire for a change of pace with the seasonal move to mountain cabins or seaside camps as they took their herds to upper pastures or went fishing. Although not primarily recreational, these seasonal homes offered a respite from everyday life. The urban poor had no such relief.

In the United States, many of the early colonial aristocracy continued their pattern of vacationing by maintaining both country homes or plantations and townhouses. But the New World also brought greater prosperity to the common man and, by the middle of the 19th century, popularly priced resort communities flourished at the seashore and in the mountains. Cape May, New Jersey, was the foremost resort of the mid-1800s with tourists flocking there—at first by steamboat and later by rail.

The 1880s saw major recreational development for both the rich and the poor, although the disparities of wealth among Americans were nowhere more pronounced than in their recreational pursuits. For the general public, transportation was opening up new areas. City trolley companies developed parks at the end of their lines to encourage weekend use of trolleys. The trolley parks often expanded into long popular picnic groves, evolving later into amusement parks. Coney Island became the prototype of American amusement parks and its development from 1860 to 1890 included huge resort hotels, ballrooms, beer gardens, bathing piers, and rides and games which attracted thousands, and later, millions of New Yorkers. Like many recreational ventures, the exotic Margate Hotel on Coney Island, built in 1881 in the shape of an elephant, was designed as an attraction for a land sales promotion. Following the example of Coney Island, amusement parks were developed across the country.

1-18 The Banff Springs Hotel near Banff, Alberta, built by the Canadian Pacific Railway in the 1880s.

1-19 First opened in 1888, the Hotel Del Coronado in San Diego was designated a U.S. National Historic Landmark in 1977.

Seasonal resort communities for the working class also were popular and often had a religious or cultural focus. The homes were modest—rustic cabins or cottages with few amenities, often densely built around lakes or at the shore. The Baptist colony in Oak Bluffs on the island of Martha's Vineyard off Cape Cod, Massachusetts, survives as an example of this type of vacation home development.

For the rich, the 1880s brought a surge of luxury resort development. The Ponce de Leon in St. Augustine was the most lavish and expensive resort hotel of its kind during this period, contributing to the recognition of Florida as a tourist destination and stimulating rail travel. The Hotel Del Coronado in San Diego was designed in the extravagant eclectic style of the day that combined Spanish and Swiss elements. The hotel was intended to promote investment in real estate on Coronado Island. Its character and charm have withstood the test of time, and although now surrounded by urban development, the hotel has maintained its prestige.

By the turn of the century, the exclusive resort communities of the wealthy sported designs for summer "cottages" that rivaled their European predecessors in grandeur and opulence. Newport, Rhode Island, Long Island, the Adirondacks, and Palm Beach all are renowned for their splendid seasonal homes.

With the automobile becoming the major means of transportation, the pattern of American recreational activity changed. No longer limited to the trolley routes, Americans began to look farther from home for a diversity of recreational experiences. A growing awareness of the physical wonders of the country and the expanding naturalist movement stimulated interest in the outdoors. The U.S. National Park Service was established in 1916 to manage and protect the nation's scenic wonders. Yellowstone Park was first established in 1872 and Yosemite National Park in 1890. Large, rustic hotels in these and other parks attracted travelers in small numbers arriving by stagecoach at first, and later, in increasing numbers, by car. This same period saw the beginning of the first recreational land booms, most notably in California and Florida.

The growth of private leisure home development ended in 1929 with the Great Depression. The Depression also took its toll of small commercial recreational entrepreneurs, forcing many businesses to close as people could no longer afford leisure time or activities. In 1919, there were 1,500 amusement parks in the United States; by 1936 there were only 500.[1] The Depression also affected the national parks, but in positive ways, since the Civilian Conservation Corps and other federal work projects brought in manpower to develop recreational areas in the parks. Not until after World War II did the recreational and second-home market begin to revive.

[1] Louis Wasserman, *Merchandising Architecture* (Washington: National Endowment for the Arts, 1978), p.54.

A brief revival of amusement parks in the late 1940s ended with the advent of television and increasingly home-based suburban lifestyles. Nevertheless, during the period leading up to the 1970s, with an unprecedented boom in family travel by automobile, the touring trip became the most popular form of family vacation, giving rise to the widespread growth of motels (which replaced the early auto courts).

The burgeoning "upper-middle" professional class was growing more affluent, mobile, and—with the post–World War II baby boom—more family-oriented. Walt Disney captured the imagination of this new market and in 1955 brought to life at Disneyland the fantasies that were pictured on television and in films. New types of commercial recreational projects appeared in the suburbs. Vacation travel began to increase and skiing, boating, and golfing centers gained popularity. Ski resorts bloomed in the Northeast and West, marinas and yacht clubs opened along the coasts and Great Lakes, and country clubs appeared across the land near suburban housing developments. Major destination resort and second-home developments expanded in Florida, California, New England, South Carolina, Hawaii, and Nevada, to mention only a few.

1-20 America's scenic highways helped establish a tradition of automobile vacation travel.

Land Sales and Government Control

The most recent boom in recreational real estate development came in the 1960s and early 1970s. Land speculation and the strong demand for recreation spurred developers into action and the market accelerated. Second-home projects and recreational lot subdivisions proliferated. A lack of regulation in most rural areas allowed developments to grow unchecked. Large corporations entered the land sales boom, subdividing and marketing huge tracts of land. High pressure salesmen sold thousands of acres to eager but naive investors.

Among the simple, low-density recreational land subdivisions proliferating in the 1960s and early 1970s, the number of lots that have been built on is estimated as low, averaging perhaps well below 10 percent. The build-out rate is higher at successful new second-home communities and at recreational subdivisions established many years ago in locations of prime accessibility. Of the estimated 10 to 15 million recreational lots in the United States,[2] approximately 30 percent were built on by the late 1970s. The remaining lots have either never been sold, are being held for investment and future use, or were bought by unwitting purchasers at prices far exceeding their expected worth.

As the complaints about misrepresentation and fraud concerning "dirt" sales began to surface, environmentalists took issue with other recreational development practices. Soil erosion, inadequate sanitary disposal, and insensitive disruptions of scenic areas caused by certain recreational projects focused public attention on the environmental concerns in development.

The response to both consumer and environmental abuses was increased regulation. In 1969, the Office on Interstate Land Sales Registration (OILSR) was established by the U.S. Department of Housing and Urban Development. It requires all developments of 50 lots or more to register a prospectus with the department if they use interstate commerce to market their properties. In 1973, there were 5,090 developments registered; by 1979, a search of the OILSR records showed 21,391 active subdivisions involving 7,766,376 lots.[3] From 1971 to 1977, OILSR received an average of 3,000 consumer complaints a year. Over this time, indictments against a number of companies

[2] Richard Ragatz, *Recreational Properties* (Eugene, Oregon: Richard Ragatz Associates, 1974), pp. 242–243.

[3] These data are somewhat confusing since they are not broken down by project type and there are duplications and computer errors. Unfortunately, no complete source exists to indicate the number of recreational land developments.

were initiated and sales were suspended at hundreds of developments pending OILSR review.

Since 1973, the U.S. Federal Trade Commission (FTC) also has been involved in land sales regulation. With authority over advertising, it has acted in consumer interests to stop deceptive practices. A landmark decision in 1974 against the GAC Corporation, one of the largest land developers, required full disclosure of the sales contract, a "cooling off" period for buyers, and refunds of down payments to certain purchasers. A further federal effort to offer protection from indiscriminate development came with the National Environmental Policy Act (NEPA) which Congress passed in 1969, establishing the format of the environmental impact statement (EIS) for all development projects involving federal lands or funding. Most states have followed suit in some way by establishing review processes and environmental regulations.[4]

The local forces often had little control over and took a low profile on issues concerning the thousands of recreational subdivisions established during the boom of the 1960s. Many local governments were without zoning or other regulations during this time, particularly in rural areas where land use controls have traditionally been the weakest. Since the 1960s, it has been widely recognized that holding to high standards is in the best interests of everyone. Although some local governments now employ highly sophisticated and tested controls, many others still have no practical understanding or tools to deal with the impact of recreational development.

The scope of environmental impact statements goes beyond investigating a developer's plans for erosion control or sewage disposal. Environmental assessment is defined as "a means to arrange, present, and evaluate the natural, economic, aesthetic, social, and cultural effects, both direct and indirect, of a proposed project."[5] Obviously, the extensiveness of this assessment has placed an enormous responsibility on the developer to collect and substantiate the plans for a new development. Environmental regulation has multiplied the front-end costs of development with its requirements for preconstruction permit approval. It has also enhanced the authority of the

[4] Robert Burchell and David Listokin, *The Environmental Impact Handbook* (New Brunswick, New Jersey: Center for Urban Policy Research, 1975), p.8.

[5] Ibid., p.215.

1-21 Maintaining open space is another part of the American heritage, the promise of which has sometimes been used in aggressive tactics to sell lots to unsuspecting purchasers.

local community as a party to the permit hearings. A developer is required to make substantial outlays for planning and presenting his project for public review, without any assurance of receiving an approval to proceed. Because of the delayed returns from projects, many individual developers were unable to finance the front-end costs, leaving the field open to corporate land subsidiaries. The success of publicly owned corporations diversifying into land development has been mixed, however, and their participation declined appreciably during the middle and late 1970s.[6]

The proliferation of environmental and consumer regulations was prompted by numerous complaints concerning abuses primarily by large-scale developers, sometimes referred to as land merchandisers, of lots sold on installment. Most of this activity was centered in the Florida wetland, desert areas of Arizona and Colorado, and arid California mountains. By some accounts, the lack of implementation and enforcement of the regulations resulted in little change in these developments.[7] But public reaction to the publicity surrounding these activities produced a strong and pervasive negative image of land sales.

1-22 High-rise, second-home condominiums fronting on the beach in Ocean City, Maryland.

Recent Trends

In spite of these problems, demand for recreational real estate continued to grow. The trend in the early 1970s was away from recreational lot sales toward high-amenity, second-home and condominium communities. This period witnessed an immense increase in the sales of condominiums to be used for recreational purposes.

The OPEC oil embargo from 1973 to 1974 and the recession of 1974 and 1975 proved disastrous for many recreational communities. In an economic downturn, comsumers cut back on "luxury" purchases, and some developers were left holding large inventories. Interest and holding costs ate up profits and a number of developers were forced into default. Some of the nation's most prestigious financial institutions were also caught in the recession's real estate debacle with their real estate investment trusts (REITs) facing huge losses.

The example of Ocean City, Maryland, illustrates this situation. "Because of rapidly increasing land

1-23 Fuel availability at secluded recreational projects, such as here at Lakeridge, Connecticut, is a reassuring sign for visitors in times of energy uncertainties.

[6] American Land Development Association (ALDA), *Selected Results of the 1978 (for 1977) ALDA Survey of Real Estate Development and Sales Activity* (Washington: ALDA, 1978).

[7] Morton C. Paulson, *The Great Land Hustle* (Chicago: Henry Regnery Co., 1972), p.213.

and construction costs and pent up demand for condominiums, prices of units expanded dramatically in 1970, 1971, and 1972. Annual increases of 25 to 30 percent were not uncommon. . . . So great was the opportunity to realize an extraordinary gain that the market was soon swarming with speculators. In fact, in late 1972 and early 1973, speculators accounted for 50 to 90 percent of all deposits."[8] Developers reacted to the speculative demand and increased construction accordingly, just as the speculators began to retreat from the market. The result was severe overbuilding which left 5,100 units on the market in Ocean City at the end of 1974 while the 1974 settlement rate was down to only 500 units per year. "The primary lesson that can be learned by the private real estate sector from Ocean City's resort condominium experience is that developers and their financial backers must distinguish between final use demand and intermediate speculative demand."[9]

In 1974, estimates projected that it would take 4 to 10 years to sell the complete inventory of resort condominiums at Ocean City. By 1979, the glut had been absorbed and new development was continuing, although cautiously. This pattern was repeated in other areas affected by the 1974–1975 recession. Gradually the recreational development industry recovered, returning to a healthy, if not exuberant state.

1-24 The Alai Kai II timeshare units on Kauai, Hawaii.

While second-home sales in 1977 were down one-third from their 1973 levels, the demand for recreation of all sorts continued to increase and vacation home development has remained an important part of that market. Forecasts of the 1980 recession found recreational developers much better prepared to weather the market. Inventories had been kept lower, with more presales and fewer speculation units, and development had generally proceeded more conservatively. Real estate investors had recalled and used the lessons of the recent past.

Consumer demand for recreation continues to change. The recreational development industry has responded to market pressures by developing a new range of products including recreational vehicle campsites and timesharing units. Timesharing is a type of ownership in which the buyer purchases a time segment, typically 1 or 2 weeks, for the use of a dwelling unit. With several buyers purchasing time segments in a unit, timesharing has become a highly practical device for getting full use of vacation properties as well as enjoying certain benefits of ownership.

Timesharing was first introduced on a large scale in the United States as a marketing response to high inventories and poor sales of vacation condominiums in 1974 and 1975. Since 1976, sales have doubled each year, and in 1980 were expected to exceed $1 billion. Improved brokerage and financing support has helped boost the reputation, popularity, and profits of timesharing. Initially used as a temporary marketing strategy, conversion of failing projects into timeshare units nevertheless could not turn a bad project into a good one. The overall upgrading of the timeshare product and management since 1976 has resulted from the fact that units and resort operations are being designed and built specifically for timeshare use.

To a large extent, those who provide opportunities for recreation have themselves shaped the demand. Interest in more active participatory recreation has spurred commercial recreational projects of many types. Recreational amenities have been so well integrated into many permanent home developments that it is sometimes hard to distinguish recreational projects from residential projects. Recreational elements have also been designed as supplements to other types of development, including shopping centers and industrial parks.

[8] Jim Haimes and Marvin Rose, "The Second-Home Condominium Boom in Ocean City, Maryland," *Urban Land* (December 1974), p. 14.

[9] Ibid., p.18.

1-25 Aerial view of the Spanish Building on International Street at Kings Island theme park near Cincinnati.

Adapting to changing markets is a constant process. Theme park developments which spread nationwide after the success of Disneyland must face the prospect of an increasingly adult population and fewer children. Energy shortages and prices continue to have an impact on recreational developments. The gasoline shortages in 1973 and 1979 disrupted vacation travel considerably. Although gasoline prices have been found to have a limited effect on decisions to take vacations—even where recreational vehicle owners are concerned—they have been responsible for reducing the distances people are traveling.[10] What is most evident is the importance of acknowledging the probability that economic cycles in some form do exist and development should be tailored accordingly. In all likelihood, recreational demands will continue to provide many development opportunities, particularly for destination resorts and recreational facilities near residential development.

[10] Suzanne D. Cook, "Let's Take a Kyack to Quincy and Nyack," *American Demographics* (July/August 1979), p.14.

1-26 Different types of thrill rides like this hanging roller coaster are primary attractions at theme parks.

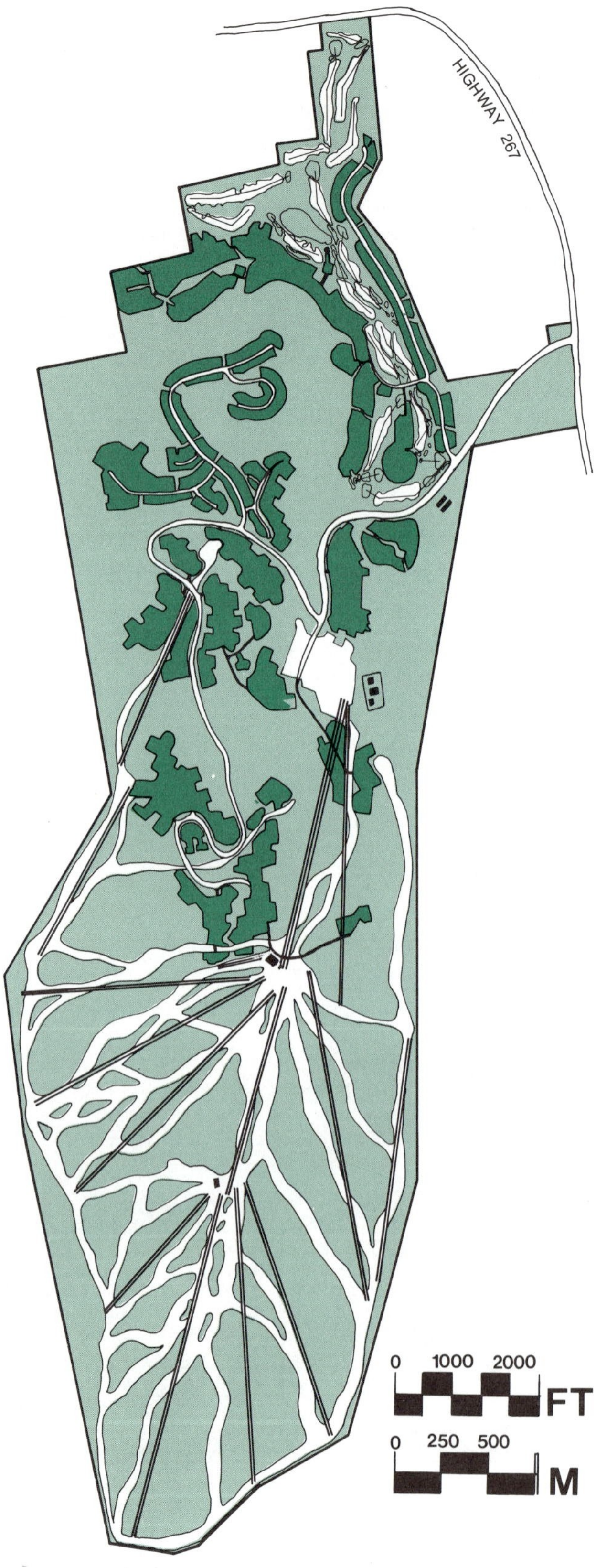

1-27 Site plan of Northstar at Tahoe, including ski runs and golf course. The risk associated with the high cost of amenities is exacerbated by seasonal markets.

General Issues

At the most, recreation may be popularly perceived as an inalienable right or, at the least, as a pastime, but the use of certain recreational products cannot be called a necessity. The strong influence of consumer preference in determining expenditures makes recreational development as defined in this volume highly vulnerable to change and uncertainties. Thus, to be feasible, a development plan, no matter what its nature, must consider many general issues which influence the way in which a project will function with respect to that ill defined activity termed recreation. The following sections introduce some of the general issues affecting recreational development, although the factors discussed are by no means all-inclusive or of equal importance in every situation.

High Risk

Recreational development is among the most risky of real estate activities. Numerous variables aggravated by prolific uncertainties affecting the demand for and supply of recreational facilities contribute to this high degree of risk. Factors contributing to the instability of consumer demand for recreation, as discussed earlier, include general economic trends, fluctuating consumer preferences, and energy supply and cost problems. Substantial risks in supplying recreational products are attributable to the high costs of financing, excessive expenditures associated with the need for front-end amenities, escalating uncertainties due to the long-term nature of the project, dependence on real estate values created through development, poor management, local opposition, approval delays, seasons, weather, and market variables.

The recreational facility which is developed as part of a larger resort area offers a quicker and often safer return on investment. But the large self-contained resort destination presents its own special risks as well as opportunities. The isolated facility can enjoy a captive market, but requires that extensive amenities be provided at an early stage along with a substantial marketing effort to create the demand. The large capital needs of a comprehensively planned, self-contained recreational development, with little or no secondary use, involves a high risk. But if by adding amenities, the value of the property is appreciably increased in the long run, the potential rewards can make the risk worthwhile.

In the final analysis, it is the potentially negative leverage which results from the high debt-to-equity ratios common in most recreational developments

1-28 Risk and seasonal effects can be reduced by providing a range of activities which draw on different markets and stretch facility use throughout the year.

that ultimately leads to financial failure. Equity funds can be increased and debts reduced, thereby lessening the financial risks, by allowing the project to ride the inevitable cycles without the cash flow shortages created by heavy interest carrying charges. Indeed, a review of the financial histories of major recreational/resort projects reveals that only those financed with a substantial amount of equity have been successful in creating long-term value for the original owner. Projects lacking adequate equity are now creating value for the third or fourth owners.

Seasonal Effects

Historically, specific recreational activity has been synonymous with a particular season of the year. As a result, a good deal of recreational development depends on a short season of intense activity and is affected by such changing conditions as weather and transportation. Prime vacation resorts are most susceptible to these conditions. Second-home communities transfer full ownership costs directly to the users who in turn tend to use their second homes all year to receive the fullest benefit from their investments.

Increasingly exorbitant development costs are forcing both providers and consumers to get more use out of recreational projects throughout the year. Many new facilities could not be built unless they are to be used for extended periods. Planning for seasonal resorts requires special design considerations to handle intensive but limited demand, pricing policies to regulate peak demand and encourage use in off periods, longer in-season attractions, and targeting of off-season markets such as conventions and tour group business. A major problem in balancing recreational supply with seasonal loads is identifying what peaks to build for. In some respects, a trade-off may be necessary between product quality and quantity, with varied price markups, making the total potential return from a small, quality project equal to that from a large volume job. The possibility of excess capacity or foregone market opportunities exists in either case, exacerbated by the short demand period.

Community Impacts

Almost every public community can be affected by recreational attractions, although to widely varying degrees. Recreational development can be a community's boom or bust, depending on the market, the interests of the population, and the capacities of the natural environment. Economically depressed areas may look toward recreational development as a means to save local employment. Prosperous communities, or those with strong preservationist interests, may be less receptive to recreational development.

Recreational development can bring additional pressures to bear on both natural and manmade environments. Although increased use and possible congestion may be signs of a development's success, paradoxically they can also diminish the appeal of the original attraction. Recreational development can affect social structure by introducing new human elements to a community, which, in the case of a sparsely populated area, might have dramatic repercussions. This potential impact applies also to the political structure and direction of a community as new residents attracted by recreational facilities begin to participate in the political process (usually with an aim to discouraging further growth). Economically, as well as providing new life, the impact can also lead to higher prices for property and general services with more expensive investments demanded. A lack of affordable housing for local employees may occur. If an economic multiplier effect becomes important, a complete new economy may emerge. For communities with small populations, this could represent an increase in size to a threshold level when a full range of urban types of services and facilities would then be economically viable.

In each area of impact, the old and the new may clash at some point. Generally, the larger and more diverse the community is, the more diffuse the impact of a recreational facility will be. The relationship between a recreational presence and the community is not unlike that between a university or college and the town in which it is located. A community's preference will be predicated on the circumstances peculiar to each situation. Public policies will most likely undergo change as the recreational development itself begins to exert an influence. Not only does the surrounding community experience change, the recreational facilities also are affected in turn by their own successes, all part of the push and pull of community growth.

1-29 Lake Tahoe is an area where intense competition for recreational land uses, be it for conservation or development, requires a sensitive planning and negotiation process.

Lot Sales

If no initial investment is committed to infrastructure development, marketing mass numbers of unimproved lots for recreational purposes in areas with inexpensive land and small populations is commonly referred to as "dirt sales." Such an approach denotes a land sales operation rather than real estate development in its proper sense. This handbook promotes practices of conscientious and sincere real estate development, not the simple sales of unimproved lots, which cannot accurately be referred to as "development" in the first place. True recreational development based on added facilities can have long-term returns that are more justified than those typical of the quick sales of unimproved lots. Community building allows value to be added to property, which an early exit from the market will deny the developer.

Controlled lot sales can be an attractive and appropriate part of a comprehensive recreational development strategy. Despite the history of abuses related to dirt sales and unscrupulous high-pressure sales tactics, lot development and sales, if done properly, represent a valid and desirable aspect of the recreational development industry. The best recreational communities offer a balanced inventory of lots and housing units. The key to the validity of lot development and sales programs—just as it is with any type of real estate sales program—is whether or not they offer real value in terms of price, location, and utility.

As a singular approach to development, however, lot sales can be an unfortunate solution. In some areas, they may no longer be a practical or likable option. The prevalence of such lots contrasts with the increased consumer preference for built housing. Furthermore, the limitations and inefficiencies of planning single-lot development often pose a greater threat to the environment than other approaches. The ultimate misfortune results when an inexpensive lot sales program not only provides the least initial return but also destroys the environmental qualities which contributed to the land's original value.

An issue that arises in relation to dirt sales is the practice of using high pressure in selling a recreational product, improved or unimproved. The promotion of recreational real estate has come under suspicion when unscrupulous sales tactics have been employed essentially to entice people into buying property they had not really wanted or intended to buy. Many persons tend to be fanciful about recreational property and are vulnerable to ill-considered or impulse buying. Protective consumer regulations help, but aggressive marketing is still a practice in the marketplace and is particularly attractive to a one-shot entrepreneur who has no intention of worrying about the future of a particular recreational community.

Regulation

Modern day recreational development is subject to major public regulations affecting land use, the environment, financing, marketing, operations, and so on. Regulations are intended to enhance and protect the public interest, which may mean, on the one hand, preserving a wilderness area or, on the other hand, increasing the supply of and access to a particular recreational opportunity. Philosophically, the regulation system operates as a series of checks and balances. Responsible recreational developers recognize the need for appropriate public stewardship of land development and enjoy the protection and assistance it affords.

Numerous problems exist, however, when the specter of regulation threatens to choke development activity, making projects so expensive that only the wealthy can afford to use them, or when it results in unexpected and undesirable solutions which seem to represent a way around the restrictions. Regulations and procedures at the local, regional, state, and federal levels consume valuable time, money, and energy —in notable cases, enough to make good development impossible (particularly for new large-scale PUDs). Such a situation can lead to piecemeal and

1-31 Although they may not have produced the highest use or returned maximum value, beach area lot sales were critical to the early financial viability of the 4,500-acre Sea Pines Plantation on Hilton Head Island, South Carolina.

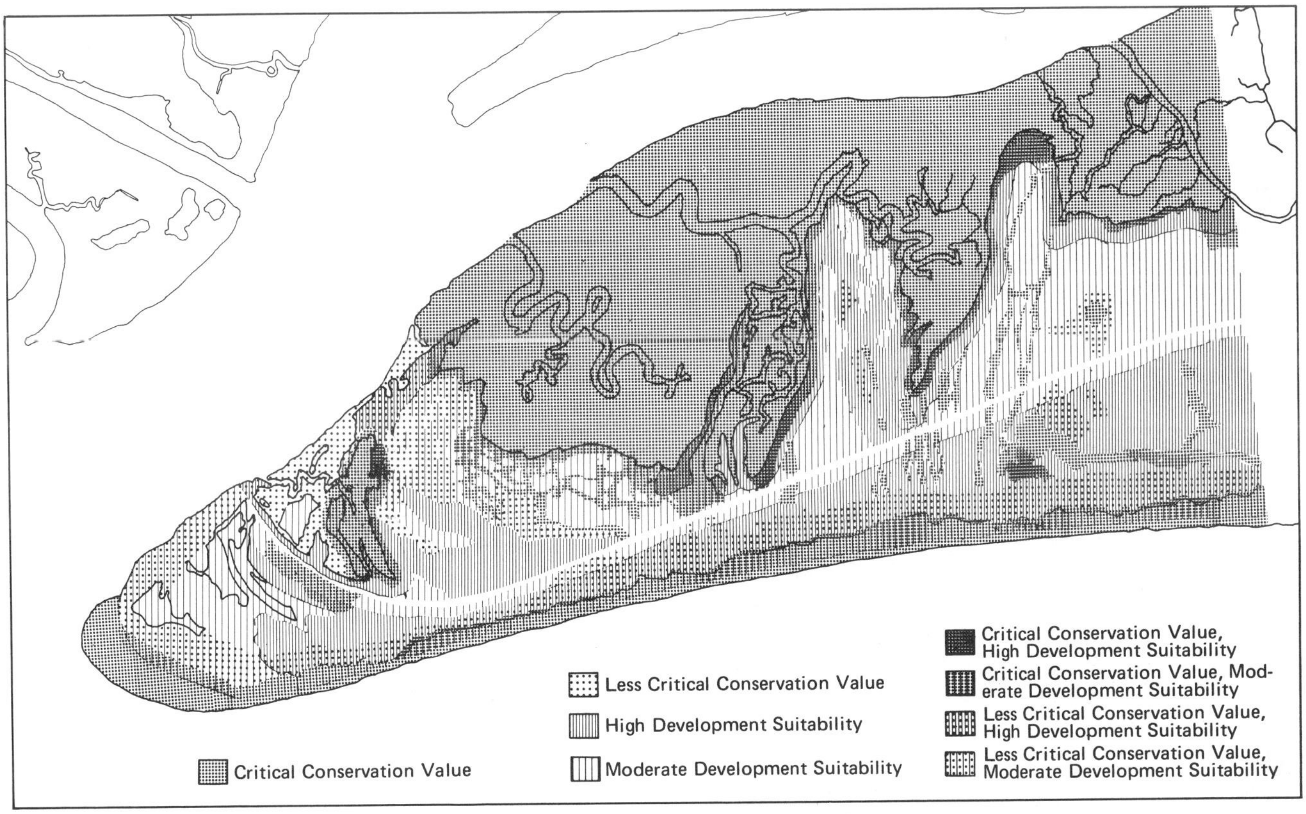

1-30 Map showing synthesis of conservation values and development suitabilities for Amelia Island, Florida. Environmentally conscious development depends on detailed and careful planning.

1-32 Vacation opportunities can be provided in many ways, whether through a Miami Beach. . .

1-33 . . . or a campground. . .

1-34 . . . or a roadside motel.

less controlled development which can over time be less satisfactory for the long-term quality of a recreational area. A multitude of expensive requirements can give great blockading power to a small active opposition. Moreover, the uncertainties associated with regulations changing after a developer's commitment has been made can make an ambitious plan too risky to consider.

Specialized Markets

The field of recreation comprises many specialized activities, whether they involve skin diving or bowling. The special requirements of these recreational activities must be carefully identified and targeted in order to justify investments made to provide facilities which cater to them. The importance of knowing the market and targeting it specifically is critical to succeeding, even where larger, more diversified resort second-home communities are concerned. Unless the type and standard of recreational development relate effectively to a particular market, a desirable consumer image may fail to materialize. The developer who is aware of the importance of catering to a specific market would help to secure his position if an alternative special market is identified for targeting, should the need arise.

Opportunities by Income

Not surprisingly, distinguished recreational development is expensive and consequently available only to a limited segment of the population. Those who can afford it demand quality, and get it to the extent that developers are skilled, motivated, and well financed.

Recreational opportunities for lower- and middle-income persons are subject to different conditions, which does not imply that less expensive recreational opportunities provide a less rewarding recreational experience. By matching one's tastes to the opportunities one's income can afford, a choice of fulfilling recreational experiences should be available to all but the most hard-pressed groups. Recreational expenditures are highly discretionary and based on the participant's interests; one participant might put all his resources into transportation, while another might prefer luxury accommodations. From the perspective of recreational development, persons with moderate incomes can choose from a myriad of less expensive lodgings, camping facilities, package tours, mass products, timesharing arrangements, and off-season incentives.

Recreational development experiences the same filtering process that affects residential real estate: as new premium developments open up, the top dollar consumer may move on to them, freeing certain areas which then become relatively more affordable to other income groups. This has been a common occurrence in the past when resort areas were free to grow and evolve incrementally from special isolated attractions into larger units catering to the mass market. In the future, however, this process may be restricted as new development is limited by the scarcity of land, high costs, and multiple regulations, at which point, higher uses must be made of existing facilities.

The recreational development practices recommended in this handbook are generally, but by no means, exclusively associated with more expensive development. It should not be assumed that people of all incomes have similar recreational preferences. There will always be exclusive facilities, as well as those which maintain heterogeneity.

What should be drawn from the handbook is that many good practices can be implemented at little or no more cost than not implementing them at all. The big challenge is to make the best practices available to consumers at a moderate cost.

1-35 Satisfying experiences, such as fishing, are the essence of recreational pursuits.

2.
Resort/Residential Communities

General Characteristics

Resort and residential recreational communities are defined by a variety of facilities appealing to the many different segments of the leisure time market. Recreational destinations offer overnight facilities in a multitude of styles and prices ranging from hotel units to private second homes to recreational vehicle sites. A combination of these can broaden the overall appeal of a particular resort. The following discussion attempts to distinguish among types of resort recreational functions and characteristics as a preamble to outlining the development process of a recreational community.

Commercial Versus Resort Hotel

The differences between a resort hotel and typical hotel can be described in terms of the purpose that the guest of each facility has for staying there. The chief difference between a resort hotel guest and a typical, or commercial, hotel guest is that the former is at the hotel in order to have an "experience," whereas the commercial hotel guest is there in order to satisfy a need for convenience. In turn, the needs of the guests influence significantly the service and location of each kind of hotel.

In some cases, both purposes can be served at the same hotel, but such situations are relatively limited and form a special category. Examples in which commercial hotels have many occupants who are there for experiential purposes are seen in such unusual cities as San Francisco, New York, and Montreal. In cities like these, people have an urban vacation and experience by enjoying the rich cultural, social, and intellectual environment. On the other hand, although the concentration of hotels in Honolulu's Waikiki was developed primarily to provide a resort experience, the extensiveness of the hotel industry in Honolulu causes those same hotels to be used by business people. The visitor needing a convenient hotel while on business usually has no objection to enjoying some recreation at the same time. Similarly, a person who is going to a resort hotel for the experience often does not want to forsake all convenience for a recreational experience. Thus, we have the phenomenon of modern, high-rise hotels in rather primitive locations.

The resort hotel, however, is more than simply an establishment providing lodging. Influenced by the increased popularity of condominiums, the fairly large segment of affluent retirees seeking a resort environment, and a younger generation seeking a life-

2-1 The Hilton Hawaiian Village, a resort and convention hotel complex on Honolulu's Waikiki Beach.

style which is somewhat removed from industrialization or intense urbanization, the resort hotel has developed over the past 10 to 20 years as an establishment more akin to a community than to a freestanding business enterprise.

The resort hotel usually provides a variety of experiences. Its surroundings, generally in some scenic or natural environment, are made pleasantly accessible because of the location of the hotel itself. As a rule, there is usually some type of key recreational activity such as boating, swimming, sunbathing, skiing, tennis, golf, or horseback riding. The rooms of a resort hotel typically have pleasant views and the building is designed to induce relaxation and extended stays. It has dining room facilities and lobbies that are informal and relaxing in their layout, offering different settings and conducive to a variety of experiences. The hotel also may provide special entertainment for its guests—not only music and typical nightlife fare but also other programs such as lectures, special tours, sports lessons, and physical fitness and weight control programs.

The commercial hotel, on the other hand, is a commercial hotel by virtue of its being located near an area where potential occupants will want to be, such as a business center, an airport, or the downtown of a principal city. Its primary aim is to provide convenience. It will have certain accommodations required by business and commercial travelers, such as travel desks, cleaning services, secretarial services, a restaurant designed for business entertaining, meeting rooms, taxi service, fast check-in/check-out arrangements, and a business-oriented shopping mix. Some of these features, such as those relating to hosting conferences, may be equally important to a destination resort.

Second Homes

Second homes are used for various purposes according to different segments of society. Traditionally, second homes have been used for vacations. This use is often seasonal, and homes may be located at some distance from the owner's primary residence.

Another popular use of the second home is as a weekend retreat. The property owner visits much more frequently but for shorter periods of time. By necessity, weekend homes are located closer to the market area—most of them are within 200 miles of a major metropolitan area. In some cases a second home may be both a weekend and vacation home, depending on the amenities. The owner will commute weekends in the off-season and spend longer vacation times in the primary season. For example, skiers whose properties are close enough to commute weekends will do so during the ski season while planning longer summer vacations at their mountain retreats.

Second homes are often purchased as investments. This is particularly important to middle-income homeowners who see a second home as forced savings and depend on its long-term equity appreciation. A second home may also be seen as a short-term investment by risk-taking speculators who perceive a vacation home in a growing area as a rapidly appreciating asset that will produce a capital gain. The investment aspect of second homes has also been realized in the United States by the owner who rents the property either privately or through a property management service and takes advantage of tax write-offs for depreciation. Many of the tax advantages of this ownership, however, were undercut by revisions of the U.S. tax laws in the later 1970s, and what benefits remain continue to come under frequent scrutiny.

Recreational second homes are being used increasingly for retirement. Consumers seek preretirement, semiretirement, and ultimately full retirement vacation homes. The home may be purchased in a resort or recreational community by a person still working who uses it occasionally and plans to retire there eventually. It may also be purchased at retirement for seasonal use, alternating with the owner's primary home. A large part of the market for retirement recreation homes is composed of "empty nesters," couples whose children are grown and have left home and whose homes consequently are too large and costly or inconvenient to maintain. Many of these couples desire to move into an appropriately sized modern home in a recreational community before complete retirement.

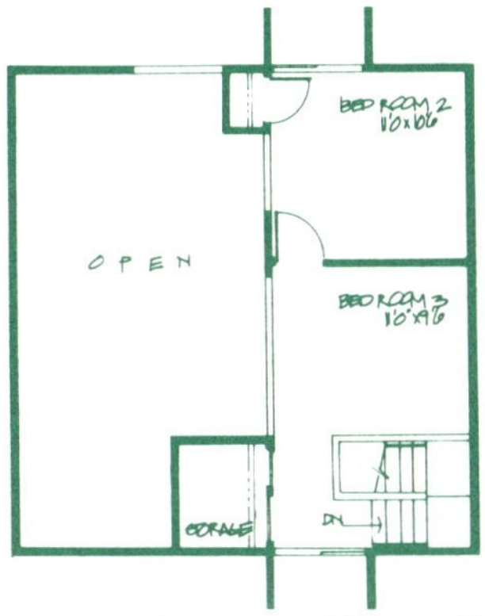

Second Floor . . . 286 sq. ft.

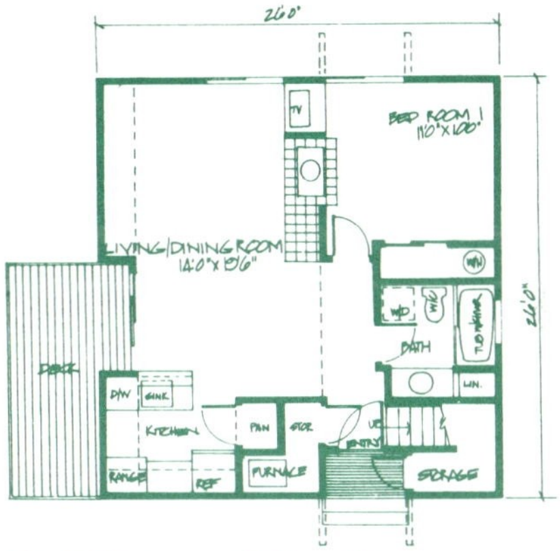

First Floor . . . 676 sq. ft.

2-2 Relatively simple homes, often built on a do-it-yourself basis, make comfortable weekend and vacation retreats.

Characteristics

The physical characteristics of second homes vary greatly—from futuristic to traditional in style, from remote to high density in location. The type of home developed must reflect a combination of factors: the market segment to be served, the physical requirements of a particular site, and the financial investment projected.

Since privacy and the relief from urban density are major motivations of second-home ownership, the single-family detached vacation home on its own lot has been extremely popular. A variety of precut, packaged homes, in styles from log cabin to contemporary, has been marketed to the vacation home buyer since the 1960s. These homes are available in a range of prices from moderate to expensive and, in some cases, offer do-it-yourself construction. Many developers of recreational subdivisions are builders as well and offer a limited portfolio of single-family home designs. Some lot sales contracts may require purchasers to select a home design for construction within a set time limit.

Recreational projects generally focus around a particular physical amenity—ski slope, lake, golf course, or special vista. Siting of homes to take best advantage of the amenity is essential to maximizing their value. The design of and materials used on the home should complement the site and surroundings. Homes in wooded areas, for instance, may best be treated with muted stains or paints to blend in rather than protrude from the landscape. In open areas, homes may best reflect the influence of local architecture in materials and scale, thus integrating the development with its setting.

2-4 Modern custom-built houses designed for more full-time use are appropriate for the semiretirement and retirement leisure home markets.

The increasing cost of land, construction, and necessary infrastructure for second homes has encouraged the development of cluster homes, townhouses, and low-rise attached units. Moreover, concentrating development allows the preservation of natural attractions such as greenbelts and open space which in turn can help offset increased density. Services are more easily managed in cluster areas and less land is taken up with roads and driveways.

With regard to services, it is important to note that since most vacation homes are constructed of wood, water is frequently scarce, access to some remote locations is difficult, and some houses must depend on volunteer fire departments, fire protection is a very important consideration in unit design.

Leisure home cluster units require careful siting and landscaping not only to maintain views but also

2-3 Clustered or attached second-home units have become increasingly popular, offering substantial flexibility in siting, competitive development costs, and shared maintenance.

to protect privacy. Soundproofing in attached units should be adequate. Attached second homes can be individualized and given added distinction from each other by combining different unit sizes to vary the rooflines. As with single-family homes, second-home attached units which enhance rather than compete with the natural setting are most popular.

Popular seaside, lakeshore, and western ski resorts have increasingly turned to mid- and high-rise buildings to accommodate the larger number of purchasers wishing to own a second home. Mid- and high-rise construction has been popular in European resorts for years, but North Americans have been less familiar with high-density, urban-styled leisure homes. Some multistory buildings are constructed of wood, and when sited on a slope allow mid-level access with walk-up (and -down) entrances to the units. Building codes and load requirements generally necessitate the use of reinforced concrete or steel framing for buildings over six stories.[1]

Mid- and high-rise construction should be carefully considered in typical recreational environments. The construction of urban-scale buildings can seriously affect the natural setting that is the area's primary attraction. In some areas, high rises have met resistance from the local community because they "wall off" the view and replace it with highly visible glass, concrete, and steel. Nonetheless, high-rise construction concentrates development and may be less environmentally damaging than scattered development.

Recreational Vehicle Sites

Having a recreational vehicle (RV) and a site for it in a private campground is one option for many who would like a recreational home site. The RV industry mushroomed in the 1960s and 1970s and elaborate family campers and motor homes are now available in many shapes and sizes. Over 6 million families own RVs suitable for camping.[2] The RV offers mobility, convenience, and comparatively low price, although one can spend from $14,000 to $60,000 or more for a motor home, and fuel supply and cost problems may pose uncertainties.

Where private campgrounds have typically competed with low-cost public camping facilities, with at most the minimal improvements of roads, plumbing, and electricity, RV parks can offer fuller amenities,

[1]Urban Land Institute, *Residential Development Handbook* (Washington: ULI–the Urban Land Institute, 1978), p. 129.

[2]*Real Estate Investing Letter* (June 1978), p. 4.

2-5 Campground advertisement featured during the gasoline shortages of 1979.

better hookups, and reserved space as part of a more expensive facility. The boom in the RV market led developers to create campgrounds with sites available for purchase.

A variant of the purchased campsite is the club campground in which a camper purchases a membership with rights to overall use rather than a deed to a specific site. This eliminates the need for platting and numerous other regulations. An exchange program with other campgrounds allows members to use the membership privilege at other locations.

Types of Consumer Ownership

The most common form of vacation property ownership is fee simple. Fee simple ownership is a whole interest in the land and the home. In recreational communities, as in residential subdivisions, the developers will impose covenants that are passed on with the deed which restrict the use of the land. The covenants ensure the continuation of specified development and use standards. Community home owner associations (HOAs) invariably are created to help guide community policy and fulfill community management needs in ways largely parallel to those characteristic of primary-home community associations, although modified to meet the needs of second-home owners.

The condominium is another common method of ownership. A condominium may be attached or detached, a townhouse or a high rise. The concept of a condominium is that the buyer purchases and owns outright the complete interior of the unit, from the surface of the lowest floor to the paint on the uppermost ceiling. The building exterior, public areas, and the land on which it is sited are owned in common with other buyers. A developer of a condominium must register a declaration which sets forth the percentage of ownership of each unit and establishes a condominium owner association to oversee the maintenance of the common areas.[3] This arrangement relieves to a degree the second-home owner of maintenance and security responsibilities while absent and allows him more leisure time when present.

A relatively new concept of second-home ownership is timesharing or interval ownership. Popular in Europe for some time, timesharing was introduced in the United States in the early 1970s. It offers equity ownership advantages for tax purposes although each buyer owns only a share of a unit. Timesharing can work in a variety of ways, but the basic concept is that a purchaser buys a share in a specific unit for a certain

[3]David B. Wolfe, *Condominium and Homeowner Associations That Work: On Paper and In Action* (Washington: ULI–the Urban Land Institute and CAI–the Community Associations Institute, 1978).

Profile of Timesharing in the United States

Essentially two kinds of timeshare plans are being offered in the United States: fee ownership and right-to-use programs. With the former, the buyer acquires fee ownership in a particular unit and a corresponding exclusive occupancy right for a specified annually recurring period of time. Under right-to-use programs, the buyer acquires an occupancy right for a specified annual period to a designated unit or class of accommodations, sometimes involving more than one location, but acquires no ownership interest in the property.

2-6 Capri-by-the-Sea, an oceanfront timeshare high rise near San Diego.

Initially, most right-to-use programs had terms of 40 years or more (life of the building). Currently, however, many right-to-use plans are adopting shorter terms (10 to 25 years) with a renewable option for additional years at either the original price or one greatly discounted.

As shown in a survey made in 1980,* the typical U.S. timeshare project had the following characteristics. It was a facility of 41 units with plans for 37 more and extensive recreational amenities on-site or nearby. It offered a trading opportunity through membership in one of two independent exchange services, Interval International or Resort Condominiums International. Units were on the market for approximately 24 months. Consumer financing was being offered at 20 percent down, with terms of 5 to 7 years and 13 percent interest.

*This survey was conducted by Stephen W. Brener's Helmsley-Spear Hospitality Services, Inc., New York City.

period of use. The most common timesharing interval is 1 week, but multiple units may be purchased for continuous blocks of time or on a revolving calendar. At least one period a year is customarily reserved for unit maintenance.

Timesharing offers advantages and disadvantages. It makes units available at low cost and allows owners to pay only in relation to the time they will spend in them. In 1979, the average cost of a timeshare unit was approximately $4,300.[4] For the developer, timesharing increases the total gross return from unit sales but net profits may not be any higher than those from conventional sales.

The fact that timesharing is complicated contributes to its disadvantages. Many individual sales must often be made to complete the full use of a unit. The cost of maintenance is higher than that of single ownership use and the marketing budget is higher, as much as 35 to 50 percent of the sales price. Finding buyers for off-season intervals in a seasonal resort may be difficult. The buyer runs the risk of insolvency or default from one of the other owners, thus making that percentage interest in the unit vulnerable to seizure. Finally, timesharing has had problems with financing though lenders have been more receptive since 1977. In spite of low prices for shares, buyers have often had to seek outside financing, with lenders initially being wary of this form of ownership. Nevertheless, timesharing has been increasingly accepted and is growing rapidly. Developers who have made available a network through which timeshare units can be exchanged have found it a highly successful marketing tool for projects.[5]

Finally, ownership through clubs has been gaining in popularity. This form of ownership involves an undivided interest in a club which owns and maintains a property. Membership use may be specified for a certain number of days a year or regularly scheduled. The "condotel" is a variant of club membership that has been used in European resort areas as a means of equity financing. A percentage of the rooms in a condotel are sold and the rest remain available for rent. A buyer who purchases a membership in the condominium/hotel receives the right to use a room for a certain period each year and shares in the expense and profit of the hotel operation. Club ownership presents risks in that the management of the facility is the key to a profitable operation. With poor management, the members will be liable for the hotel's excessive expenses.

[4] ALDA, *Resort Timesharing* (Washington: American Land Development Association, 1979).

[5] For a full discussion, see William B. Ingersoll and Stuart Marshall, eds., *Timesharing* (Washington: ULI–the Urban Land Institute, 1977).

Approximately 415 resort locations—principally in the United States, Mexico, the Caribbean, and Europe—had announced or were offering timeshare plans as of June 1980. In that year, the average resort was 63 percent sold out.

The most common types of units offered are one- and two-bedroom configurations. The two-bedroom unit, most often offered in a timeshare program, can have a gross yield of $295,398 or $299 per square foot, approximately twice the yield from the sale of a whole unit of the same size to a single buyer.

A timeshare is, of course, a two-part purchase. In addition to the one-time purchase price, all programs have an annual maintenance fee. Newer programs tend to peg annual fees higher than older programs in order to reflect the actual costs.

The cost of marketing when compared to other real estate offerings appears quite high. There are several reasons for this high cost. Consumers must be educated regarding timesharing. Since each unit may be purchased by over 50 different consumers, compared to one consumer per unit in conventional whole-time units, a developer must screen many more prospective buyers to sell a unit. In order to draw prospects to the project, off-site sales offices are often established, greatly increasing marketing costs. Sales commissions for timesharing sales personnel are higher than in conventional real estate transactions due to the much lower purchase price.

2-7 Interval ownership is offered for highly popular two-bedroom, two-bath units grouped in fourplexes here at Shell Island Beach Club, Sanibel Island, Florida.

Location

Discussion of the locational characteristics of recreational communities involves both a review of the locations of existing recreational real estate as well as an examination of the criteria that determine the location of new projects. Determining the location and number of existing second homes and recreational lots is a difficult problem. In the first place, it is difficult to define a recreational home, and second, the sources of information are limited and outdated.

The Office of Interstate Land Sales Registration (OILSR) sheds some light on the general geographic distribution of recreational projects. In 1979, the states having the most projects registered with OILSR were Florida and California, followed by Texas, Arizona, New Mexico, and Colorado. Because many of the projects in the Southwest are unimproved lot developments with a low build-out, data are skewed toward lot locations. The 1970 U.S. Census counted 2,143,434 leisure homes, approximately 3.1 percent of the total housing units.

As of 1979, estimates of the number of second homes in the United States exceeded 3 million, with a higher percentage of increase attributed to the southern states. Texas, for example, has experienced tremendous growth in leisure homes, with 215,000 estimated in 1979, up one-third from the 165,000 counted in 1970. It is logical that second-home demand will follow both the national demographic shifts and climatic conditions favoring the South and West.

The location selected for a recreational project reflects the influence of the two main players in the market—the developer and the buyer. From the developer's point of view, incremental recreational projects traditionally have been built around established resort areas. Pioneering a new area presents a far greater risk than making a new offering in an established area. Public recognition and acceptance of an area as a vacation spot have been important factors in persuading buyers to purchase homes or lots. Established resorts provide built-in entertainment and physical amenities that consumers desire. Recreational projects can take advantage of the preexisting public demand to own property in these recognized areas.

Developers have also sought to create a destination—in essence, open up a new area—which will attract second-home buyers. The concept of the new community which offers a variety of recreational opportunities designed for leisure living has been popular with several large and well-financed developers and has been well received by consumers.

Destination developments are typically large-scale

2-8 Water-based locations such as Harbour Town shown here at the Sea Pines Plantation are ever popular vacation destinations.

operations that expand on an already existing natural feature such as a body of water or a mountainside by the construction of golf, tennis, skiing, boating, or swimming facilities in some combination to create a number of recreational alternatives. This type of project is much more expensive to develop since all the amenities must be established by the developers and substantial marketing efforts are necessary to make the public aware of the property. The recreational development in Orlando, Florida, is a case in point. Before the construction of Disneyworld, recreation was not an important factor in the local economy. But the theme park and its satellite developments formed an important mass of recreational alternatives that have truly created a new destination to which thousands flock.

Although a plan to locate a recreational project may be highly orchestrated, based on complex marketing analyses, the fact is that many developer decisions with respect to a particular site are often made quite fortuitously. A certain piece of land may represent a "good deal" or suddenly become available, meaning a use must be found for it, and by its very development will help form the consumer's impression of the market.

Consumers prefer to have their leisure homes located within a 4-hour driving radius of their primary residences so they may be used frequently. A minimum distance of perhaps 50 miles is also important, however, to provide an adequate change of venue. Increases in air travel have meant that consumers are willing to travel farther than 200 miles to a recreational site if it offers unusual or outstanding amenities. The Rocky Mountains, Florida, and Hawaii have been notably successful in attracting purchasers living thousands of miles away.

Developer decisions must reflect consumer preferences. Water is the prime recreational amenity and is consistently selected as the most preferred option for leisure home projects. Water offers both active and passive enjoyment and appeals to all ages with the variety of its recreational opportunities. Swimming and fishing are two of the most popular outdoor sports and the passive pleasures of peaceful and relaxing water views are universally enjoyed.[6] Aquatic theme parks have been developed in response to the American love of water and the demand for active, organized recreation.

Mountainous areas are another popular locational choice. They offer cool and fresh climates, an atmosphere of physical ruggedness, interesting flora and fauna, and panoramic views which give one the feeling of spaciousness and isolation. Mountain developments frequently offer both summer and winter recreational activities. Water bodies located in mountain environments can be prime recreational attractions.

A variety of other factors influences consumer preference in choosing leisure home locations although the extent to which these factors determine demand is undocumented. Climate obviously plays a part, as well as one's previous exposure to an area and the decisions of one's family and friends to purchase on a particular site. Other factors include cost, taxes, and proximity to public lands.

Development Process

Predevelopment Planning

A recreational developer embarking on a development process must first consider the options and identify a general project concept. Many variables will determine the development concept which is most appropriate. The interested party might begin with a certain site whose best use is readily apparent (although this should not be too easily assumed). In another instance, the developer might be interested in tapping a potential market and would need an appropriate site. Experience has shown that the latter approach stands a better chance of success. Too frequently problems stem from attempts to make a project happen on a particular site simply because it is already owned or controlled and not because it is the right or best site. Nevertheless, while the initiating factors will differ from one case to another, the development practices employed to plan a project and make it succeed may have some similarities.

Essential to a calculated recreational development process in piloting a project through to maturity are the constant thinking and rethinking of the development concept and the continual reevaluation of available information and refinement of projections. This requires surveying the prospective market at the same time that the product type, project densities, and build-out periods are conceptualized and then testing this material against the real estate development constraints anticipated over the development period. All these items will first require preliminary investigation, and as each step of feasibility is established and used in refining the concept objective further, more detailed steps will need to be pursued. Without this careful coordination and matching of development considerations, a recreational project may easily be flawed from the start.

[6] Managing water surfaces is outlined in Joachim Tourbier and Richard Westmacott, *Lakes and Ponds*, Technical Bulletin 72 (Washington: ULI–the Urban Land Institute, 1976).

2-9 View from inside the Kapalua Bay Hotel on Maui, Hawaii.

Fundamental to creating a design concept is establishing the nature of the development or its desired image. Establishing a psychological goal will help determine a project's image or intended ambience which will in turn influence decisions on the type of facilities, their arrangement and quality, the operational needs, marketing techniques, and many other details.

The importance of early long-range conceptualizing of resort/residential recreational developments cannot be overstated. Certainly, a small project will entail fewer complications in this regard. But in any situation involving phased development, the initial actions must be made as supportive as possible of the goal sought, which means establishing certain development standards. Questions must be answered such as whether or not employee housing should be integrated into the development. In these matters, building recreational communities is not unlike building new communities in general. The recreational developer will need to consider what roles the developer should play throughout the development of the project—from its beginning to its maturity. Those roles will include an involvement in hotel and recreational operations, original sales, real estate resales, or whatever.

Products and Amenities

By targeting an image for the development, a recreational developer can begin to identify the product and services needed. Market surveys should help suggest an appropriate mix of hotel, condominium, and single-family products, along with some indication of size, style, ownership types, and price range.

As a preliminary step, the developer will want to consider what amenities to include in the project. It will be most important to identify those natural amenities which must be protected and how those amenities can be enhanced—for example a beach can be developed on an already existing lake. An existing built facility, such as a ranch, may also serve as an attraction. Another early procedure is to determine those amenities which should be built at the beginning of development, allowing for additional future facilities in the projected plan. Such "created" amenities will depend on the orientation of the project. If golfing and tennis are to be seed attractions, they will require an early and obvious commitment.

Four major questions should be considered in determining the amenity package:

- How does the amenity fit in with the total project physically, economically, and as part of its image?
- What quantity of the amenity should be provided?
- What should be the timing for construction?
- Is the cost justified?

In general, whenever amenities are created they should be planned and constructed well or not at all. Since the purpose of a resort is to offer a pleasant and substantive experience, it may be worse to have facilities that frustrate the user than to have no facilities at all.

The selection and quantity of facilities will depend on the type of consumer, the significance of other attractions, and the type of lodgings in the project. Amenities can be added to provide an alternative to heavy use of other recreational elements, but only as they reflect consumer interest. To some degree, amenities can be added or extended as demand grows.

The type of residence used in a recreational development can be significant. A conventional hotel

2-10 A natural amenity such as a beach may provide the initial and primary attraction of a resort. Manmade facilities may be necessary early investments, depending on the requirements of the target markets.

room is likely to create more demand for recreational services than a single-family home which is considerably more self contained and less intensively used. Condominiums available for rental fall somewhere in between these two kinds of residences in the amount of use they receive and the demand for recreational facilities they generate. Some condominiums, however, emphasize one particular amenity such as skiing or golf, which contributes to maximum use of key facilities.

The nature of these residential uses may not matter to the short-run investor, but for the master developer, future land values and potential profits from overall operations may be greatly affected by residential types, user habits, and satisfaction with the quantity and quality of the recreational amenities demanded and provided.

The developer must relate the amenity package to the surrounding community as well as to the outside visitor who must travel to reach the project. This relationship is particularly important when facilities depend on an operating cash flow to support themselves and are competing with off-site attractions or will rely at some time on off-site consumers for a substantial part of their support. In other cases, the amenity package is designed for the exclusive use of owners and guests.

Making a profit from or at least breaking even in commercial recreational operations should be an objective in a development plan. However, when recreational development occurs in an isolated location without a threshold community population, it may sometimes be worthwhile to subsidize certain facilities for activities, such as a limited version of golf, swimming, restaurant dining, and special convenience services. If a large community is anticipated, these facilities should ultimately pay directly for themselves. Recognition of the cyclical nature of real estate should convince developers and investors of the wisdom of incorporating the operation of facilities into their overall investment strategy.

A primary obligation of the recreational developer is to maintain expected standards of quality in meeting the demand for recreational facilities. For example, golf may be promoted as the key amenity. If the facilities provided allow for 300 active members for each 18 holes, and this number is exceeded, another recreational facility on or off the development should be provided as an alternative activity. Otherwise, as the project is built out, the facilities will become overloaded and users dissatisfied.

Tennis, for instance, is a simpler amenity to develop than golf. Courts can be added relatively easily. A golf course consumes over 25 times as much land as a tennis facility capable of handling a comparable number of users. Golfing areas, however, offer substantial aesthetic, environmental, and other values which may more than justify the expense.[7] Other facilities to consider will include those for water activities, walking trails, outdoor cooking areas, equestrian operations, retail services, conference accommodations, and community facilities such as transportation services and security.

2-11 Security is a principal concern of prospective second-home purchasers, both to maintain exclusivity, and more importantly, to protect property when the owner is absent.

In working up an amenity package the recreational planner will need to apply the same careful evaluations of demand and suitable standards that should characterize the whole recreational development process. To some extent, the developer is in a position to influence demand through the amenities provided, but this is no guarantee that such amenities will contribute effectively to the development. It is impossible to describe here a well-conceived amenity package since each one will evolve as a part of the particular recreational development project. The case studies in this handbook provide examples of ways in which individual projects have dealt with different concerns.

Site Selection

The only good site is one that will be marketable and capable of making the recreational development work. Therefore, a developer should not fall in love with a site, expecting the site to justify any development. The primary rule is to match the concept and the site. This means identifying a concept suitable to

[7] For planning a golf course amenity, see Rees L. Jones and Guy L. Rando, *Golf Course Development*, Technical Bulletin 70 (Washington: ULI–the Urban Land Institute, 1974).

a given site or finding a site suitable for a chosen concept.

The criteria for selecting a site for a major resort/recreational community involve setting, accessibility, and price. The determinants of setting include: aesthetic and climatic attributes; cultural attractions; recreational opportunities related to the setting, whether it is isolated or in an urban environment; and the availability of services. A simple but significant factor in choosing a setting is whether a project will be near an already established recreational destination. All these factors should be assessed for consistency with the image of the proposed development.

The marketability of the project depends on its distance from population centers and the types of transportation services available. For the exotic destination, distance from the consumer markets may not be as crucial (if jet travel continues to be affordable). Whatever the case, the appeal of the destination must compensate for the distance or inconvenience in getting there.

Ease of access also depends on transportation service—its frequency, quality, and cost. A resort in a location which is inaccessible will have high construction costs and, more than likely, an inadequate labor pool, which adds further costs to the infrastructure, management training, and labor importation. Improving the major means of transportation to a resort is usually beyond the resources of the normal development, which would require that the resort be positioned to take advantage of existing operating transportation facilities which, if not adequate, could be upgraded.[8] This is especially true for those locations that have been or would be dependent upon the private automobile for access. The development of transportation access involves extremely long lead times and heavy capital investment. The lack of access or its substandard condition should not be overlooked or underemphasized. Building roads is expensive and establishing service stations, rental car services, and bus lines is a formidable task. To construct an airport and operate a commercial air service is almost an impossibility. Obviously, the larger the contemplated resort, the more important it is that high volume commercial transportation be available in the area.

A third locational factor is financial in nature, namely the cost of development and the cost of operating the project when completed. These costs translate into the price the consumer must pay. Although price is affected by many factors, the major one is location which essentially affects: (1) the cost of the land; (2) the cost of building on it; and (3) the operation and marketing. These items relate closely to the physical setting and accessibility of the site and are all important to the success of a resort.

The absence of an outstanding natural amenity often requires higher front-end costs in order to create an attraction—for example, Disneyworld. Expensive construction required at a certain site can magnify this problem. Furthermore, expensive construction may create a lifetime of higher promotion costs to sustain business volumes if a manmade amenity is not exciting enough.

Phasing and Timing

Phasing and timing are the principal dilemmas in a resort development. An adequate set of recreational amenities should be provided at the beginning in order to draw and satisfy customers in sufficient volume to meet the growth needs of the developer. Heavy front-end financing is required to create these early recreational amenities, as well as cover their high initial operating losses until the number of visitors or residents and the concomitant revenues begin to support the operating costs. These front-end capital costs and early operating losses are usually sizable and lasting enough to cause the initial returns on the total investment to be unsatisfactorily low.

[8]Consequences of development in rural areas are discussed in Glenn V. Fuguitt, Paul R. Voss, and Joseph Doherty, *Growth and Change in Rural America* (Washington: ULI–the Urban Land Institute, 1979).

2-12 Construction economies may mandate building interrelated elements at the same time, such as a golf course in tandem with a water drainage system. A golf cart trail may double as a bike path.

The developer, however, need not go to extremes to create amenities in the beginning stages. A common misconception is that all amenities must be completed in order to attract visitors or buyers. The location of a resort or recreational community next to or within a strong existing attraction can provide, at no cost, much of the front-end amenity that a development might need to get started as well as ease some of the long-term burden of providing other kinds of amenities which require capital. If a location has been selected properly and is based on a nearby existing amenity, some people may be attracted to it even in its earliest stages when the developer has not yet created a full array of amenities. If not too much is promised them, visitors will not expect too much and will continue to return. Furthermore, a project will most likely appeal to different patrons at each stage of its development.

The amount of existing recreational consumer traffic in the area of a new project is an important consideration in sizing the initial amenities. For example, a resort community located where a substantial user market is established is in a better position to start with sizable amenities because of the already existing demand for them, thus helping to keep these facilities from operating at a loss from the outset. On the other hand, if little or no consumer traffic exists in the project's general or immediate vicinity, rather than start with numerous amenities, one should rely on the natural amenities already there, which require little extra capital investment, and start with the construction of accommodations. At this stage, certain people will become interested in the development because they are drawn to it in its purely natural state. This gives low front-end exposure, and as the number of accommodations increases, a sizable enough base will eventually be established to make it feasible to install the operating amenities, such as a golf course or tennis courts, and so forth. When these amenities are added, the developer would then intensify the promotion campaign and speed up the rate of growth so that the amenities producing revenues can break even as soon as possible.

Planning Approaches

The traditional approach to planning a site has been to consider the normal constraints of engineering demands, local ordinances, and marketing strategies in order to develop a site plan that is largely superimposed onto the land. Under this approach, amenities usually fit in as ancillary to the general site plan. A more environmentally sensitive approach, particularly important to recreational developments, is that of basing the construction on the unique personality of the site. With facilities and amenities carefully introduced, the ambience of the land can be emphasized. Only at this point, after cataloging how to enhance the character of the natural setting, should an overall site plan be prepared. In final form, such a product makes its own marketing statement.

2-13 In a special environmental setting, land uses should mold naturally with the landscape, enhancing the integrity of manmade facilities and optimizing view potentials.

Apart from integrating the development with the natural environment, the primary problem in planning the layout of a resort/recreational development is to arrange the accommodations in such a way as to provide every unit with some type of view or access to an amenity. The price differential accorded a prime location unit—for example, an oceanfront dwelling or one fronting a golf course as opposed to a unit in an interior location—is sizable, ranging from 20 percent to 30 percent, if not more. Therefore, it is to the developer's advantage to maximize the orientation of each unit toward any amenities.

Each recreational community has its own hierarchy of preferred locations based on views and proximity to amenities. In a beach resort the prime location would be near the waterfront; in a ski area it would be next to the ski run. The next preferred location might be frontage on or a view of some other secondary amenity, such as open space or a golf course. The third ranking location is what might be called an "overview." That is, from the unit one is able to look over other property or units and see the overall amenity, such as the ocean, golf course, or ski hill. The fourth ranking location offers a more intimate garden-type landscaped setting, possibly providing some privacy, or it is a location adjacent to another facility such as tennis courts, a swimming pool, or shopping center. The planner of a resort should examine all of the alternative primary layout schemes in order to test which ones will produce the highest yield, meaning the highest number of units which have the highest level of amenity associated with them. Such a plan will produce the highest gross sales value for the project. Generally, all other considerations such as utility and road extensions will be secondary to this one.

In view of increasing energy costs, all new resorts will most likely be more pedestrian in scale. This might suggest a movement toward a more concentrated land use plan or a multiple village concept rather than a highly disbursed plan. Because automobiles are sometimes thought to detract from a resort environment, a resort community scaled toward pedestrians can have additional advantages.

Tried and true residential development practices offer a number of alternatives for resort/recreational communities in meeting the special design priorities appropriate to a recreational environment. Typical residential planning alternatives include small- to large-scale subdivisions, unit clustering, planned unit developments, and other variations.[9] The conventional recreational lot subdivision is the least intensively planned approach and allows the private purchaser to exercise a high degree of individual discretion in designing and carrying out the development. While standards of design are still important in recreational lot development, as exercised in large part through platting, design committee controls, and restrictive covenants, environmental planning may be limited by the need to maximize lot counts and thereby occupy as much of the site as possible. Subdividing requires extensive road and utility construction and, with the implied lower densities, reduces the number of units which can enjoy direct amenity access.

The arrangement of structures in closely related groups, or unit clustering, is based on the concept of concentrating density in physically suitable locations, consequently, freeing open areas. To achieve the optimal effect, cluster planning requires more substantial design control than does subdivision planning. Planned unit development (PUD) is a special concept widely applied to recreational land development which is comprehensively planned as a single entity, grouping dwelling units into clusters, mixing housing types and land use, and preserving natural features and open space. PUDs are a legal concept whereby a developer is allowed planning flex-

[9] Urban Land Institute, *Residential Development Handbook*, op. cit., pp. 112–118. Also see Urban Land Institute, *Large-Scale Development: Benefits, Constraints, and State and Local Policy Incentives* (Washington: ULI–the Urban Land Institute, 1977).

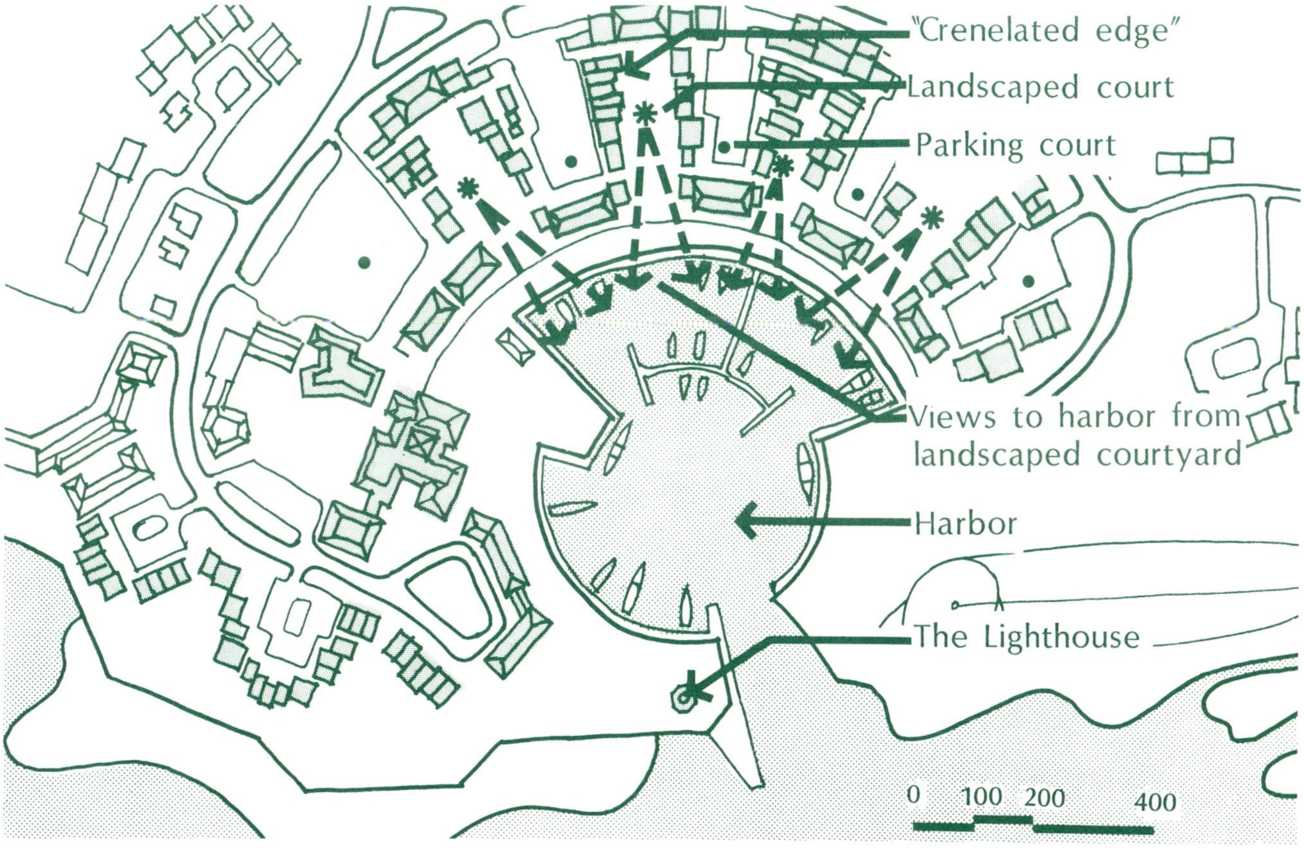

2-14 Dwelling units must be sited to highlight views in resort residential planning as portrayed here at Harbour Town.

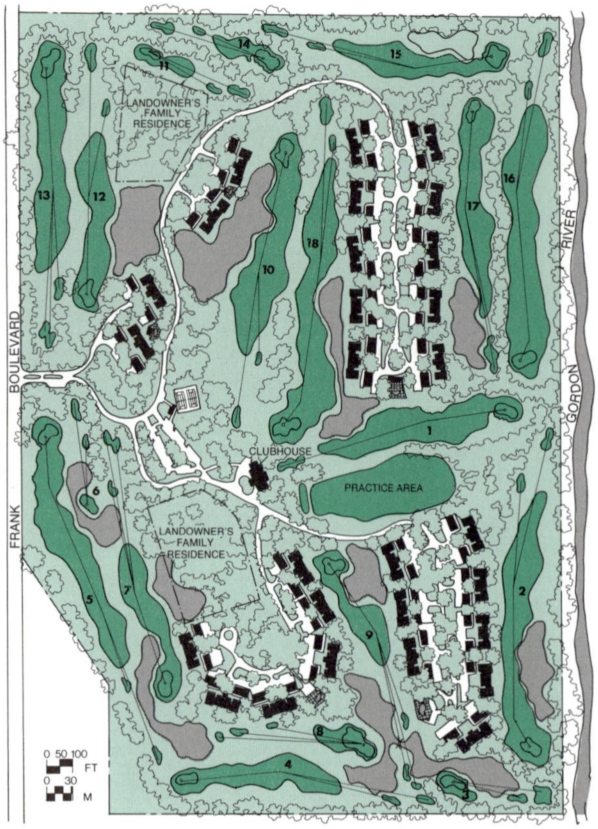

2-15 Lakes and golf fairways are used to create an attractive setting for The Wilderness, a second-home and retirement community in Naples, Flordia.

ibility in negotiating with the public regulating interests. Formal approval processes stipulate the appropriate planning procedures. These vary from place to place and are widely used, as they encourage comprehensive and flexible planning of recreational developments.

The overall scale of resort/recreational development will depend on many variables relating to site, financing, market, and regulations. Large-scale PUD-type development is an important recreational development tool which can provide a more efficient use of the land and greater aesthetic attributes than traditional development methods. For more isolated recreational destinations, large-scale development can provide a level of community services and amenities which would otherwise be uneconomical.

Development Strategy

Land Sales

Lot sales have historically represented the largest and most profitable type of recreational development. The strategy for land sales requires less capital investment and less managerial skill than other development alternatives. Depending on the improvements added, land sales transfer the bulk of the carrying costs, construction, and operational responsibility to others. The responsible recreational land developer, however, has long-term stakes. Building extensive amenities, roads, and utilities as part of a lot sales package can be extremely burdensome. Because competitors can enter into lot sales development relatively easily in rural areas, and because of the nature of their frontier appeal and low utility when undeveloped, lot sales can be a risky commitment. Moreover, unimproved projects cannot compete with the fully improved second-home subdivision having a complete amenity package.

One land sales strategy is to sell large tracts to builder/developers on a controlled and phased basis. Coordinated land sales in which different tracts of land are released for purchase under specific restrictions and covenants can help maximize returns on the land by allowing land values to increase before sales as a result of a calculated development program.

Built Dwelling Units

In recent years, a popular technique has been to develop and market a complete recreational product, even including interior furnishings and housewares. The recreational developer in this market has the opportunity to profit not only from land sales but also from constructing and marketing the product. Building the units provides a recreational developer with additional control over the product, giving him the flexibility to combine open space and unit density, which would not be possible under many lot sales programs. When a recreational community is in an isolated location with no suitably equipped local industry to develop a project, the developer may need to initiate a building program of his own.

Although the construction of units can increase the gross profits, it also increases the capital needs and risk. In an economic downturn, the developer/builder may have to carry not only the land but also the buildings. At any rate, this combined land development and building approach requires special managerial and marketing skills.

Operations

A further strategy is that the recreational developer operate the resort's facilities, whether that involves leasing commercial space, managing a hotel, operating a unit rental pool program, providing maintenance services or a resales program, or operating a golf course or health spa. This alternative provides the ultimate degree of developer control over the destiny of the project with such benefits as:

- Long-term profit.
- The potential for continued cash flows when the project has been completed and when real estate sales are slow.
- Influence over and capture of the phased increase in market values.
- Help in maintaining project standards (perhaps through subsidization).

Again, a successful operations program depends on extensive management expertise and financial backing.

Combined Alternatives

With various strategies available, the astute recreational developer can benefit from a flexible business plan combining the advantages of each approach. Occasional land sales may help generate funds for debt service or new capital expenditures. Joint ventures involving partners in ownership and operations can reduce the risk and the management requirements. A building program can add momentum and activity during a lull in land sales and help generate sales that increase the market for the existing amenities and facilities. The developer risks less by spreading his investment over the many business aspects of a resort/residential development. As a further incentive, certain tax benefits may also be derived from balancing profits and losses across the various facets of resort recreational development. And always prerequisite to these strategies is the builder's long-run commitment to new community development.

Development Team

Resort and recreational development is a highly complex multidisciplinary process. Recreational community development demands simultaneous work involving many areas of expertise. Numerous variables affect each possible procedure in a step-by-step development process whose every step can present a new question.

A team of tested professionals from several fields, unified under the owner/developer's objectives should plan, design, and construct the project. The developer may or may not be the owner, who could be an individual, a corporation, or a consortium of investors (which may include the developer). Regardless of who the owner is, however, the developer should be a skilled team manager with responsibility for coordinating successfully all the parts of the complex development process including its financial backing.

Effective organization and management are fundamental to success. To maintain strong management the developer needs a core staff through which management programs can be executed. Part of the developer's or team manager's responsibility is to ensure good communication among the various elements of the team, including those persons involved in market and financial analysis, planning, design, engineering, marketing, and operations. Team review and coordinated meetings are essential in optimizing efficiency and making sure the overall effort is on the right track.

2-16 Well-managed recreational facilities can become profit centers for a developer who is interested in long-term operations.

2-17 A team of experts from a variety of disciplines considering a development question. The isolated and specialized nature of recreational destinations invariably requires an experienced development team whose members come from a wide geographic area.

The question of whether to staff the development team from inside or to contract from outside is often debated. Its resolution depends on the experience and capability of the individuals involved, the development company's overall structure, the nature of the task, and the particulars of each situation. Participants can be involved under various contracts. They can work for a negotiated lump sum, on a cost-plus basis, or for a direct interest in the project.

One advantage in using consultants is that they can be used only when needed. A price must be paid for this method, both in terms of money and in terms of the effect on continuity, but it is an attractive approach because of the cyclical nature of recreational development. Consultants can offer expertise which is often indispensable to a developer new to an area. There are those consultants whose constant monitoring of the national market is crucial in assessing recreational demand, just as there are the specialized design and engineering experts on marinas, golf courses, or ski hills, as well as those knowledgeable individuals with insight into the local political system.

Feasibility and Planning

Market Analysis

With predevelopment ideas established and a site identified, detailed feasibility studies should be completed. An unfortunate problem in the study of recreational development has been the tendency to emphasize physical planning and architecture while giving inadequate attention to basic economic, political, and managerial concerns. The result is sometimes an attractive physical plan which cannot be implemented or which fails to optimize financial potentials.

Detailed market studies should be conducted to indicate the potential rates of absorption and revenues associated with:

- Residential properties in terms of price, rental rates, ownership types, lots versus units, single-family versus multifamily units, owner occupant versus vacation user;
- Hotel rooms in terms of quality classification, facilities, and average room rates;
- Potential revenue-producing facilities such as tennis or golf;
- Retail commercial areas in terms of tenant mix, supportable square footage, and obtainable lease rates; and
- Other types of development opportunities such as recreational vehicle parks.

The market analysis should include, but not necessarily be limited to, the following tasks:

- Defining a primary market region from which buyers and tourists could be expected to be drawn. Market area definitions should be based on such factors as time-distance relationships, comparable travel costs, available information at competitive projects, and tourist origin and destination data.
- Estimating the potential demand for various types of development within the defined market region. Demand estimates should be based on past preferences of different income groups in their purchase of recreational lots and homes, modified to reflect current and projected economic conditions and buyer attitudes toward recreational properties. Estimates should be established according to the type of product and the price range and further reflect the regional buyer's ability to purchase.
- Identifying and surveying related competitive projects in the primary market region. Projects should be surveyed based on such factors as physical features, recreational orientation and facilities, locational characteristics and access to markets, and real estate products. The intent of the survey is not only to develop a profile of competitive projects but also to synthesize from recent project histories relevant trends in both products and markets, and to determine how successful such projects have been in the current market.

A thorough evaluation of supply and demand characteristics should indicate what product and ownership type, pricing, and sizing would maximize the market opportunities for a new recreational development. An analysis of the effect of various recreational

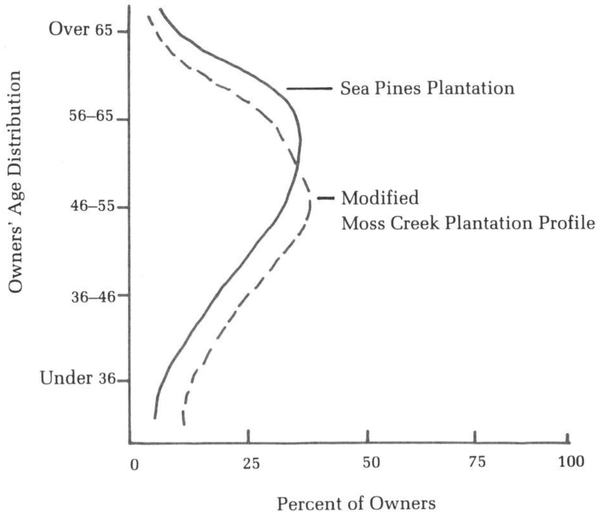

2-18 Data from the established Sea Pines Plantation on the age distribution of owners were used to assess the markets for a new development called Moss Creek Plantation near Hilton Head Island.

development programs and facilities on potential sales and prices should suggest a suitable recreational amenity package. Based on the anticipated increase in visitors, an estimate of the potential demand for various types of retail and commercial recreational facilities should be possible. The market study findings will allow physical and economic planners and market analysts to develop jointly a realistic plan for land use allocations for the various development components.

2-19 Analyzing this physical situation includes asking: Is this oceanfront suitable for dwelling units, or is golf a better use with respect to the overall project?

Physical Analysis

The analysis of the physical opportunities and constraints of recreational development will involve collecting all existing base data and identifying future information needs. Physical analysis studies should include assessments of:

- Topography and slope.
- Hydrology—major and minor drainage and water source features and resources, including flooding hazards and erosion.
- Geology—surface and subsurface conditions.
- Oceanography—shoreline; littoral drift; soundings; and wave action.
- Vegetation—major vegetation covers; forests; and agriculture.
- Wildlife.
- Meteorology—wind; temperature; humidity; rainfall; and sun angles.
- Ecological and environmental factors—views; sounds; and special conditions.
- Utilities—power; water; sewerage; and communications.
- Circulation and related infrastructures—highways and roads; railways; airports and air routes; ports and harbors; and bridges and dams.
- Natural resources.
- Historic and cultural sites and landmarks.
- Existing land uses and proposed future changes or developments.
- Permitting process and legal restrictions—zoning and building codes and restrictions which are applicable (including proposed changes); certainty of approvals over time; and easements and deed restrictions.

Information from these studies should be synthesized into a series of analysis drawings and reports to provide a factual basis for ongoing planning, engineering, and design. Also included at this stage should be the identification of potential site development areas and concepts, the identification of the areas of cost sensitivity, and the identification of areas possessing special physical characteristics and development potential for high-priority recreational attractions, which should be given more concentrated study.

Concept Design

Preliminary programs for various types of facilities and attractions should be further developed and tested using the data and studies formulated during the analysis. Based upon these studies, the economists and planners along with other team members can evaluate various development areas and make recommendations for the specific area or areas having the greatest potential. Their work will include:

- Conceptual diagrams.
- Ideal functional relationship diagrams.
- Site-related functional diagrams, with special attention to land which would be particularly suitable for recreational development.
- Preliminary land use diagrams.
- Capacity studies of gross acres available for development, as well as of probable areas for preservation.
- Suitability studies of various alternate land uses.
- Alternate density and yield evaluation.
- Other illustrations and perspective drawings which may be required to show more fully any special features or characteristics of the project.
- Preliminary project staging plans.

While planning and engineering studies are being carried out, architects should:

- Evaluate architectural forms and construction methods which might be appropriate for construction in the general area, and those specifically appropriate for the recreational market.
- Establish design criteria and standards for building construction (especially as they relate to orientation and siting, available local building materials, and other special problems such as construction access and distance to sources for materials).
- Research local construction costs.
- Research existing building codes, requirements, and restrictions which must be followed, as well as other requirements needing changes, modifications, or updating.

When the physical analysis and program concepts have been further refined, the conceptual land use studies will then require modification. More detailed studies will be made as sites are selected and given relative priority and projections suitable for financial negotiations are prepared.

Financial Analysis

Mandatory to successful implementation of recreational projects are analyses that evaluate the financial feasibility of the proposed program, assist in the process of revising the recommended phasing and composition of development to optimize financial returns consistent with development goals, and provide a data base and convenient means of monitoring and maintaining financing control throughout the implementation phase. To achieve these objectives, the following procedures are recommended:

- Development of input parameters not otherwise generated in the market analysis. Examples would be infrastructure costs for roads, sewers, drainage, utilities, and so forth; hotel construction and furnishing costs; residential site development and construction costs; development costs for such amenities as golf courses, swimming pools, bike paths, tennis courts, and the like; and assumptions regarding items such as depreciation rates, capitalizing development costs, financing costs, engineering and consultant fees, real estate taxes, promotion and adver-

2-20 Artist's drawings help clarify development concepts . . .

tising expenses, project management and overhead costs, and expenses for maintenance and utilities.

- Analysis of inflationary effects on both revenues and costs for the project and inclusion of adjustment for inflation in financial modeling of the project.
- Preparation of a pro forma annual balance sheet, income statement, cash flow statement, and profitability analysis by detailed land use components. These pro forma statements should be provided for a period as long as necessary to reflect the full build-out and absorption of the property, or at least to the point where a positive and continuing cash flow is established after financing charges are deducted.[10]
- Revisions to the proposed development plan based on review of the financial analysis and discussions between the developer and his physical planning consultants.
- Interpretation of the results of the financial analysis and recommendations concerning the feasibility of the development's timing, phasing, strategy, marketing program, and potential for joint venture or bulk sales.

Preparation of a Preliminary Plan

Based upon the land use plans and facilities programs developed in the conceptual design phase of a resort/residential project, the planning team will:

- Prepare preliminary cost estimates for all facilities to be reviewed and refined by the marketing/economic planners.
- Update and refine facilities programs with the marketing/economic planners.
- Prepare detailed plans of land use areas to allow for continual physical refinement and financial analysis.
- Refine capacity studies of gross acres of developable land and facilities.
- Prepare studies of alternative densities and yield.
- Prepare interim projections portraying development alternatives for financial evaluation by the economic planners.
- Prepare preliminary project design guidelines.

Upon completion of these studies, which will evaluate all aspects of site planning, physical design, engineering, architecture, and market and financial considerations, the physical planners will proceed with preparation of general overall plans. At this level of design, alternative land uses appropriate to the recreational market and the site and compatible with the constraints dictated by government authorities will become evident.

Financing

There is no single formula for financing recreational development. Different projects with their various characteristics of ownership, development needs, and market will have different financing arrangements, as even identical projects will. The unique financial package that is the life blood to any recre-

[10]Examples of pro forma statements can be found in ULI, *Residential Development Handbook*, op. cit., pp. 91–94.

2-21 . . . and market a plan to financial backers, as well as potential buyers.

ational development will be determined by, among many variables, the merit of the particular proposal, the business reputation and development experience of the applicant, the applicant's equity and collateral, the type of financing institution involved, the mood of the lender, and the general economic prospects of the times.

Recreational development financing has its counterpart in many other types of real estate development, from small-scale land sales which may be entirely financed internally on up to large-scale new communities requiring direct long-term ties with money sources. The financing needs typical of real estate development include:

- Early planning in which developer/owner equity investment is essential.
- Land acquisition, possibly first through land options, with purchase by mortgage, seller's note, or other traditional methods.
- Site improvements, commercially financed with the land as collateral, through presales or other means.
- Construction financing, a short-term funding proposition requiring guarantees to satisfy the risks to lending institutions.
- Permanent financing in which the evidence of market viability permits long-term mortgage repayment of interest and principal on the full development.

The sources of money are many and relate to the type of financing. Money may be obtained from individuals, banks, insurance companies, pension funds, foreign investors, savings and loan associations, public bonds, and others, and might be structured in a variety of ways such as conventional mortgages, loans with equity kickers, loans with options to acquire ownership, and joint ventures. Depending on the nature, size, and organization of the real estate project, financial sources more typical of commercial businesses might be available, such as unsecured lines of credit, inventory and receivables loans, and preferred stock, though the last example is unusual.

These forms of financing are not unique to the resort/recreational community but rather are fairly common in the real estate industry generally and have been discussed at length in other publications. However, recreational development, and specifically the development of resort/recreational communities, has unique financing requirements and problems, as well as opportunities which should be discussed.

To oversimplify, the uniqueness of resort/recreational community development, as it affects financing, is based on the principal fact that resort/recreational community development involves, in varying combinations, specialized facilities, services, activities, and amenities not normally associated with other types of real estate development, examples being golfing, boating, eating, and dancing. The economics of providing facilities for these activities have either not been carefully studied and documented for long-term use as elements of a larger development project or, where studied and documented, are not understood by the financial community at large. Needless to say, it is difficult to finance an activity which the would-be lender or investor does not understand, or is nervous about, or, further, is convinced is uneconomical.

Attempts at analyzing the economics of a given project are complicated in particular by the typically long-term nature of resort/recreational land development. A project of this kind is subject to a host of changing conditions over time, both intrinsic and extrinsic to the project itself, including the economy, market attitudes and tastes, inflation, interest rates, availability of credit, availability of gas, labor strikes, climate, and many more. Most real estate developments, with the exception of large land developments, are relatively short-term projects in which many economic conditions can be identified in advance, such as construction costs, interest rates tied to permanent financing, and revenues associated with presales or preleasing. Compounding the difficulties associated with long-term recreational developments are the often required heavy front-end costs during the period of negative cash flow and the fact that investments can be recovered and profits made only in the last phases of development. The long-term nature of resort/recreational community development makes it more difficult to evaluate a project's economics and thus increases the investment risk, at least compared with other forms of real estate development.

In part because of these considerations, the financial community has not developed an understanding of long-term resort/recreational community development. Certainly, short-term development and land loans (provided in some cases by real estate investment trusts) were and are not the answer. As a result, the resort/recreational developer may have to make do with financing techniques and attitudes designed for quite different undertakings. Perhaps the best solution to this dilemma is to rely heavily on equity in the early stages of resort/recreational community development. The more prudent heavy equity approach to an inherently risky, long-term venture will likely require creative partnership arrangements with equity partners willing to sacrifice short-term returns for

2-22 The economics of community scale facilities in recreational developments such as Sea Pines are not well understood; they lack the closely comparable and more stable market conditions typically shared by other types of development.

long-term values. The alternative solution is for the resort/community developer simply to revise, modify, and tailor his development program to the financing available, or face abandoning any plans altogether.

In most instances, those projects that do proceed do so with the developer deciding to go ahead with whatever financing he can obtain—however inadequate or unrealistic it may be. This accounts in some measure for the high failure rate of resort/recreational properties and the easy assumption that a resort project must go through much hardship before it can be successful or that it is the second or third owner who will make the money. While these statements may be true, it is not true that resort/recreational community development is necessarily unprofitable, but, as this discussion has emphasized, that few people genuinely understand the complex long-term economics of such developments and that these projects are often financed in such a way that they are doomed to failure, except under the most favorable circumstances.

The circumstances can be optimized by making the financial proposal as attractive as possible. Money markets are highly competitive, and lenders naturally seek investments having the lowest risks. The developer's interest in maximizing the return on his equity by maximizing the leverage used must be balanced against the relative risk incurred by the lender.

The applicant's proven skills and the project's physical appeal alone will not impress the lender. A sophisticated and well-presented feasibility analysis is an indispensable tool in soliciting financing support. Pro forma statements are essential to indicate the "go/no-go" situation and obtain a financial commitment.

2-23 Because there is no general formula with which to determine the cost effectiveness of amenities in real estate development, the assumed value of amenities must be carefully scrutinized.

2-24 A viable financial plan may need to include provision for sustaining operations such as cleaning and maintenance of resort rental units.

A strong managerial commitment is also necessary. Over the last two decades, the mixed success large diversified corporations have had in real estate development, without having real estate expertise, attests to the need for specialized managerial skills in the development process. The developer may be well advised to include on the development team an intermediary with expertise in financing who would seek out funds in what is generally an imperfect capital market. Financing opportunities will be improved by the experienced financial middleman who has personal contacts and who is knowledgeable, creative, and flexible.

Approval Process

Some of the early measures to take in preparing a development plan involve cataloging the public agencies and regulations, preparing to meet them in proper sequence, and considering a plan for negotiating the needed approvals. As mentioned previously, initial community analysis should begin with conceptual planning. In addition to the approval requirements mandated for typical urban development, recreational development may have to overcome serious environmental hurdles (because of its natural affinity for special environmental areas), concerns such as traffic congestion and public service demands associated with the extraordinary impact of a large project in a rural area, and the unfamiliarity of local institutions with planning for such development.

As part of the approval process, a developer must meet certain requirements in order to obtain the government permits and community approvals needed to undertake and complete a project.[11] This process is extremely important to the developer since denial of a permit or approval could kill or indefinitely delay a project, resulting in financial disaster. Even when the project proposal represents the best land use practices, is environmentally sound, and meets all the stipulated requirements, it is not assured of a timely approval or an approval at all. In order to obtain permits and approvals in the shortest time, the developer should, at the earliest possible stage, prepare a community analysis and a plan of action.

The community analysis should identify all the factors, conditions, and forces, both adverse and supportive, which could influence the decisions and ac-

[11]For further discussion of the approval process, see Fred Bosselman, Duane A. Feurer, and Charles L. Siemon, *The Permit Explosion: Coordination of the Proliferation* (Washington: ULI–the Urban Land Institute, 1976). Also see Frank S. So, David R. Mosena, and Frank S. Bangs, Jr., *Planned Unit Development Ordinances* (Chicago: ASPO–the American Society of Planning Officials, 1973).

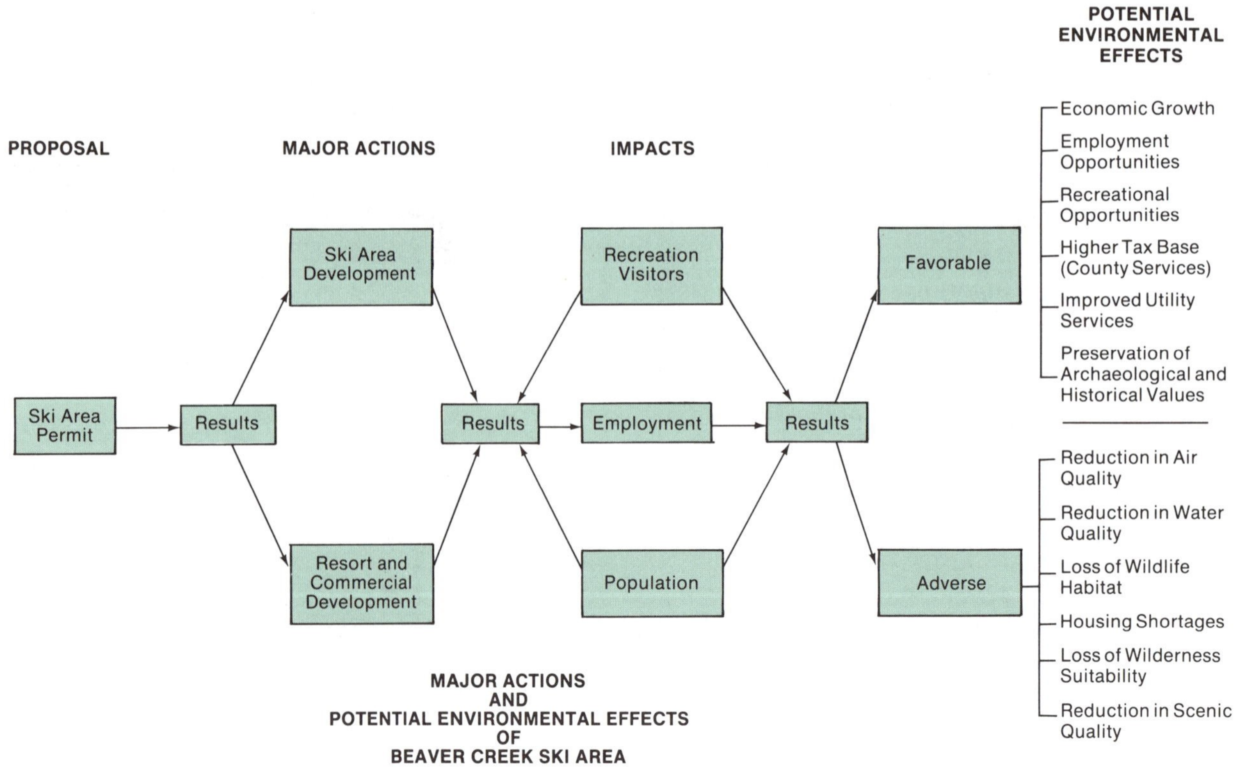

2-25 Flow chart showing development process for the Beaver Creek mountain resort located just west of Vail, Colorado.

2-26 Public and private regulations stipulating ocean setbacks and measures for dune preservation help protect recreational projects from the ravages of nature.

2-27 Employee housing can take many forms. In expensive resort areas, providing affordable employee housing may be part of the business expense of the resort developer and operator.

tions of public officials, community leaders, and special interest groups. The analysis should present a thorough and fair assessment of the predicted impact on the community. Rapid changes in social, political, and regulatory conditions require the developer to update this information continually.

Included in the community analysis should be as much relevant information as possible about potential issues of public concern and individuals whose involvement can be anticipated. In this assessment, the developer should determine the likely position that public officials and interest group leaders will take regarding the project. Obviously, these persons may have significant influence in controlling the permits and approvals required for development. Also evident is that while some information will be confidential to the developer, any action the developer takes in securing approval must be acceptable to the public.

With the benefit of basic community political data the developer will be able to prepare a plan of action for dealing with the appropriate issues and individuals in obtaining the required permits and approvals. All the formal permits required by the project from each of the various federal, state, and local agencies must be identified and the amount of time and work estimated to obtain each. This procedure should identify the most appropriate times and methods for working with the public agencies and special interest groups. The developer's strategy, if well conceived, will help to avoid unpleasant and costly surprises and identify appropriate tools to be used in overcoming anticipated opposition. Programs and studies should be set up which mitigate adverse environmental impacts, document beneficial economic and fiscal effects, and accomplish whatever else may be required to address each particular issue and concern, most of which should be accepted as legitimate community interests.

After completing the community analysis, the developer or representative should meet with the various elected and appointed officials to brief them on the project and learn firsthand of their concerns. With this meeting arranged before the project is presented to the community and special interest groups, officials will have a chance to express opinions on the proposal and suggest any revisions. Conceptual approval might be possible at that point, justifying more detailed planning.

The developer's firm commitment to satisfying public concerns will help rally support and a sense of public investment in a proposed project. In this role, the developer should meet early and as often as necessary with the various community and special interest groups.

Regardless of the developer's best efforts, a comprehensive recreational development proposal may be subject to years of exhaustive study, negotiation, and waiting, particularly in working through what may often seem to be an endless process of duplicative steps. The developer must anticipate delays and in trying to expedite the process remain respectful of the various participants, encouraging cooperative arrangements rather than falling into adversary roles. The public and private sectors have many common interests in development, and cooperative planning—with time to work out problems—can go a long way toward achieving mutual satisfaction. As a contingency, however, the developer's legal position must always be well understood, and when all reasonableness has been spent, that legal prerogative may have to be applied. Litigation may be required so that a developer's rights can be exercised, just as community issues may make it necessary to impose constraints on development. In any case, the developer's performance during negotiation and afterwards in implementing his proposals will be the primary test of his integrity along the way.

Overall Plan

Before final public and financial approval of a recreational project, the overall plan must be completed. It should delineate the following land uses and facilities to the extent that they are components of the project concept:

- Residential areas—hotel sites, multifamily housing, single-family housing and lots, and employee housing.
- Commercial areas and special features—town center, and entertainment and commercial activity centers.
- Recreation—water- and land-oriented activities, parks and playgrounds, and open spaces and natural zones.
- Circulation—major and minor vehicular routes, parking and service areas, pedestrian paths, bikeways, and equestrian trails.
- Historical/cultural features.
- Vegetation patterns.
- Land for future development and/or acquisition.
- Utilities and maintenance—water supply, power and electricity, waste treatment plants, telephone, other communications systems, and maintenance center.
- Community and public facilities as required—fire, police, schools, and churches.
- Related infrastructure—drainage, bridges and dams, primary access roads, and airstrip.

In addition to the illustrative plans, the following documents should also be prepared:

- Perspectives showing character of the proposed project.
- Large-scale site plans which examine selected areas in greater detail.
- Design guidelines consisting of sketches, sectional diagrams, elevations, and language which demonstrate the design intent of the plan.
- Phasing plans.
- Utility plan showing location, size, and phasing of major utility systems.
- Documentation of the long-term ownership of common facilities, designation of maintenance responsibilities, and specific structuring of developer, public, and owner roles.

When the overall plan has been completed (in conjunction with continuing economic analyses) and survived the scrutiny of all parties concerned, the development team can select specific areas within the project and proceed with the design and construction. This will involve the preparation of working drawings, contract documents for construction, a bidding process, and construction supervision.

Detailed Design

Design schematics should include detailed studies of the layout, grading, building plans, lighting, and landscaping. The design of recreational development should carry over the practices and basic standards of quality found in residential development, while focusing on consumer needs in recreation.[12] Dwelling units could probably be smaller, more open, and informal than primary residences, depending on their intended uses. For the second-home market where purchasers would otherwise be forced to furnish their units completely on their own, furniture and decorating "packages" with a choice of treatments may be highly practical. Security can be a major issue since owners may be unfamiliar with the surrounding community and concerned for their property and possessions during their prolonged absences. Security and privacy suggest the importance of physically orienting the recreational development internally. Security may involve a long-term expense and deserves practical consideration in the design stages. For example, a controlled single entrance, planned in the original design, may increase considerably the safety of a project.

Access and entranceways should be carefully designed into the development. Circulation will depend on the size, nature, and layout of the development. Automobile-oriented destinations having single-family lots will require extensive roadways with parking provided by the purchaser on each lot. A high-density/open space development may require some form of central parking complemented by an internal transit system. When autos are seen as impinging on the character of a particular resort, their use may need to be discouraged altogether or appropriately hidden from view.

The architect, landscape design architect, graphics designer, and interior designer should develop a detailed design vocabulary which will complement and reinforce the project image. It should be reviewed by the market analyst and marketing manager before final adoption. Such a vocabulary should include most or all of the following: exterior and interior building materials, a basic color palette, and a palette of plant materials.

[12] As one of many books on residential design, see Robert Engstrom and Marc Putman, *Planning and Design of Townhouses and Condominiums* (Washington: ULI–the Urban Land Institute, 1979). Also see David R. Jensen, *Zero Lot Line Housing* (Washington: ULI–the Urban Land Institute, 1981).

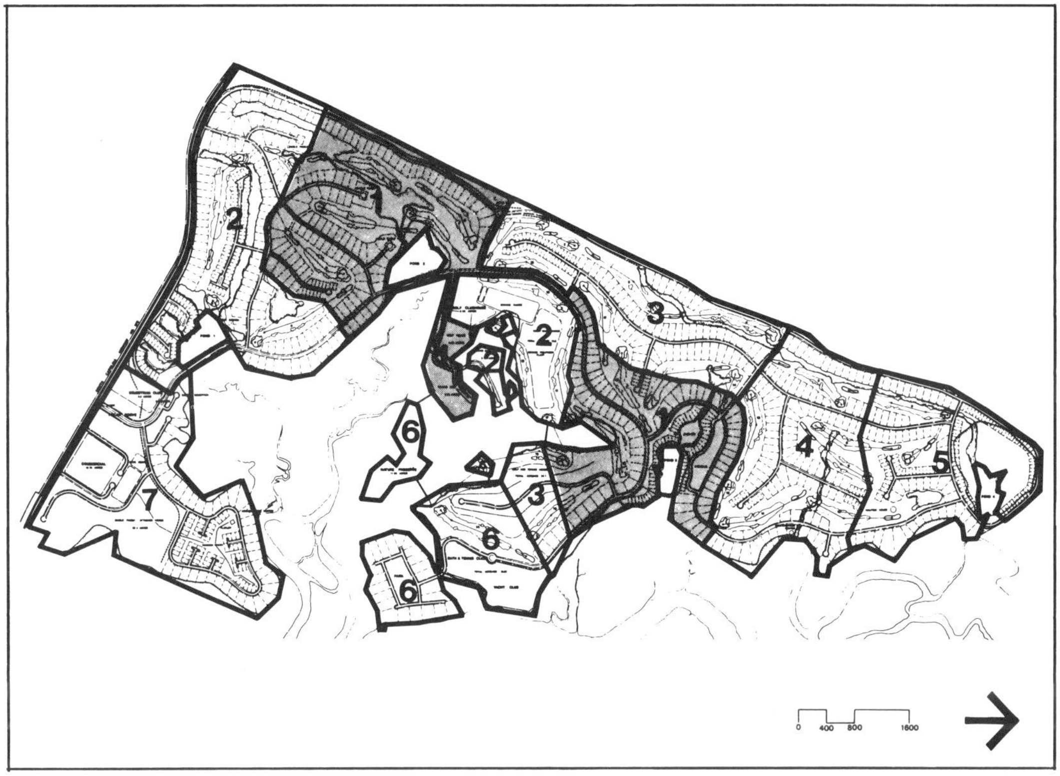

2-28 Site plan showing phases of development for Moss Creek Plantation.

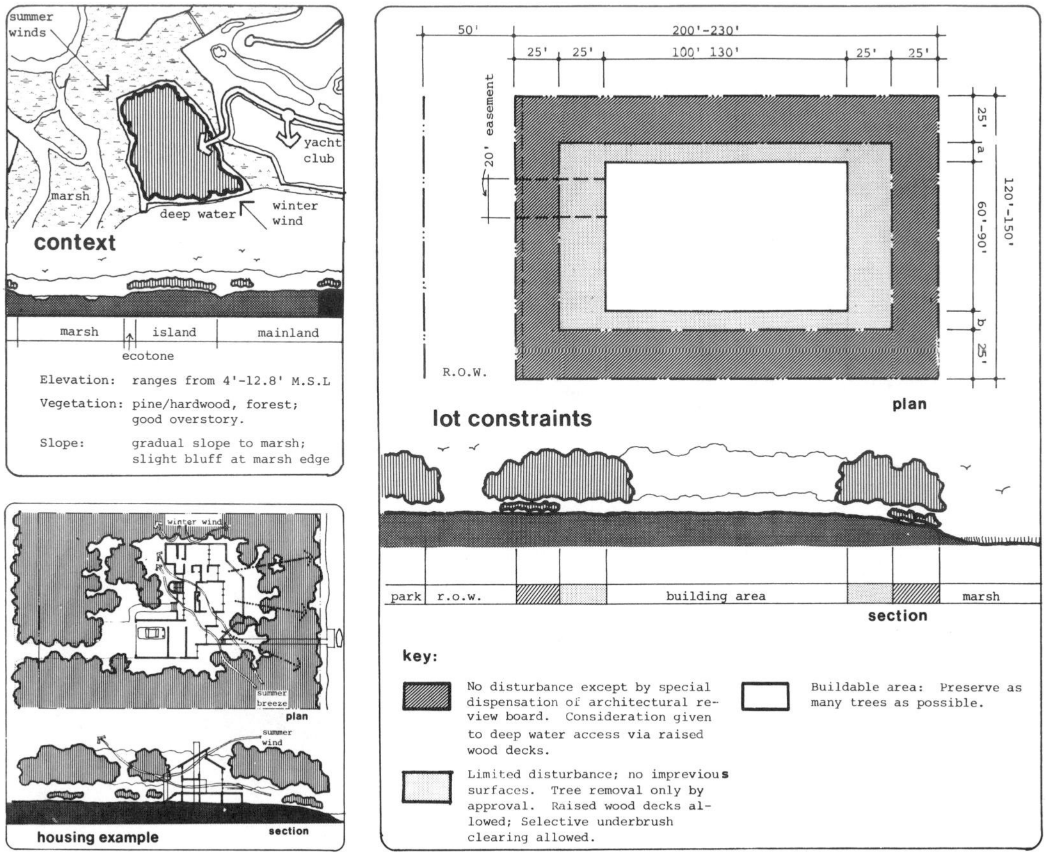

2-29 Plan study of one of 15 housing types included in the Moss Creek Plantation planning report.

Site Plan Techniques

The enhancement of real estate values by natural and manmade amenities is the hallmark of site and architectural design at recreational development projects. To achieve the potentials of each landscape, creative site solutions are often required, particularly in the face of diminishing well-positioned land and the need to use lands previously passed over which may have one or more serious physical impediments to development. For example, although they contain an abundance of natural amenities, the heavily wooded sea islands off the U.S. southeast coast present particularly difficult drainage problems associated with heavy annual rainfall and the low-lying character of the land.

At The Landings, on Skidaway Island, Georgia, the "hammerhead" street was developed to increase the depth of real estate frontage against the golf course fairways and to resolve the engineering costs associated with the provision of drainage. The hammerhead consists of a short private street for four to eight one-third acre lots. The street consists of a 22-foot-wide pavement designed as an inverted drain without curb or drainage structures. The hammerheads are tied to collector roads containing the standard complement of curb, gutter, and drainage structures. At The Landings, the hammerhead reduced public right-of-way requirements by two-thirds from the required width of 60 feet to 22 feet, and pavement requirements by over one-third. The project became economically feasible in large part because of the savings which would be realized from rights-of-way, pavement, and elimination of curb and drainage structures. Moreover, the special street helped preserve the woods and enhance the private, safe, residential character of each small neighborhood.

2-30 This narrow street maximizes the lot area and is designed as an inverted drain.

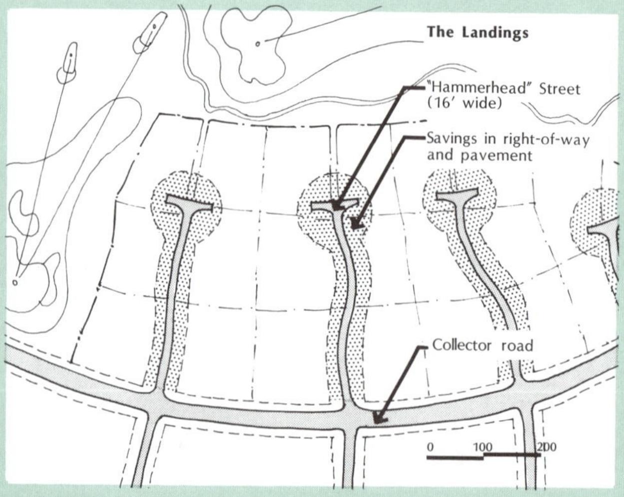

2-31 The "hammerhead" street layout at The Landings on Skidaway Island, Georgia.

Of particular importance if the developer is to sell building sites to subdevelopers in a recreational project is the establishment and enforcement of design standards. Standards should deal with some or all of the following: exterior building materials and colors; signs; plant materials and landscaping; outdoor storage; architectural guidelines for style, size, and height; building siting; building and grounds maintenance; conservation; and resource management.

Signs and graphics are also important to consider at this stage. A well-designed symbol or logo can assist in establishing and reinforcing the project's image. Once adopted, it should be used in all promotion, advertising, brochures, signs, and business forms. Ideally, the project's name will fit the project image and will be presented in an imaginative logo—a subtle but nonetheless important factor.

The signage program itself is an important design challenge and should be entrusted to a specialist in the field. An opportunity to establish a strong single identity (if desired) for the recreational project will be lost if architects sign the buildings, interior designers

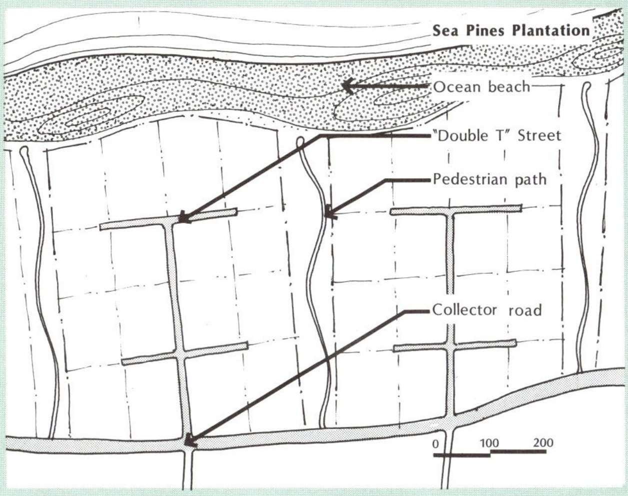

2-32 The "double T" system helps optimize proximity to the beachfront at Sea Pines.

2-33 Lake and park systems, small development parcels, varied street patterns, and landscaping can provide visual diversity. Pictured here is The Hammocks, under construction in Dade County, Florida.

At Sea Pines Plantation, in response to the obvious potential real estate values of the ocean beach, a "double T" residential street network was designed for the ocean beach frontage. In contrast to the typical coastal road with strip development paralleling the beach, the double T was a series of cul-de-sac streets thrusting toward the beach from a parallel road deep in the interior. The culs-de-sac are crossed twice at the beach end with short intersecting streets to increase the capacity for lots, hence the term "double T." A pattern of culs-de-sac and paths creates a private and secure residential environment, affords each resident direct and safe passageways to the beach, and has the effect of dramatically increasing the wedge of high value real estate against the ocean face.

In Harbour Town at Sea Pines, the concept of a "crenelated edge" was used to triple the frontage real estate around the circular harbor (see illustration 2-14). Deep landscaped courts radiate from the harbor edge around which townhouses and condominium apartments are sited. The landscaped courts alternate with parking courts so that each residential unit has its required auto access but also has a direct view of and physical access to the harbor through a landscaped court. A total linear architectural face of 5,600 feet was achieved for a harbor frontage of 2,000 feet.

Much of the sunbelt area of the United States, where a great deal of the large-scale recreational development is occurring, is dominated by the engineered grid pattern of roadways. In southern Florida, a chief objective of site design is to soften the hard, engineered look of the dominant grid pattern and to ameliorate the impacts of high-density residential development with the use of soft and irregular land forms, highlighting lakes and open spaces to give the appearance of a natural landscape, in contrast to the grid pattern.

sign the interiors, landscape architects sign pedestrian ways, and civil engineers pick standard traffic signs out of the manual. All signs should be unified in theme and designed as part of an overall graphics program which would include everything from matchbooks and paper napkins to the entrance sign.

Construction

Because of the customarily more remote or undeveloped location of a recreational project, its construction can be complicated by uncertain lead times, a shortage of skilled local labor, difficulty in obtaining materials, and weather problems affecting the length of the construction season and daily productivity. (A lot sales program may have a problem associated with a lack of appropriately experienced local contractors.)

The quality of the construction should match the overall image of the development; the project's reputation will most likely be determined by those components having the lowest quality. To control costs

2-34 New construction at the Sea Pines Plantation.

2-35 Attention to detail carried through to utility buildings helps establish consistency in the design and quality of the project.

and maintain quality, small units or fewer amenities may be necessary. Accepting the trade-off between quantity and quality is preferable to otherwise frustrating the expectations of the consumer, and is an issue that should be resolved when the project is first conceived.

After construction contracts have been negotiated and construction begins, a full-time representative of the development team will be required on the site, with periodic visits by other team members. On-site supervision is mandatory to ensure that the project is on schedule, within the budget, and constructed with the quality specified in the contract documents. Progress reports will keep all team members informed of the job status.

Marketing

The primary marketing task is to develop the right product at the right place at the right price and time. Direct selling is only a small part of the overall marketing effort. Because of this, a marketing person must be an integral member of the development planning team. The questions which must be answered in identifying the target market(s) include: Who will be the buyers and for what reasons? Where are the consumers located? Is immediate personal use anticipated or will the purchase be for investment or future use (retirement)? How will this product lend itself in particular to location, amenities, and quality? Will buyers'/users' friends be a main drawing point?

Preparation for specific promotional and sales activities should begin well in advance of the release of the product. Marketing is a large up-front budget item which can substantially increase the cost of the product. Market variables and marketing strategies will determine the appropriate sales techniques. If a major presales effort is programmed, direct selling can begin almost at project conception. Post-construction sales will require constant monitoring through the development phase, but may employ different tools when actual selling commences.

As has been stressed previously, a critical function in planning the product is pursuing target markets. Reassessing the target markets should be an ongoing activity of the marketing group. The project's whole image should be carefully presented as a reflection of the interests of these targets. Targets provide a standard by which to maintain and evaluate the project's success and direction, and will include maintaining the appropriate reputation for the project, as well as programming expected sales figures and the use of facilities.

The marketing strategy beyond these basic guide-

Kapalua

2-36 The symbol of Kapalua, a resort residential community on Maui, Hawaii. A distinguished logo can be an important element in the creation of a new project's identity.

2-37 Signage is needed for practical purposes, but used attractively, it can also help support the project's image.

lines will depend on the circumstances of each situation, but must specifically relate to the identified market and project appeal. The strategy should be comprehensive and flexible. It is imperative that each marketing program be evaluated for its cost-to-sales effectiveness. This will require a systematic and rigorous analysis of customer characteristics and responses with respect to the marketing program. Significant benefits can be realized by scrapping high-cost/low-return programs and reallocating expenditures to more productive approaches.

Sales Procedures

Recreational project sales can be operated internally or handled outside. A marketing director and an appropriate marketing system are essential. The sales effort should be directed by a primary member of the development team and conducted in a manner consistent with the objectives of that program. Where a high-amenity resort/recreational community is being promoted, an in-house sales effort may be most appropriate because of the interdependence of many facility functions.

Recreational developments typically sell a particular lifestyle, making it important that marketing personnel interpret and convey the project's strengths and appeals accurately. A potential obstacle to achieving this is the fact that many salespersons have not been and do not stay in recreational development a substantial length of time to give them the experience and understanding needed. This fact, compounded by the many private and public pressures to have a responsible professional sales staff, make it worthwhile to provide sales incentive compensations and strong sales management in major recreational development marketing. A salesperson for a large resort PUD typically receives a base salary plus a 3 percent commission, although commissions can run as high as 10 percent on lot sales and 5 percent on built units.

Numerous complexities usually require that recreational development be sold at markups well above the costs of the physical assets. The high gross profit is substantially eroded by steep marketing costs that can command 25 to 40 percent of the sales price for a land sales project with low capital investment and 5 to 25 percent for a built unit marketed and sold in-house.

Another approach is to invest dollars earmarked for marketing purposes in developing income-producing resort facilities which add permanent long-term value to the development. Resort operations of quality can satisfy visitors and help achieve land and housing sales objectives with little marketing expense. The extra expenditures made in developing a quality resort can be well worth it by encouraging sales and thus acting as a strong marketing strategy.

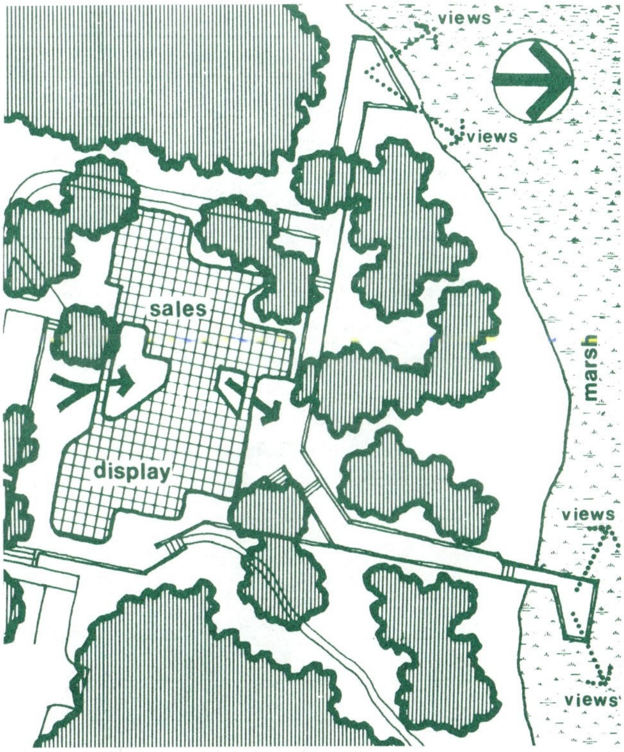

2-38 The atmosphere of a sales and reception center should instill confidence. A display area should include a montage of informative material, and vistas of amenities should be readily accessible.

2-39 Hilton Head Inn which is associated with the Sea Pines Plantation.

Resort Marketing in Real Estate

The most cost-effective markets to tap for the sales of recreational projects are often those closest at hand—existing property owners, their acquaintances, and resort guests. Major resort community destinations can benefit in particular by combining resort and residential activities in their marketing campaigns.

Through proper pricing and target advertising, resort activities can attract qualified buyers to a recreational project. Because the resort guest is also a prospective buyer, an ongoing program geared toward a sale should be incorporated into his stay.

At the same time resort guests provide a market for real estate, they enhance property value by helping pay for common resort elements and by establishing a demand for property rentals. An active and vital atmosphere established through recreational amenities can be essential to the ambience of a project and thus justify the expense of the amenities even if they operate at a loss to the developer.

2-40 Social events supplement the experience of a resort guest in a recreational community.

Sales Tools

There are numerous tools for promoting a resort/recreational development. They include rental management programs, special resort packages, sales offices, model units, prospect follow-ups, referrals, advertising, and community relations efforts. The following are suggested:

- Collateral materials required for resort operation. They include: resort brochures for both the consumer and travel agents, package brochures and rates for tour operators and airlines, folders with maps for guests, service directories, lists of internal and outside activities, card/questionnaires to evaluate service and provide profile information, direct mail pieces with letters to previous guests, as well as items needed to maintain amenities such as menus, room cards promoting facilites, golf course score card, napkins, place mats, matches, and so forth.
- Collateral materials required for real estate sales operation including: sales brochure/folder incorporating total community concept; site plan; buyer guide giving all basic project data such as areas of development, building design, floor plans, and prices; room card inviting guests to visit sales center or attend social mixer and see property products; direct mail pieces; and all other documents used as sales tools.
- Advertising targeting local consumer sales and use of amenities as well as national consumer and trade markets.
- News releases concurrent with the advertising program—accompanied by photographs wherever possible—to send to editors of magazines and various sections of newspapers in all market areas. First-hand stories should be encouraged and related to all facets of activity and to the developers themselves. Editors should be invited to visit the project.
- Newsletters to residents, purchasers with property in the rental program, prospective purchasers, visitors, and resort guests, keeping them informed of progress.
- Individuals and groups to enhance the activity level. In this regard, ongoing promotion of various types such as buffets and on-site parties should be planned to attract different groups. Further suggestions for promoting an image and enhancing the activity level include: (1) arranging major on-site activities (possibly for charity) such as golf and tennis tournaments and outings which provide maximum exposure via the media and actual spectators; (2) having a celebri-

ty officiate as host; and (3) inviting residents, local officials, prospective purchasers, and others to appropriate social and promotional activities.

- Records on prospective customers and follow-up procedures which will not only encourage greater sales but also provide for assessing the cost effectiveness of advertising and information in order to fine-tune the marketing program.

Market Example

Different income and social groups will require different types of recreational products. The opportunities and parameters for development associated with these various segments of the population should be identified in the marketing program. For example, the characteristics of a particular group of moderate-income consumers might include:

- a strong fishing and hunting orientation;
- a preference for barbecue cookouts;
- a tendency to allow equipment to accumulate;
- a desire to act quickly in purchasing and occupying a unit;
- a preference for freestanding units with a minimum of community obligations; and
- little interest in renting or selling a vacation unit; instead, relatives and friends will be invited to use it.

As previously stressed, any marketing effort should be closely attuned to these consumer tastes and habits. For instance, building with such characteristics in mind may involve low maintenance requirements to allow for as many individual liberties as possible without infringing on the surrounding community.

Management and Operation

Although the management of resort/residential property is similar to that of primary residential development, the type of ownership differs in that owners reside in their units only periodically.

Recreational communities and facilities can be owned and managed as commercial for-profit enterprises or as part of a not-for-profit community association of the property owners. Facilities owned either by private developers or by other private commercial interests will require a profit to be realized, except where potential profits in interrelated areas justify subsidizing certain operations. A thorough economic analysis of the business prospects is important to the developer in evaluating the potential for a commercial operation. A good indicator of financial opportunity is the level of outside investor interest in a proposed amenity. One problem with developer-owned facilities in residential recreational communities is that users tend to expect more than the developer can afford.

2-41 Popular competitions such as this tennis tournament at the Amelia Island Plantation in northeast Florida attract resort business, and, more importantly, bring media attention to a recreational project.

Transferring project management functions to community associations can help shift the burden off the developer. When a community association is to be empowered, the particulars of control should be clearly disclosed in consistent documents covering land covenants, bylaws, sales literature, sales contracts, and property reports. This underlines the importance in the early planning stages of designing the final management structure effectively. The period of developer ownership and support should be clearly defined with an appropriate transitional phase and and legal documentation of the specific terms and conditions. The access rights of nonproperty owners to facilities (for example, through club memberships) should be clearly defined. Furthermore, property owners should pay certain fees to support community maintenance associations.[13]

Specialized contracted management can be particularly useful when commercial ownership or community association expertise is not available or is uneconomical. This strategy demands that a contract for management services be carefully negotiated, covering the level of involvement to be applied and the financial objectives. The use of specialized management is particularly attractive where there is a substantial resort operation. Good communication between the owners and operators is important to ensure the proper level of management.

Covenants

Covenants are the essential legal tools for sustaining desired project standards as ownership becomes dispersed. They are user restrictions which can be attached to the land for varying terms up to perpetuity. Covenants must be consistent and clear on key issues. They should thoroughly support and guarantee the continuance of the established philosophy of the project. Association bylaws, sales contract disclosures, and sales documents should reinforce the covenants. Enforcement should not be delayed or allowed to slip. As the project matures and conditions change, there should be a mechanism by which covenants could be modified and upgraded.

Community Associations

Community associations are necessary if the community is to manage the project after the developer terminates his management responsibility or if ownership of the common facilities is otherwise conveyed to the property owners. It is in the highest interest of the developer to maintain the best possible relationship with the community association, recognizing that his interests and those of the association may not always coincide. It is also appropriate and can be beneficial for the developer to take an active role in the community association. Informal sessions with the association's board of directors can help to assure good communication between the two entities.

2-42 Maintenance responsibility can be a delicate issue for the developer and owners to deal with, underlying the importance of clear documentation of reasonable terms early in project plans.

Well before the conclusion of the development phase of the project, the developer should instigate a transitional period when the community association and its members can be brought up to date on various activities within the community which will become their responsibility once the developer has terminated his involvement with the project.[14] It is important, however, that the developer maintain control until the project is sold out. The community association should consider using the assistance of a professional management group to ensure competent operation of the association. Typically, owner associations change officers each year, although it is preferable to stagger the tenure of members of the board of directors for terms of 3 years. When associations change officers, the developer has to establish rapport and basic lines of communication with the new officers.

Occasionally, associations are pressed to assume control over numerous community services rather than forcing local government agencies to fulfill their responsibilities. For instance, although fire protection and garbage service can often be provided by local governmental agencies, owner associations may assume these responsibilities (and debts) in order to be in control, but more probably because they have been presented with no alternative. Often local governments, particularly in rural areas with few services, are reluctant to assume responsibility for such services and must be prodded into action. To whatever degree an association chooses to become involved

[13]David B. Wolfe, op. cit.

[14]For further discussion, see C. James Dowden, *Creating a Community Association: The Developer's Role in Condominium and Homeowner Associations* (Washington: ULI–the Urban Land Institute and CAI–the Community Associations Institute, 1977).

in community services, its effective and efficient operation will depend on the association's internal management.[15]

Maintenance Assessments and User Fees

Maintenance budgets for amenities and natural features must be carefully prepared and reserves for major repairs or rebuilding programs at a future date must be established. A good technique is to account for costs by the type of activity or facility and review them periodically against the budget. Even so, objectives and operations must be kept flexible to adapt to various levels of service demands and income streams.[16]

User fees must be carefully monitored in terms of increasing maintenance costs and in the continuing development of common areas and recreational facilities. The single most important concern should be to avoid overbuilding amenities. Establishing a high level of services through developer subsidy can be dangerous later if the economics turn sour or the developer steps out.

User fees and assessments must be reviewed objectively in light of the level of services provided, the collection rate expected, and the impact on property sales. Entrenched inflationary cycles require that measures be taken to assure that user fees can be escalated unthwarted, if so needed, for either the responsible operation of common facilities or those that are privately owned. From the beginning, the developer should estimate maintenance and operating costs realistically and apply a cost adjustment index to any maximum assessments established in the covenants. Part of this developer responsibility involves raising assessment fees only in reasonable increments. The temptations to raise user fees to generate cash flow to cover cost overruns in other areas should be strictly resisted.

Rental Programs

Rental programs represent a continuing long-term involvement with a recreational property and are a means by which investors/buyers receive some financial return on their investments. Care must be exercised concerning the legalities of rental programs. One caveat is the Securities and Exchange Commission's requirement that rental programs be kept completely separate from real estate sales activities. Rental programs are difficult when neither the community nor individual living units have been designed with rental use in mind (for example, without provision for owner closets and central laundry).

A rental program must be structured to pay for the high marketing and management costs it entails. Using a rental program as a sales incentive without charging fees substantial enough to offset costs is a serious mistake. More than 50 percent of any rental receipts may have to be retained for management costs.

If the furnishings of a unit are individually owned, it is important that they be specified to the prospective tenant. It can be disastrous for a rental program and its management personnel to have tenants demanding to be changed to other units because their units lack a certain furnishing, such as color television.

It may be in the best interest of the developer to control the rental program rather than assign it to local brokers. As many projects have demonstrated, resort guests can be a great source for prospective buyers. If more than one entity is handling rentals, resort guests will receive different "benefits" and services, which can create dissension among the renters and detract from their desire to purchase property. Consistent, responsible, and successful rental pool programs are often managed by resort hotel operators. Furthermore, continuity in the management of various resort facilities is important in order to provide efficient and effective customer service.

Where there are other rental operations, the developer should maintain control of as many recreational outlets as possible to keep a competitive edge in terms of a rental program as well as to generate prospective real estate purchasers.

Even if a developer is interested in obtaining outside brokers to manage rentals, it may be difficult to find one willing to spend enough time to do an effective job, especially during the early stages of a project. When a program is refined and has proven successful, consideration can be given to the use of a local broker, under appropriate terms and controls. The unique requirements of condominium management are different from hotel management, and the value of specialists in this field should not be underestimated.

Future Phases

The best sales tools for future phases of development within a project are satisfied property owners and a well-designed community association performing its services effectively and efficiently. The relationship

[15]See Urban Land Institute and Community Asssociations Institute, *Managing a Successful Community Association* (Washington: ULI–the Urban Land Institute and CAI–the Community Associations Institute, 1976).

[16]See David B. Wolfe, *Financial Management of Condominium and Homeowners' Associations* (Washington: ULI–the Urban Land Institute and CAI–the Community Associations Institute, 1975).

or effect of a community association on future phases can be significant particularly if the form of development is uncertain. It might be advisable for the developer to have whatever master plans and/or detailed development plans processed and accepted by the appropriate governmental agencies before an association becomes too active. More often than not, even though the community has been properly informed of the intentions of the developer, its attitude may change with time until it becomes an adversary of the development plan as initially conceived and subsequently processed by the developer. The developer should make every effort to inform the community and the association of the development plan and keep them up to date. Inherent risks can be countered by proper developer design, leadership, and control of the community association.

The developer may need or want to consider alternative land use plans for undeveloped areas. Presentations to prospective owners and others should allow flexibility for future phases. To strengthen this flexibility, the economics of one phase should not ultimately rest on the development of other phases. Property owner associations may themselves be developed in phases and incorporated into a master association to provide a smoother legal structure as a mix of land uses is added to the recreational development.

Considerations by Special Type

If they are broken down by type, there are easily hundreds of variations of resorts and other recreational destinations. The following section will discuss a sampling of specialized elements that are behind some of the numerous examples of recreational development. Because the intent of this handbook has been to focus on the real estate component of recreational development, the specifics of providing particular amenities are not typically discussed. It would be negligent nevertheless not to reiterate the importance of treating amenity planning with great care in any recreational development strategy. Ski hills and lifts, golf courses, marinas, and equestrian facilities, for instance, represent large capital investments and potential sources of income, requiring highly specialized planning and development.

Consumer demands for recreation have become increasingly sophisticated, supported by broad and varied expertise from those who provide leisure time activities. The result has been a generally better facility and service being offered the consumer. New investments in recreation are prepared to compete head on with other facilities for customers, a significant evolution from the past dominant pattern of building marginal facilities which an underserved and expanding market quickly absorbed.

This competitive recreational climate has necessitated the use of qualified persons, if not specialists, to execute feasibility studies and planning analyses in order to structure the appropriate recreational attractions and amenities. The diversity of recreational demands and environments generally precludes the use of highly standardized, formal approaches to amenity planning. For example, the fact that skiing conditions can vary by geographic area, based on mountain and snow types, not to mention market differences, is a fundamental that should be considered in planning a ski resort. This kind of attention to detail should condition all planning for recreational facilities, whether they be golf courses or swimming pools.

The Retirement Community

Retirement communities are either specifically created or result from the natural evolution of well-suited second-home development into permanent or primary seasonal use. The locational characteristics of retirement communities are highly similar to general leisure use property, depending on the degree of recreational amenities the market can afford.

Many retirement communities are located in warm climates, often where living costs are lower. Others are situated in colder climates serving the needs of retired people who want to remain close to their native communities, families, and friends. A study of demographic trends is necessary to determine the opportunities for developing this type of community.

A retirement community can be self-sufficient, offering a broad range of facilities to provide for the needs of its residents. In other cases, it may be part of a larger urban setting and should be situated so that residents will have ready access to key services such as shopping, medical facilities, transportation, cultural facilities (for example, museums, libraries, adult education) regional recreation, and religious institutions.

As with second-home communities, locational nuisances should be avoided. Such nuisances might include heavy automobile traffic, high-crime areas in the vicinity, industrial areas, and airports. Children could represent a nuisance to some retired people. Competing retirement facilities nearby as well as negative attitudes of the surrounding community might also be factors to consider in the location of a development.

2-43 In retirement communities such as Rossmoor Leisure World in Maryland, security is a top concern.

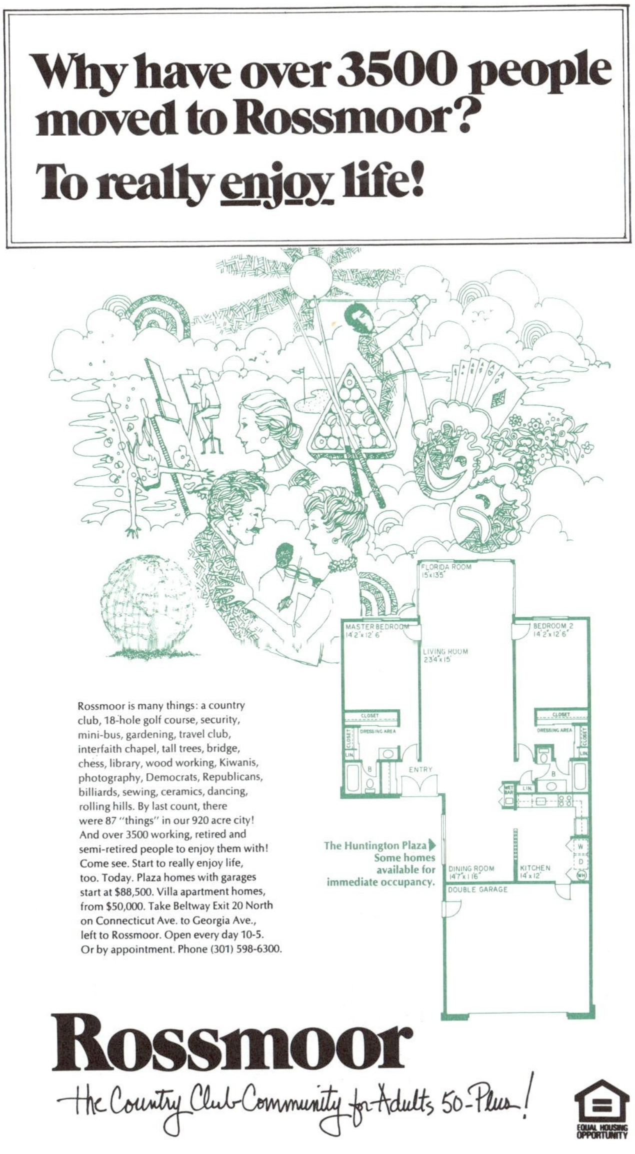

2-44 Advertisement promoting numerous activities available at Rossmoor.

Site Development

Hilly sites may pose problems for older people although certain segments of the retirement market may prefer a site with varied terrain. Stairs and steep slopes should be avoided and special considerations, such as provision for handicapped people, are essential in planning a retirement community for a specific market. Retired people may demand a fully landscaped environment, not one that will require years to mature. This underscores the advantages of a naturally wooded site, and especially the attraction of a well-established second-home community.

Determining the Market

Young retired persons from 50 to 60 years old will usually want individual access to many activities typical of a resort, second-home community. As retired persons grow older (from 60 to 70 years old), they may need fewer facilities for active recreation and more guided programs as well as greater security measures. Retired persons over 70 years old may eventually require increased health care. For those who are semiretired, access to major centers of employment will be important. Fully retired persons will probably rely largely on community activities to keep them occupied.

Affluent persons will usually expect more amenities and services than those on limited incomes, who will probably depend more on public services. The affluent, mobile retired person who spends only part of the year in the community requires few services other than maintenance. The year-round resident expects more in services and programs. The physically able will need little in the way of on-site health care other than access to nearby medical centers. The physically infirm or otherwise disabled residents, on the other hand, will require substantial on-site health care. Specialized health care facilities could be added to a second-home development as the need becomes more apparent.

Community Types

The complete, self-contained retirement community will have a supporting infrastructure—sewers, water, streets, utilities, and fire and police protection. It must have some form of government and provide a complete amenity package including recreation, shopping, transportation, and social services.

Occupying approximately 20 to 30 acres with 250 to 600 units, the smaller retirement community within a larger urban center can take advantage of existing public facilities, draw on the surrounding community for residents, and require less in up-front development costs. Apart from market attractions, it would not be appreciably different from the urban neighborhood the average retiree might come from.

Mobile homes can provide one type of retirement community without the need of a housing developer.[17] However, the larger surrounding community may oppose mobile homes. A retirement hotel is a further alternative. It may be well suited to persons needing more care, or for those of limited income, or for those who need or want minimum housing space. It must be located within easy access to a large range of community services, which may already be present in an established second-home development.

Housing Considerations

The market will determine whether units are rented or purchased. A more affluent market will be inclined to purchase, using equity from the sale of a former residence. The less affluent market will be more likely to rent. There are substantial risks in mixing rental and sales units because of different outlooks and expectations on the part of the potential occupants.

Communities can consist of apartments, single-family homes, cluster housing, or a combination of all these. Smaller units are most popular but not to the total exclusion of larger homes which are suitable for lodging visitors, entertaining, or are reflective of some personal need.

For the older retiree, specific design considerations may be needed. Doors and passageways may need to be wider than normal to accommodate the handicapped. Ramps should be provided instead of stairs or curbs, and elevators can be essential even in two-story buildings. Electrical outlets should be placed high to minimize stooping and other electrical facilities should be placed for easy access. Bathrooms should have grab bars and nonslip surfaces. Bright lighting is needed in halls and an intercom and emergency signal system are desirable. It is extremely important for this market that interior and exterior maintainence requirements be minimal.

Amenities

Central entrance security and/or patrolling, is essential, particularly at night. Guard personnel should be trained to handle a variety of emergencies.

A program of planned activities making use of standard recreational facilities should be provided which would include a swimming pool, shaded deck areas, and a recreation center. Depending on the market, additional amenities may include tennis courts, golf facilities, shuffleboard, a comfortable but not too elaborate clubhouse, an on-site restaurant with catering service, a marina, and bikeways.

Maintenance services are a key to retirement communities. Many retired people will need periodic help with their units and those who are affluent and travel will want their property looked after while they are away. Staffing is also important. Members of the staff should be relatively mature and sensitive to and respectful of the needs of retired persons. Assistance with transportation may be an important community need. Guest suites for children and grandchildren should be incorporated and should be of a superior hotel/motel decor.

Recreational Vehicle Parks

Recreational vehicles (RVs) offer opportunities for outdoor recreation in numerous and diverse locations, with the conveniences of home brought along. Camping, under canvas or in fully equipped motor homes is particularly suitable to families for whom other forms of overnight travel are prohibitively expensive or otherwise restrictive, and for retired persons with extended leisure time.

Over 60 million people were estimated to have gone camping across the United States in 1979, and approximately 6 million owned motor homes, camping trailers, camper trucks, and other recreational vehicles suitable for camping.[18] As the descendent of the simple campsite, the sophisticated recreational vehicle requires multiple user facilities. While the demand for all types of camping has generally remained strong, especially across the South, the demand for equipped recreational vehicles has had the greatest proportional growth.

[17]Considerations for planning and developing mobile home parks are reviewed in Robinson Newcomb and Max S. Wehrly, *Mobile Home Parks: Part I, An Analysis of Characteristics; Part II, An Analysis of Communities*, Technical Bulletins 66 and 68 (Washington: ULI–the Urban Land Institute, 1971 and 1972).

[18]This information was reported by the RV Industry Association, 14650 Lee Road, P.O. Box 204, Chantilly, Virginia 22021.

2-45 Despite different markets and design needs, the development issues pertinent to RV parks in many ways parallel those of other resort types.

Historically, camping has been associated with publicly owned campgrounds. Rapid growth in the market for space in private recreational vehicle parks is attributable to the overall popularity of camping, the slow rate of growth in the number of public campsites, and the consumer's desire for more varied recreational amenities than offered by most public campgrounds.

Recreational vehicle parks have many similarities to other lodging and recreational facilities; the practices appropriate to their respective development differ only in the structural sense and not in the general nature of the service.

Recreational vehicle parks have various purposes. The overnight park serves primarily as a stopover during travel and is most effective when highly accessible to major highways, with direct ingress and egress to level sites and essential facilities. The destination park provides for a longer stay and features fuller amenities, privacy, and ready access (seldom more than 20 miles) to a major attraction, such as a resort beach, mountain preserve, or major theme park. The camping resort goes the furthest in providing the full vacation experience with a complete range of amenities. Combining a mix of types in one park is possible, although this has its limits.

Climate can play a key role, with areas such as Florida and Southern California which enjoy favorable year-round weather being the most profitable for recreational vehicle parks. Developments located in the Northeast and Midwest near winter recreational centers can also operate throughout the year. Otherwise, the operation of facilities will be limited to 4 or 5 months of the year.

For practical weekend convenience and to economize on fuel, a destination park should be located well within a 4- or 5-hour drive of a major metropolitan area.

Site Development

Recreational vehicle park projects require the same comprehensive feasibility analysis and sensitive planning as does other major recreational development. The standard business procedures of identifying the market, optimizing the location, and following responsible engineering and financial and management practices are crucial prerequisites. As with other recreational land uses, RV parks must comply with various municipal ordinances and zoning regulations.

In a 1977 survey published by the American Planning Association, the following standards for recreational vehicle parks were reported:[19]

2-46 Destination RV parks typically require a fuller range of amenities than simple overnight stops.

- The minimum park size can vary from 3 to 50 acres.
- The maximum number of sites permitted per acre ranges from seven to 25.
- The minimum size of an RV space should be 900 to 4,500 square feet.
- Recreational vehicles should be at least 10 to 15 feet apart from each other.

A recreational vehicle park should obviously be designed for the type of use targeted. Overnight sites can be smaller and should facilitate pull-through parking patterns. Destination sites should be at least 1,800 square feet and have good screening. RV users seem to like proximity to each other, making an overall density of seven to 15 plots per acre quite respectable. If it is possible to accommodate different preferences, it might be wise to allow for some spaces which are private and some which are closer together. In any case, congestion must be avoided.

Utilities (electricity, water, sewage, television, and telephone) are a major investment to be considered. Many park users—even those on tent sites—have grown to expect these provisions. Convenient sewer facilities are particularly important in order to maintain environmental standards both in the park and downstream. Providing various utility services and extensive road networks emphasizes the value of studying building conditions and utility capacities at the earliest planning stages.

[19] American Planning Association, *Zoning for Recreational Vehicles*, Report No. 326 (Chicago: American Planning Association, 1976).

2-47 Provision for vehicle storage is a must at RV parks that have repeat weekend and vacation use.

Where mixed camping demands are anticipated, segregated uses can be designed into the park, for instance by emphasizing utilities and easy vehicle maneuvering in an area designated for larger vehicles. If lot sales are a probability, single metering of utilities and other site-by-site destinations may be advisable. It is essential to complete and follow a master plan and preferable to build in stages. Using architecture with various themes is a popular way to establish a special identity and park atmosphere.

One approach to help cover park amenity costs is to attach a recreational vehicle development to some other development such as a motel. A second-home developer may recognize a recreational vehicle park as a means to increase the visibility of his product, with the further potential of its functioning as an interim land use.

Ownership

Independently owned campgrounds offering sites for short-term rental are by far the most common type. Chain operators or franchising affiliations have made large inroads into the site rental market, with nationwide reservation services, standardized quality, and other services. Kampgrounds of America, (KOA), established in 1962, is the largest chain with hundreds of KOA campgrounds across North America.

A minimum required occupancy for a rental park is difficult to determine for the industry as a whole, but a 35 percent annual figure is considered typical for a well-serviced park. Some popular locations enjoy occupancies of more than 80 percent.

Other forms of park ownership include various club arrangements entitling members to exclusive use at one or more destinations. Condominium lots and timesharing are further types, shifting the greatest financial burden directly to the consumers. Such ownership of a lot gives the purchaser a guaranteed site at a given time period, use of shared common facilities, the opportunity to participate in park management, the possibility of rental income and equity appreciation, and other advantages.

Financing

The mid-1970s recession combined with the growing energy crisis dealt a heavy blow to RV park developers. Zoning problems and competition from inexpensive public campgrounds have been further deterrents to development. Nonetheless, financial prospects seem reasonably good for well-planned, less distant parks, particularly as recreational vehicle owners become less inclined to make long-distance trips in vehicles getting low gas mileage.

The minimum cost of opening a recreational vehicle park in 1979 was approximately $2,500 per plot, excluding land costs. Even with an investment of $3,000 to $4,000 per site, a developer was limited in the amenities that could be provided. As the RV park and campground business grows in professionalism and stature, competition will dictate that such facilities as tennis courts, recreational buildings, pools, and modern laundries will be more of a necessity than a luxury. Full-scale development can push costs up to $10,000 per site, hardly qualifying this type of campground as a low-cost land use.

Because of the assumed uncertainties of the recreational vehicle market, and lender skepticism attributed to the fragmented history of the industry, the equity needed by a developer can easily run over 50 percent, though with a good financial plan and strong development and management prospects a development might receive financing of as much as 70 percent. The land to be used may act as sufficient collateral if it is owned, particularly in locations of increasing land values near metropolitan areas or special natural attractions. Large national corporations have not participated as strongly as projected before 1974–1975; the number of national participants dwindled from over 50 to less than 10 during the 1974–1975 recession.[20]

Should rising fuel costs and economic reversals persist in adversely affecting disposable personal income, leasing recreational vehicles instead of buying them may gain popularity. Under these and other circumstances, the number of registered vehicles may not increase as projected, but parks situated in good

[20] *Real Estate Investing Letter* (December 1978), p. 1.

recreational environments close to major population centers would not be hurt. Other trends influencing campground development might include advances in lightweight equipment, a resurgence of canvas accommodations in response to the escalating costs of other recreational lodgings, and perhaps such innovations as urban high-rise camping.

Conference Centers and Recreational Development

Through the 1970s, conference centers emerged as significant generators of income associated with recreational development. This resulted from a dramatic growth in the multibillion-dollar meetings market and the increased popularity of holding meetings in resort settings.[21]

Resorts as Conference Settings

One of the original motives for planning meetings away from business premises was to place the meeting in a change of scenery. Early conference facilities often provided a "monastic" environment with intense and cloistered sessions uninterrupted by other activities. During the last several years, however, the psychological environment sought by meeting planners encourages an integration of meetings, meals, and recreation with the meeting/communication process itself. Meeting planners require a variety of recreational amenities convenient to the meeting site. Numerous surveys have confirmed the importance of recreational facilities in the choice of a conference site. This has provided great marketing strength to resort conference settings with high-amenity packages.

The trend toward holding meetings in resort environments has also encouraged a growing use of nonhotel resort facilites with meetings frequently held in rented private dwelling units. This establishes both the informal setting and the feeling of privacy and self containment, which corporate meeting planners seek.

Small meetings are particularly service-intensive in their requirements. The high level of service required of the meeting facility staff has encouraged planners of small corporate meetings to choose resort sites which do not emphasize major conventions and large meetings, or centers that set aside separate facilites to meet the service needs of smaller groups. Resorts and conference centers doing a significant amount of group business report that repeat business is a key to the success of a conference site. For example, the Silverado Country Club resort in California's Napa Valley books between 350 and 400 small conferences a year, with an average group numbering 45 persons. Of these conferences, 65 percent are repeat business. The best guarantee of receiving return visits is to provide a continuing high level of service.

The generally seasonal and discretionary market typical of recreational development has obliged re-

[21]Economic Research Associates, unpublished report (Los Angeles: Economic Research Associates, 1979).

2-48 The Broadmoor in Colorado Springs, a resort hotel popular for conferences.

sort operators to pursue group business, particularly during off-seasons or "shoulder" seasons such as the spring and fall when many business meetings tend to occur. Group business has a broad meaning, encompassing conferences, executive board meetings, social groups of people banding together for a vacation, regional or state association meetings, sales meetings, and conventions.

Many groups who had traditionally considered only downtown hotel locations for their particular functions have become strongly receptive to resort settings. As a result of their successful marketing campaigns, many of the major resorts attract 50 percent or more of their business from groups. Prestigious resorts such as The Greenbrier in West Virginia and The Homestead in Virginia both receive between 65 and 70 percent of their business from groups. Increasing efforts to attract group business, whether for meetings or for vacations, have given resorts much more economic stability than they have had in the past.

Conference Facilities

Three principal forms of conference centers associated with recreational amenities have appeared: (1) the conference center that has been added to an existing resort hotel; (2) the conference center that has been developed to improve the occupancy and profitability of a residential resort; and (3) the center that has been established as an independent executive conference facility.

The principal rationale for adding conference facilities to existing resort hotels is to increase overall room occupancy by attracting groups to the resort during slack seasons. Older resort hotels which have either constructed new conference facilities or renovated their existing spaces include The Homestead, The Greenbrier, The Boca Raton Hotel and Club; The Arizona Biltmore; and The Broadmoor in Colorado. All of these hotels at one time catered primarily to resort guests but now derive a substantial portion of their business from meetings. They are included among the top 23 resorts most frequently used by conference planners.

The purpose of adding conference facilities to a residential resort is basically the same as that for a traditional resort—to increase occupancy during the shoulder season and off-season and, thus, increase profits on operations. Further, higher occupancies mean higher rental yields to private dwelling unit owners, which facilitates sales of additional units. Although no guarantees of rentability can be made to purchasers, many buyers are interested in renting their units for at least a portion of the year and are sensitive to potential rental incomes. Some of the best known examples of residential resorts used for group business are Sea Pines Plantation in South Carolina, Innisbrook Resort in Florida, and Silverado in California's Napa Valley.

Executive Conference Centers

Self-contained executive conference centers offer a specific product which is distinct from those facilities acting as appendages to resorts. The original executive conference centers were designed to offer seclusion, a minimum of distractions, the best possible audiovisual and meeting facilities, and considerable staff expertise in handling groups. Recreational amenities were few and schedules were tough and demanding, starting at 8:00 in the morning and concluding with homework after midnight. Small, hard working groups were the rule and leisure time was limited.

The 1970s gave birth to a very different conference center with extensive recreational facilities such as golf courses, tennis courts, swimming pools, jogging trails, and health clubs being the rule rather than the exception. Accompanying the dramatic change in facilities was a change in the programming of the conference. Meetings shifted their emphasis from classroom responses and audiovisual materials to active participation and role playing. Recreation is an essential element of the program. Many programs start early, break for tennis or golf, then continue in the afternoon and on into the evening.

Highlights of a survey of executive conference centers indicated that the typical center provides 13 conference rooms averaging 800 square feet, 125 hotel rooms, and 297 restaurant seats.[22] Most of the centers surveyed offer a full range of services including assistance in conference planning and the use of audiovisual equipment. None of the centers charge fees for use of the conference rooms, but some charge for special equipment. All operate on the American plan for conferees, but on the European plan for vacationers and other transients. Substantial rates are typically charged by chain-operated centers, with little resistance from the market. The corporate market places high value on consistency, purpose, and quality of service and on an overall environment conducive to productive meetings. It is willing to pay for these attributes. All of the conference centers surveyed have swimming pools, and all offer tennis, golf, and bowling either on or off the premises. Nearly all have a game room, gym or exercise room, and saunas

[22]This survey was conducted in 1979 by Laventhol and Horwath, 1845 Walnut Street, Philadelphia, Pennsylvania 19103.

Silverado Country Club, Napa, California

Located in California's Napa Valley wine country, Silverado is a successful condominium/second-home resort built on a 1,200-acre, 19th century estate. As of 1980, the project had over 700 dwelling units, with approximately 60 percent comprised of condominiums and the balance in single-family products. Lodging accommodations available for conference business are entirely in luxury condominium rentals of one and two bedrooms. These units are oriented to the resort's seven swimming pools and two 18-hole championship golf courses. There are 20 tennis courts to serve 430 guest rooms. In addition to the banquet facilities in the historic Miller Mansion, which serves as a clubhouse, there are two restaurants, two cocktail lounges, and tennis and golf pro shops.

Silverado is less than a 2-hour drive north from San Francisco. Five daily flights are scheduled from San Francisco to Napa Valley and Silverado provides courtesy limousine service to the resort. Roughly 70 percent of Silverado's annual occupancy is from conference business, and 65 percent of that is said to be from repeat clients. The 350 to 400 meeting groups booked per year are typically small; approximately 40 to 60 percent are groups under 20.

As of 1980, Silverado had an inventory of 285 condominiums in their rental pool. One hundred new two-bedroom units sold rapidly in 1979 at $90,000 to $95,000 each. The Amfac Silverado Corporation builds the condominium units itself. At a planned building rate of 60 new units a year, the project will be completed in 1987, 22 years after its conception in 1965.

In late 1979, a new 9,000-square-foot conference center was completed, costing $3 million, or more than $300 per square foot. The high cost is due to the high quality in design, features, and equipment and will accommodate groups of up to 500 persons.

The management at Silverado feels that meeting rooms can no longer serve as a loss leader; they must produce some revenue to help defray the high service costs of conference use. The meeting space charges are usually waived, however, for groups making significant use of food and beverage service, so the imposition of these charges is somewhat discretionary.

2-50 Silverado books around 400 small conferences a year, with target sizes of 50 to 100 persons.

2-49 The mansion for the original 1,200-acre estate was developed into a golf clubhouse in the 1950s and became the focal point of the expanded Silverado recreational community in the late 1960s.

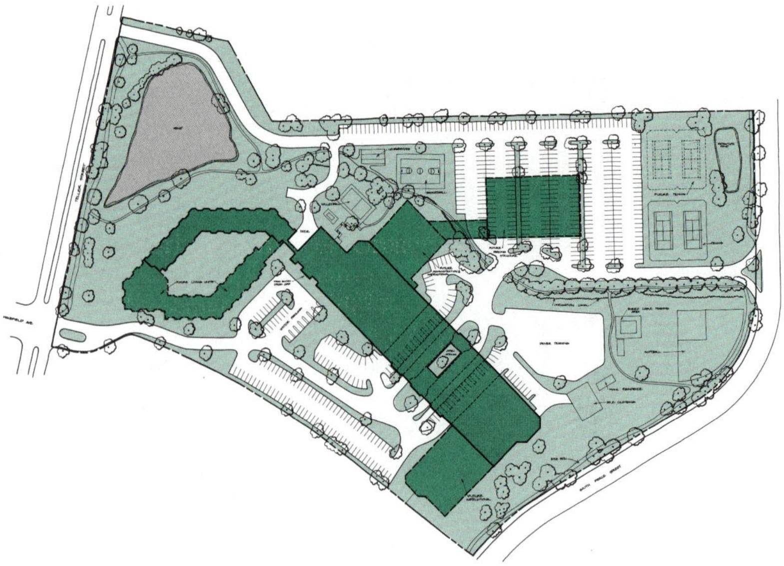

2-51 Site plan of the Mountain Bell Training and Education Center, a self-contained conference facility with on-site recreational amenities located in Lakewood, Colorado.

or steam baths. Most facilities are available without extra charge.

Economic Considerations

The conference center business has been expanding rapidly and in effect is challenging downtown, suburban, and resort hotels by offering substantial curricula programming and facilities completely tailored for groups. From a standpoint of economics, the basic purpose of conference centers is the same as hotels—to sell rooms, food, and beverages. Many conference centers have done well, but by concentrating exclusively on groups, they are vulnerable to some of the same seasonal and weekday-weekend fluctuations which conventional resorts and hotels are subject to. For those centers not pursuing resort business, weekends pose more booking problems than weekdays, unlike resorts and hotels.

The most difficult challenge to the development and management of conference centers is adapting them to increasingly more complex demands for facilities, services, and programming. Their continued success will depend on their ability to keep up with these demands. The services required for high-level executive conferences are labor-intensive and expensive and have enabled centers to charge substantial premiums accordingly.

Contingencies and Workouts

Every recreational development program should include strategies for accommodating some unforeseen change such as an economic downturn, financial problems, government policy changes, or altered competitive conditions. Contingencies can entail applying a reserve equity, refinancing, accelerating land sales, halting construction, or even selling out.

On the extreme downside, a recreational development may require a complete strategic and functional overhauling. This usually occurs when the existing owner—or more probably, the project's creditors—loses confidence in the direction the project is heading. It may accompany a foreclosure, further funding, or outright takeover by creditors. Whatever the circumstances, a recreational development in such a precarious financial position must be turned around toward better fortunes in order for investments to be recovered. The term "workout" refers to piloting a depressed project through this unfortunate phase with the hope that it will turn losses into profits, or at least minimize further losses. Workouts are particularly common in recreational development and are a consequence of the high risks associated with the business.

The typical workout strategy is to aggressively overhaul the development program and operation. The sale of the best assets helps regain financial stability and characterizes the dominant goal of a workout, that is, to maximize immediate returns. Thus, if a project can be sold for a price greater than the outstanding debt, it would be advisable to sell it.

An extremely important relationship during a workout is that between the developer and lender. In successful workouts, the developer has managed well the political process of negotiating with the lender; otherwise an unnecessary bankruptcy can result. Often the decisions are not clear. Lenders do not want to sue or foreclose. The developer, however, must present a variety of alternatives to the lender if he wants to continue to manage the project. Besides being responsive, competent, and honest, the developer must convince the lender that he is as good or better than any other management choice. He can help achieve this by preparing some of the detailed work—in short, informative reports—for the lender. If the developer's restructure proposals are rejected, further alternatives should be made even up to foreclosure. Continuing attempts to negotiate are essential, even if it involves going to the president of the bank. A workout between a developer and lender is not just economics: it is a political process. From the beginning, lenders and developers must realize that through their interdependent involvement in a large real estate development, they may eventually become active partners, in spite of different interests.

Management personnel may or may not be shifted and changed according to the needs in a workout situation. It is nevertheless advisable to retain certain staff members to provide the continuity needed to maintain a project's image which is crucial to a workout program. The development must maintain a viable and confident image, radiating good prospects for the future. Building confidence in the development company is important to the workout. Detailed commitments to the existing residents must be upheld or, if this is impossible, every effort to show good will to the owners should be made. Owners may then be more understanding of a developer's position and support a positive workout program.

Workout programs often include diversifying the market appeal and product line. One option is to expand a resort rental program to help carry the operation and introduce potential buyers to the property. Lowering prices is not always a good practice unless the product was overpriced to begin with. Price cuts can seriously undermine the true value of the project.

In any event, an effective and detailed development program, with proper contingencies and a good measure of luck, should make a workout unnecessary.

Rehabilitation

Three factors reflecting the urban rehabilitation phenomenon are playing an increasing role in strengthening the prospects of existing, though aged, resort/recreational facilities. The first factor is the diminishing frontiers for new domestic recreational development. Certain older facilities should enjoy fresh attention since new locations either do not exist or are unavailable because of environmental regulations and other restrictions. A second factor is escalating construction costs and restricted financing, which make existing facilities increasingly attractive for rehabilitation. The third factor is the influence of transportation costs which can act to place in greater demand highly accessible locations which underwent early development.

2-52 The Ahwahnee resort hotel, built in 1927 in Yosemite National Park, California, was renovated over a 7-year period for $1.5 million.

However, the economics of restoring old structures to meet modern requirements for living units may not always generate much enthusiasm. For example, the developer recycling the Glenbrook Inn dining hall on Lake Tahoe in Nevada to provide living units budgeted costs at 25 percent more than the cost of new construction in 1980. At the same location, however, rehabilitated structures have provided relatively inexpensive space for low-intensity community uses, including small offices, employee housing, and a recreational cooperative.

The rehabilitation of older facilities may represent a significant approach to providing quality recreational opportunities for consumers at all income levels. Applying techniques to modernize older structures should benefit recreational development as a whole and in sum represents the improved use of otherwise limited resources.[23]

The following section of Chapter 2 comprises a series of resort/residential case studies. The selected projects are intended to provide hard examples of recreational development products, practices, and experiences. For purposes of comparison, these case studies have been divided into six groups: coastal projects, Hawaii Island projects (Maui), mountain projects, created amenity projects (focusing on golf courses and manmade lakes), a recreational vehicle project, and workouts.

[23]See Urban Land Institute, *Adaptive Use: Development Economics, Process, and Profiles* (Washington: ULI–the Urban Land Institute, 1978).

Coastal Projects

Amelia Island Plantation
Amelia Island, Florida

Amelia Island Plantation is a 900-acre resort, second-home community located 30 miles northeast of Jacksonville, Florida, on the Atlantic coast. Major attractions of the project include its wide 4-mile beach, dramatic sand dunes, thick vegetation, bountiful sea marshes, and moderate temperatures.

Development (as of 1980) comprises 545 lots, 100 single-family homes, 580 condominiums, and the 24-room Amelia Island Inn. Facilities include a 27-hole golf course, a beach/pool complex, a 19-court tennis center, a health spa, and various nature pathways. There are five dining facilities, approximately 27,200 square feet of conference space, and an eight-store shopping village.

The project was opened in 1974 by the Sea Pines Company, famous for its second-home community on Hilton Head Island, South Carolina. It had a difficult start-up period due to declining market conditions following the opening and a developer whose resources were spread over a number of new large-scale projects experiencing similar problems. This unfortunately typical faltering of a recreational project of this size was resolved in part with new ownership in 1978. The new private investors formed the Amelia Plantation Company and introduced a new residential product, built an executive conference center, spent over $1 million in refurbishing, and generally upgraded the resort.

Development is scheduled to follow the original master plan, though construction will occur more slowly and at a somewhat lower density than it did previously. A build-out over 10 to 12 years is anticipated, with 30 to 50 condominium units being added annually. There are 120 acres of land currently remaining for multiple unit development. No further single-family home sites are planned. Additional facilities are expected to include expanded golf and other recreational amenities.

The Site

The project is located in Nassau County, Florida, 8 miles south of the county seat of Fernandina Beach (population 10,000). The property is bisected by Route A1A, which connects by bridge with Interstate 95, 20 miles away. Commercial airline service is provided 29 miles from the project at Jacksonville International Airport. A general aviation airport is 4 miles away on the island, and marinas are also located near the project.

Amelia Island is the southernmost of the major sea islands along the southeast coast of the United States. The project covers the entire width of the island near its southern end. There has been little development in the immediate vicinity of the property which was originally part of a larger 2,450-acre tract. This area of the island is protected from the Atlantic by 30- to 40-foot-high sand dunes that are being strictly safeguarded in placing development and in providing access to the beach. A unique sunken forest can be found in parts of the natural trench parallel to the beach between the rows of dunes. On the west side of the island tidal marshes extend 3 miles across to the

2-53 A divided and heavily landscaped entrance leads into the project.

2-54 Waterways and golf spaces provide valued visual diversity.

2-55 A wide beach and tidal marshes border Amelia Island.

mainland at its widest point. Between the sand dunes and marshes is a low lying subtropical forest averaging one-half mile in width.

Amelia Island has a four-season climate, with temperatures averaging 80°F., often with high humidity, in June through September and 55°F. in December and January. As elsewhere along the Atlantic, hurricanes occasionally pose a threat although minimum building site elevations and drainage provisions are maintained at the project to help prevent potential storm damage.

Planning

The Amelia Island Plantation property offered its developers the opportunity to apply highly sophisticated ecological planning to a rich and unspoiled natural environment. The final plan won national acclaim for its excellence in preserving the environment. A primary element in the master plan is the protection of the dunes, closely following the dictates of the land where construction occurs and providing boardwalks for passage through the fragile dunes. The marsh areas are protected from almost any intrusion or change. Interior drainage is handled by an interconnected canal system in which the water hazards of the golf course play an integral part. The project's private roadways wind gracefully and unobtrusively through the project, and parking is well screened. Landscaping is used extensively to separate uses and enhance the lush tropical setting. Several acres are designed as permanent nature preserves.

Site characteristics and the desired resort use mutually determined land use patterns. Since the beach was the primary attraction, relatively high-density development needed to be located near it and concentrated in a manner compatible with the constraints imposed by the dunes. A golf course provided a means for using the dunes while maintaining the natural terrain. The golf course also serves to vary the visual patterns on the interior of the island and provides a buffer between the roads and residential areas. The marsh area offers a different type of vista, with the adjacent land suitable for both single-family homes and some condominium units.

Major resort lodgings and guest facilities are separated from the primary residential area by the main highway which splits the property. The majority of the multifamily units available for rental are located closer to the beach and major activity centers than are the single-family residences. There are extensive provisions for walking and bicycling, as well as for a

2-56 The Amelia Island Inn (left) has a central location and unique view.

2-57 Condominiums with ocean views and private amenities are strategically placed in the dune areas.

2-58 Townhouses with marsh vistas are set within lush subtropical vegetation.

shuttle bus service that is required to connect separated activity centers for tennis, golf, swimming, and commercial facilities. Activity centers have been separated to minimize congestion during peak periods and preserve the natural setting as much as possible.

The real estate product inventory includes regular home sites of up to one-half acre, smaller zero lot line lots, and various condominium groups. Strict controls and covenants assure the environmental and aesthetic integrity of the project. An architectural review board, for example, counsels home builders. Condominium groups are clustered and architecturally varied to offer greater identity and product choice, and private recreational amenities are provided within some of the condominium groups. Activities for children were also an important planning concern; tot lots, bicycle paths, and other play facilities are provided.

A recent new product is a 33-unit oceanfront sand dune condominium cluster completed in 1980. The prices range upward from $200,000, and the units were largely presold. Each townhouse and apartment unit has an ocean view yet is oriented to an internal common area. They are designed for flexible, second-home or primary-home use and range in size from 1,600 to 2,900 square feet.

Several large tracts are designated for future development, as both joint venture and in-house projects. Moderately priced oceanfront condominiums well suited for rental are a likely future product to support the new conference center.

Resort oriented businesses have been encouraged to locate in a centrally established commercial village. At the entrance to the project is a reception center which serves as a check-in for guests and as a sales information center and is tied in with a security gate. A full range of dining and lounge facilities are provided in association with the main activity centers.

Utility distribution lines are all underground. Residential units have access to a central antenna television cable. The water system is supplied by a deep on-site well. The sewer system feeds a modern sewage treatment plant just off the property, and the discharge is used in the golf course sprinkler system. The water and sewer systems are owned at this time by a mortgage company. Trash collection service is contracted to a local company and paid for by individual owners.

Resort Operations

The ownership and operation of the Amelia Island Inn, conference center, beach, and tennis and golf clubs are major long-term commitments of the developer, as well as adjuncts to the real estate marketing. The company also operates a rental management program based on a 45 percent management fee for 340 condominium units, itself a revenue source, but more significantly a marketing tool and a means to achieve higher occupancy and greater use of resort facilities. The completion of the conference center in 1980 is expected to strengthen the overall use of the resort, particularly in the off-season.

The company-owned club facilities are available for private use to guests and club members. Property owners and those outside the resort area are eligible by invitation to participate in club activities through a variety of membership categories.

A common issue in a resort, second-home community of this kind is the mixing of resort functions with the interests of owners. In many ways, property owners benefit from the support the temporary resort guests give the common facilities. The Amelia Island Company believes conflicts between owners and resort users can be minimized when the character and quality of the resort operations reflect that of the community and when internal management rather than outside operators, who may not be sensitive to the interdependent aspects of a residential resort development, is used. Single-family residential areas are, by and large, segregated from the predominantly investor/rental condominium units.

2-59 Site plan of Amelia Island Plantation.

2-60 A park with picnic facilities overlooks sea marshes.

2-61 A pool complex also serves as a beach club.

Market

Property owners at Amelia Island Plantation are family oriented and tend to be over 40 years old with relatively high incomes. The project is an attractive vacation destination although as the original purchasers mature, more and more retirees are expected to take up seasonal residence. There are a few primary residents as well.

Resort guests tend to be upper-middle-income couples and families. The peak season is between Easter and Labor Day although the full season stretches 9 months from March to November. The bulk of the vacation market comes from Florida and Georgia, as well as the Northeast Corridor, the Midwest, and, more recently, Europe. There is a distinct family orientation during the summer months, with heavy golfing and tennis activity during the spring and fall.

The Plantation also caters to conferences of up to 500 persons, appealing mainly to associations and corporations throughout the country. A new $3 million executive conference center was recently completed, expanding the project's capacity to handle conferences and meetings.

Oceanfront rentals enjoy full occupancy during peak periods and are the most popular investor units. Later buyers have been generally more interested in using their property themselves over time than were many original purchasers. Approximately 85 percent of the buyers come to Amelia Island through referrals. The newest condominium product was 86 percent presold. Indications are that succeeding projects may sell out prior to construction.

Community Association

Property owners are given responsibility through the community association for the project's infrastructure, nature preserves, and various self-governing covenants. The community association maintains a high profile in security and environmental affairs. The property owners participated in the recent refurbishing of the entire property. The Amelia Island Company is a contributing member in the association, and retains veto power until 1986.

Experience Gained

- In promoting the use of its resort and conference facilities, Amelia Island Plantation could use perhaps 100 hotel rooms compared with the 24 it has and would benefit from a smaller condominium product for sales and for rent.
- More expensive sales units are simpler to manage but may generate fewer visitors and less associated demand on resort facilities than a more moderately priced rental unit.
- Given proximity to the primary attraction of a recreational development, such as a beach or other natural setting, people will buy units with or without convenient ancillary amenities.
- The expense of maintaining rigid environmental standards is well justified by the response in the marketplace.
- The original Amelia Island development was achieved too quickly. Unsold units competed with those bought by early investors who later wished to sell them.
- A developer is well advised to consider developing a core area adequate for initial activity and expand to other "villages" as market conditions prevail.
- Separated facilities at Amelia Island Plantation disperse activity but entail high transportation and management costs. When activity is high, this approach may be desirable to minimize congestion, but when activity is low it may make

activity seem almost nonexistent.

- Accounting losses and subsequent reporting undermine consumer confidence, with the potential of leading to disastrous declines in property values. However, such financial reassessments may be helpful in restructuring a development's position.
- Patient private investors can accrue advantages by assessing development losses against other income through tax mechanisms available to private owners. Such tax advantages may make the inevitable interim losses for new community development acceptable while still allowing investors to anticipate greater long-term profit.

PROJECT DATA—AMELIA ISLAND PLANTATION

Land Use Information:

Site Area: 900 acres

Total Dwelling Units:

	Existing	Planned at Build-out
Multifamily	594[1]	1,190
Single-Family	100	560
Total	694	1,750

Gross Density: 1.95 per acre at build-out

Net Density:

	Multifamily	Single-Family
Average	4.6 per acre	3.7 per acre
Maximum	15 per acre	7.3 per acre

Parking: Minimum of 2 spaces per d.u.

Land Use Plan:

	Acres	Percent
Single-Family Lots	160	18
Multifamily	80	9
Commercial	35	4
Recreational[2]	245	27
Common Areas[3]	260	29
Undeveloped Multifamily	120	13
Total	900	100

Economic Information:

Original Development (1973):

Site Improvement[6]	$12,000,000
Beach Club	$ 1,000,000
Tennis Center	$ 1,000,000
Golf Course (27 Holes)	$ 2,000,000

Newest 33-Unit Oceanfront Condominium (1979–1980):

Site Cost	$900,000 ($150,000 per acre)
Site Improvement Cost[7]	$192,000
Amenities[8]	$165,000
Landscaping	$150,000
Construction Costs	$52 per sq. ft.

Community Association Dues: $32 per month

Notes

[1] Includes 24 hotel units.

[2] Golf course is 190 acres; tennis is 20 acres; and miscellaneous and access are 35 acres.

[3] Includes open space, road network, lagoons, and some marsh area.

[4] Condominium rental rates per day range from $71 to $156 in the low season to $100 to $207 in the high season.

[5] A swimming pool is incorporated into each unit.

[6] Approximately $6 million was spent on project-wide infrastructure improvements with another $6 million going for site preparation specifically for dwelling units.

[7] Includes off-site extension of services to site.

[8] Includes pool, cabana, restrooms, boardwalks to beach, and other access.

Single-Family Lots:

Size: 6,000–25,000 sq. ft.

Cost (1980): $10,500–$70,000

Unit Information (1980):

Type	Unit Size	Number	Sales Price[4]	Bedrooms	Bathrooms
Condominium					
Cluster	1,200 sq. ft.	62	$65,000–$ 85,000	2	2
Townhouse	1,500–3,000 sq. ft.	180	$80,000–$150,000	2–4	3–4
Specialty[5]	1,000 sq. ft.	21	$85,000+	1	1
Mid-Rise	1,200–2,800 sq. ft.	331	$65,000–$350,000	1–4	2–4
Single-Family	1,200–4,000 sq. ft.	100	$75,000–$300,000+	2–6	2–5

Developer:

Amelia Land and Development Company
Amelia Island Plantation
Amelia Island, Florida 32034

Planning and Architecture:

Nichols Carter Seay/Grant
5314 14th Street, N.E.
Atlanta, Georgia 30309

Original Planning:

Wallace McHarg Roberts and Todd
Philadelphia, Pennsylvania 19103

The Homestead, Glen Arbor, Michigan

The Homestead is a 221-acre destination resort, second-home community located in the northwest quarter of Michigan's lower peninsula. It features 1.2 miles of beach frontage on Lake Michigan and 2 miles of frontage on the Crystal River, year-round recreational amenities, food service facilites, conference areas, condominiums, and single-family homes.

By 1979, the project included 63 single-family home sites (66 percent of the total proposed) and 225 condominiums (45 percent of the total proposed). The project's core facilities have also been completed. These include central water and sewer systems; paved roads; two restaurants; and two recreational facilities (a beach club and a racquet club, representing about 65 percent of the total projected costs of amenities).

Upon completion, the project will comprise approximately 5 miles of roadways; four food service facilities with seating capacity for 300 people; conference areas able to accommodate groups up to 200; a beach club with bike rentals, seven tennis courts, a pro shop, and a pool; a sailing harbor; a racquet club with six tennis courts and three platform tennis courts; 3 miles of paved bike paths; 20 miles of cross-country ski trails (located primarily on parkland adjacent to the site); ice skating; downhill skiing with three double chairlifts and five runs; a ski shop; and about 100 single-family homes and 500 condominiums, some of which will be owned as timeshare units.

The Site

The project is located in Glen Arbor Township and is served by the Cherry Capital Airport in Traverse City, about 30 miles to the east. Traverse City, the commercial center of northwest Michigan, has a permanent population of about 18,000. The area is generally regarded as one of the most scenic on the Great Lakes.

2-62 The Homestead stretches across an escarpment on the shore of Lake Michigan.

The Homestead is bordered on the west by the large expanse of Lake Michigan and on its other sides by the 70,000-acre Sleeping Bear Dunes National Lakeshore. Beyond the National Park boundaries lies Leelanau County.

The site's extensive beach area is sandy and gently sloping and includes a dune located between Lake Michigan and the Crystal River. A portion of this dune has been deeded forever as open space. Approximately 200 to 300 feet to the east of the beach area, a steep slope (45 percent) rises to a heavily timbered ridge located some 350 feet above the water elevation. Located beyond this ridge is a series of deep valleys and ridges.

Planning

The Homestead's objective has been to develop a year-round destination resort focusing on two core areas: the waterfront during the summer season and a sheltered valley during the winter season. Within each core, an activity center with commercial, food service and recreational facilities is provided. A system of interconnecting bike paths and cross-country ski trails is interspersed throughout the project. These trails link the facilities and allow pedestrians, bikers, and skiers to reach much of the property with minimal contact with roadways. Automobile use by property owners and resort guests has been discouraged. A jitney service is available in peak seasons.

The project is an excellent example of environmentally sensitive design. Emphasis has been placed on the preservation of a beautiful natural setting. By clustering core facilities and housing, a majority of the site has been maintained in its natural state. Upon project completion, less than 12 percent of the site will be covered.

To avoid a suburban appearance, buildings have been sited at irregular distances and angles to present natural contours. Residential views are oriented toward wooded areas and Lake Michigan rather than toward adjacent structures. A maximum number of trees have been saved, and in many instances, they are located within several feet of buildings.

Paved areas have been minimized. Boardwalks have been provided instead of concrete or macadam sidewalks, allowing trees of significant size to be saved. Common driveways have been provided and are required by deed restrictions, and parking areas have been kept small and separated by heavily landscaped areas. Road clearings and pavement widths have been minimized. The municipality has permitted two-way roadway widths to be reduced to 22 feet. Roads have been intentionally curved to avoid long views and driveways have been offset.

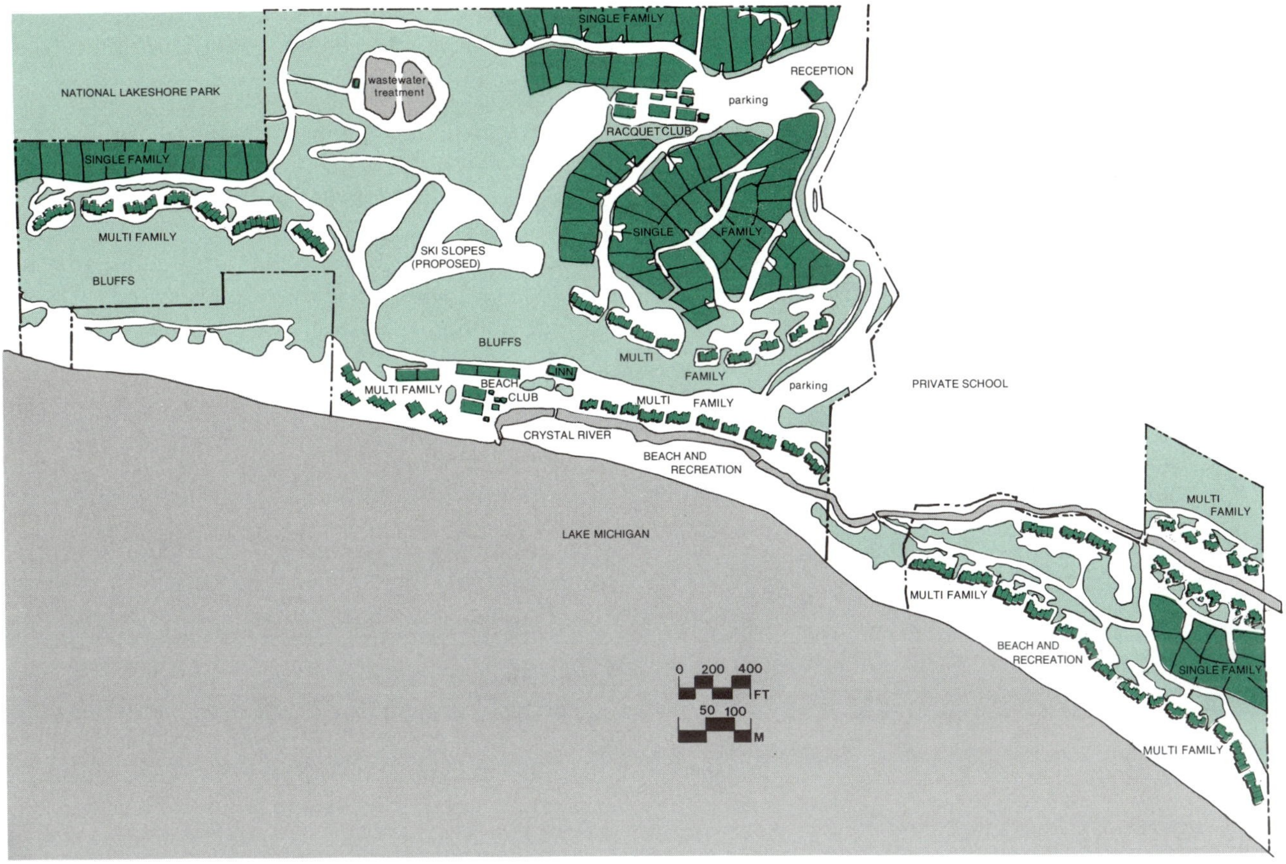

2-63 Site plan of The Homestead.

The steeply sloped building sites (up to 40 percent slope) have required extensive piling, retaining, footing, and foundation work. Preservation of natural vegetation, which is vital to the marketing concept, has required special construction on virtually every site. Where necessary, wooden tie retaining walls and landscaped terraces have been constructed and steep slopes adjacent to roadways have been hydroseeded. Jetty walls have been constructed to protect the fragile dune area between the lake and the Crystal River.

Electric, telephone, and television lines have been installed underground, except in a very few areas where grades or soil conditions are such that underground installation is not feasible. Central water and sewer systems serve all units. These include three large wells, chlorination buildings, two elevated storage tanks, and a wastewater system comprised of collection mains, lift station, pump houses, and aerated lagoons which function with an air-aqua oxidation system and seepage fields. A fixed monthly charge for water and sewer services is levied on each unit.

Architecture

Structures have been designed to be pleasant and unobtrusive so that they complement the land rather than making a statement independent of it. Natural materials and colors are stressed. Rough sawn cedar exteriors have been stained in forest colors. Buildings are characterized by low eave lines, steeply pitched roofs (8:12), multiple floor elevations, and frequent breaks in building lines. The extensive use of courtyards, patios, and screen fences has helped to deemphasize scale.

A detailed set of protective covenants regulates The Homestead's architecture. The covenants require that all building plans, including a detailed survey, a topographic map, and a tree survey, be submitted to and approved by The Homestead's management prior to construction on any residential home site.

2-64 Units have been stepped up the steep slopes.

2-65 A network of trails is used in winter for cross-country skiing.

Community Association

The Homestead has both an overall community association and individual associations for the various residential complexes. The overall association consists of an ad hoc board composed of a representative from each of the individual associations and deals with property management and insurance matters. It has no legal standing.

Rental Management

The Homestead offers the services normally associated with a major resort and a rental program for those owners who wish to rent their units. Housekeeping and maintenance services are provided by a year-round staff.

For its rental management services, The Homestead receives a commission equal to 40 percent of the net rental of the home. Rental rates are set by The Homestead according to a detailed pricing formula, with daily rents ranging from $40 to $150 in 1979. The Homestead will only accept rental management responsibilities from those owners who adhere to its rate structure. As of 1979, about 65 percent of the owners made use of The Homestead's rental program.

At the time an owner offers his house to The Homestead for rental management, and on a semiannual basis thereafter, the home is inspected using a set of written criteria to evaluate its condition, furnishings, and equipment. Homes which do not meet these criteria will not be rented by The Homestead.

Market

The Homestead has been designed for a young, affluent, activity-oriented, family clientele from the Great Lakes region. Most resort guests are in their early 30s, well educated, with annual incomes in 1979 of about $40,000. Property owners are generally in their 40s, well educated, and have annual incomes of greater than $80,000. Guests and owners tend to be professionals (physicians, lawyers, accountants, etc.) or are self employed. Units are purchased both for personal use (an average of 5 weeks a year) and as investments.

Advertising has focused on the varied recreational amenities available at The Homestead, particularly the natural amenities such as the clear, clean water of Lake Michigan, the extensive beach and dune areas, and the scenic, unspoiled countryside. The preservation of these natural amenities has served as one of the most effective sales tools. Activities for the entire family have been stressed.

The resale market for The Homestead has been excellent. As of 1980, the average resale had increased in value approximately 32 percent a year, with about 5 percent of the units being resold annually.

Experience Gained

- While costly and difficult to carry in the early years of a project, a quality site with natural amenities is far more marketable than a site with manmade amenities in a less desirable natural setting.
- An environmental assessment and plans for preservation should be made early, documented, continuously updated, and communicated. This will not only help to expedite the various governmental approvals required but will also have very positive marketing benefits if the environmental preservation plans are well formulated.
- A master plan should be formulated early, communicated to all governmental agencies, published for resort guests, and given to property owners in order to help minimize later "no growth" attitudes which are, to some degree, inevitable.
- Design consistency is imperative in order to ensure compatibility with existing natural features. This requires a detailed set of design covenants which must be strongly enforced.
- Amenities should be designed and built to be at least self-supporting. The long-term drain from unprofitable facilities cannot be charged to real estate sales indefinitely.

- An overall property owners' association is beneficial to both the developer and the property owners but budgeting for it on a long-term basis is difficult. While maintaining control of the association, the developer should also listen with care to suggestions from the owners.
- Sensitivity to the property owners' pride of ownership/partnership will lessen management problems. It is important to provide owners with facilities, activities, and privileges not available to resort guests or local patrons. Frequent, candid communication with owners is of considerable value.
- The preservation of the natural environment will be the strongest sales tool, particularly with a well-educated, affluent market, and in the long run will be well worth the additional construction costs.

PROJECT DATA—THE HOMESTEAD

Land Use Information:

Site Area: 221 acres
Total Dwelling Units: 600
Gross Density: 2.7 units/acre
Maximum Gross Density Permitted: 4.3 units/acre
Parking: 1,100 spaces (2 spaces per lot—single-family; 1.5 spaces per unit—condominium)

Land Use Plan:

	Acres	Percent
Single-Family Areas	47	21
Condominium Areas	115	52
Recreation	13	6
Commercial	2	1
Undeveloped	44	20
Total	221[1]	100

Unit Information (1979):

Type	Unit Size	Lot Size	Number	Sales Price	Bedrooms	Bathrooms
Single-Family Detached	900–2,000 sq. ft.	20,000 sq. ft.	63	Lot $25,000 House $75–$85 per sq. ft.	2–4	2–3
Single-Family Attached	1,400 sq. ft.	10,000 sq. ft.	10[2]	$126,000	4	3
Condominium—Efficiencies	400 sq. ft.	n/a	8	$25,000	1	1
Condominium—1 Bedroom	600 sq. ft.	n/a	22	$60–$75,000	1	1
Condominium—2 Bedroom	1,150 sq. ft.	n/a	112	$75–$90,000	2	2
Condominium—3 Bedroom	1,350 sq. ft.	n/a	80	$90–$115,000	3	2–2½
Condominium—4 Bedroom	1,700 sq. ft.	n/a	3	$125,000	4	3

Economic Information

Site Cost: $1,120,000 (1972–1979)
Site Improvement Costs:

Water and Sewer	$1,000,000
Roads	250,000
Utilities (relocation underground)	150,000
Total Improvement Costs	$1,400,000

Construction Cost (1979 average): $50

Amenities:

Tennis Courts and Platform Tennis	$190,000
Beach Club	225,000
Cross-Country Skiing Trails	60,000
Racquet Club	400,000
Total	$875,000

Condominium Association Dues (1979): $114 to $178 per month.

Notes

[1] Upon completion of the project, coverage of the site, including roads, parking, buildings, and recreational facilities, will be less than 12 percent.
[2] Proposed.

Developer/Management:
Kuras Properties
Wood Ridge Road
Glen Arbor, Michigan 49636

Architecture:
Community Design Services
223 Lake Street
Traverse City, Michigan 49684

Planning:
Guidelines
Juniper Ridge Road
Lincoln, Massachusetts 01773

Sea Pines Plantation, Hilton Head Island, South Carolina

Sea Pines Plantation is the Sea Pines Company's original resort/residential community. It is widely considered to be the national prototype of this type of development. Begun in 1957, the 4,500-acre sea island plantation has become a mature, community with over 1,700 homes, 1,300 villa condominiums, and the 202-room Hilton Head Inn. As of 1980, Sea Pines Plantation was valued at several hundred million dollars and was more than 80 percent complete. Amenities include four golf courses, 55 tennis courts, horse stables, playgrounds, two marinas, a farm, a child care center, a variety of beach, pool, and water facilities, and abundant shopping and dining.

The Sea Pines Company pioneered the use of comprehensive plans for community recreational development, using ecological studies to determine the best use of the land. Strict, privately administered controls on land use through extensive deed restrictions and architectural covenants ensure that buildings meld with the natural setting and produce a homogeneous contemporary effect. The developer is heavily committed to preserving extensive greenbelts, parks, and natural areas. The successes at the Sea Pines Plantation have been recognized with numerous awards and with widespread application of its ideas and land use concepts to other residential resorts.

2-66 The creation of Harbour Town was part of a strategy to open the marsh face of the island to real estate development.

2-67 The island style of architecture uses natural woods and stains to blend with the natural hues of the forest.

The Sea Pines Plantation includes four distinct areas. Harbour Town, with its famous Mediterranean port basin and historic architecture, is the commercial heart of the plantation. South Beach is a strongly family-oriented beach and ocean cove with a New England flavor. Middle Beach is an older area concentrated around the full-service Plantation Club. The club course area is intended for private single-family residences with golf course and salt marsh views and a minimum of intrusion from resort operations.

The Sea Pines Company operates a variety of resort services and facilities that add to the comfort of living in the community and to the value of privately owned properties. The company operates the Hilton Head Inn and manages the rental of over 900 villas and houses throughout the year. A property owners' association in conjunction with the company handles the civic and operating affairs of Sea Pines. No zoning ordinances were in effect during development, and historically, local government has been essentially uninvolved in land use planning at Sea Pines.

Development Strategy

The basic business activities of the master developer at Sea Pines have been sales of home sites and other land, development of residential units for sale, and operation and sale of resort facilities. During the many years required to build Sea Pines, the master plans have been altered in response to changing government and financial requirements, changing resident and visitor needs, evolving community planning techniques, and changing conditions affecting the developer's financial position.

The Sea Pines Plantation procures professional land development services by contract rather than maintaining in-house staff as it once did. Profit-incentive management arrangements are used for profit center operations, and programs to improve profits are followed to increase returns from buildings. The company recently reunified its resort and real estate marketing programs, reducing the percentage of revenues spent on marketing from 8 to 6 percent.

Approximately 80 acres of a total 2,400 acres owned by the company remain to be developed. The developer has and will continue to expand its resort facilities in joint venture arrangements to meet growing demand and to take advantage of the significant real estate values that have been created because of the growth at Sea Pines.

2-68 The "treehouse" consists of second level living quarters above a utility core, representing a design solution for lands which are otherwise undevelopable at Sea Pines.

2-69 The South Beach area at Sea Pines takes advantage of a protected cove at the southern end of Hilton Head Island.

Experience Gained

- The key factor in generating purchases and repeat business is quality of product in planning, development, and service.
- Home building, brokerage sales, and resort amenities are worthwhile areas for diversification. They directly affect values while property is under development and are potential long-term sources of profit.
- Recreational development requires constant executive management. Excessive overhead and marketing costs can cut deeply into profits. As in any business enterprise, growth of sales is not the only gauge of success.
- Careful management of recreational development can balance investment costs and operating expenses against market and financial uncertainties. Good management can attract financing and markets, but equity is still critical to weathering economic fluctuations. While growth at Sea Pines was relatively slow, it was steady and distinctive financially (and environmentally), testament in part to the advantages of using cash flows and accrued property values to fund expansion.
- A rental management program needs adequate rates to cover services and sufficient occupancy to justify the overhead. The Sea Pines experience indicates beach and other activity areas are appropriate for rental units, while quieter, more isolated locations are more suitable for home ownership.
- In year-long resort operation, lower seasonal occupancy is unavoidable. Marketing directed at the general consumer may not be cost effective in overcoming seasonal preferences, making it better to concentrate efforts on specially targeted groups and offering attractive price incentives.
- Commercial facilities benefit most from high dollar-volume rental visitors. Conference facilities are needed to attract group rentals in off-peak vacation periods to help support resort facilities.
- The Sea Pines Plantation story is one of success, though it is not readily replicated elsewhere. Large-scale new communities of this sort may no longer be possible, given the increased uncertainties of the 1980s. Nonetheless, a developer can benefit from obtaining as much land as financially feasible and tailoring a flexible development plan to it.
- Established and growing resort destinations like Hilton Head Island are in strong enough demand so that even a relatively poor development can succeed.

2-70 To protect distinctive plants and wildlife, 600 acres at Sea Pine Plantation have been set aside as a nature preserve.

Kiawah Island, South Carolina

Kiawah Island is one of the newest and certainly among the last of the major planned residential resorts on the U.S. southeast coast. Opened in 1976, the project gained quick acceptance and by 1980 included over 725 dwelling units.

The project is located 21 miles south of Charleston, South Carolina. Surrounded by 45 miles of tidal inland waters and more than 10 miles of broad Atlantic Ocean beach, Kiawah Island is a 10,000-acre barrier island, half of which is thickly vegetated marine forest. Unlike most other barrier island beaches in the region, the Kiawah beachfront—100 to 150 yards wide at low tide—is building up at a rate of 8 to 10 feet annually instead of eroding.

Development History

The present development of Kiawah Island began in 1974 with the purchase of the island by the Kiawah Investment Company for approximately $17.3 million. A planning and marketing team from the Sea Pines Company of Hilton Head Island, South Carolina, was contracted to develop the first phase of the project as a destination resort community reflecting the state-of-the-art in planning and development. Master planning began after an exhaustive 16-month environmental study was completed by a team of consultants representing 13 scientific disciplines. The resulting concept of clustering resort activity in several self-contained villages was structured to minimize the environmental impact of development

2-71 The 10,000-acre Kiawah Island is being developed in a series of resort villages and private residential neighborhoods.

and to separate intense visitor activity from private residential areas.

The acceptance of the Kiawah Island project is demonstrated by dramatically successful real estate sales since opening in 1976. Through October 1979, gross real estate sales volume totaled more than $72 million from approximately 1,370 company transactions and an additional $17 million from 230 brokerage sales. Because of carefully limited inventory, real estate offerings have never met market demand. All of the housing units have been sold before completion of construction, and since 1978 all units and lots have generally been sold on the day of release. The island presently has more than 1,400 property owners and a residential community comprised of some 175 homes and 550 villas and cottages. Roughly 700 home sites have been sold but are yet to have homes constructed.

Prices for lots in 1980 ranged from $30,000 for a wooded interior lot to $250,000 for an oceanfront lot. Lots vary in size, with the average lot approximately 100 feet by 150 feet, or 15,000 square feet. Housing prices range from approximately $80,000 for a one-bedroom condominium to $300,000 for a four-bedroom oceanfront condominium.

The first phase of development, West Beach Village, is now essentially complete. The Village is anchored by the 150-room Kiawah Island Inn and 250 rental villas, which together accommodated more than 110,000 visitor-days in 1979. Ten meeting rooms with capacities of 10 to 300 persons are available.

Existing development at West Beach Village also includes an 18-hole golf course designed by Gary Player, a racquet club with 16 tennis courts, and a 16,000-square-foot shopping center. Other recreational facilities include miles of bicycle paths, a children's and two adult swimming pools at the Kiawah Island Inn, a men's and a women's sauna and whirlpool, and a 25-meter owners' swimming pool and cabana club. To be added in early 1981 are a golf course with a major clubhouse and pro shop featuring fine dining and a complete line of golfing merchandise. The 27-hole golf course will feature three spectacular oceanfront holes carefully placed in the dune line along the ocean. It is expected that this new golf complex will match any in the country and be a symbol of the project's overall quality.

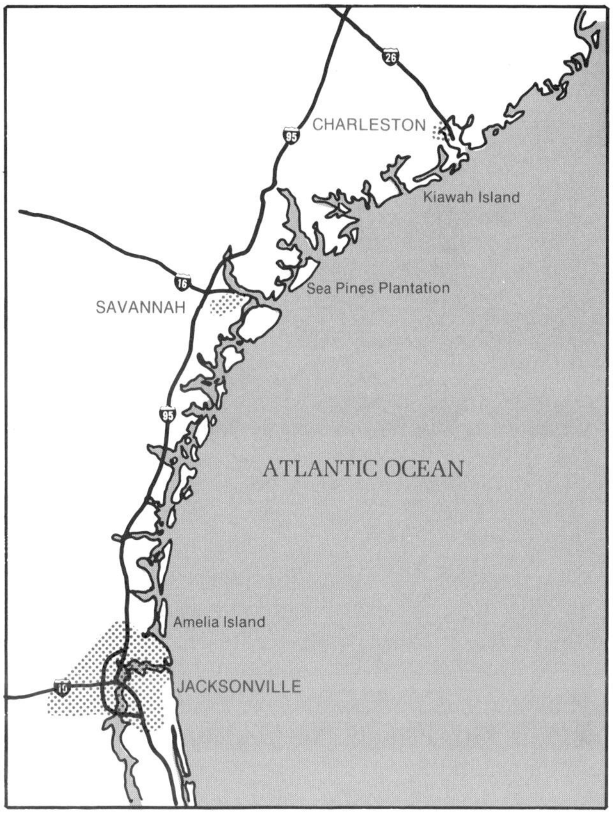

2-72 Coastal sea islands of the southeast United States.

Market

The typical Kiawah buyer is an individual with high income and high net worth in his mid- to late forties, motivated to purchase property at Kiawah by the island's beauty, natural environment, master land use plan, and investment potential. Based upon buyer surveys, competitive analyses, and input by marketing consultants, Kiawah's major markets are found to be segmented into three categories: primary homes (5 percent), second homes (55 percent), and preretirement/retirement homes (40 percent).

Primary Homes. This segment represents established households, both families and couples, who are actively employed in the Charleston area. Household size varies from two to five, and age of adults is predominately over 35. Location is usually the prime motivational factor for this market, but product design, exclusiveness, appreciation, and protected property values are also important. The primary-home buyer is seeking a neighborhood atmosphere with all the advantages of a resort and none of the disadvantages; therefore, privacy and security are essential. The primary-home buyer usually purchases a home site and then contracts for the construction of a single-family home.

Second Homes. Most of Kiawah's buyers have been second-home buyers. As of 1979, this market segment generally comprised three subgroups: investor (50+ percent), investor/user (25+ percent), and user (25+ percent). Research has shown several general characteristics and motivations are common among these subgroups.

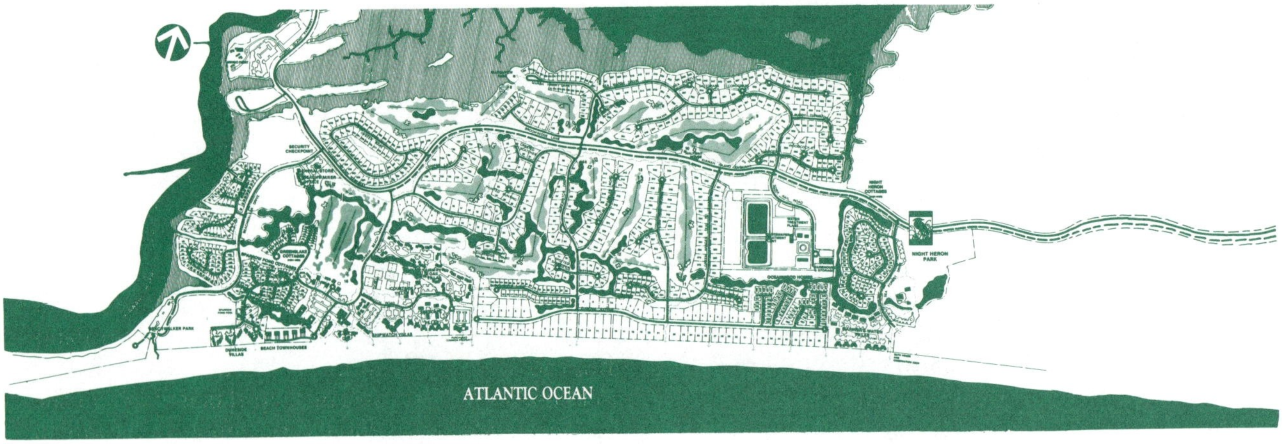

2-73 Site plan for West Beach Village, the first phase of the Kiawah Island project. Resort and residential areas have been separated to inhibit intrusion on private neighborhoods.

The investor typically purchases housing and is generally over 35 years of age with sufficient income or net worth to invest in real estate. He is motivated by potential appreciation, resale, and tax shelter benefits and uses his unit a maximum of 2 weeks each year to conform with income tax regulations, offering the unit for rental the rest of the year. The investor is concerned with security and controlled growth to the extent that they relate to the protection of his investment but generally rates an easily rentable product, high potential for appreciation, and proximity to major resort activities above security and growth.

The investor/user is motivated by many of the same factors as the pure investor but uses the unit more frequently. Therefore, depending on how often this buyer chooses to occupy the unit, personal preferences in location and product type more strongly influence his decision to purchase a unit than they do the investor.

Although also motivated by investment, the second-home user is more interested in long-term appreciation than in the cash flow and tax advantages which are important to the investor. The user market is generally comprised of established families and empty nesters with households of two to five persons. The second-home user wants all the conveniences of home with the advantages of a resort. Controlled growth and maintenance-free living are important factors to this market. Because of the desire for maintenance-free living, part of the user market is inclined to buy condominiums. Lots and speculator-built single-family houses also interest this segment, however.

Preretirement and Retirement Homes. Preretirement (35 percent) and retirement buyers (5 percent) at Kiawah have in the past bought primarily lots or single-family speculator-built houses. These buyers may start as second-home users and then change to a better location and product. This buyer is generally over 55 years old; the household usually includes two persons. The prime motivations for purchase are security, development stability, recreational amenities, and proximity to major services, including medical facilities. Kiawah's sales will reflect a higher percentage of these buyers as the community matures and basic resident services become available at or near Kiawah. Secondary motivational factors for purchase include location, climate, amenities, and product design. This market is the most consistent in terms of motivation and preferences. To attract it, Kiawah must be capable of demonstrating its immediate ability to cater to its resident community with respect to security, commercial and medical services, and recreational amenities.

Regional Markets

Important to the planning of the initial Kiawah marketing effort was the knowledge that during the real estate slump of 1974 and 1975, more affluent vacationers were still traveling to southeastern resorts, were willing to pay high rates, and were capable of buying property. The strategy from the beginning, therefore, was to provide a high-quality resort that would bring a steady supply of qualified buyers to the island. According to annual buyer surveys, each year of development has brought increasingly more affluent buyers from a wider geographic market area. The most recent buyer survey shows a continuation of the shift in demand from regional to national markets, with 45 percent of the 1979 buyers residing in midwestern, mid-Atlantic, and northeastern markets more than 500 miles from Kiawah. Only 13 percent of the 1976 buyers lived more than 500 miles away.

Because there is little developable oceanfront property along the southeast coast, most of the competition for Kiawah's major markets will come from existing regional developments. A 1979 survey of 10 competitive projects extending from Charleston, South Carolina, to Jacksonville, Florida, ranks the competition as having generally strong sales activity and relatively rapid absorption, particularly for attractive investor-oriented housing units and sales linked to the availability of permanent financing. Kiawah's lot and housing prices are consistently high compared to the competition.

The 1979 analysis of competitive projects identifies some comparative opportunities for Kiawah, based on several factors:

- Competitors for the most part are well along in development plans, and none offer truly distinctive quality—as Sea Pines did in the 1960s.
- Kiawah has some of the most attractive beaches and vegetation and the greatest amount of undeveloped ocean frontage. Many of the regional competitors have problems with beach erosion and will be sold out of company-owned products by the mid-1980s.
- Buyers will for some time perceive Kiawah to be in the early development stages and will want to get in on the ground floor. The excitement of new facilities and amenities planned throughout the 1980s will give Kiawah a distinct and constant momentum, unlike its more mature competitors.
- Facilities and activities for investors will draw vacationers to rental units, ensuring adequate occupancy rates.

As real estate prices increase and sales continue to shift to the generally more affluent distant markets, major competitive influences will emanate from resort communities nationwide and selected areas outside the country. It will be critical to the success of future sales to identify top competitors outside the region and to develop marketing strategies for Kiawah's advantage.

Plan to Completion

Planning for large-scale, long-term resort recreational development involves constantly refining the planned direction of the project based on the continuing assessment of the results of preceding concepts tempered against projected market conditions. During 1979 and 1980, Kiawah Island enlisted a multidisciplinary team of development professionals to prepare a comprehensive Plan to Completion (PTC). The need for a major update of the 1975 master plan before proceeding with major capital investments over the 1980–1985 period that would irreversibly determine the final scale of Kiawah development precipitated the preparation of a thorough Plan to Completion.

The basis of the PTC process was to prepare and evaluate three separate alternatives that effectively simulate reasonable and achievable development concepts for the undeveloped portions of the island in terms of type and density of residential products, level of amenities, and construction of commercial facilities. The development alternatives considered were termed intensive, moderate, and least intensive.

The intensive alternative concentrates on the development of finished, built-for-sale residential products (4,000 units in appropriate tracts of the project) and a limited supply of 2,000 single-family home sites at completion. The moderate alternative is structured to provide a balanced offering of 2,000 residential built-for-sale units and 2,600 home sites, with the finished units located primarily in parcels close to planned water and harbor amenities. The least intensive alternative focuses on the development of residential home sites, with only a limited offering of built-for-sale units provided in the short term. Sellout for the most intense development alternative was projected for 1996, generating annually by that time over 1.2 million visitor-days. The moderate and least intensive alternatives would be completely sold out in 1991 and 1989, respectively, generating annually approximately 900,000 and 350,000 visitor-days each.

Preparing the three development alternatives for analysis required the generation of a substantial base of assumptions about land planning, marketing, engineering, finances, and operations. To ensure their accuracy and detail, a planning team composed of inhouse staff from the Kiawah Island Company assisted by outside consulting organizations in planning and engineering prepared the assumptions. The outside

2-74 Tennis instruction at the Kiawah Island Racquet Club. Tennis ranks with golf as a major attraction at recreational developments such as Kiawah.

2-75 Resort specialty shops directly across from the Kiawah Island Inn. Resort facilities at Kiawah are located within a short walk to guest lodging.

consultants were selected on the basis of demonstrated capability in resort and recreational community planning and the ability to dedicate key staff members to the work so that the experiences of other high-quality resort projects could be applied to Kiawah Island development. The planning team approach resulted in highly sophisticated planning—a process that exceeds typical planning efforts at comparable resort projects but is anticipated to prove extremely valuable in meeting the changing conditions of a competitive marketplace and volatile economic environment.

A basic objective of the PTC planning process was to properly integrate the physical and financial aspects of the planning efforts. Physical and business planning teams were each headed by an in-house administrator responsible for coordinating the activities of company staff and outside consultants.

The physical planning team, composed primarily of land planners and architects and engineers, defined islandwide development opportunities and constraints by tract for each of the development alternatives. The team documented these findings in a set of master plans for each alternative. In addition, the physical planning team evaluated parcels within tracts to determine the implications of different types of development from a physical standpoint. An offshoot of these evaluations was the further definition of standards for development of individual parcels for Kiawah Island.

The business planning team, comprised primarily of financial and marketing analysts, evaluated the assumptions about land planning, engineering, marketing, finances, and operations for each of the development alternatives. These assumptions, after evaluation by the business planning team, were fed into a computer simulation model called the Land Development Model, which performed a series of economic analyses for each of the alternatives. The Land Development Model was specifically designed for analysis of large, complex land development projects containing a variety of residential, commercial, resort, and recreational land uses and facilities. The model evaluates the profitability and cash flow generation of both the overall project and specific project components and functions as a planning tool by maintaining an information base of all the project assumptions. Each of the three development alternatives was subjected to a series of iterative economic analyses designed to optimize the specific alternative's project plan in terms of the mix of residential products, commercial, resort, recreational, and infrastructural land uses, and phasing of capital costs. After each computerized economic analysis, the physical and business planning teams reviewed results and revised the assumptions as appropriate. This procedure produced the desired integration of physical and business planning and kept all team members aware of planning progress.

Included in the PTC alternatives was essential consideration of risk and flexibility. The PTC process gave special attention to the risk related to the length of the development period—the longer the time estimated to sell all units, the greater the implied risk of actually being able to achieve estimated absorption. Long-term planning increases the difficulty in reasonably assessing the vagaries of a volatile marketplace.

Two other factors of risk measurement needed to be considered. The first was the length of time required for the project to generate sufficient cumulative cash flow. The payback coverage, or safety margin, is calculated by dividing project cash flow by the original investment.

A further important characteristic the PTC process evaluated was the flexibility of the development plan to conform with future changes in business conditions—the ability to adjust overall company strategy between real estate and resort elements.

By summer 1980, the PTC process reached the stage where a reasonably optimized development program for each of the three alternatives was available for analysis by the Board of Directors of the Kiawah Island Company. For each of the alternatives, the development program includes a master plan, a phased schedule for absorption of residential units, requirements for development of amenities and commercial facilities, and factors affecting resort operations. The Board of Directors was asked to consider the key issues and define the direction needed to finish the final business plan.

Hawaiian Island Projects: Maui

The Hawaiian recreational market has been growing rapidly since the 1960s with projections of visits doubling again from 1980 to 1990. The affluent Islands market seems to have been relatively insulated from recessions. Recent development has spread to the neighboring islands, such as Maui, on which a less intensely developed environment is offered compared with the island of Oahu and the city of Honolulu. Visitors to Maui seeking a natural, rural setting are willing to pay a premium for quality development projects. In this handbook, three master-planned resort/recreational destinations on Maui are discussed—Kapalua, Wailea, and Kaanapali, the last being treated as a more typical case study.

A major vacation resort and high-quality residential community, Kapalua is the newest of the large, developer-controlled destination resorts on Maui. It comprises 750 acres of oceanfront and includes a hotel, golf course, tennis courts, shops, and four condominium projects, with additional development on line. Kapalua's success has been due to its developer's reputation and its high product and marketing standards. Compared with Wailea and Kaanapali, Kapalua projects perhaps the most low-key profile while catering to the most exclusive market.

Wailea is also a luxury-oriented residential resort community on Maui. The slower pace on Maui is considered Wailea's major market appeal. Like Kapalua, Wailea is a product of the 1970s and, with the beginning of the 1980s, was beginning to show its first profits. Wailea is larger than Kapalua with 950 hotel rooms and a planned total of 3,500 condominium and single-family lots. The developer does not wish to own or operate hotels and subcontracts residential construction. Wailea's shopping and dining facilities are important growth areas.

The Kaanapali Beach Resort is the most mature and intensely developed of the three planned recreation destinations. It is similar to a standard resort, with more than twice as many hotel rooms as condominiums. Its first hotel completed in 1963, Kaanapali was a pioneer on Maui, going through a number of phases as it matured. The master developer, Amfac, made use of land sales and subdevelopers to supplement development. The beginning of the 1980s sees Kaanapali at a crossroads. Like many resort destinations for which success has led to high volume business, the increasing maturity of Kaanapali raises serious questions about maintaining its market appeal and product quality. Competition for tourist markets and the potential for further on-site development are major concerns.

The success of a recreational community on Maui has depended on four factors: government objectives, large land holdings, quality product, and strong marketing. Maui's overriding attraction, however, lies in its natural attributes of outstanding white beaches, island mountain scenery, exotic microclimates, and the historic whaling town of Lahaina. All the resorts across Maui share the benefits of promoting these features. The focus of the affluent market may shift, but in Hawaii older facilities remain much in demand. Island regulations are comprehensive and restrictive, adding value to approved developments. Competition over construction resources among projects and employee housing are mutual problems of resorts. Through 1979, property on Maui was generally sold quickly and at high prices, although the uncertainties that prevailed in 1980 proved that a time may come when this activity slows.

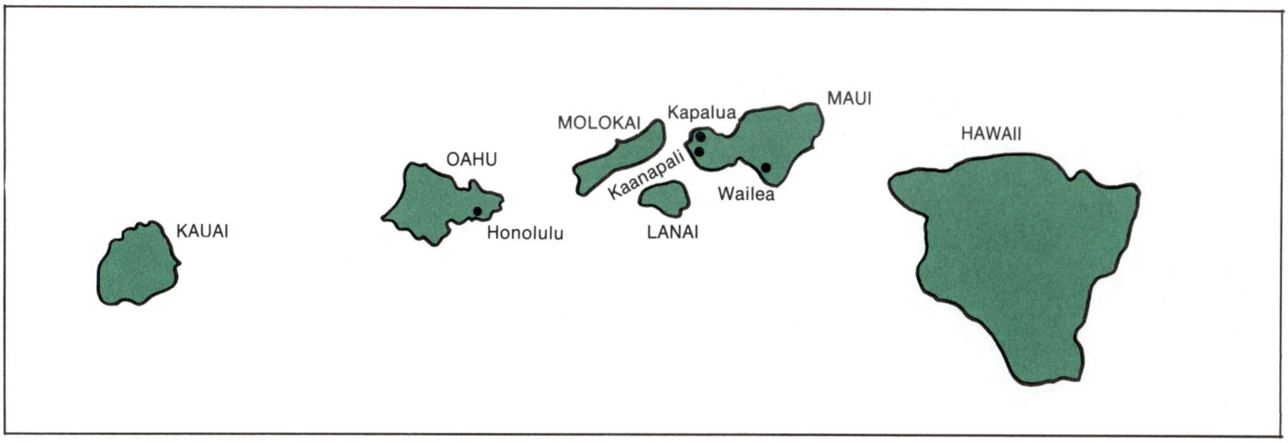

2-76 Map of Hawaii.

Kaanapali Beach Resort

The Kaanapali Beach Resort, owned, developed, and managed by Amfac, Ltd., a billion-dollar Hawaii-based corporation, is located on the shores of west Maui. It was the first major destination resort established in Hawaii off Oahu and, with the opening of a golf course and the first two hotels in 1962, has served as a model of planning, marketing, and profitability.

By 1980, about 600 of the more than 1,000 acres had been developed or were under development, including construction of six hotels with a total of 3,700 rooms, seven sold-out condominium projects with a total of 1,300 units, 130,000 square feet of commercial space, 350 custom home sites, two 18-hole golf courses, and an airstrip served by a commuter airline. Plans for expansion continuing into the 1990s include the addition of two more hotels, three condominium projects, 17 apartment sites, a neighborhood shopping center, two theme cultural attractions, a number of residential subdivisions, and an executive golf course.

The Site

The resort is 26 miles from the main airport on Maui at Kahului, approximately 100 miles from Honolulu on the island of Oahu, and 3 miles north of Lahaina, an old whaling port with a population of about 6,000 people. Lahaina was the first capital of Hawaii; its historic significance serves as a major attraction to the west coast of Maui.

2-77 Sheraton Maui Hotel, Kaanapali Beach Resort.

Kaanapali Beach is predominantly dry and sunny. Annual rainfall is 15 to 20 inches with an average of 355 days of sunshine and breezes. The project is bordered by 3 miles of sandy beach on the ocean side and sugar cane fields that reach up a gradual slope on the mountainous inland. The most intensively developed area of the resort proper immediately fronting on the beach is relatively flat and is bisected by the main highway which separates the sloping residential areas from the resort area.

Planning

When conceived in the late 1950s, the Kaanapali Beach Resort was intended to be a self-contained island resort, ultimately including all the recreational, commercial, entertainment, social, and medical facilities necessary. Provision was made to build residential apartments as a secondary land use, primarily for the limited number of local business executives.

Golf courses were planned as important areas of open space and landscaping is profuse throughout. In addition to the beach and golf courses (handling 85,000 rounds annually, with an effective capacity of 100,000), recreational facilities include 22 tennis courts scattered throughout the resort along with numerous other land- and water-oriented activities typical of a major ocean resort.

The desired but somewhat weakly coordinated architectural image is tropical, relying on Hawaiian style rooflines, natural rock, and open air design. Amfac maintains an architectural review committee of five experts who serve as advisers. The resort was already well established when zoning was introduced; consequently, urban development is permitted over most of the property. Public regulations stipulate a 12-story maximum height for buildings, setbacks from the ocean, special permits for construction seaward of the highway, landscaping requirements for parking lots, and public access to beach spaced at a maximum of 1,500 feet apart (the state of Hawaii owns the land seaward of the vegetation line). Amfac provided central water and sewer service, and is blessed with access to fresh water in an otherwise water-short area.

Management

Amfac is primarily a master planner and bulk lot developer and prefers to sell or lease finished lots to developers. It manages the resort as a whole but not the individual properties, with the exception of those owned by Amfac. Among the company's $20 million in current assets—most of which are profitable—are the golf courses, commercial centers, common areas,

2-78 Kaanapali Beach. A mountain (out of view) which begins a slow ascent a few hundred yards behind the beach dominates the island backdrop.

and the airport and jitney services. There is no central owners' association. The Kaanapali Beach Operators' Association (KBOA), which has as members the hotels, the various condominium managements, the shopping complex, Amfac, and the commuter airline, acts as a marketing arm for the resort, as well as an organization to consolidate operations.

Market

Kaanapali is heavily oriented toward hotels—operated by Interisland Resorts, Sheraton Hotels, and Island Holidays, a subsidiary of Amfac—whose independent advertising and promotional efforts benefit the entire resort. Kaanapali pioneered the advertising approach whereby all of its attractions were identified with it as one, a marked contrast to individual projects advertising solely for themselves. The Kaanapali Beach Operators' Association has a full-time executive director and a budget, contributed on a per-room basis, which is used largely to promote Kaanapali to the travel trade. As a result of the various hotel organizations and KBOA's marketing efforts, the hotels have in recent years averaged over 90 percent in annual occupancy rates. About 50 percent of the travel trade are groups and 50 percent are individuals. The total number of visitors ranges from 400,000 to 500,000 annually and represents almost half of the Maui market. The primary tourist area is the West Coast of the United States mainland although the number of visitors from Canada, Asia, and Europe has been increasing. Approximately one-fifth of condominium purchases are made by foreigners (90 percent Canadian) with most U.S. buyers being from the West Coast. The buyers are primarily from upper-middle and upper incomes.

For its size, Kaanapali does little convention business. There are no central meeting or exhibition facilities and no plans for them. Existing hotels have small- to medium-sized banquet/meeting facilities, the largest being 10,000 square feet. The new Hyatt-Regency, however, has a substantial capacity and will focus on attracting conventions and business meetings.

Nevertheless, it is expected that Kaanapali's marketing efforts will continue to be geared toward the vacationing traveler—individually or in groups—primarily along the West Coast from California to Canada. The United States East Coast and Asia are targets for expanding the market.

2-79 Compared with manmade amenities, water-oriented activities require almost no fixed capital investment.

2-80 A jitney service at Kaanapali provides for essential internal transportation.

Property Development

As of 1980, the combined values of the developments at the Kaanapali Beach Resort represented an estimated $250 million. The resort employs over 2,200 persons, paying $15 million in salaries, and produces well over $3 million in gross excise and real property taxes.

From the opening of the first hotel in the early 1960s to the 1980 debut of the 820-room Hyatt Regency, said to have cost $100,000 per unit, the Kaanapali Beach Resort has gone through a number of development phases. The master developer committed heavy investment through the later 1960s and the entire resort was highly successful during the next decade. The addition of new hotels and second-home properties has helped sustain momentum and growth and, with the 1982 opening of a new Marriott Hotel, should continue to attract attention. Despite its established success, however, the Kaanapali Beach Resort has felt some of the pains of increasing maturity. The original master plan and organization strategy failed to anticipate the significance of certain environmental, circulation, marketing, and general development concerns that are commonplace today. In a number of ways, the resort shows its age, both in its basic planning (for instance, there is no interconnecting beachfront walkway or common signage) and in its facilities. Kaanapali is striving to maintain its established standards by adding new products but also by maintaining and upgrading the older facilities. In 1977, a new golf course was added, the original course was

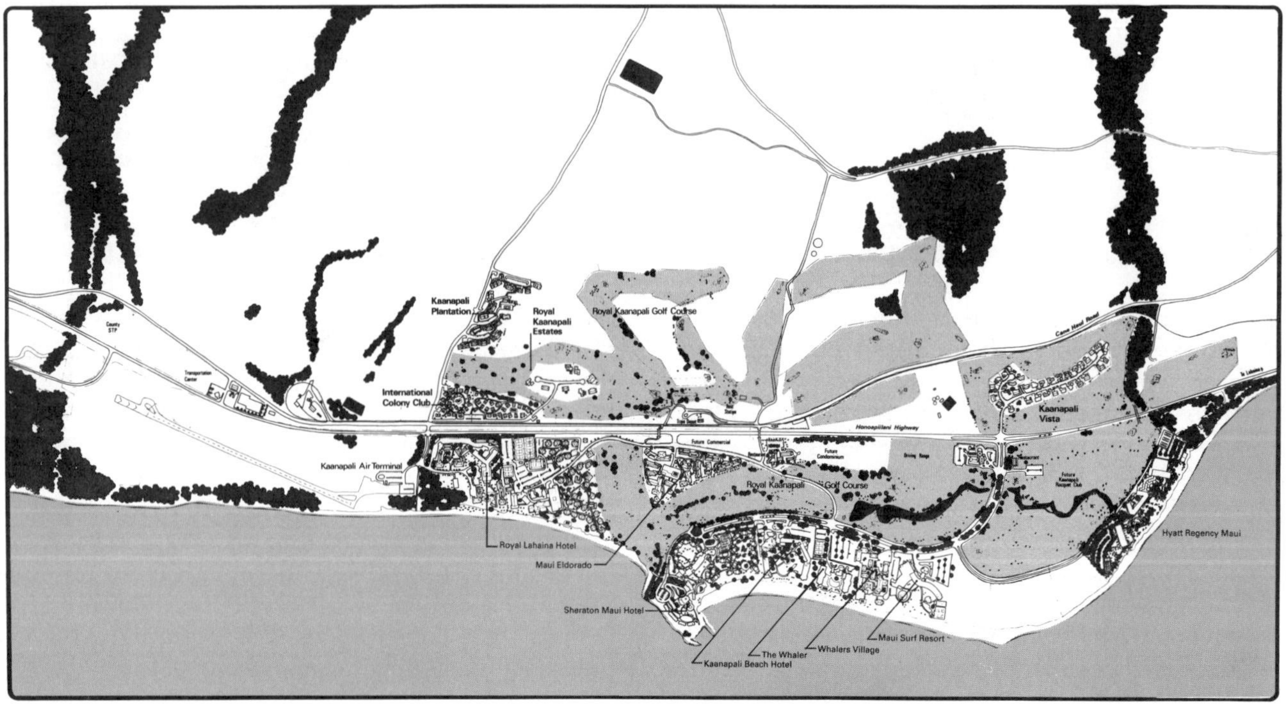

2-81 Site plan of the Kaanapali Beach Resort.

renovated, and a $2 million clubhouse was completed.

For the future, new attractions will be added, and Amfac is continuously reevaluating its plans to ensure a sound future. Preparing to double its present investment through build-out, Amfac is giving careful attention to the essentials of open space, view channels, recreational facilities, the adequacy of utilities, employee housing, economic feasibility, and the proper mix of unit types.

Experience Gained

- The success of the Kaanapali Beach destination is attributable to climate, proximity to the town of Lahaina, ambience of resort, friendliness of local people, range of services, and amenities.
- The concept of selling properties to help finance development limits the master developer's control over orchestrating resort development as well as the quality of service. Amfac believes leaving the development planning to the owners and operators is a less expensive strategy and more effective in creating a natural, vital, and rich built environment. (Without this liberty allowed to subdevelopers, the Hyatt Regency Maui, for instance, may not have been constructed.)
- The strategy of using bulk land sales or leasing minimizes risks for the master developer but requires skillful negotiation.
- Negotiations are important, not only for development deals, but to ameliorate conflicts, which in Kaanapali include dealing with adjacent sugar cane operations, as well as with conflicts between golfers and nongolfers.
- An operators' association is helpful in achieving goals of mutual benefit. The Kaanapali Beach Operators' Association serves to provide consensus and direction for resort operation.
- Initial planning should consider many details, such as security, transportation, organizational responsibilities, and, ultimately, the potential for an increased number of permanent residents. Poor control of signage and graphics, for instance, can seriously undermine the magic of an exotic resort atmosphere.
- In a strong growth setting, it is desirable to expand facilities during a slow market period to be best positioned to take advantage of an upswing.
- At Kaanapali, the ratio of demand is two hotel units to one condominium unit.
- Ocean vistas are by far the prime values. The new Hyatt at Kaanapali offers ocean views in 90 percent of its rooms.
- Growing resistance to "overbuilding" can result in a community opposing any further construction. While this is a typical and familiar problem to all developers, it is of particular concern in resort development because of the need for a return on the heavy front-end costs of infrastructure.

PROJECT DATA—KAANAPALI

Land Use Information:

Site Area: 1,055 acres

Total Units:	Existing 1980	Planned
Hotel Rooms	3,700	5,700
Condominiums	1,300	2,500
Commercial Space	130,000 sq. ft.	700,000 sq. ft.
Apartments	—	1,000
Single-Family	350	1,500
	Total planned	10,700 units

Gross Density: 10.7 units per acre

Parking Spaces: 1.25 units per space

Land Use Plan:

	Acres	Percent
Hotel	150	14
Condominium	110	10
Commercial	55	5
Single-Family	300	29
Apartment	70	7
Golf Courses	370	35
	1,055	100

Economic Information (1980):

Site Cost: $4,000–$5,000 per acre book value, appraised over $3,000,000 per acre
Site Improvement Cost: $80,000–$100,000 per acre
Construction Costs: $100,000 per hotel room, $100.053 per sq. ft. for condominiums
Golf Course: $200,000–$250,000 per hole
Tennis Court: $25,000
Sales and Rent Information: hotel rooms average $50+ per day; condos, $100,000–$700,000; single-family lots, $100,000–$150,000; house packages, $300,000+

Developer/Owner:

Amfac Property Corporation
P.O. Box 696
Lahaina,
Maui, Hawaii 96761

Planning:

HKS Associates
220 Jackson Street
San Francisco, California 94111

Marketing:

Weiner Associates, Inc.
Pioneer Plaza, Suite 1555
900 Fort Street Mall
Honolulu, Hawaii 96813

Whalers Village, Kaanapali Beach

Whalers Village is a specialty commercial complex created to serve the resort recreational market and using as its theme the island's historic whaling industry. It is a 15-building complex consisting of 65,543 square feet of net leasable area divided into 31 shops, eight restaurants, and several offices. Painted in earth tone colors, the low-rise concrete and wood frame construction is located on an 8.5-acre lot and has an oceanfront of 352 feet. There are 100 displays throughout the open areas of the complex depicting the history of the whaling industry in Maui. Whalers Village offers tourists a pleasant, leisurely, and educational shopping experience. The complex is the only shopping center in the Kaanapali Beach Resort although each hotel has commercial retail space.

The theme of Whalers Village is carried through in the architecture of the buildings, which are fashioned after ship hulls and cabins. Skylights and open-air areas resemble ship decks. Whaling artifact displays are strategically located throughout the village to create a traffic pattern which leads tourists through the entire shopping area. A Polynesian show is held weekly on an outdoor stage.

The project opened in 1970 and approximately 10,000 square feet were added in 1975. Expansion will contain 10,000 to 15,000 square feet of additional retail/restaurant space while retaining the open space and landscaped character of the project and strengthening the museum theme.

Amfac owns and operates the $3.5 million complex. An architectural review committee controls exterior signage. All operating costs are passed on to tenants. Experience has shown that short-term leases of 3 years are best, that basement space is not advisable, and that cleanliness should be a top priority.

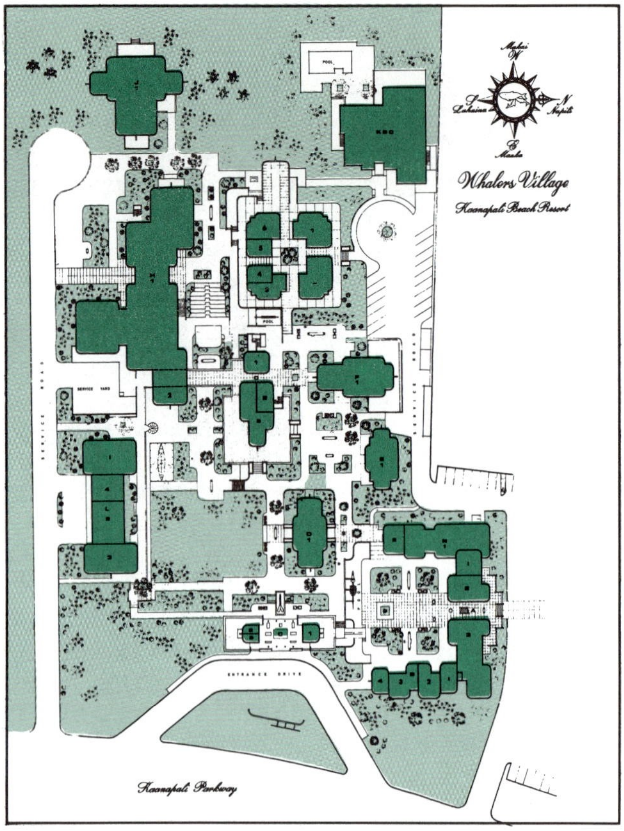

2-83 Whalers Village site plan, highlighting opportunities for relaxed and varied pedestrian movement through the project.

2-82 Displays portraying the whaling industry support the theme of the shopping complex.

2-84 The complex is located between the main resort roadway and the beach at Kaanapali.

The Whaler, Kaanapali Beach Resort

The developer of The Whaler purchased the land for it from Amfac. The project comprises two 180-unit, 12-story towers, and includes four tennis courts, two paddle courts, a beach-side pool, a sauna, a Jacuzzi, a work-out gym, and a pantry. It is designed for transient occupancy, with the necessary management and storage spaces. The 6.7-acre property is surrounded on one side by the sands of Kaanapali Beach and on the other side by the Royal Kaanapali golf course. This project enjoys the distinction of being the only condominium complex at the Kaanapali Resort fronting on the beach. Next door is the Whalers Village museum and shops complex, and on the other side is the Kaanapali Beach Hotel.

When the project was put on the market in 1974 prior to construction, all 360 units were sold in approximately 1 week. The first tower was completed in July of 1975, and the closings were effected during that summer. The second tower was completed in early January 1976 with closings between November 1975 and February 1976.

The developer retained 38 units, which were later timeshared, primarily through on-site sales over a period of approximately 2.5 years. Since that time, the owners have moved to prohibit further timesharing at The Whaler, after first allowing some 14 additional units to be timeshared, on a grandfather basis.

As of 1980, the unit values had increased five or sixfold and the last of the timeshare units was offered for sale. The management of the home owners' association is under contract, as is a high-quality, hotel-style rental program. A rental management advisory board was nominated by the rental management company and elected by the owners.

Planning

The two towers which run perpendicular to the beach afford ocean views from about 90 percent of the units, and the courtyard between the two towers is handsomely landscaped. Open spaces are designed to create foreground and distant vistas, complemented by the adjacent Whalers Village which is low-rise and the Kaanapali Beach Hotel which is mid-rise. The project makes maximum use of the allowable density.

Special design elements of the project include: Italian marble throughout the lobby and bathrooms; azure blue ceramic tile on the spacious lanais that adjoin each unit, as well as in the elevator lobbies; a security system limiting access to each tower to owners or guests with keys; covered parking for 218 cars, with elevator access to the two towers; and air conditioning separately controlled in each living space, which cuts off when the lanai doors are open to admit the trade breezes. In addition, each unit was originally sold with a standardized furniture package of good quality.

Because of the sandy subsoil near the water's edge, it was necessary to drive pilings to support the front of the two towers. A faulty membrane between the underground parking and the landscaped courtyard above caused some engineering difficulties.

Management

The project is governed by standard legal documents for condominiums. A board of directors manages the common areas for the association through an appointed managing agent, Management Consultants of Hawaii, Inc.

The ownership use patterns of the 360 units can be broken down roughly as the following: permanent owner/residences, 3 percent; rental units, 3 percent; units of absentee owners who do not rent, 11 percent; units rented occasionally by absentee owners, 8 percent; timeshare units, 17 percent; and units in the resort rental program, 58 percent. The rental program,

2-85 The twin towers of The Whaler, completed in 1975 and 1976.

PROJECT DATA—THE WHALER

Land Use Information:

Site Area:	6.7 acres
Total Dwelling Units:	360
Gross Density:	54.5 d.u. per acre
Parking Spaces:	281[1]

Economic Information:

Land Aquisition (1973):	$750,000 per acre
Off-Site Improvement Cost Allocated to Site:	$20,000 per acre
Construction Costs (1975):	$24,500,000

Developer: Pacific Building Corporation
Hadley Properties
2200 Sixth Avenue
Seattle, Washington 98121

Rental Management: Village Resorts, Inc.
3620 Mt. Diablo Boulevard
Lafayette, California 94549

Real Estate Marketing: Mike McCormack Realty
P. O. Box 3204
Honolulu, Hawaii 96801

Residential Units:

Size	Bedrooms	Price (1974–76)	Resale Price (1980)
542 sq. ft.	Studio	$ 40,000	$185,000–215,000
905–914 sq. ft.	1	50,000–65,000	300,000–500,000
1,444 sq. ft.	2	100,000–120,000	575,000–750,000

Rental Program:

	1977–78	1978–79	1979–80
Gross Revenues	$2,379,633	$3,436,607	$3,842,766
Total Expenses	$1,236,273	$1,610,379	$1,839,407
Total Return to Owners	$1,143,360	$1,826,228	$2,003,359
Average Return Per Unit	$8,335	$11,110	$11,571
Average Daily Rate	$54.02	$66.74	$76.60
% Occupancy	82.2%	81.0%	74.5%
% Return to Owners[2]	48.0%	53.1%	52.1%

Rental Rates 1981: $70 to $185 per day

Notes

[1]218 underground, 63 outside.

[2]Percent return to owner figures reported with monthly checks includes 4% tax; audited figures do not.

operated by Village Resorts of Lafayette, California, is based on a long-term lease with the association for the use of the management spaces and on rental agency agreements with each owner. The rental agreements are based on the hotel formula whereby: (1) the revenue is credited directly to the unit in which the guest stays; (2) expenses are pooled between all owners in proportion to revenue; (3) profits are accrued to the owners; and (4) management fees are based on a percentage of the profit returned to the owners. Six percent of the gross revenues are allocated to marketing.

The concept of the rental program has been to identify strongly with the owners' objectives for maximum cash flow and enhancement of real estate values. This was accomplished by providing extremely high levels of guest services, as would ordinarily be expected from a first-class hotel. An aggressive rental marketing program involving $400,000 annually has resulted in extremely high occupancies, premium rental rates, and an average net return to owners that increased to $11,571 in 1979–1980.

Market

The Whaler was well-positioned to meet the down-market of 1974–1975 due to its unique location on Kaanapali Beach, the high quality of its units, and an attractive financing package. Buyers were offered mortgages of 80 to 90 percent of the sales price at 8¼ percent for 30 years. The developer had negotiated the financing before the energy crisis. Because of the extreme desirability of the area and the many hotel guests who had stayed there previously, there was considerable built-in demand. A model was set up to initiate sales and little additional promotion was required to sell all the units in a few days. The typical owner is a business executive from the West Coast of the United States and Canada, although Hawaii is also well represented.

Kapalua

Kapalua is the newest of the three large master-planned, developer-controlled destination resorts on Maui. Collectively, these resorts have contributed significantly to the image of Maui as a place of magic not only to visit but to invest in.

Kapalua comprises 750 acres of oceanfront land on the northwestern coast of Maui. The development is owned and managed by the Kapalua Land Company, Ltd., whose parent company, Maui Land & Pineapple Company, Inc., owns an additional 22,000 acres surrounding Kapalua, lands which are now planted in pineapple or used for pastures and watersheds, and which start from the 5,800-foot summit of the west Maui mountain peaks and extend down to the sea and 9 miles along the coast.

Kapalua is a full-scale planned destination resort community including a hotel, golf course, tennis facilities, resort shops, restaurants, and four condominium projects. Approximately half of the Kapalua area is in golf course, park, or other open space use. The rest will be developed as condominium and other residential projects, a second hotel, and, possibly, a lodge and conference center. An old plantation village will be redeveloped into commercial and residential areas. Although no specific timetable has been set for the completion of these projects, it is expected that it will take at least until 1990 to accomplish. When completed, Kapalua will be both a major visitor facility and a residential community of high-quality.

Market

From the beginning, the marketing thrust of Kapalua has been aimed toward the affluent visitor or buyer. The 196-room Kapalua Bay Hotel, for example, is geared almost entirely to the individual visitor. This hotel is operated on the modified American plan, at

2-86 Villas at Kapalua. Condominium projects are located on leasehold land, and, as of 1980, each project had been entirely sold before construction.

2-87 Development at Kapalua has been carefully integrated into the natural setting.

2-88 Open space for golf combined with sloping terrain and the ocean afford dramatic vistas.

2-89 View of the 198-room Kapalua Bay Hotel.

1979 rates of $135 to $170 per day for double occupancy, with guests having a choice of four dining facilities.

The condominium projects have been equally selective. As of 1980, four projects of low-rise, one-, two-, and three-bedroom apartments have been completed and sold. Sales for the 530 condominium units totaled $93 million since the fall of 1975—all sold on site and essentially from brochures and tabletop models.

All of these condominium projects are on leasehold land with a substantial monthly land rent payable to the developer. For example, the rents for one project started at $142 a month for one-bedroom units and $227 a month for two-bedroom units, escalating every 5 years so that at the end of 25 years they will almost double. A leasehold runs for 55 to 60 years. Since no resistance has been encountered, the monthly lease rent appears to have had little, if any, effect on the pricing of the four projects.

The major reasons for Kapalua's success are attributed to:

- Location—the most important criterion in any real estate analysis.
- Quality of product—including good design and strong design control for Kapalua as a whole. Since each individual project was sold before construction, this quality was early recognized.
- Confidence in the developer—Kapalua benefited by being developed by a long-established company under strong family control and management, which had another profitable business (in pineapples), as well as adequate cash and credit.
- A strong institutional advertising program—emphasizing the fact that the quality of the product will not be compromised. Resort occupancy is expected to look after itself once Kapalua is well established.

Planning

Serious planning for the development of Kapalua began over 10 years ago when the parent company, once a part of a larger firm located in Honolulu, became an independent public company, although with over 40 percent of the stock still controlled by the private family which founded it. Construction of the golf course and the various infrastructure improvements began in 1974 and continued through 1979.

Physically, the site extends from sea level where the three major beaches are located, up to 700 feet in elevation where the second golf course is situated. Most of the active development, however, is occurring in an area between sea level and 300 feet. The average grade is approximately 10 percent, making it

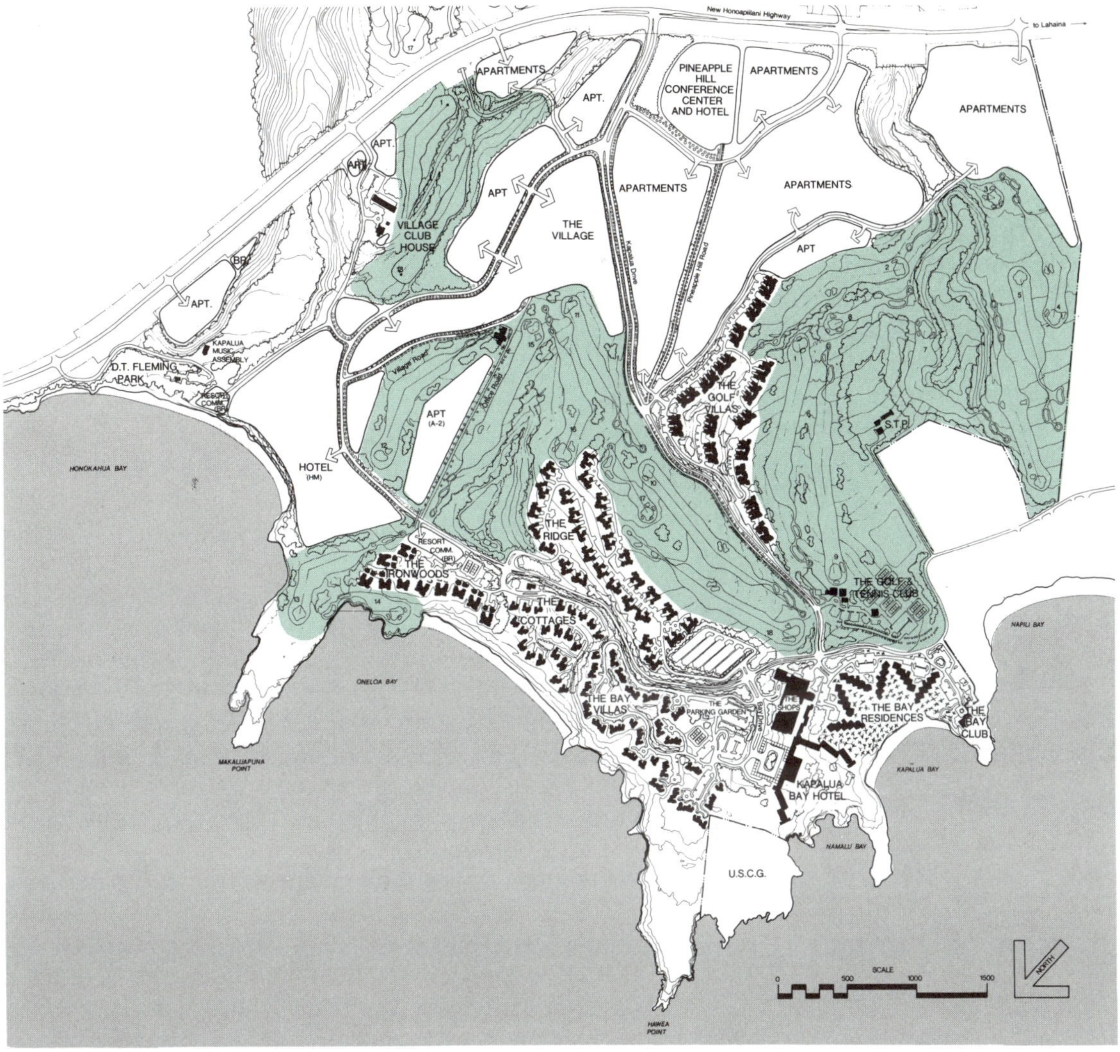

2-90 Site plan of Kapalua.

possible for individual projects to have unobstructed ocean views. This grade, however, makes site development more difficult and increases costs. The site is at the end of a 10-mile section of west Maui development and is located approximately 30 miles and a 60-minute drive from the main Maui airport at Kahului, although a small commuter airline has hourly flights into the Kaanapali airstrip, 5 miles south of Kapalua.

In the beginning, plans were designed to take advantage of the natural site variations and to compensate for limitations (Kapalua has somewhat stronger trade winds and more rain than Lahaina and Kaanapali) in terms of the seclusion of the site. The project was therefore planned as a destination resort aimed particularly at the more affluent guests who might be potential buyers. The varied terrain, beautiful scenery, and protective surrounding lands owned by the developer offered the opportunity to provide many kinds of resort experiences. Future additions include a music assembly hall, a botanic garden, a park, and various historic and artistic projects.

Experience Gained

Costs of construction on the small and remote Maui site have easily exceeded what was anticipated. Delays are costly, particularly with high interest rates. The problem of attracting and holding employees is difficult in an area where housing is inadequate. In order to help alleviate this situation, Kapalua, in partnership with the state of Hawaii, developed some 174 fee simple houses just south of the project and also agreed to donate land to the county of Maui for the construction of further housing geared primarily toward employees or potential employees of Kapalua. Even so, the rapidly developing Kaanapali project as well as other development in west Maui will continue to increase the housing needs.

Wailea

Wailea is defined as a residential resort community, in contrast to Kaanapali which is a resort community with certain residential aspects. The property is approximately 3.5 miles long and nine-tenths of a mile wide, extending from the oceanfront to an elevation of about 350 feet. While the property focuses on its natural setting with five beaches and a 10,000-foot mountain backdrop, it is also highly oriented toward manmade amenities. Wailea has 36 holes of golf and a tennis complex planned ultimately to have 24 courts. It offers golf and tennis memberships to residential property owners and hotel operators. The annual fees entitle members to preferential use and priority in obtaining reservations. Both golf and tennis have produced operating profits at Wailea.

2-91 Wailea Beach Hotel, Wailea.

With over 500 dwelling units completed as of 1980, the Wailea Development Company hopes to achieve a rate of development of approximately 175 condominium units and 75 single-family lots per year for the term of the project. Obviously, such factors as location, parcel size, topography, and market conditions will influence the average rate; however, based on development so far, the 3,500 dwelling units planned would be completed in the early 1990s.

As of 1980, Wailea had two hotels, totaling 950 rooms and a third hotel was being considered for construction. As a residential development with some resort aspects, Wailea also caters to a higher income market than Kaanapali. Sheer volume in numbers of patrons is considered incompatible with its real estate development activities: thus, hotels are restricted to a total of 1,200 rooms. Group tours are not as a rule composed of prospective purchasers who can afford expensive real estate.

Market

Despite the targeted real estate market, Wailea's uses are varied. The hotel patrons are of all ages and backgrounds. The winter visitor tends to stay longer and spend more than the summer visitor, whereas the summer patron will likely be part of a tour arrangement.

Condominium unit occupancy experiences a similar pattern in terms of a visitor's length of stay; however, winter visitors tend to be either single couples or two couples sharing a large, two-bedroom unit, whereas summer travelers tend to be families taking advantage of the lower summer rates and of being able to cook in and do their own housekeeping.

During the winter, many owners—particularly those who live in northern climates—spend 4 to 6 months of the year in their condominiums. Many of them do not rent during the off-season but occasionally allow friends to use their apartments. Other owners also use their units for short periods during the year; however, they rent their units and tend to have a less personal interest in them. Finally, there are those owners who are strictly investors and seldom use their units. Sometimes a group of people invests in a unit together in order to use it both for vacations and as an investment.

Because of required costs and compromises, Wailea no longer pursues interstate registration in order to facilitate real estate sales. The one project in which Wailea became involved early took so long to complete that it was sold locally before registration. It is believed that through promotion of the resort facilities and superior hotel accommodations enough potential buyers will be attracted to Wailea to fill its market needs. The drawing power of the other areas on Maui is also valuable in that most buyers will try to assess the full range of the market before making a decision.

Wailea has sold all of its product in fee simple. Timesharing programs are not included because they would in effect create problems similar to those of hotels. The hotel or timeshare occupant typically has only a short time in which to vacation and therefore wants intense recreation during that period. Such intense use of the facilities could overtax the beaches, golf course, or tennis courts.

The master developer does not wish to build tract or custom homes on the single-family lots, recognizing they would probably lose money and present problems with custom warranties. At some point, however, it may be necessary to build sample custom homes. This should help to set the desired architectural standards, and by introducing building activity to a new area, encourage lot owners to proceed with their own building plans.

Wailea has a variety of condominium products to offer. Each site determines the product with regard to such factors as size, price range, and orientation. Typically, prime waterfront locations call for large and expensive luxury units. Farther back from the ocean, a smaller unit was found more appropriate, though the product can vary based on the opportunity for views, the proximity to core facilities, and other similar considerations.

As a matter of policy, the owners of Wailea decided to develop the condominiums as low-rise units. The only major structures rising noticeably above the coastline will be the three hotels and one mid-rise condominium which was approved earlier.

Public Review

Like other development on Maui, Wailea is subject to a multi-tiered zoning process. The State Land Use Commission has jurisdiction over four classifications of land—urban, rural, agricultural, and land used for purposes of conservation. Nine hundred of Wailea's 1,450 acres are zoned as urban with the balance zoned as agricultural.

The county of Maui has a general plan that covers approximately 1,000 acres of Wailea, including the 900 urban acres, which are further zoned for specific uses. In addition, Wailea is subject to the planned development process of the county of Maui and to the special management area (SMA), that is, the shoreline management area affecting coastal properties.

2-93 Wailea Ekolu Condominium Village. Plentiful and meticulous landscaping is a trademark of quality resort residential development such as that found at Wailea.

2-92 The 16-court tennis club includes a 1,500-seat facility for tournament play.

2-94 The two-story tennis clubhouse with a restaurant and pro shop. Resort operations at Wailea are programmed to become profit centers as the community grows.

The planned development process calls for a three-step presentation of schematic plans, design development, and final working drawings to the county planning department. A public hearing is required as the first step; thereafter, the process is administered through the planning department, followed by the normal building permit process.

The SMA requirements subject properties to scrutiny within what is defined as the coastal zone. At this stage, in addition to all of the submittals necessary for the planned development, a developer must prepare an environmental impact assessment which is a shortened form of an environmental impact statement. A photographic analysis of the property must also be provided and an additional public hearing held.

The Master Developer

The Wailea Development Company participates in all land and condominium development. It is not involved in the ownership or operation of the hotels and tries to avoid involvement with small businesses. For the present, the company does not offer bulk parcels of condominium or single-family lots to other merchant builders for development.

All construction work is contracted. The Wailea Development Company consists of a project development coordinator, a construction supervision department which also takes care of warranty and customer service problems, an in-house brokerage subsidiary with eight to 10 salesmen, a sales manager, an escrow coordinator, and a marketing coordinator. All recreational activities are headed by professionals, and financial and treasury functions are handled by a controllers division. All other functions are managed by a general department of operations and administration. The organization uses outside legal and planning services, as well as architectural and engineering consultants. Advertising and public relations services are also provided by consultants.

Financial planning for the Wailea Development Company is kept simple. A forecast of the term of the project until completion is made and updated annually. The components are straightforward, dealing principally with the budget for each project and various department budgets. After completing major expenditures for infrastructure, the company was able to turn the corner of profitability in 1979.

Mountain Projects

Sunriver, Sunriver, Oregon

Sunriver, a 3,370-acre resort, second-home community located in central Oregon, is surrounded on three sides by the Deschutes National Forest. As the name implies, the sun and an unpolluted river, as well as a rich mountain environment with pine forests and open meadows, are the natural amenities which this recreational project has built upon and which attract families and retired couples from the rainy coastal cities of the Northwest and the urban centers of California.

The original 5,555-acre project was reduced in size by the 1978 sale of 2,185 acres to the U.S. Forest Service in order to optimize the project's operation and economic viability. As of 1980, there were 826 acres of dedicated common land within the developed portion of Sunriver. Since the project is a planned unit development with a maximum gross density of 1.5 dwelling units per acre, the developer was able to achieve a significant allocation of open space. River setback requirements further enhance the adjacent open spaces and make it possible for residents and guests to fully enjoy the river.

Environmental planning and quality have been the hallmarks of Sunriver since its inception in 1967. It has attracted mostly upper-middle-income professionals who have bought lots, homes, or condominiums. Alternative recreational projects in the area are primarily standard large lot (1 to 5 acres) subdivisions of mountain cabins, lodges, second homes, and mobile homes.

The project's peak season is summer but conference/meeting bookings begin in early spring and last into the fall. Except for the holidays, winter is Sunriver's slow season, even though the project is near a major downhill skiing facility.

Sales activity fluctuates with the seasonal activity. The main lodge with its condominiums nearby is the facility which is key to the developer's total program of land development and resort operations. Coupled with the recreational amenities, these facilities usually present a visitor with his first impression of Sunriver, whether he is visiting a current resident, attending a conference, or vacationing. As with other projects, the resort operation and recreational amenities are subsidized at the outset by the developer to support his main interest—the lot sales program. For this reason, developing this kind of resort/recreational community requires balancing the wishes of permanent residents with those of resort visitors, the up-front amenity costs and operation costs with the uncertainty of real estate sales in the future, and the economy of operations with the maintenance of quality. Only by having a well-managed development team with in-depth experience in all facets of the development can a resort/recreational project of this magnitude succeed.

As of early 1981, the developed area of 2,768 acres contained approximately 2,300 home sites with 857 private homes and about 508 condominiums constructed on 104 acres. The resort facilities include a lodge with two dining areas, a lounge, conference rooms, a golf pro shop, saunas, and an art gallery.

The recreational amenities consist of two 18-hole golf courses, an olympic size pool, tennis courts, paved bike paths, a marina, riding stables, and a 4,500-foot paved and lighted airstrip. In addition, the project has a jogging course, an arts and crafts center, a nature center, a hot tub complex, a park and picnic area, softball diamonds, a hill for sledding, ice skating areas, and cross-country ski trails.

Commercial facilities include a shopping mall with a grocery store, bakery, delicatessen, boutique, men's store, sports shop, beauty salon, drugstore, fabric shop, bookstore, jewelry store, interior furnishings store, and professional offices as well as a nearby gas station, hardware store, casual dining establishments, and a bicycle shop which also functions as a Nordic ski pavilion in the winter.

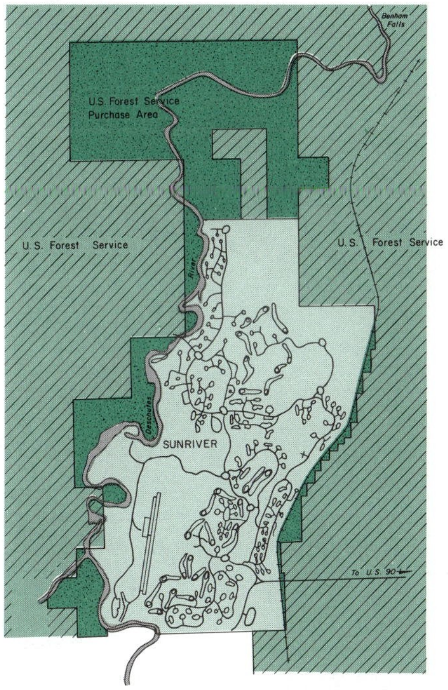

2-95 Sunriver is largely surrounded by national forest.

2-96 In the foreground—the Sunriver Lodge and condominiums; middle ground—golf course, meadow, airstrip, and the Deschutes River; and background—the Cascade Mountains with the 9,000-foot Mt. Bachelor.

The remaining undeveloped area of 1,602 acres represents approximately 1,775 new home sites and 20 acres of condominium land, planned to yield 360 units. Plans for further recreational amenities include a swimming pool, a golf course clubhouse, and tennis courts. The project build-out is expected to occur around 1987.

The Site

Sunriver is located in Deschutes County, Oregon, 15 miles south of the county seat of Bend (population approximately 20,000), and 175 miles southeast of the city of Portland. U.S. 97, a major highway connecting Washington, Oregon, and California, is 2 miles east of the project with a paved county road leading to the Sunriver entrance.

Situated in the high desert country at an elevation of 4,200 feet above sea level, Sunriver enjoys a moderate year-round climate with an average of 263 days of sunshine. Daytime temperatures range from 70 degrees to 90 degrees F. from June through October. Precipitation, most of which occurs during the winter months in the form of snow, amounts to approximately 12 inches annually.

Sunriver attracts buyers through the extensive recreational opportunities it offers. The adjacent pine forests and nearby plains are among the most popular deer hunting areas in the state. Large herds of antelope have been restored to the sagebrush-covered plateau to the southeast. The Deschutes River which flows along Sunriver's western and northern boundaries is one of the most famous streams for fishing in the Northwest. Except for some privately owned land to the south, the Deschutes National Forest encircles the project. Surrounding mountains and numerous lakes, reservoirs, and fishable streams, offer a variety of opportunities to campers, picnickers, fishermen, hikers, mountain climbers, horseback riders, and skiers. Eight miles north of Sunriver is the Lava Lands Geologic Area. The 9,000-foot, volcanic Mt. Bachelor is 39 paved miles northwest of Sunriver. There are eight chair lifts at Mt. Bachelor and slopes and trails for both downhill and cross-country skiing. During the 1979–1980 season, Mt. Bachelor had 505,000 skiers, a record for the mountain. As part of its winter promotional program, Sunriver provides ski-bus transportation to and from the mountain.

Land Sale to the Forest Service

Since the early 1970s, the U.S. Forest Service and the Sunriver developer had been interested in a land exchange of about 1,000 Forest Service acres for nearly an equal parcel of Sunriver land. The Forest Service wanted more riverfront land for the national forest, and Sunriver wanted to consolidate its ownership. The exchange was approved in 1975 by the county commissioners, who must approve federal land acquisitions under the requirements of a combination of federal and state laws. However, after 8 years of operation and experiencing a squeeze from the recession, the development came under new management during which the project owners lost interest in the Forest Service exchange, preferring instead to sell acreage before starting another phase. The intent of this decision was twofold: to diminish the heavy front-end debt incurred during the initial years for site improvements and amenities, and to make any development projections more valid based on a 7-year development period instead of a period of 15 years or more. Otherwise, if deciding to continue the project into the next phase, the developer would be committed to develop the entire 5,555 acres to justify the investment in the amenities required by the approved county PUD plan.

2-97 The Sunriver Lodge is the focus of resort activities.

The developer's potential buyers were other developers, a lumber company, and the Forest Service. The lumber company was eliminated as a buyer because it did not want to pay the high price for land that was zoned residential. Other developers were eliminated so that the Sunriver developer could control the quality of development on adjacent parcels. The Forest Service became the logical buyer because it would properly manage the ecologically sensitive migration routes of elk and deer and nesting areas of birds and would protect Sunriver's existing development from other projects.

In November 1976, the developer suggested a sale of 3,187 acres to the Forest Service. In October 1977, after negotiations and appraisals, the county commissioners voted down the $6 million sale for the following reasons:

- Sunriver Properties had promised its property buyers that the 3,187 acres would be developed.
- The Sunriver community association would be unable to maintain the facilities if additional phases of development did not occur.
- The Deschutes National Forest already consisted of 1.5 million acres, including 235 miles of fishable streams.
- Approximately 80 percent of Deschutes County was in public ownership.
- Sunriver was a highly lauded type of development which merited expansion.
- According to the county assessor, tax benefits to the county if the land was developed by Sunriver would be $1.52 million greater annually than if the Forest Service purchased the property.

During the negotiations with the Forest Service, however, the developer continued planning sections for development in the second phase and, therefore, was prepared to offer the Forest Service a sale of 2,185 acres and to develop an area north of the existing first phase of development which would double the number of potential Sunriver dwelling units—a compromise to all the parties involved. With the new proposal, Deschutes County would receive three-fourths of the revenue of the total 5,555-acre development; Sunriver residents would have a second phase of development, and the property owners along the northern line of the first phase would have, as they had counted on, an area for similar development; the Forest Service would save 90 percent of the river and keep most of the deer migration routes at the northern end intact; and the developer would have the proceeds of sale to decrease outstanding loans as well as a more realistic period in which to project and complete development.

On October 30, 1978, Sunriver Properties, Inc., sold 2,185 acres to the U.S. Forest Service for $2.8 million. This price was lower than the $1,800 per acre offered in the original 3,187-acre proposal since Sunriver kept some of the more valuable land to develop in the second phase.

Planning and Engineering

Sunriver's objective from the start has been to develop a residential area with the resort as a support facility, both being complemented by a variety of recreational amenities, while retaining the natural environment as much as possible. Permanent residents numbered approximately 717 at the end of 1980. It is anticipated that 20 percent of the ultimate population will be permanent. At peak periods, residents and visitors can now swell Sunriver's population to approximately 5,000.

In pricing home sites, the developer allocates costs to specific tracts based on acreage, the original cost of land, capitalized real estate taxes and interest (given that the accumulated project cost does not exceed market values), and the estimated costs of common facilities and general development. Costs of lot development are charged directly to each tract. The total cost assigned to each tract is charged to the cost of sales, based on an average cost per lot, as sales are recorded. The developer acted initially as the builder of several detached homes and condominium units. This involvement with construction helped to establish the project image and architectural standards and to stimulate home construction. The developer, in joint venture partnerships with other builders, also acted as a builder of model homes, providing lots and making certain payments for 1 year for the exclusive right to sell the units in various locations throughout the property. In addition to operating the resort facilities and a home and condominium leasing program, the developer leased space at the project's shopping center, The Country Mall, and has sold 1- to 5-acre commercial lots near it and in a 32-acre business park designed to accommodate light, nonpolluting industry and office sites. The developer no longer owns The Country Mall.

The master plan reflects a concern for the natural environment. The clustered single-family lots provide a sense of community for each neighborhood while still retaining accessible views and open spaces. Large portions of the river frontage have been left undeveloped for the enjoyment of all. Tree thinning was done selectively to enhance living areas and at the same time provide a healthier environment for the remaining timber. A comprehensive system of bicycle trails throughout the project offers easy access to any given point on the property and substantially reduces the need for automobiles. The recreational and commercial facilities are located in the central core area near the lodge, both for easy access and to protect the privacy of the residential areas by minimizing traffic. To further promote the privacy and environmental appeal of the project, each single-family parcel touches common areas.

The private road system within Sunriver of all-weather oil mat finish (except for asphalt main collectors) encompasses a pattern of circles and culs-de-sac which slow the traffic flow yet provide easy access to all areas throughout the project. The roads have no curbs or gutters and vary in width from 20 to 22 feet.

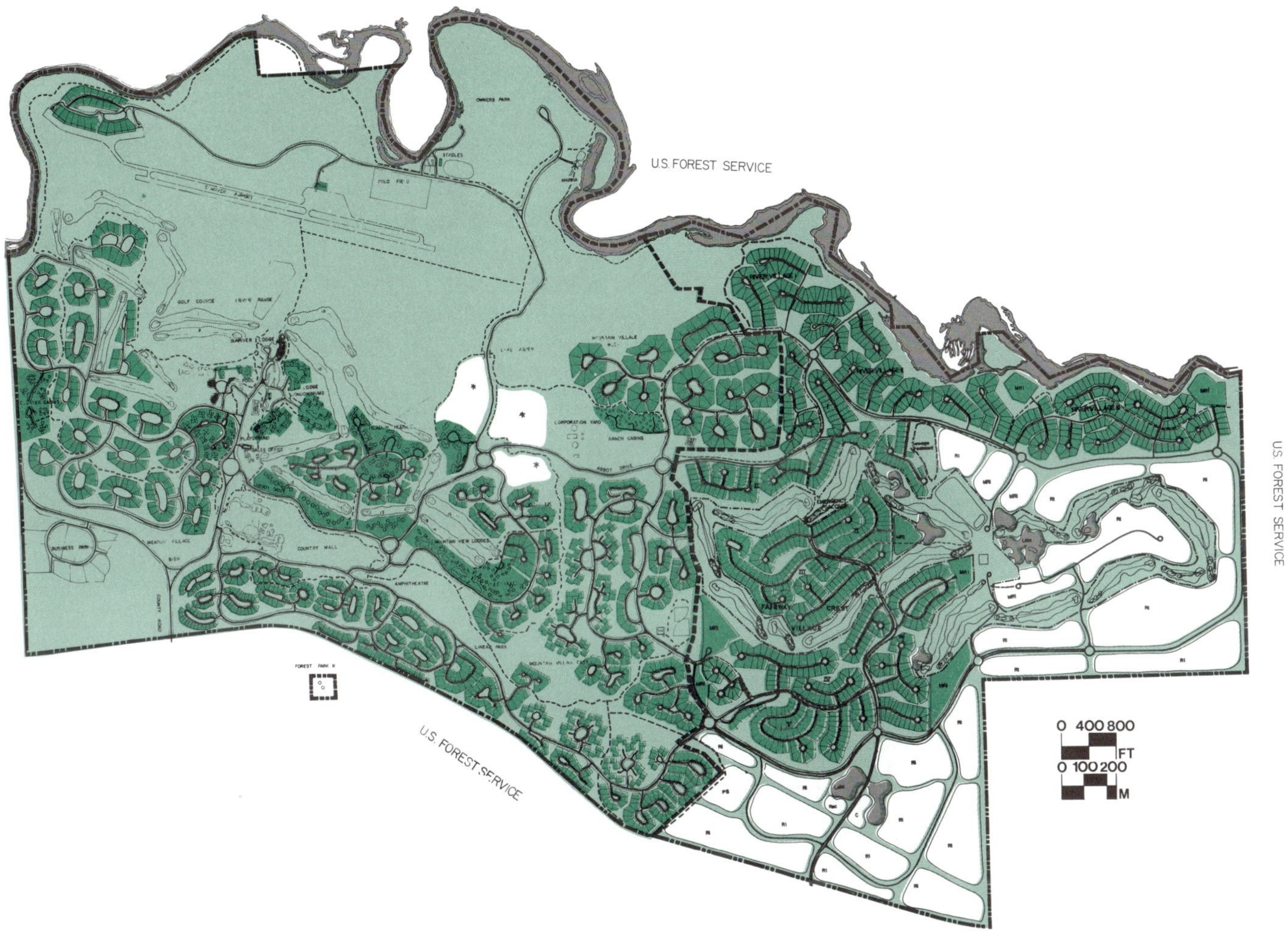

2-98 Site plan of Sunriver.

The oil mat surfacing is relatively inexpensive and the roads have proven resilient to both use and weather extremes over the years. With many of the residential courts culminating in culs-de-sac, privacy is enhanced for the residents.

The Sunriver Utility Company provides all water and sewer service underground to each individual lot line. No individual water systems or private wells are permitted. A central sewage treatment facility employs tertiary treatment and no effluent is discharged into the Deschutes River or other surface waterways. Effluents are instead collected in golf course ponds, which serve as wildlife refuges and irrigation sources for the golf course, and any surplus is evaporated or percolated into the soil. The Sunriver Utility Company is subject to regulation by Oregon's Public Utility Commission for the water service. The developer installs water and sewer lines and coordinates the installation of the other utilities (gas, telephone, electric, and cable television) with its installation of the water and sewer lines. Except for electricity, no alternative fuel sources such as propane or butane are permitted. Stormwater drainage follows the natural drainage courses and a minimal storm sewer system is utilized. Individual television receptors are not permitted and available television is via cable. The standard hookup fee for cable television service in 1980 was $150 and the monthly fee $12.

The development process for a new home tract follows a 3-year cycle: the first year—the section is platted, a sales road is graded, and lots are sold; the second year—utilities are installed; and the third year—the roads are hard-surfaced. Lots in a new section may be presold on a reservation basis with a deposit held in escrow until required reports are received from the Interstate Land Sales of the U.S. Department of Housing and Urban Development and from the state of Oregon. Deposits range from $500 for lots less than $25,000, to $1,500 for lots over $25,000. After the HUD registration, there is a 10-day grace period during which time a purchaser can withdraw his offer and have his deposit returned. Once the utilities are provided in the second year of the tract development cycle, a lot owner can begin to build. No final approval is granted by the Design Committee until the utilities are in, and the county planning commission will not issue a building permit until it has final approval from Sunriver's Design Committee. When construction is started, however, the exterior of the house must be completed within 1 year.

Architecture and Design Control

With the construction of Sunriver Lodge in 1969, the developer began an architectural style and standard which has been continued throughout the project in private residences as well as in condominium projects. The use of native woods and stones, together with soft, semitransparent external staining, softens the effect of construction and helps blend the structures with their environment. In addition, similar standards have been set to minimize the impact of directional signs, which are routed wood, lighted from below.

Each structure proposed at Sunriver, whether a private residence, condominium project, or commercial building, must first be reviewed and approved by the Sunriver Design Committee. Besides having architectural control over initial construction, the Design Committee controls additions, exterior remodeling, exterior lighting, and all major landscaping elements. In its first review, the committee considers aspects of the home such as siting, shape, size, color, design, height (limited to 26 feet), and whether it will disturb the existing terrain and vegetation and impair views. Surrounding property owners are notified in advance of the review in order that their concerns and comments may also be considered. The owners' association is responsible for the Design Committee which is comprised of six Sunriver residents and one project employee. The committee is financed in part by a fee for checking plans ranging from $25 to $125 and a $50 building permit fee with additional support from the community association's maintenance fund.

Resort Operations

Subject to the easement rights of Sunriver unit owners, the developer retains the title to the swimming and recreation area, eight tennis courts, open spaces and scenic areas, and the bicycle paths on common areas. The developer as the administrator of phase I is to maintain and operate these facilities out of the maintenance assessment and is required to convey title to the phase I owners' association no later than January 1, 1999. Portions of open spaces and bike paths submitted to the Plan of Sunriver phase II, are owned by the phase II owners' association but operated and maintained by the developer as the administrator of Sunriver phase II.

2-99 Besides reviewing initial designs, a design committee controls additions, exterior remodeling, and landscaping at Sunriver.

2-100 The pool and other recreational activities are near the resort's lodge.

The remaining recreational facilities—the golf course, dock facilities, 10 tennis courts, riding facilities, bicycle and ski pavilion, the main lodge, and the Great Hall—are owned by the developer. These facilities are open to the public and are subject to user fees competitive with similar facilities in Oregon.

Sunriver has a planned program of activities for children. Arts and crafts, nature tours, hayrides, boating, fishing, swimming lessons, riding lessons, and junior tennis clinics are a few of the many scheduled events. The outdoor playground is well equipped with swings, slides, and even a miniature fort. Current films are shown once each week throughout the year. The Establishment, a supervised youth center complete with its own game machines and adjacent snack bar, is the teenagers' domain.

The Sunriver airport is an integral part of Sunriver's operation; over 175 property owners own their own planes, and air traffic into Sunriver is increasing annually at a substantial rate. During the summer, an average of 300 planes, consisting mostly of single-engine and twin-engine private aircraft, fly into Sunriver each week. The airport has a 4,500-foot paved and lighted runway, complete fueling and tie-down facilities, a modern flight plan center, ground transportation to and from the lodge, and a limited fleet of rental cars. A local charter service is available for 24-hour service between Sunriver and major Oregon cities. During 1979, Air Oregon, a regional commuter airline, began commercial air service directly to the Sunriver airport.

The 54,000-square-foot lodge contains two restaurants (totaling 460 seats), a cocktail lounge, banquet and convention rooms (totaling 18,000 square feet), a barbecue deck, sauna baths, an information center, golf pro shop, and administrative offices. The Great Hall supplements the lodge conference facilities, seating 350 people for meetings and banquets. The condominiums near the lodge are in the rental program, as are various privately owned resort homes and condominiums located throughout the project. The visitor has choices ranging from one- to two-bedroom suites with kitchens to fully equipped private houses for as many as eight persons. In 1980, the resort operation had a total of 40,658 room nights and 177,521 guest nights. The total gross revenues for 1980 were $4,875,924. The number of employees for the resort varies from 105 to 321 during the year. The total number of employees at Sunriver varies from a low of 210 to a high of 470. Sunriver has a comprehensive employee manual and training program. The developer recruits students from various colleges in the region via a poster program.

Project Market and Sales Program

Sunriver property owners tend to be in the upper-middle-income group. Median annual family income in 1979 was $37,500 and the median age was 42 years. Two-thirds of those owning Sunriver property have children under 21. While recent market surveys reflect these characteristics, a broad range of professionals, incomes, and age groups are represented in the overall Sunriver ownership. Buyers purchase Sunriver properties primarily as investments, although they also purchase them as recreation, retirement, and permanent homes.

Surveys indicate that Sunriver's market lies chiefly in the Pacific Northwest and California, although property owners come from other states across the country, as well as from other countries. Fifty-five percent of the owners surveyed reported they first became aware of Sunriver through friends, relatives, or business associates. Advertising was the second most commonly named source of information. This includes informational displays, project brochures, newspaper and television ads, and ads in regional magazines. The on-site sales offices are located in the Great Hall with a sales staff of 15 full-time and 3 part-time employees. An off-site sales office is maintained in Portland.

The Home Owners' Association

The Plan of Sunriver creates a self-governing community which is administered by the developer until the authority is transferred to the home owners' association by January 1, 1999, or when 90 percent of the total land within Sunriver is sold, leased, or converted into common areas. As the administrator, the developer maintains control over all community functions, which, when appropriate, can also include fining those who infringe on community codes.

The owners elect a five-member board of directors who represent the entire ownership in dealings with the administrator. As well as other aspects of the project's operation, the home owners' association board monitors the administrator's activities relating to the maintenance fund activities (security, fire protection, first aid, snow-plowing, road maintenance, common area maintenance, and maintenance and operation of dedicated recreational facilities). This becomes an intensive liaison relationship in a community such as Sunriver which has a resort operation in addition to the usual community activities. Contributions paid by each Sunriver property owner for the maintenance fund were $23.50 per month in 1980.

PROJECT DATA—SUNRIVER

Land Use Plan (1980):

	Acres	Percent	Proposed Acres	Proposed Percent
Lots[1]	827.93	24.6	1,106.41	32.8
Condominium Areas	184.20	5.5	221.10	6.6
Commercial	89.22	2.6	99.62	2.9
Recreational	394.60	11.7	400.20	11.9
Common/Open Areas	1,271.74	37.7	1,542.67	45.8
Undeveloped	602.31	17.9	—	—
	3,370.00	100.0	3,370.00	100.0

Unit Information (typical sections):

Type	Unit Size	Lot Size	Number	1980 Sales (Rental Price)	Bedrooms	Bathrooms
Single-Family Detached	1,300–3,000 sq. ft.	13,218–15,749 sq. ft.	368	\$ 75,000–\$300,000[2]	2–3	2–3
Single-Family Attached	1,360 sq. ft.	n/a	52	\$ 95,000–\$110,000 (\$90–\$125 per night)	2	2
Lodge Condominium	1,215–1,527 sq. ft.	n/a	77	\$ 85,000–\$105,000 (\$64–\$82 per night)	1–3	1–2

Economic Information:

Site Cost: \$1,375,800 (1965–1968)

Site Improvement Costs (1980 per lot):[3]

Professional Services	\$500–\$700
Site Preparation	\$0–\$90
Roads (in-tract)	\$400–\$650
Underground Utilities (power and telephone)	\$150–\$300
Water (in-tract)	\$700–\$1,100
Sewer (in-tract)	\$900–\$1,500
Total Improvement Costs	\$6,900 per lot[4]

Amenities:

	Existing	Proposed
Pool Complex	\$276,977	\$265,000
Tennis	\$227,890 (18)	\$220,000 (10–12)
Marina	\$59,689	—
Stables	\$62,503	—
Bicycle Paths	\$200,082	\$384,000
Golf Courses	\$2,370,610	\$130,000
Club	—[5]	\$300,000
Equipment	\$173,170	\$47,000
Central Playground	\$4,000	—
Fort Rock Park	\$56,523	—
Amphitheater (incomplete)	\$24,658	—
Par Jogging Course	\$958	—
Contingencies	—	\$250,000
Total	\$3,457,060	\$1,596,000

Community Association Dues: \$23.50 per month

Notes

[1] Includes platted roadways.

[2] Lot prices vary from \$20,000 to \$135,000 depending on size, location, and views.

[3] For single-family detached tracts; condominium site improvement costs are lower.

[4] Includes land, capitalized interest, taxes and interest, utilities, roads, and amenity program.

[5] The club facilities for the initial course are a part of the main lodge facility which cost \$2 million.

Land Use Information:

Site Area: 3,370 acres

Total Dwelling Units: 4,450 — 3,105 Lots; 1,345 Condominiums

Gross Density: 1.5 d.u. per acre (maximum)

Net Density:

Average .... 3 to 8 d.u. per acre
Maximum (condominiums) .... 14 d.u. per acre

Parking: 2 spaces per d.u. (to include condominiums)

Developer:

Sunriver Properties, Inc.
Sunriver, Oregon 97701

Planning:

EDAW, Inc.
San Francisco, California

Royston, Hanamoto, Beck & Abbey
San Francisco, California

Market and Financial Planning:

Urban Projects, Inc.
Los Angeles, California

Management:

Alpert Corporation
Dallas, Texas

2-101 Condominium units can be rented under a program operated by the developer.

Experience Gained

- The front-end investment for amenities and resort facilities must be in proportion to the income generated by sales activity. Sunriver's initial infrastructure costs were so far and above any revenue generated that the project simply dug itself into a "financial" hole which is an extremely difficult position to build from. However, the initial facilities constructed play a notable role in establishing credibility with prospective buyers. Clearly, one of the aspects of Sunriver which potential buyers appreciate most is the fact that the developer lived up to certain promises and commitments.
- Dwellings built on lots of 5,000 to 6,000 square feet were found to be too close together and in the developer's judgment have too much of an urban appearance. At present, the minimum size for lots is 10,000 to 12,000 square feet.
- The concept of mixing the resort with the residential community is basically sound, especially in a remote area. However, provisions must be made to separate the resort guest and the resident, particularly in terms of certain recreational amenities, so that a given facility will not be overrun by resort guests during the peak season. For example, two separate pools would have been more appropriate than one olympic size pool. One pool could possibly have been indoors for year-round use.
- Bicycle paths are a great asset and the concept is sound, but the minimum width should be 8 feet even though costing $39,000 per mile (as of 1980). Furthermore, the path should be cleared and opened sufficiently to be safe.
- Having a maintenance fund or a general association is a sound concept, but a flexible method of setting the monthly assessment should be available, simply because costs and revenues never materialize as initially expected. Because of this, the maintenance fund at Sunriver ran a deficit for almost 8 years before breaking even, costing the developer a total of $450,000.
- The resort/recreational development business is sufficiently specialized, if not complex, to require that senior management expressly schooled and experienced in this particular area lead the development team. The remainder of the development team should be composed of key people as determined by the senior management. Nevertheless, an all-encompassing development and operations department, such as Sunriver initially had, may be too expensive. Outside consultants and contractors should be hired for a specific purpose at a specific price.

2-102 Clustered development helps establish a sense of community while preserving views and open space.

2-103 Shopping complex at Sunriver.

- It is preferable to establish a high density initially and reduce it later if necessary, rather than start with a low density and later increase it.
- The concept of clustering a development, having a variety of lot sizes, and utilizing private streets, is a definite asset and, if properly executed, can create value for the purchaser. A lack of curbs or gutters along the roads, coordinated project signage constructed of natural materials, and traffic circles give the project a less urban appearance.
- If the capital is available, utilities should be installed before the sale of properties.
- Although initially costly, the underground utilities have proven a positive environmental aspect of Sunriver and a definite selling factor.
- A strictly controlled in-house property sales operation is mandatory.
- Since construction of condominiums and homes is specialized, a developer should not act as a building contractor, if at all possible, unless he is going to have selected and trained personnel devoting all their energy to a building program.
- A full service resort depends on year-long occupancies to break even. For a resort to weather a winter season in a northern climate, it should be located close to a ski area.
- Since land immediately around the main lodge is dedicated common area, expansion of the resort facilities in this area is limited. Adequate land should be dedicated to an operation during the earliest stages, giving the developer greater control over the resort operations and increasing the value for possible sales later.
- The land sale to the U.S. Forest Service further enhanced Sunriver's image. By its protection of this land, the Forest Service would also protect the environment of Sunriver.
- Although the project has security guards and is under the jurisdiction of the county sheriff, there is limited law enforcement. Establishing a police district would be more effective. At present, county deputies must be appointed by the sheriff, and they feel that Sunriver should police itself.
- Security measures, such as the use of entrance gates allowing only selective entry, should be considered in the initial design concept. This is particularly important in a combination resort/residential development.
- In the second phase of development, amenities will be clustered to make their operation more manageable than that of the more scattered amenities of the first phase.
- In a seasonal area, golf course income will never, in a reasonable period of time, amortize the cost of a course. Therefore, the sale of property adjacent to a course is necessary to justify its existence.
- Extreme care must be exercised in locating a project. The principal market area in Sunriver's case is 175 miles away and has a relatively inefficient transportation system. This has proven to be a detriment; consideration should be given to a location where commercial transportation is readily available.
- Resort packages can build business by including recreation as part of the room cost. Drawing resort guests, especially in a somewhat remote location, can be done through the provision of an inclusive package for each guest group to enjoy.

Lakeridge, Torrington, Connecticut

Lakeridge is a 235-acre planned unit development of multilevel townhouses located in northwestern Connecticut. The project has been designed primarily as a second-home and recreational community, with approximately 70 percent of all units being purchased as second homes. A wide variety of year-round recreational facilities has been provided.

In addition to the townhouse units and recreational facilities, the project contains a village center which presently includes a post office and gas station. Plans call for the village center to be expanded to include a restaurant and inn, a convenience store, and additional shops and services for Lakeridge residents.

The property was purchased by the developer in the late 1960s. After several years of planning, construction began in 1973 and the initial occupancies took place in 1974. As of 1980, 310 units were finished and occupied. With an annual building rate of approximately 85 units, it is anticipated that the project will be completed in 1983. Upon completion, the project will contain approximately 670 homes. The annual absorption (sales) rates has been about 100 units (including 25 resales).

The Site

The project is located in Litchfield County, long considered one of the most desirable and scenic second-home and vacation areas in Connecticut. Located in the foothills of the Berkshire Mountains, Litchfield County is characterized by wooded hills and valleys, lakes and streams, picturesque vistas, and quaint historic villages. The area offers a distinct four-season climate, with colorful autumn foliage, winter snows, and lush spring and summer greenery. Despite its rural character, Litchfield County is less than a 2½-hour drive from New York City.

The project's mountaintop site is heavily wooded with numerous hills and valleys. Vegetation includes pines, hemlocks, birches, maples, and a variety of smaller plants which are indigenous to the area. The site is extremely rocky, with shallow bedrock and many boulders. It is almost completely surrounded by 2,000 acres of state forest, containing miles of hiking and riding trails. A 100-acre natural lake with 5 miles of unspoiled shoreline lies within the state forest and is available for sailing, canoeing, fishing, and swimming.

Planning

The project is a superb illustration of environmentally sensitive planning and design. The basic planning objective was to preserve as much of the natural environment as possible. Upon completion of the project, 80 percent of the site will remain in its natural state.

In order to minimize the developed area, the townhouse units have been located in a series of small village clusters. Units have been carefully sited to preserve as much of the existing vegetation as possible and to minimize the intrusion on the natural setting. The preservation of existing vegetation on the heavily wooded site has allowed many units to be nearly hidden from view. Views have been oriented toward the undeveloped, wooded portions of the site instead of toward paved areas or adjacent structures. All recreational amenities have been located away from the homes.

Roads have been designed to follow the natural contours of the site. The amount of cut and fill has been minimized. In addition, roads have been curved to avoid the disturbance of significant vegetation and other site features, and to minimize pavement visibility. Parking areas have been kept small and have been screened and separated. All utilities have been placed underground and follow the road layouts. The project is served by municipal water and sewer systems. A system of uniform signage directs visitors and residents to the various townhouse clusters and recreational facilities. All signs are of rough-sawn lumber with white lettering.

2-104 Units have been sited to allow maximum preservation of existing vegetation.

Architecture

The townhouse units have been designed to be unobtrusive and to complement the rugged natural landscape. The multilevel units are of a rustic, contemporary design. The exteriors are rough, cedar shingles which are stained a light gray and blend with the color and texture of the natural surroundings.

Large windows and sun decks maximize the opportunity for outdoor views. In many cases, balconies, walls, and windows were positioned to take advantage of special views and to save specific trees.

Existing units are either two- or three-levels, and many contain lofts and skylights. Together with the large windows, the skylights provide unit interiors with a light and airy atmosphere. Architectural variety is provided through a series of horizontal and vertical offsets.

All units have been designed to provide maximum privacy. The entrance to each unit has been screened from adjacent entrances and all rear sundecks have been shielded from the view of neighbors. In addition, all units are totally soundproofed. Where common walls exist, they are double-partitioned, separated by air space, sound board, and double insulation.

Recreational Amenities

A full complement of year-round recreational facilities has been provided. Most of the facilities were completed before any units were occupied. Two large activity centers, the East and West Lodges, serve as the focal points for both recreational and social activities. The East Lodge, which overlooks a large outdoor pool and terrace, contains a children's club, arts and crafts rooms, a kitchen, gyms, locker rooms, saunas, Ping-Pong and billiard tables, and a central lounge. Adjacent to the lodge are seven tennis courts and two platform tennis courts, some of which are lighted for night play. The 27,000-square-foot West Lodge includes three indoor tennis courts, an indoor pool, a whirlpool bath, saunas, locker rooms, and a spa. The lodge overlooks a spring-fed pond and a sandy beach. The pond is available for swimming in the summer and skating in the winter. Three outdoor tennis courts adjoin the West Lodge.

In addition to the two lodges, Lakeridge includes a private ski area, with three trails, a double chairlift, snowmaking and grooming equipment, a licensed ski patrol, and instructors. The ski area is lighted for night use. Other facilities include a fully equipped stable which offers horseback riding, a softball field, a basketball court, shuffleboard courts, six additional tennis courts, a small animal farm for the children of the community, and garden plots for the use of individual owners.

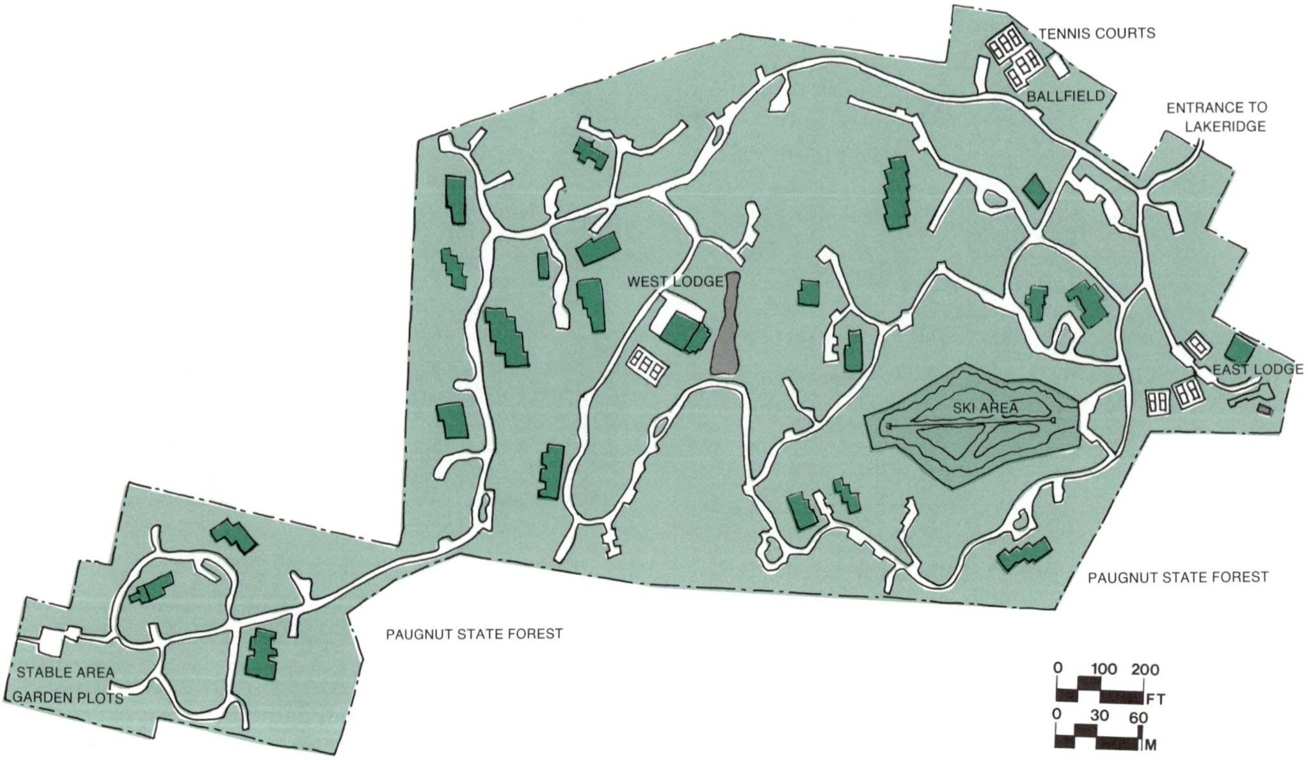

2-105 Lakeridge site plan.

2-106 One of two activity centers at Lakeridge includes an indoor swimming pool and three indoor tennis courts.

Home Owners' Association

All home owners at Lakeridge are members of the home owners' association. The association owns and operates all of the project's recreational facilities and is also responsible for all exterior maintenance of homes, walkways, landscaping, roads, and other common areas. The actual maintenance of these facilities is provided by an on-site management company which is paid from association dues. In 1980, monthly dues ranged from $147 to $167 per unit depending on the number of bedrooms. The association is governed by a six-member board which is elected by the owners for a 1-year term.

Marketing

Lakeridge has been geared to a relatively young, affluent, professional second-home market within the New York City area. Most buyers are married, in their early 40s, have two children, and in 1980 had annual incomes of more than $80,000. Many live in Manhattan. Most advertising has been through the media in the New York City area.

Advertising has stressed the quiet, secluded natural setting, the recreational facilities, the proximity to New York City, the 24-hour security, the private gas station, and the availability of low-interest rate financing. The focus has been on the sale of a pleasant, relaxed lifestyle rather than on the sale of specific units. The prestige of owning a home at Lakeridge has also been emphasized through advertisements which contain profiles of some of the many prominent home owners.

Market surveys are a key aspect of the marketing program. Questionnaires are distributed to all buyers and visitors. These contain questions such as why a unit was or was not purchased, where one first heard about Lakeridge, and the geographic location of one's primary home. The responses to these questionnaires are tabulated weekly and monthly and are carefully analyzed. They are used extensively in decisions on what modifications are needed in the project and in the marketing program. Several changes have been made in the architectural design of the units based on the data compiled through the questionnaires. For example, single-level units are under construction after an analysis of responses revealed that many prospects did not buy because only multilevel units were available.

Experience Gained

- The original units were built using post and beam foundations in order to preserve existing vegetation as much as possible and to facilitate construction on the rocky, hilly terrain. These foundations, however, proved to be unpopular with the market and impractical in the cold climate and were abandoned in favor of standard foundations. All of the post and beam units have been enclosed and insulated to prevent the pipes from freezing and reduce heat loss.
- Recreational communities are frequently viewed with skepticism by potential buyers who are concerned that promised recreational facilities will not be delivered on schedule. In order to eliminate such skepticism, recreational facilities should be completed up front. Although this approach will increase front-end costs significantly, it will allow the project to sell itself.
- One of the keys to project success is the creation of a marketing program which has sufficient flexibility to adjust to rapid changes in the market. The marketing program must also have the creativity to convert problems to opportunities. For example, Lakeridge dealt with the gasoline crisis of 1973–1974 by constructing its own gas station.
- The developer must be willing to allocate sufficient front-end money to an ambitious and sophisticated marketing program. The market must be thoroughly tested from the outset and the project must have the flexibility to be redesigned to assure compatibility with the market. The additional front-end costs will be quickly recouped as a result of the successful marketing program.
- With an established community such as Lakeridge, a substantial percentage of sales should be from referrals. However, many buyers have been reluctant to refer others to the project and thus possibly contribute to a rapid growth in population which they feel would diminish their lifestyle.

PROJECT DATA—LAKERIDGE

Land Use Information:

Site Area: 235 acres
Gross Density: 2.8 d.u. per acre
Net Density: 16.8 d.u. per acre
Total Dwelling Units: 670 (upon project completion)
Parking Spaces: 1.5 spaces per d.u.

Land Use Plan:

	Acres	Percent
Residential	19	8
Recreational Facilities	7	3
Common Open Space	188	80
Roads and Parking	21	9
Total	235	100

Economic Information:

Site Cost: $40,000 (1966)
Site Improvement Cost: $1,952,160[2]
Construction Cost: $39 per sq. ft. (1980)
Amenities Cost:

East Lodge	$ 300,000
West Lodge	1,404,000
Ski Area	106,000
Stable Area	84,000
Tennis Courts	320,000
Platform Tennis Courts	14,000
Total	$2,228,000

Unit Information (1980):

Unit Type	D.U. Size (Sq. Ft.)	Number[1]	Sales Price	Bedrooms	Bathrooms
Berkshire	1,350	8	$91,600	2	2
Tanglewood	1,612	103	$85,600	2	2
Hideaway	1,154	39	$80,100	2	2
Woodhaven	1,410	32	$83,100	3	2
Hearthstone	1,584	41	$85,100	3	2½
Sundown	1,888	8	$96,000	3	2½
Lookout	2,284	47	$106,600	4	2½
Villager	2,073	24	$102,600	4	3½

Notes

[1] Does not include unit types which have been discontinued.
[2] Site improvement costs to date. Includes on-site and off-site improvements.

2-107 A system of uniform signage has been provided at Lakeridge.

Developer:

George Giguere
1019 Burr Mountain Road
Torrington, Connecticut 06790

Architect:

Philip J. DiCorcia
Hartford, Connecticut 06105

Planning:

Storch Engineers
Wethersfield, Connecticut 06109

Management:

Lakeridge Management Company
Torrington, Connecticut 06790

Landscape Architecture:

Raymond Jefferson
Hartford, Connecticut 06114

Snowmass, Colorado

First opened in 1967, Snowmass is one of the premier ski resort complexes in the United States. It is second only to Vail, Colorado, in amount of skiable terrain. The Aspen Ski Corporation owns and operates the ski facilities, while the Snowmass Company and the Benedict Cattle and Land Company are the master developers of the resort community. This case study focuses on the activities of the primary Snowmass developer, the Snowmass Company.

At the beginning of 1980, the resort community comprised 1,977 dwelling units (1,067 condominiums, 500 hotel rooms, 334 single-family houses, and 76 employee units) in the 3,600-acre Town of Snowmass Village. Of that total, 1,737 units are part of the 2,800-acre Snowmass Company development. In 1979, the town's population capacity was 7,300 persons, including an estimated 1,385 permanent residents. The development is scheduled for completion by 1992, and the Snowmass Company has retained approval for 2,549 additional units, comprised primarily of condominiums with some town houses and new lodging units. Single-family build-out between 1979 and 1992 would mean the construction of 238 additional homes. The Snowmass ski facilities and community are in the fortuitous position of being an approved development in a rapidly growing market subject to strong growth and environmental controls.

The Snowmass Company purchased the substantially completed Snowmass development in 1977 from previous corporate owners. The time was right for the purchasers. The infrastructure was already in place; its depreciated value was necessary for the deal to be arranged. The market was well established, and the ski facilities were owned and operated by a very reputable company. In addition, the town and the developer were interested in promoting the area.

The Snowmass Company is owned by a limited partnership and develops most of its projects through a variety of limited partnerships. The two general partners in the company offer expertise in development management based on their personal record (with the Sea Pines Company), their personal investment, and the value of the property itself. The new developers follow a conservative financial posture, with a low debt-to-equity ratio and low overhead. The limited partnership was syndicated through the personal efforts of the general partners, securing private equity investors to ensure a cushion for uncertain times and to absorb any initial losses. The development strategy has been to start with a small project to gain experience with subdevelopers, contractors, pricing, and so on. Financing is arranged project by project. The limited partners have the right of first refusal in participating in a proposed project.

2-108 Villas under construction at Snowmass.

Joint Planning

The negotiated annexation in 1978 of the company's property into the Town of Snowmass Village provided a preferred alternative to county control. A unique relationship has developed through a process of joint planning, characterizing a psychological contract between the town and the developer. Major negotiated elements of this arrangement cover transportation (autos are deemphasized), employee housing, land use, and the expansion of community facilities. As one of only two primary developers in the town, the Snowmass Company works cooperatively with the town to prepare plans, which can be changed by mutual consent each year.

Snowmass land has been overzoned, permitting practical flexibility for the developer. The flexibility of a PUD ordinance is also useful, though each project must undergo thorough conceptual, preliminary, and final steps in the application process.

Under the provisions negotiated with the Town of Snowmass Village, 161 dwelling units per year can be added to the Snowmass Company development. Out of the potential 2,549 new units, 650 must be designated employee housing, to be made available at less than the market rate for unit sales, running in 1980 at $200 to $300 per square foot.

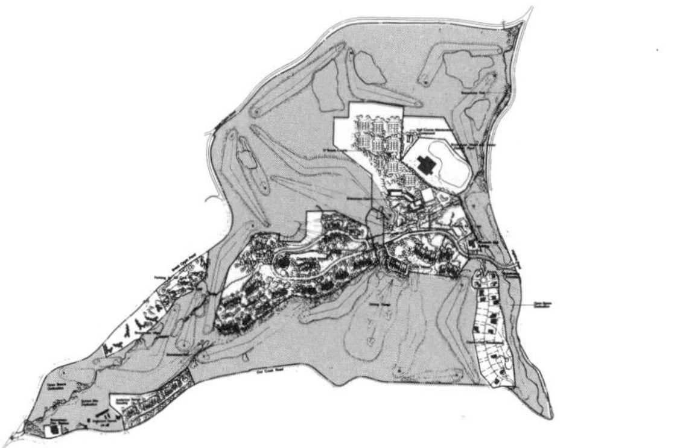

2-109 Site plan for The Snowmass Club, featuring country club facilities for summer use.

Community Development

The Snowmass Company is working as a full-scale community developer. Increased year-round occupancy (presently three-fourths of the more than 500,000 guest nights per year occur in the winter), with less dependence on skiing, would help to contribute to the resort's maturity. Snowmass needs more and higher quality commercial operations, and specific, improved amenities are being targeted.

Development by the Snowmass Company is phased project by project, with some site sales and some land kept for its own account. The master developer's control over site developers is stipulated through state regulations that require plans to be approved before sale and backed by strict controls on design. The mix of residential and resort population is slated to be housed largely in high-density horizontal structures.

Ski operations are conducted by the highly reputable Aspen Ski Corporation (ASC). While the conditions for skiing are an external constraint on potential community growth, ASC is committed to the most efficient expansion of ski capacity possible, given the strict public policies and regulations controlling it. ASC provides free mass transportation for skiers and employees between Snowmass and nearby Aspen.

The Snowmass Company maintains a small staff, hiring consultants and subdevelopers as necessary. A separate resort association at Snowmass annually spends over $500,000 on marketing, reservations, and so forth for the independent businesses and condominium rental groups occupying the existing Snowmass development.

As of 1980, few housing units were available for purchase at Snowmass—as few as 1 percent of the units. Supply is anticipated to lag behind demand in the near future. Primary attractions at Snowmass are the many ski-in/ski-out units.

Experience Gained

- The best plan is one that looks to the long term of community building, including a socioeconomic balance among employees, year-round residents, and visitors. A developer must recognize that profit cannot be made on everything; some functions may have to be subsidized.
- Clustering development on a hillside, as was done originally at Snowmass, presents considerable challenge for providing convenient and functional circulation of pedestrians and vehicles. Single-family units on a mountain can be more expensive to build and maintain than they are worth for the return they provide.

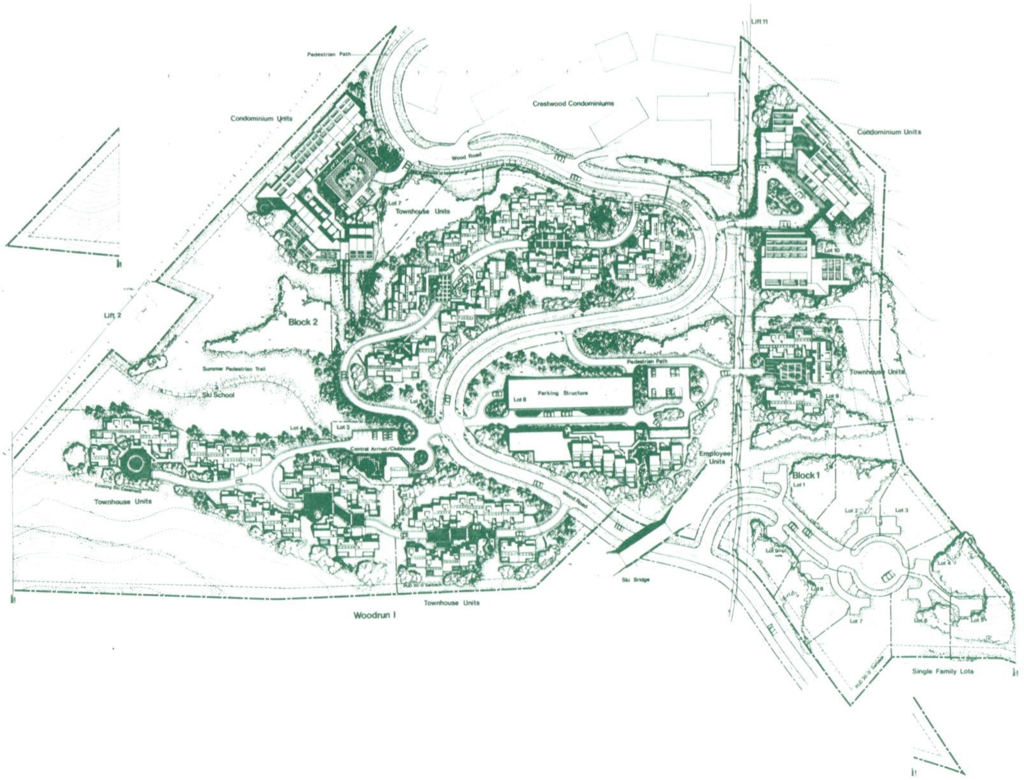

2-110 Site plan for hillside townhouse clusters including employee units.

- The developer must remain committed to involving the public in the planning process and follow through on those commitments to maintain credibility. He must deal comfortably with increasingly sophisticated communities. Joint planning provides both the town and developer with many benefits. One advantage is that potential partnerships with public bodies give private investors access to tax incentives. The possibility of an unfortunate failure sometime in the future of joint planning (as the town grows and the company stabilizes financially) might force a return to a less flexible and more traditional planning process and the possibility of litigation.
- The developer should be a businessman, have clear market objectives, be able to maintain tight management control, and be flexible in community relations. There should be substantial equity in the project, as a highly leveraged position is vulnerable to economic cycles, regulations, and delays. The developer must be ready to sell his ideas personally, both to investors and to the public. Given this commitment, a developer can transfer his skills to another market and area, anticipating differing political and engineering conditions.

2-111 Direct access to ski slopes gives a premium value to units at Snowmass.

Beaver Creek, Colorado

First opened for daytime ski use for the 1980–1981 season, Beaver Creek is one of the largest and possibly one of the last ski projects in the United States to be developed on public lands.

Beaver Creek is a 1,400-acre, year-round destination resort, located 10 miles west of Vail and 110 miles west of Denver. The master plan for this PUD was developed over 7 years and is the summation of contributions from many consulting firms. A high-density ski village at the end of a mountain valley 2.5 miles from I-70 is designated to contain 70 percent of the project's 3,200 dwelling units. Spread down the valley and in the meadows is the remainder of the project units, including 275 home sites and an 18-hole medium-difficulty golf course. The project is planned to contain a total of 10,500 hotel beds.

The buyer profile is similar to that of the skier who goes to Beaver Creek—young, affluent, professional. Most buyers come from Colorado, but many also come from California, Texas, and Illinois. For projects like Beaver Creek, the average winter stay was 6.5 days and the average summer stay 4 days in 1979.

Planning

All visitors must confirm their reservations in the reception center at the entrance to the project. Overnight visitors may drive their cars to their dwelling units, but day visitors must park their cars in surface lots and are shuttled by bus to the village and the base of the ski hill. Buses run every 5 minutes during peak periods. Studies on the feasibility of a monorail between the entrance and the village indicated cost would be prohibitively expensive—over $3.5 million per mile.

Vail Associates, the developer of Beaver Creek and owner of the nearby Vail ski development, is building all the structures in phase 1 of the village except the gondola terminal building and a hotel. The developer's buildings will be multi-use structures with retail space on the first floor to floor-and-a-half and 40- to 50-room individually operated hotels above. The retail space for phase 1 will total 15,000 to 30,000 square feet. All structures have a height limit of 50 feet and will be serviced from underground tunnels. Many areas of the village core have been designed for pedestrians only. Under the ski school area will be an 18-foot truck service corridor and a 375-car parking garage. The village core will also include a performing arts center with a 475-seat amphitheater that will be used for the project's conference/meeting activities. An in-house planning and architectural staff pre-

2-112 View of ski runs at Beaver Creek; golf course is under construction in foreground. (Photograph: Jill Vig.)

pared detailed site massing studies for all structures to verify their feasibility before contracts were given to outside architects.

When the project is completed, the mountain's daily ski capacity will be 9,000 (Vail Mountain is 12,000). The hill has 3,350 feet of vertical drop; the village is at an elevation of 8,150 feet and the highest ski area at 11,500 feet. Approximately 50 percent of the slopes will be for intermediate skiers, 25 percent for beginners, and 25 percent for experienced skiers; the latter area will be isolated from the other slopes. In the project's early years, 75 to 80 percent of the skiers will be day skiers; at completion, the percentage will drop to only 20 percent, similar to Aspen and Vail.

Planned facilities for summer activities include 30 tennis courts, riding stables, and lakes for fishing. The 130-acre golf course starts at the village core and extends down the valley.

The project's architectural theme is derived from the rustic architecture of the area when it was first homesteaded in the 1880s and from southern Europe. From a distance, the buildings will appear to blend into the landscape. Roofs will be consistent in color and massing. Architecture at street level will have more detail, adding to the street life and human scale of the project. Landscaping will be informal and natural, such as stone fences.

Vail Associates purchased the 2,200-acre site in 1973 from a sheep rancher for $4.4 million. In 1968, the Forest Service first studied the area for a possible ski area. Planning for the project began in 1971, and the environmental impact statement was completed in 1974. Colorado voters defeated a state issue in 1974 attempting to designate Beaver Creek as the ski area for the 1976 Winter Olympic Games, which in hindsight saved the project from piecemeal completion and becoming a total financial disaster. In 1976, the Forest Service issued the ski permit, which is subject to annual review, much to the dismay of the project's lenders (a ski permit is subject to a review process similar to that for a public utility). In 1977, the Forest Service approved the mountain plan and the county government approved the PUD master plan in the spring of 1978. Many of the plan's limitations were self-imposed, such as limiting fireplaces to 1,000 at first (one out of three dwelling units) to see how air quality is affected. One limitation that was not self-imposed was replenishing the water in Beaver Creek at January low flows by pumping it from a creek in the valley over 2 miles away.

The developer is committed to 600 units of employee housing. About 540 units will be located near the entrance to the project with the remainder being rental apartments attached to individual units. No industrial revenue bonds or public monies are being used for these units; if they were, the units could not be restricted to project employees. The developer is donating the land for this housing; rents will cover expenses only.

Development Strategy

Vail Associates has used the operating cash flow from Vail and Vail Mountain to build Beaver Creek. The developer's strategy at Beaver Creek is aimed at preserving the project's assets (land and building) for long-term reoccurring income through land and building leases and business partnerships in the hotels. This unconventional approach to a ski project is different from the developer's strategy at Vail.

- The project is being financed by commercial banks, long-term fixed interest loans, or industrial revenue bonds where available. A project like a ski resort that requires large front-end investment and therefore is considered a high risk usually cannot obtain financing for less than 4.5 percent over prime (1979).
- The developer can afford to deemphasize sales of home sites which are usually relied on as a major source of cash flow, so that amenities and improvements can be built. The entire project has only 275 home sites. Their not being sold is not critical to the project's financing; if they do sell, then the prices are too low.
- Because of the developer's staying power, the project's economic viability can be established sooner. As studies of other large-scale recreational projects have shown, a critical mass must be established before the project becomes economically viable (i.e., shops must stay open). During the initial stages, the cost of construction always exceeds operating cash flow of the income properties and profit centers until the project reaches a critical point on its way to maturity. For example, Snowmass was slow to mature because nearby Aspen provided the diversity, mixture, and quantity of amenities (especially shopping and dining) to keep potential Snowmass skiers in Aspen. Although the same situation could happen at Beaver Creek because Vail is nearby, the critical mass at Beaver Creek is thought to be 600 to 800 guest beds and 75,000 square feet of commercial space, aimed at the week-long destination guest. Therefore, Beaver Creek guests should not be compelled to go to Vail to dine or shop, except perhaps once or twice during their stay.
- Until the economic critical mass is reached, the developer subsidizes the project by owning the land and leasing it as well as by becoming partners in certain hotel deals. Not only does the project have to maintain occupancies during the ski season of at least 85 to 95 percent, it must also maintain acceptable occupancy levels in the off-season with conferences and meetings so that the resort operates 10 months per year. This level of use will reduce the developer's project subsidies and the length of time that the subsidies will be needed. Even so, no positive cash flows from the lodges can be expected in the first few years.

2-113 Architectural style typical of Beaver Creek.

Beaver Creek is being developed and operated by a collection of wholly owned subsidiaries of Vail Associates: B.C. Mountain Company owns and operates improvements on the mountain (for example, the ski area, lifts, and food service); B.C. Land Company improves the land for development (roads, water, and sewers) and leases project land; B.C. Venture constructs the site improvements and the village core; and B.C. Operations manages and operates the various improvements in the resort itself.

Beaver Creek's quasi-municipal organizations include:

- B.C. Metropolitan District, which finances the operation of project utilities. The district has the power to assess taxes, charge user fees, and sell bonds.
- B.C. Resort, a nonprofit arm of Vail Associates, responsible for land use and design controls, police protection, marketing, central reservations, conference operations, and management of the resort property.
- Village Parking District, a pending entity responsible for close-in parking.
- B.C. Foundation, a nonprofit group whose responsibility is to own and control the project's open space and to fund educational activities for the project.

Jack Frost Mountain, Poconos, Pennsylvania

In 1964, the Blue Ridge Real Estate Company began to examine its 30,000-acre Pocono holdings for potential recreational sites, paying particular attention to a heavily wooded tract of land of some 2,600 acres only 4 miles from the Pocono exit on the northeast extension of the Pennsylvania Turnpike. This wilderness area had been a private preserve leased to a few hunters and trout fishermen.

A land plan for the area provided for a ski resort to be constructed on the northeastern facing slopes overlooking the Lehigh River. Resorts were visualized in both the summit and base areas, including resort accommodations and housing in varying densities. Entrance to the ski area would be from a 2.3-mile-long private roadway constructed to the summit area. The initial plan called for all skier services in one structure, the Summit Lodge, which would be designed not only to serve skiers in the winter but also to accommodate other seasonal activities—tennis, golf, and so forth.

Planning

Planning consultants determined that approximately 130 acres would be needed for ski slopes and support facilities, another 112 acres would be reserved for future expansion of the ski area, and the ski area would be built as the first stage of a year-round resort and recreational community. The basic elements of the ski facility were to include a lodge, 11 slopes of varying difficulty, four double chairlifts, one dual double chairlift, a J-bar lift, a completely electrified snowmaking system, and parking for 1,500 vehicles. Water would be supplied from two deep wells, and a tertiary sewage treatment plant would be installed with a capacity of 30,000 gallons per day and the capability of expanding to 90,000 gallons per day.

The slope's design took into account functional and environmental considerations. The developer recognized that the ski area would attract novice and intermediate skiers, thus requiring slopes of different difficulty. Construction and operation could only minimally disturb the natural surroundings overlooking the river in its valley, some 475 feet below.

The lift towers were to have a relatively low profile not to extend above the tree line adjacent to the slopes. This environmental consideration produced a second useful effect: greater stability of operation under windy conditions. A helicopter was used to install the lift towers after their assembly in the west parking zone. The "sky drop" not only was quicker but also enabled the installation to proceed without

2-114 Aerial view of Jack Frost Mountain taken from a point over Interstate 80.

damaging the slopes and ground cover. The lifts were designed to handle 6,400 skiers per hour—2,400 per hour on the dual double chairlift (one of the first of its kind built in the United States), 1,200 per hour on the double chairlifts, and 600 per hour on the J-bar surface lift.

A reasonably long season is a must if the ski operation is to be profitable, particularly in the Mid-Atlantic states, where the average annual natural snowfall amounts to 50 inches. Therefore, a snowmaking system was designed for Jack Frost Mountain to produce manmade snow on all 11 slopes.

The electric-powered system relies on compressed air and a water delivery system capable of producing 1,000 gallons per minute from a tributary of the Lehigh River, just a few hundred yards from the mountain's base. The air and water are delivered through a 10-mile network of welded steel piping placed in the wooded areas adjacent to the slopes, to rubber hoses, and then to mixing chambers in the tripod mounted "guns" on each of the slopes. Under ideal conditions, as much as 6 inches of snow can be produced in an hour. Other "guns" varying in size and design have been added to the snowmaking system since the original installation. Since its opening, Jack Frost Mountain has expanded its water delivery system by approximately 40 percent. Production expenses for snowmaking, including labor, maintenance, and power, were well over $100,000 for an average season of 4 months in the late 1970s.

The Summit Lodge, capable of serving 2,500 skiers, is contemporary in styling. It provides food and beverage service, sanitary facilities, lockers, equipment rentals, a ski school, a first aid room, and central staff quarters.

Jack Frost Mountain opened in December 1972. It was immediately successful: on some peak weekends and holidays as many as 4,000 skiers use the property. In 1975 the Summit Lodge was expanded to provide larger quarters for the ski school, a sport shop, and ski rental facilities, and in 1977 the east dining room was expanded. The lodge now contains a total of 30,700 square feet.

Blue Ridge's investment in Jack Frost Mountain will approach $4 million by the end of fiscal year 1980, excluding land. The direct costs to date of the principal components of the ski area construction are as follows: general planning and design of the ski area only—$52,000; roads and parking lots—$359,000; construction of slopes and trails—$150,000; chair and surface lifts—$719,000; snowmaking equipment—$808,000; grooming equipment—$150,000; buildings—$867,000; utilities—$318,000.

2-115 A helicopter assisted in chairlift construction.

Services

In a ski area catering to novice and intermediate skiers, the ski rental, food service, and ski school facilities are critical to a resort's successful operation. They represent significant profit centers as well.

The Jack Frost Mountain ski rental shop has over 2,500 complete sets of rental equipment (skis, boots, and poles), placing it in the top 10 percent of United States ski areas in volume of inventory. The ski shop offers leading lines of equipment and clothing priced competitively with most urban ski shops. Because of the proximity of the Poconos to metropolitan areas, the Jack Frost Mountain customer, unlike the destination skier, can readily shop elsewhere, so pricing must be competitive. Both ski and rental shops are operated under a concession arrangement.

Market

The marketing strategy for Jack Frost Mountain has been successfully keyed to its proximity to the residents of New York, New Jersey, Pennsylvania, Delaware, Maryland, the District of Columbia, and Virginia, and to the huge beginning skier segment of this primary market. The ski and rental shops and the ski school cater to new or novice skiers, as the advanced skier usually owns his own equipment and depends on the ski school only for special instruction.

Jack Frost Mountain, located only 4 air miles north of another ski area, Big Boulder, has joined that area

2-116 Summit Lodge at Jack Frost Mountain ski area.

in promoting "Ski the Big Two," offering the advantages of a same-day reciprocal lift ticket and the choice of two full service ski areas with a combined total of 21 slopes and 13 lifts. Jack Frost Mountain has also innovated a "First Day on Skis" package, multiple "Learn to Ski" programs, and midweek specials. Discounts for the purchase of season lift tickets during the preseason period are available. Of special significance as fuel costs increase, Jack Frost Mountain emphasizes group skiing for schools, industries, ski clubs, and the like, a marketing approach stressed from its beginning. This program is offered in conjunction with bus charter firms, travel agencies, and various organizations to encourage groups to use mass transportation, with the extra inducement of a group discount for equipment rentals, lessons, and lifts.

Jack Frost's 150,000 customers exhibit similar demographic characteristics to most nationwide skier patterns: 56 percent male; 44 percent female; 55 percent ages 12 to 25; 29 percent ages 26 to 35; 10 percent ages 36 to 44; 6 percent age 45 and older. Singles comprise 60 percent of the skiers. The average skier visits Jack Frost Mountain six times a season.

The Blue Ridge Real Estate Company planned the Jack Frost Mountain ski area as the "seeding operation" in the creation of a four-season recreation community. In 1977, consulting engineers and land use planners were engaged to prepare an updated conceptual master plan for the Jack Frost Mountain tract. The master plan identifies locations for a resort hotel, commercial shops, year-round recreational facilities at the summit, and a variety of housing types. A real estate consulting firm prepared a marketing study to use in future arrangements with investors and/or developers who would actually develop the parcels leased from Blue Ridge or otherwise made available for such purposes.

Each land use is directly related to the type and density of proposed residential or commercial use. The consultant's reports have played an important role in determining and evaluating the size and location of the various land use areas that are best suited for the specified type and density of development activity. Acreage programmed for low-density residential development at one dwelling unit per acre has been sited in an area that includes some steeper slope conditions overlooking the Tobyhanna Creek. Other acreage surrounding a proposed golf course has been programmed for medium-density residential development at two dwelling units per acre. Cross-country skiing can be scheduled within this sector.

Two areas have been programmed for higher density residential development because of their prominent location near the summit of Jack Frost Mountain with an outstanding panoramic view of the Lehigh River Valley and because of their proximity to the existing Summit Lodge, the planned resort lodge, and the planned commercial village.

As of early 1980, the resort hotel/convention center was proposed to occupy the highest point on the property. The planners and consultants think a 300-room facility with public meeting and convention space is feasible. Their opinion is based on current convention demands experienced by other resorts. The winter resort shoulder periods of late fall and early spring will depend on conference business to maintain high occupancy levels.

The creation of the resort community at Jack Frost Mountain is expected to take place over 15 or more years. The developer intends to maintain a relatively passive investment role, with his involvement confined to leasing certain portions of the tract and operating the ski area and other commercial facilities.

2-117 Snowmaking is a necessary provision—at considerable expense.

Created Amenity Projects

Boca West, Palm Beach County, Florida

Boca West is a 1,436-acre PUD leisure community for retirees, second-home buyers, and primary-home buyers other than retirees. Planning was initiated in 1969 and construction got underway in 1973. When completed, the project will have four golf courses, a major tennis and club center, extensive commercial facilities, and numerous lakes. As of 1980, 11 residential villages were completed or under construction, representing slightly over 2,000 units out of approximately 4,500 projected for completion between 1986 and 1990 (permits for 7,975 have been granted). Midrise and low-rise units dominate, with only a few single-family homes. Approximately 70 percent of the owners are seasonal users, 15 percent are retirees, and 15 percent are other primary-home owners. General land development and amenities have cost almost $10 million, most of which was invested before 1976.

Boca West was the first planned unit development to be approved in Palm Beach County. It is being developed by the Arvida Corporation, which has extensive land holdings in the city of Boca Raton and adjacent areas, including the Boca Raton Hotel and Golf Course. The Boca Raton Hotel was very important in providing a market for the use of Boca West's front-end amenities. The project is part of a larger development program which has transformed Arvida's Palm Beach County properties into a comprehensively planned array of residential developments, convenience shopping areas, an office/industrial park, a regional shopping center, and other uses compatible with the high standards established by the community of Boca Raton.

The Site

Boca West is situated within the urbanizing corridor which stretches more than 100 miles along the southeastern coast of Florida between Miami and Palm Beach. The development lies between the Sunshine State Parkway, along which it has 1.75 miles of frontage, and the western city limits of Boca Raton. A tollway interchange at the southwestern edge of the property provides access to Boca West via State Route 808, and Interstate 95 lies approximately 2 miles to the east. Development in this part of Palm Beach County is edging westward from the coastline.

Planning and Engineering Features

Because of the size of the property, the developer recognized that it would be necessary to provide a variety of unit types appealing to a broad leisure-oriented market in the middle- to upper-income ranges. Consequently, Boca West is open to children and is a primary-home community for residents other than retirees.

Residential development is grouped in a series of villages which are interconnected by an internal collector street and bicycle and pedestrian paths. These individual neighborhoods are defined by a network of open space, including the golf courses and the lake system. Wherever possible, golf fairways have been grouped in twos and threes to avoid placing residential areas close to one another across single fairways. With over one-half of the total site remaining permanently in open space, the visual effect created by

2-118 Golf course fairway and an interconnecting lake system provide a setting for mid-rise and townhouse homes.

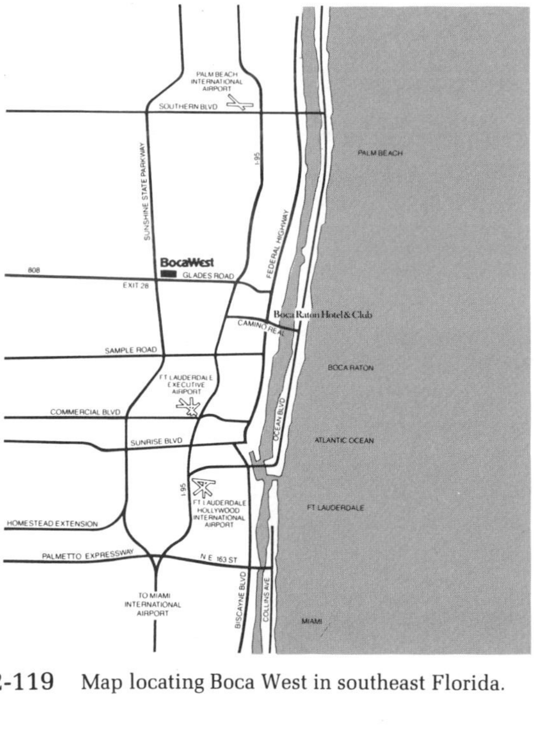

2-119 Map locating Boca West in southeast Florida.

2-120 Village of Bridgewood, one of a series of interconnected residential clusters at Boca West.

this design scheme is one of residential islands in a sea of green. The open space also buffers the community from adjacent areas and forms a grand main entrance.

The villages include clusters of mid-rise and garden apartments, groups of townhouses, fourplexes, zero lot line patio homes, and areas of detached homes and rental villas, in a range of product types and costs. A primary advantage of the village concept is that it permits maximum development flexibility, both with respect to accommodating changes in market demand over the 10-year build-out schedule, and in mixing otherwise incompatible resident types within a single project.

The site is entirely flat, and is being developed according to a master plan for a drainage system approved by the Lake Worth Drainage District. A high water table has made it possible to create a series of interconnecting lakes by excavating to a depth of 12 feet. In addition to its aesthetic value, the lake system is connected with the district canal system and provides for storm drainage throughout Boca West.

Residential Environment

The dominant architecture which has always proven most successful in this market is typical of that found in south Florida, and is constructed of concrete block and stucco with contrasting wood trim. Townhouse units have been individualized by the use of setbacks, irregular rooflines, fencing for privacy, and other varied exterior detailing.

Townhouses are clustered in groups of five to nine units. The seven-story elevator buildings contain 38 units each. Among the most unusual residential unit type found at Boca West, however, is the golf course villa. Twenty villas are clustered around a paved courtyard. A single Ficus tree grows in a circular brick planter at the center of the courtyard. The tree provides a central focus for the villa courtyard, which is further highlighted by alternating bands of textured concrete radiating outward from the planter—altogether an impressive design solution. The basic elements of this design have been repeated in later villages.

Amenities

Three of four golf courses planned for Boca West are complete. In order to broaden the recreational appeal of the community, tennis has been emphasized as well. As of late 1980, there were 27 courts with more planned. The existing club facility was expanded in 1979 and construction began on the first phase of the major club center, which will include a tennis center with additional courts, pool complex, and other facilities. A second phase will include the main club dining room, grill, lounge, health club, and golf facilities. These facilities, which are open to hotel guests and to all property owners on a fee basis, are owned and operated by the Arvida Corporation. Property owners hold title to the recreational facilities within their residential areas and villages. In the case of the village of Bridgewood, these consist of six neighborhood pools and cabanas, and a village center with pool, community center, and parking areas.

Home Associations and Governance

Boca West maintains a three-tiered governmental structure. The Boca West Maintenance Association is responsible for provision of security and maintenance and operation of communitywide common property, including entrances, the loop collector streets, and the lake system.

The village associations own and maintain bicycle paths, bicycle shelters, and recreational centers. Local streets are owned by the developer. Current maintenance of the streets and roads, if required, is handled through the master association.

2-122 Townhomes grouped around courtyard used for parking.

Each condominium association owns and maintains common open space and parking areas, and also maintains the building exteriors. Each association has its own maintenance budget and has as its management arm the Arvida Management Company, a legal entity completely separate from the Boca West Maintenance Association.

Ordinance Provisions

Boca West is being developed under the Planned Unit Development Provisions of Palm Beach County. The ordinance permits a maximum of 16,694 units, but the developer has agreed with the county to limit the number of units at Boca West to 4,500. This was done in order to conform to a 1973 revision of the county plan which reduced densities in many areas.

2-121 Amenities at Boca West include a large resort tennis complex and private village pools.

2-123 Village of Lakewood, composed primarily of mid-rise units.

Market

The typical purchaser has a high income and is looking for a vacation or second home for personal use. Mid-rises have been very popular. Over 40 percent of the sales in 1979 were generated from referrals. Eighty percent of the first purchasers attracted to Boca West were golfers, many of whom had been introduced to the development through the Boca Raton Hotel. It soon became apparent that the potential demand for golf would exceed the supply, making an alternative attraction necessary. This led to the aggressive promotion of tennis which has since helped reduce the anticipated pressure on golf courses. Also, it became obvious that the original total of 16,000 approved units needed to be substantially cut.

2-124 Real estate promotion emphasizing club activities at Boca West.

From 1974 through 1976, soon after Boca West was brought on the market, real estate sales slowed. Although Boca West had a relatively low inventory at the time, sales lagged in the midst of a general slump in south Florida of properties not on the oceanfront. In response, Arvida spent \$0.5 million in 1 year promoting Boca West. Additional product lines were added to those already offered. By 1979, sales momentum had been well established at significantly increased prices. The objective through 1984 is to refine the product and the marketing so that they are consistent with growth and the evolving character of a maturing Boca West community.

Arvida builds units for its own account as well as selling land to builder/developers, subject to tight controls. The corporation concentrates on starter units ranging from \$80,000 to \$130,000 and move-up units costing from \$145,000 to \$200,000. Arvida builds about two-thirds of Boca West's product. Outside builder/developers are used to round out the product line with specialty products each costing approximately \$200,000. The result is that Arvida concentrates on building those products it builds best, thereby lessening inventory risk and concentrating management effort. Arvida markets the entire Boca West product.

A starter product is a smaller unit, more moderately priced, for the new Boca West owner who desires to make a modest initial commitment. These units will ultimately total approximately 2,000. Other units are designed for the buyer who prefers a larger, more expensive unit. A portion of this demand will stem from first-time buyers, and increasingly so as the development's life cycle progresses. Nevertheless, in ensuing years, a significant portion of demand in this category is expected to come from owners of starter units who wish to trade up to larger units after being convinced of the stable character and growth of Boca West.

Resort Program

Through its resort program, Boca West manages slightly over 200 rental rooms owned by investors. These units are concentrated near the club and recreational facilities. The club is also incorporated into the resort program as a meeting and conference facility.

Boca West has benefited from its resort program through which qualified potential buyers have been exposed to the project. It has also attracted the attention of the media. Certain facilities and programs have grown much more quickly than would have been possible through normal patterns. In addition, the program broadens the potential real estate market by offering a villa product oriented to the investor-purchaser.

Nevertheless, a definite balance must be struck in a resort program within a project like Boca West. Friction between residents and resort guests could arise should the resort sector expand to a size that significantly alters the feel of the community, or should resort use of key facilities put undue pressure on existing or planned capacity so that owners would have only limited use of the facilities. Accordingly, Arvida carefully gauges usage patterns of resort and owner segments and matches these patterns against the capacity of the facilities. The maximum number of resort units in Boca West is currently planned not to exceed 7 percent of the total project units.

2-125 Mid-rise under construction in the village of Willow Wood.

Experience Gained

- The economic staying power of the Arvida Corporation and its long-term commitment to the area have been significant advantages in a difficult market. Buyers are attracted by the fact that they will be living in an area being developed in a comprehensively planned fashion.
- Some resident groups mix well, others less satisfactorily. Those who mix well include retirees and second-home buyers; retirees and young families relate less well. Since the developer chose not to limit Boca West to a single resident type, the rationale for using a village design concept becomes very persuasive.
- Before development began, portions of the site were leased to farmers. Interim agricultural use has had the combined benefit of generating sufficient income to carry the property and of obviating the need to carry out extensive land clearing operations once development got underway.
- The Boca West property was bought in 1967 for $3,200 per acre ($4,520,640 total), saving considerable carrying costs assessed against current development compared with those a more recent purchaser would face. This is a particularly important factor in the lengthy development period of a large community-scale project.
- Block land sales to outside developers can be an effective strategy in a tight financial situation. This will still necessitate substantial work with builder/developers to maintain the desired character of a project. Controlled land releases and umbrella marketing by the master developer are helpful in such instances.
- Being tied in with a hotel operation can help weather a down period. Also, referrals and the affluent south Florida retirement market help maintain sales during slow periods.
- A developer must remember that bought units are still part of the available product.
- Amenities and service operations, including a well-run rental management program, can be profitable.
- The return on land for single-family and low-rise development at Boca West is clearly less than that for mid-rise development. Nonetheless, the addition of less dense development broadens the Boca West product line and allows the project to offer a diversity of living alternatives, which adds value to the community as a whole.
- Development momentum has many marketing benefits and helps sustain the volume of building necessary to economize in construction costs.
- Golf obviously is a great land consumer, supporting only three households per acre of golf course compared with 80 households per acre of tennis courts.
- Development strategies should be expected to change over the build-out period. Despite initial plans, many short-term needs will override long-term concerns.
- Government procedures in Florida are thwarting the establishment of new large-scale PUDs despite the many advantages of these comprehensively planned projects.

PROJECT DATA—BOCA WEST

Land Use Information:

Site Area: 1,436 acres
Total Dwelling Units: 7,985 (permitted)
4,500 + (planned)
Gross Project Density: 5.5 units per acre (permitted)
3.2 units per acre (planned)

Land Use Plan:

	Acres	Percent
Circulation	60	4
Commercial	29	2
Residential and Mixed Use	569	39
Open Space[1]	778	55
Total	1,436	100

Economic Information:

Land Acquisition Costs (1967):	$4,520,640
General Land Development and Amenities[2] (1973–1979):	$9,918,000

Developer:

Arvida Corporation
Charles E. Cobb, Jr., Chairman and CEO
One Biscayne Tower, 20th Floor
Miami, Florida 33131

Planning:

Harland Bartholomew and Associates
Building D, Suite 216
1401 West Paces Ferry Road, N.W.
Atlanta, Georgia 30327

Team Plan, Inc.
Forum III, Palm Beach Lakes Boulevard
West Palm Beach, Florida 33401

Landscape Architecture:

Edward D. Stone, Jr. & Associates
2400 East Oakland Park Boulevard
Fort Lauderdale, Florida 33306

Residential Unit Characteristics (1980 Product Line):

Unit Type	Size	Bedrooms	Price	Developer
Villas	1,400–2,000 sq. ft.	2–3	$100,000–$190,000	Arvida
Townhome	2,000–2,500 sq. ft.	3	190,000–210,000	Subdeveloper
Patio Home	2,500–3,000 sq. ft.	3	250,000–300,000	Subdeveloper
Mid-Rise	1,000–1,250 sq. ft.	2	90,000–120,000	Arvida
Mid-Rise	1,750–2,000 sq. ft.	3	150,000–200,000	Subdeveloper

Notes
[1]Includes golf courses, tennis, and clubhouse areas.
[2]Includes golf courses, tennis, and clubhouse costs.

2-126 View at the main entrance to Boca West.

The Pointe, Bloomington, Indiana

The Pointe is a 389-acre, year-round resort/residential community located in Bloomington, Indiana. As of late 1979, it contained 305 condominium units in a variety of architectural styles and a full array of recreational amenities, including an 18-hole golf course and tennis courts. Upon scheduled completion in 1990, the project will contain approximately 1,900 units, with about 160 units per year to be built over the next 10 years.

The condominium units at The Pointe have been constructed in four complexes (La Salle's Woods, Woodridge, Greenridge, and East Bay) with a different architectural style for each, including attached ranch units, stacked units, stacked flats, and attached multilevel units. Sizes vary from 822 square feet to 2,058 square feet and in 1979 prices ranged from $50,000 to $120,000. The basic development philosophy was to provide units which would appeal to a variety of primary and secondary shelter markets. Thus, units have been provided for both the higher and lower priced primary and secondary home buyers. The absorption (sales) rate has been about 100 units per year.

Rental management services are another feature. Participating owners must adhere to The Pointe's rate structure. There are periodic unit inspections which must be passed to continue in the rental program. At the present time, about 60 owners are participating in this program.

The Pointe is a member of Resort Condominiums International (RCI), which enables owners at The Pointe to make their units available to owners from other participating resort communities for up to 4 weeks each year. In return, The Pointe owners can vacation at reduced rates at any of the participating resorts for the same amount of time that they have made their units available. Owners participating in the program pay annual dues to RCI. As of 1979, about one-third of the owners at The Pointe were RCI participants.

The Site

The Pointe is located on the shores of Lake Monroe, a 12,000-acre, manmade lake located in Monroe County, Indiana, approximately 60 miles south of Indianapolis and 10 miles south of Bloomington, the home of Indiana University. It is readily accessible from State Highway 37 and is served by the Indianapolis and Bloomington airports. The 22,000-acre Hoosier National Forest is nearby.

Most of the site is gently rolling and was previously farmland. However, as the land approaches Lake Monroe, it slopes off sharply to the water's edge, providing a contrast to the flatter, more open areas of the site. There are two peninsulas which jut out into the lake.

2-127 Clustered condominium units and a golf course help provide a feeling of low density and openness at The Pointe.

Soil depths are extremely shallow with rock protruding through soil surfaces. The area is known for its limestone quarries and contains limestone layers in depths of 4 to 10 feet. Rock shale separates the shallow soil from the limestone.

Planning

The basic concept was to provide a high net density while maintaining a sense of low density and openness. More than 50 percent of the site has remained as open space. Residential units have been clustered in several areas and are surrounded by open space and natural amenities. The rolling hills have been left open with the golf course occupying most of this area. Many of the units have been constructed on the steeper slopes and have views of either the golf course or the lake.

In order to preserve the natural beauty of the lake shoreline, a dense band of foliage provides a buffer between the lakefront and the units. The residential complexes have been isolated from each other as much as possible with foliage and topographic buffering. Those units closest to the lake have been constructed on the steep slopes and, except for the rooftops, are not visible from most locations.

Roads have been curved to minimize their visibility. Buildings have been set back and separated from the roads with heavily landscaped driveway areas.

2-128 The Pointe site plan.

The Woodridge residential complex, which has the greatest percentage of resort guests, has a service road to provide for convenient loading and unloading of vehicles. A dense buffer is located between the service road and the parking area. The Pointe has one entrance gate which is manned 24 hours a day by security personnel.

Architecture

Buildings were designed to be compatible with the natural beauty of the lake area and the remainder of the site. Natural wood exteriors were used. Although many units have been constructed on the steep slopes which abut the lake and a nearby ravine, grading has been avoided by stepping the units down the slopes, using post and beam and caisson construction. This, as well as the varied rooflines, has made the units appear smaller externally than their square footage would indicate. In addition, the use of post and beam construction has minimized tree removal, reduced construction costs, and allowed the units to be placed closer to the water.

Units have been designed to provide maximum flexibility. Many have lofts which can be used as either an extra bedroom or a family room. Multilevel units have separate entrances at both the upper and lower levels to allow one level to be closed off and rented separately.

Buildings have been sited to maximize views of the lake and the golf course and to avoid looking at adjacent buildings. Units designed as primary homes have features such as eat-in kitchens and attached garages. To avoid monotony, rooflines have been broken and setbacks are irregular.

Amenities

The 18-hole golf course meanders throughout the project and contributes greatly to the sense of openness. An extremely challenging course, it is considered to be one of the best in the Midwest and has hosted several LPGA tournaments. Golf memberships are mandatory for all buyers. The golf course also includes a practice area, a clubhouse with facilities for business meetings, and a restaurant with the capacity to serve 100 people. Five tennis courts and a swimming pool are also located adjacent to the club-

2-129 Units at The Pointe have views of either the golf course or the lake.

2-130 Natural wood exteriors have been used.

house. Two additional tennis courts, a platform tennis court, and two other pools are spread throughout the residential complexes. Lake Monroe is available for boating, swimming, and fishing. Winter activities include cross-country skiing on marked trails, ice skating, ice fishing, and ice boating. There is an annual winter festival with a variety of activities. A trail for walking and jogging winds throughout the site.

Community Association

The Pointe includes an overall association, known as The Pointe Services Association (PSA), and four additional home owner associations, representing each of the four residential complexes. PSA monthly dues were $7.50 per unit in 1979 and cover the cost of security, maintenance, management fees, the television antenna system, legal fees, and related services.

Home owner association dues, which ranged from $50 to $110 per unit each month in 1979, cover the cost of ground and road maintenance, insurance, legal fees, snow removal, exterior maintenance of buildings, pest control, management fees, maintenance of recreational facilities, and related services. One person from each unit is entitled to vote at association meetings.

Marketing

Eighty percent of those purchasing a condominium at The Pointe are second-home buyers. Only one of the four complexes at The Pointe (Greenridge) has been designed for primary-home buyers. Most buyers are from Indiana, with out-of-state buyers coming from Illinois, Michigan, Ohio, and Kentucky.

Marketing has been directed primarily at the Indianapolis area, but has recently been expanded to Chicago and Louisville. Most advertising has been done in newspaper leisure and travel sections. However, surveys have indicated that more than two times as many people have heard about The Pointe through friends and acquaintances as through advertising. The typical owner is a married professional from 40 to 50 years old with two or three children and in 1979 had an income of about $50,000.

The Pointe is actively promoting the use of its clubhouse facilities for business meetings. This has proved beneficial to the restaurant and has helped to increase unit rentals and use of the golf course, particularly during slack midweek periods in the off-season.

Experience Gained

- Security is an important selling feature in a second-home community since units are not always occupied. However, 24-hour manned security is expensive and requires considerable front-end money. This expense may be minimized by having only one entrance to the development, thereby reducing the number of guards required; or by using a mechanical security device at the gate instead of guards; or by providing security only at night rather than 24 hours a day.
- A large-scale development should start with multiple products which will appeal to a variety of markets. Broad market appeal will increase the absorption rate and help to recoup front-end costs more quickly.
- It is often wise to sell the secondary sites first and the premium sites last. If this is not done, there will frequently be buyer resistance to the fact that secondary sites are being sold for more money (due to inflation) than the original purchasers paid for premium sites.
- The cost of recreational amenities can be reduced by centralizing all amenities instead of scattering them throughout the project.

2-131 The gatehouse to The Pointe reinforces the project's security.

- Clubhouse facilities should be designed to allow for expansion as the community grows.
- The extensive front-end costs required for golf course construction will take time to recoup. Mandatory golf memberships for all purchasers will reduce the time required to recoup front-end costs. Allowing nonresidents to become members the first few years will also help in this regard.
- It is extremely important to communicate actively with buyers and to encourage their participation in a variety of advisory committees. Regularly scheduled meetings should be held. Residents should be given periodic budget updates, and future plans for the community should be discussed.

PROJECT DATA—THE POINTE

Land Use Information:

Site Area: 389 acres
Total Dwelling Units: 1,900 (upon completion)
Density:
Gross: 4.88 d.u. per acre
Net: 11.31 d.u. per acre
Parking Spaces: 1.5 per d.u.

Land Use Plan:	**Acres**	**Percent**
Residential	168	44
Golf Course	110	28
Common Open Space	111	28
Total	389	100

Economic Information:

Site Cost: $2,917,500 (1973)
Site Improvement Cost: $5,000 to $7,300 per d.u. (1979)
Amenities Cost:

Golf Clubhouse	$700,000
Golf Course	$1,500,000
Tennis Courts	$100,000
Pools	$200,000

Community Association Dues (1979): $50 to $110 per month

Unit Information (1979):

Complex	Unit Size (Sq. Ft.)	Number	Price	Daily Rent	Bedrooms	Baths
Woodridge	822	36	$55,000	$70[1]	1 + loft	1
	929	9	$59,000	$85	2 + loft	1
	987	36	$56,000	$85	1	2
	1,088	9	$64,000	$90	2	2
	1,269	9	$68,000	$120	2 + loft	2
Greenridge	1,401	36	$75,000	n/a[2]	2	2
	1,776	24[3]	$83,000	n/a	3	2
East Bay	906	55	$50,000	$60–105	2	2
La Salle's Woods	835–2,058	115	$60,000–$120,000	N/A	1–3	1–3
		329				

Developer/Management:

K & D Development Co., Inc.
1 Fairway Drive
Plainfield, Indiana 46168

Planning/Architecture/Landscape Architecture:

Maitland/Strauss/Behr Architects
80 Mason Street
Greenwich, Connecticut 06830

Notes

[1] Rents shown are those charged during the vacation season—April 20 through November 20.
[2] These units are primary homes and therefore are not rented to resort guests.
[3] These units are not yet existing.

Lake Arrowhead, Georgia

Lake Arrowhead is the closest major mountain resort to Atlanta (56 miles from downtown). The 8,100-acre mountainous site has as its center Lake Arrowhead, a 540-acre private manmade lake. First opened in 1973, the development has 2,800 platted single-family building lots, of which approximately 700 were still available at the beginning of 1980 at prices from below $10,000 to $35,000. As of that time, the development included 142 private residences, 32 condominiums, and 20 cluster homes built or under construction at prices ranging from $40,000 to over $200,000. An additional 1,000 lots and 1,000 density units are envisioned, with sell-out near the year 2000.

The resort features rustic and contemporary design elements in a natural setting, enhancing the feeling of rural living not far from a major metropolitan area. Approximately 2,000 acres are reserved as open space. The area includes one golf course, a 35,000-square-foot clubhouse, a separate tennis/pool complex, horse trails and stables, a small campground for members, and other related facilities.

Lake Arrowhead is one of a group of major recreational developments owned by Diamondhead Corporation. Lake Arrowhead operates independently of Diamondhead but has behind it the experience and financial support of the parent corporation. The development company finances all lot sales itself, taking the building lot as collateral after a minimum down payment of 10 percent.

One major feature of the mountain development is a central sewer system with 29 pumping stations and a gravity water system under the network of paved roads. Apart from the savings home builders can realize from this system, it assures that Lake Arrowhead (which is fed from within the project) is unpolluted. Another major feature is internal and external security. A formidable entranceway establishes a sense of security, as well as a distinctive identity for Lake Arrowhead.

Lake Arrowhead's strong club membership program covers resort activities and social events. Membership is obtained by the purchase of a membership building lot, available for a minimum of $3,900. Such lots are generally unsuitable for construction, but if building is possible, comprehensive covenants and restrictions govern the type and appearance of construction.

2-132 Lake Arrowhead features a 540-acre manmade lake and a 35,000-square-foot clubhouse.

2-133 A golf course winds along the lake and through the rough, mountainous terrain, requiring the use of heavy-duty golf carts to negotiate the inclines.

2-134 Mountain View condominiums at Lake Arrowhead, available for resort use within a rental program.

Market

Construction of all its amenities was an important marketing tool for Lake Arrowhead. Because of escalated costs and increased regulations since the early 1970s, Lake Arrowhead may be fortunate the investment was made when it was. In its first year, 1973, lot sales totaled $13 million, reflecting the ready market for single-family lots. By 1975, however, the market had reversed, and sales that year were only $1.8 million. Housing starts picked up in 1978–1979 when the company opted to expand from land development into housing. A two-story condominium offering in 1977 was slowly received, but in 1978–1979, the company was more successful with single-level detached cluster units that were entirely presold with no marketing required.

Lake Arrowhead's market for land sales is the local area and for housing, the state of Florida. For the future, the company expects that an expanded variety of housing units stimulated interest in primary homes, and the completion of a nearby divided highway to Atlanta will increase sales. The proportion of investors (currently 50 percent) is expected to drop as more serious home owners enter. The company looks to the resale of units and club operations as long-term business activities.

Experience Gained

- To facilitate their management and use, resort amenities may best be centralized. The separate pool/tennis complex, country club, and sales office have been expensive to operate at Lake Arrowhead. On-site lodging would be desirable for those using the club or investigating opportunities for purchasing a membership.
- A choice of housing units, responsive to a realistic assessment of the market, is valuable to an overall development program.
- Development must comply with the engineering needs of a given location and use. Weather and topography created substantial problems in the construction of the initial infrastructure and the golf course. Even with the best initial preparations, high maintenance costs are unavoidable.
- Business and management skills supported by economic staying power are indispensable for the operation of a major recreational development.
- A recreational development project is vulnerable to economic change, particularly when it is heavily committed to a highly speculative marketplace.

Treasure Lake, Clearfield County, Pennsylvania

Treasure Lake is an amenity-oriented second-home project consisting of over 8,000 acres located 6.5 miles northwest of DuBois in rural western Pennsylvania. The site is typically rolling and heavily wooded. It is convenient to the primary markets of Pennsylvania, Ohio, and New York by way of Interstate 80, which passes near the front entrance of the development.

The project comprises 7,000 platted lots of which approximately 5,500 were sold and 700 built on as of 1980. The average one-third acre lot ranged in price in 1980 from $8,000 to $25,000, with the single-family homes running from $25,000 to $250,000.

Extensive facilities are built around two manmade lakes of 280 and 200 acres and several smaller lakes, including a 202-slip marina and six beach complexes. There are two 18-hole golf courses, 10 tennis courts, three swimming pools associated with three activity centers, a 38,000-square-foot country club, a campground with 400 sites, and a winter sports complex centered on a ski lodge and small downhill ski slope. The dominant architectural style of the common facilities is a traditional rural style using rock, exposed wood, and shake roof treatments. Unfortunately, design for energy efficiency was generally missing and has resulted in excessive utility costs. Single-family dwellings are subject to minimum size requirements, design approval, and architectural controls—measures which are consistent with a project of this nature.

If lots continue to sell at the rate of 500 a year, the existing lots should be sold out by 1983. Roads and utilities are to be completed in phases after the first 4,000 lots are fully served by 1982. Central sewer and water systems as well as hard surface roads are main elements in the project's development. Although Treasure Lake was originally planned to have 10,000 lots, it is anticipated that only a portion of the 3,000 single-family lots remaining to be recorded will be platted. Instead, the lots will be used for recreational vehicles and other uses to complement the existing inventory.

Development Strategy

The development history of Treasure Lake can be broken down into three ownerships. The original developer's strategy was to build and aggressively sell as many lots as possible, basically at 10 percent down with a 10-year contract on the balance. The plan was conceived in the late 1960s when second-home developments of this nature were very popular. Basically, the intent was to provide as many single-family lots as possible, with little consideration given to topography, traffic flow, the location of community facilities, and other features which have become commonplace in planning. Open space was planned in the form of greenbelts between sections of terrain which were generally rough enough to preclude other uses.

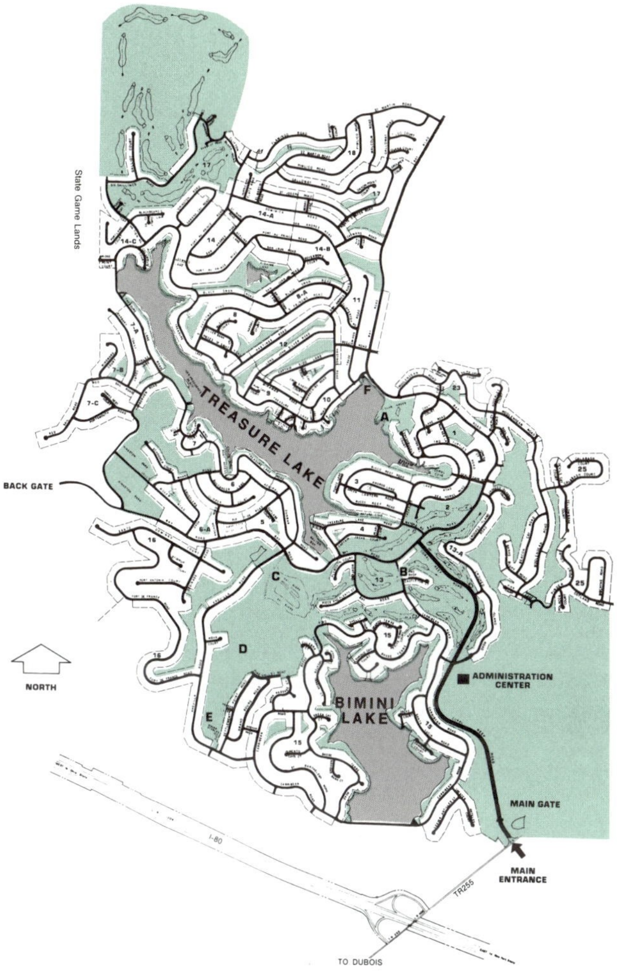

2-135 Map of Treasure Lake.

In 1972, even before the industry as a whole started having serious problems, the initial developer suffered severe financial problems which forced the suspension of the marketing operations. When the developer's creditor, Westinghouse Credit Corporation, foreclosed in 1973, over 70 percent of the 7,000 platted lots had been sold but only 10 percent of the promised improvements had been completed. After an unsuccessful retail marketing program in 1974 and 1975, Westinghouse Credit Corporation chose to get out of the lot sales business altogether and follow three guidelines: honor the commitments made, prepare the entire project for sale, and sell it to a reputable and competent developer. After Westinghouse

Credit Corporation completed the development work promised by the initial developer to purchasers of lots, the new owner would be responsible for development and construction in the unrecorded areas.

Treasure Lake was "sold" in late 1979 to National American Corporation. Westinghouse Credit Corporation received a minimal down payment and took back a long-term note and mortgage, which in essence will be paid as lots are sold at the project. Lot contract financing is being provided by Westinghouse Credit Corporation. Because of the small down payment, Westinghouse Credit Corporation established strict operating control and will strongly influence the management of the project until it is paid in full. National American Corporation had a successful sales season during 1980, selling about 500 lots. It generates prospects primarily through direct mail with some telephone soliciting and offers various incentives for 1-day site visits. It plans to continue marketing through winter, and the new owner is expected to be able to develop and market successfully the balance of the project. Despite its problems in past years, Treasure Lake still ranks as one of the quality projects in the United States with its beautiful setting and superb amenity package.

Property Owners' Association

All single-family lot owners are required to join the Property Owners' Association, which is currently responsible for the security of the entire project and for the maintenance of the roads and common facilities which have been turned over to it as part of the development strategy. The association could also be responsible for ownership, operation, and maintenance of the amenities and sewer and water facilities, should the developer decide to turn them over to it, free of any encumbrances. The Property Owners' Association enforces public safety at the site, levying fines for speeding, illegal hunting, and other offenses. It also participates in enforcing deed covenants and strictly enforces collection of association dues and annual assessments.

Experience Gained

- Development commitments for amenities were up front and too heavy for the developer to support with only limited use of the facilities until the population increased. Even at sell-out, operation of the amenities will place a heavy burden on property owners.
- Careful design of the amenity package is mandatory for efficient operations. Since the main clubhouse at Treasure Lake was not near either of the golf courses, additional clubhouse facilities had to be built at each course. The ski slope was isolated from other activity areas and also required its own clubhouse facilities. A further oversight in design was that the slope faces south, catching all the winter sun which melts the snow.
- Lots in the inventory should be released with some systematic regularity to overcome spotty sales.
- Lots should be reserved for home building in areas where improvements are in place. A trade-out requirement should be included in deed restrictions so that a build-out of homes will not trigger a build-out of improvements to undeveloped areas not needing it.
- Deed restrictions should be closely written and cross-checked with other documents so that they are consistent with each other and provide continuity in management operation.
- A turnover agreement on amenities, roads, or other facilities should be included as part of the original documentation of a project of this size. The agreement should be signed by each property owner as part of the lot sales package.
- If sewer and water are to be extended to lots and the economics of the system are contingent on the receipt of "availability fees," then individual contracts agreeing to such fees and their collection should be included in the lot sales package and signed by each and every lot owner.
- Strong consideration should be given to the formation of public sanitary and water districts where possible, or to the formulation of an agreement with established local facilities for the ownership and operation of sewer and water systems at the project. If this is not possible, property owner cooperatives or public utility companies owned by the property owners should be formed and extension agreements made in the initial stages prior to development.
- When possible, all property owners should be required to join the association to support the amenity operations. At Treasure Lake, club membership was not made mandatory, and as a consequence, there was not enough income to run the facilities without incurring large losses.
- Before sales on the site, the property owners' association and the developer should agree to share the costs of road maintenance and security during the development and sales.
- All marketing, sales, and promotion documents should be consistent from one property owner to another. Maps, site plans, and pictures should be illustrated accurately and should clearly disclose multifamily, commercial, and other future development areas.

Foxcross, Mariner Sands, Florida

Foxcross is a 10-acre village within the 720-acre planned unit development of Mariner Sands, located 6 miles south of Stuart in southeast Florida along U.S. Highway 1. Mariner Sands is a 980-unit private country club community comprising a variety of dwelling types. It is being built in two phases; Foxcross is part of the first phase. The project is a 72-unit condominium neighborhood incorporating both one- and two-story residences in configurations of four units. As of 1981, prices ranged from $118,000 to $150,000. The developer is Phoenix MacNab Properties of Cleveland, Ohio.

Phoenix MacNab purchased the Foxcross site from the master developer, Mariner Sands, for $600,000 in early 1980. Mariner Sands was responsible for putting in all roads, water, and utility lines to the site. Phoenix MacNab is responsible for all development within the site. It did all its own financing for Foxcross and negotiated with its own professionals for the job. Mariner Sands retains control of approval for the site plan, architecture, and landscape designs, and handles marketing and sales for Foxcross and all residential units within Mariner Sands.

The first phase of Foxcross, incorporating 26 units, was completed and sold in early 1981 before the second phase was offered for sale. The developers

2-136 Site plan of Mariner Sands, showing Foxcross in the upper left.

anticipate the project will be completed in 1982. From initial planning to completion is expected to encompass 2.5 years.

Foxcross is located in the northeast quadrant of the Mariner Sands property. The project is accessible from the main entry road, Mariner Sands Drive, with

2-137 View of units recently completed at Foxcross.

the project's own central drive culminating in a cul-de-sac at either end of a U-shaped parcel. Foxcross overlooks a large lake, several smaller bodies of water, and the eleventh, twelfth, and thirteenth holes of the Mariner Sands golf course. The site is relatively flat with some existing vegetation such as Florida pine and palmetto. The existing foliage was supplemented by substantial landscaping.

Planning

The lake that surrounds most of Foxcross was enlarged to create more exciting opportunities for residential siting, affording all residences views of the lake and golf course. The single entry from the main road provides security and eliminates through traffic. The project is virtually an island of development.

Foxcross encompasses substantial open space and green expanses. Gross density is 7.2 units per acre. The master developer's guidelines for landscaping encourage natural massing of plants rather than formal hedges. Within the Foxcross site itself, green areas are provided between each four-unit structure.

2-138 Foxcross site plan.

The buildings are angled to provide spaces of varying size and shape. A large expanse of green area is located at the rear of all residences, and the street side is also heavily landscaped. A landscaped mound is situated in the center of each cul-de-sac. Foxcross is surrounded by open space, and single-family home sites are visible across the water on one side of the property.

Foxcross has its own pool and cabana area. Membership in the private Mariner Sands Country Club is contingent upon approval by the membership committee. A variety of memberships is offered, including golf, tennis, and social. Bass are plentiful in the lakes and waterways of Mariner Sands, and fishing is a popular pastime.

Two different floor plans in both one- and two-story configurations are incorporated in the four-unit structures at Foxcross. The single-level residences are on either end with the two-story residences in the center, providing an aesthetic exterior configuration. Structures were designed to blend with their surroundings and are finished in natural wood with cedar shake roofs.

2-139 Foxcross is marketed through the master developer of the Mariner Sands community.

Management

Foxcross has its own condominium association; Phoenix MacNab is responsible for its formation. Mariner Sands arranges for a management company to provide management services for the association. The condominium association may appoint its own directors and management.

Market

The market for Foxcross is the same as for the entire Mariner Sands community—primarily semiretirees interested in golf and country club activities. As Mariner Sands retains exclusive rights for sales and marketing for Foxcross and any housing unit, it can ensure coordinated marketing for the entire community. Prospective buyers are often sold on Foxcross when they first see the Mariner Sands property and lifestyle.

The master developer charges a 5 percent sales commission and a 1 percent marketing fee, which are contributed to the master advertising program, for the life of the project. Foxcross benefits from Mariner Sands' overall media advertising campaign, public relations, and newsletters. The overall marketing cost to Foxcross (payable monthly) is $95,000 over the life of the project. Phoenix MacNab bears the cost of all collateral material. Mariner Sands' management believes it is more palatable to the subdeveloper to split the percentage in this manner.

Experience Gained

A small developer can buy a tract of land within a large community and concentrate on his area of expertise. As the overall developer, Mariner Sands has created the package of amenities—all the things that require major front-end investment. It provides large-scale marketing and sales, a rental program if necessary, and ongoing management of the condominium association, all of which are not economically feasible for a small tract. Based on the success of the master community, the subdeveloper can estimate the rate of sales and readily determine the proper product. On the minus side for the subdeveloper, however, is that he is paying retail prices for the land and his profit is derived only from building and development. His fate is also controlled by the fate of the master community: if it flourishes, so does the subdeveloper.

It is imperative that the master developer retain all control of approval over the site plan, architecture, and landscaping. The master developer must be certain that the subdeveloper is financially sound. Similarly, the subdeveloper must determine the master developer's credibility, extracting the appropriate guarantees and assurances relating to the project. One of the great benefits of being a developer within a planned unit development is that the master developer obtains all zoning approvals, eliminating a time consuming and costly effort for the subdeveloper.

Recreational Vehicle Project

Marina Village Campground, Trinity County, Texas

Marina Village is a 2,016-member timeshare camping club on Lake Livingstone, 90 miles north of Houston. Members receive the right to use any site in the campground for an average total of 45 days per year during one of their reserved, weeklong intervals. The camping club holds title to the land and improvements, and no ownership is conveyed with club membership. But by sharing campsites instead of owning one full time, the Marina Village club member can lower his camping costs and receive the flexibility to select any site within the campground each time he camps. A greater amenity package is also made possible by the greater return realized from multiple sales of each campsite. Amenities include a marina, separate recreation areas for adults, teens, and children, a general store, and internal tram service.

The project was developed as an adjunct to the 1,200-acre Westwood Shores, a second-home, full-ownership recreational community. Land in the Marina Village site could not be used for permanent dwellings because of a flowage easement held by the Trinity River Authority, but camping was a feasible use and planning for the campground began in March 1975, followed by construction in August 1975. The first timeshare intervals were sold in October 1975. By 1978, all the campsites and amenities were completed, and the project was successfully sold out in 1979.

The Site

The Marina Village property is a 57-acre tract on Lake Livingston, an 88,000-acre manmade reservoir which serves as one of several backup water sources for Houston. The river authority samples soil and water throughout the watershed to maintain minimum pollution levels, and the Texas Parks and Wildlife Department protects marine life and wildlife in and around the lake. Trinity, 3 miles away, is the nearest community for emergency services. The area around the project is rural, undeveloped, and without zoning controls. Except for an increasing recreation industry centered around Lake Livingston, the local economy is based on farming and lumbering.

Campsites are reached by a main collector road in the Westwood Shores development. The campground site is long and in places quite narrow and as a consequence has considerable frontage along the water. Terrain is rolling and varies 20 feet in elevation over the site. Some areas are open but most are wooded with native pine and hardwoods. Besides the drainage easement, part of the property lies within the 100-year floodplain.

2-140 Campsites at Marina Village are located at least 50 feet apart and have utility hookups and paved pads.

Timeshare Program

Marina Village campsites are shared on the basis of guaranteed reservations. No member may use a particular campsite to the exclusion of other members. The $3,550 (1978) membership, for which the developer provided financing, assures 42 to 49 camping days per year. At the time of purchase, each member is assigned one of two arrival dates (Monday or Friday) and a particular week in a revolving 8-week calendar. To each of the 16 membership types, 125 members are assigned. In any given week in the 8-week calendar, half the campsites will be used by the Monday arrivals, half by the Friday arrivals. Each of these groups leaves by 10:00 A.M. of the Monday or Friday a week later, and a new group begins to arrive at 3:00 P.M. All campsites and recreation facilities are available on a first-come, first-served basis. Memberships can be sold at any time.

To use one of the guaranteed camping dates on the calendar, a member calls a toll-free number 48 hours before arrival. If no call is made, the campground assumes that the member will not use his date and opens the space to other reservations. To reserve a space on other than a guaranteed date, a member calls 24 hours before arrival, allowing him to take advantage of a space yielded by another member who has a guaranteed date but has chosen not to use it. Unscheduled camping is limited to not more than 7 successive days. No reservations are required for daytime use. In practice, most campers are not on guaranteed time and are staying 3 or 4 days over a weekend. Peak holiday weekends are Easter, Memorial Day, the Fourth of July, and Labor Day.

Marina Village members automatically belong to a campground exchange program which entitles them to stay at about 80 other camping parks in various

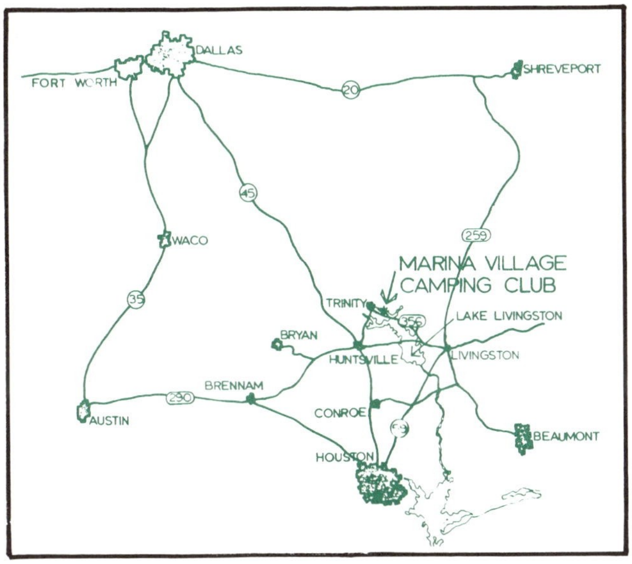

2-141 Location map.

2-142 A security ranger checks each camper.

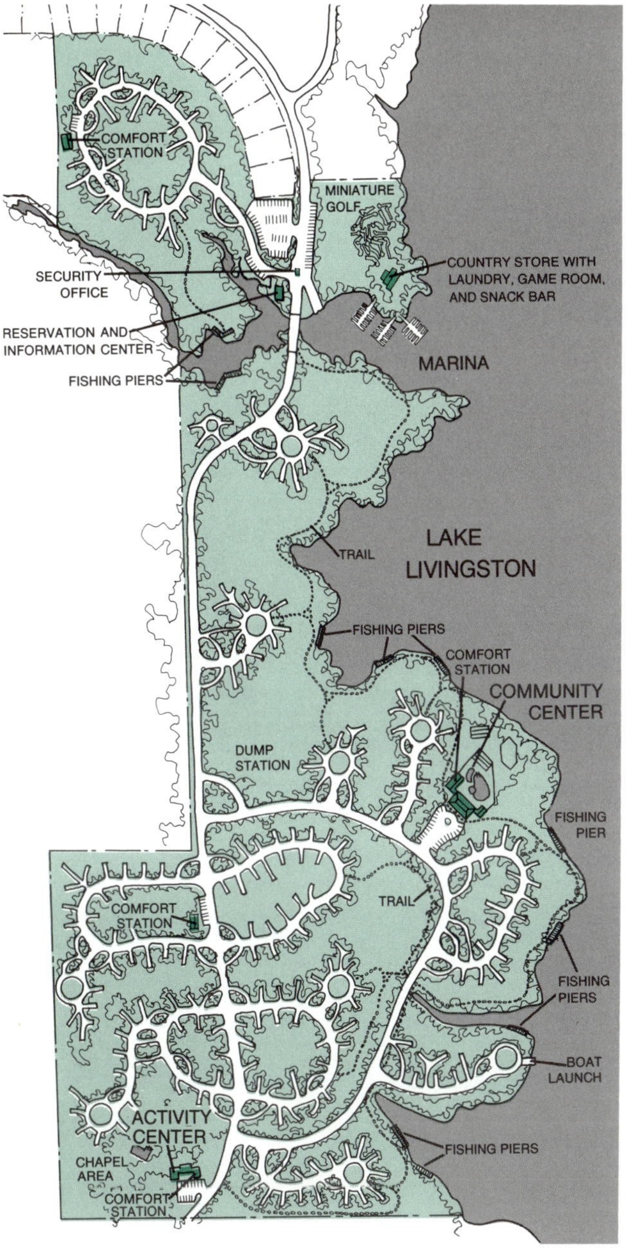

2-143 Marina Village site plan.

parts of the country. Through the exchange program, the Marina Village members may stay a total of 30 days per year at other parks, and up to 7 days at any one park. Members of other campgrounds who belong to the exchange program have the same opportunities and restrictions for camping at Marina Village. Guests may camp at Marina Village if they come with a member, register on arrival, and occupy the member's reserved campsite.

The owners' association, Marina Village Camping Club, Inc., which will be controlled by the developer until most of the timeshare units are fully paid for, is charged with all operations of the campground. Monthly dues of $12.50 (1980) pay for utilities, maintenance, campsite cleaning, amenity operation losses, and other expenses.

Planning and Engineering

The planning objective was to create a comfortable, enjoyable, and uncrowded setting for campers while providing a full range of amenities. Each campsite has a level, paved pad with picnic table, barbecue grill, and trash container. All sites have water and electrical hookups, and two-thirds of them have sewer service. A dump station is provided for those sites not serviced by sewers. Campsites are spaced at least 50 feet apart, with a gross density of 4.3 campsites per acre. Only one recreational vehicle is allowed per campsite and no more than eight people may use a site without special permission. The camper has a choice of inland, upland, or shoreline sites.

Four comfort stations are located to serve about 60 campsites each. These stations are heated and air conditioned and each contains at least three showers, four toilets including one or more urinals, as well as wash basins and dressing areas. Pay telephones are located at the adult center and the country store.

A series of culs-de-sac and looped roads lead from a main collector road to the campsites. The light-duty asphalt road system was built 28 feet wide to accommodate recreational vehicles. A security guard at the campground entrance checks in each camper. A free tram service, which operates during weekends and vacation periods, and a separate pathway system enable campers to go from their sites to the various amenity areas. No trail bikes, motor bikes, dune buggies, or other similar vehicles may be operated within the campgrounds.

Marina Village provides parking spaces for day-time visitors and storage areas for boats, and a member may leave his recreational vehicle at the campground for short periods while visiting other attractions in the area. RV storage for 500 units is also provided at $9 per month for longer periods when the member is not camping. This has been a very popular service.

Sewer inlets were waterproofed to protect against possible inundation from the lake. Pumps and lift stations were required to carry effluent to the higher sewer interceptor lines. Stormwater runs directly into the lake.

Amenities

Recreation and social activities at Marina Village center around three areas—the community center, the activities center, and the Westwood Shores marina area. Although children can use the community center at certain times, it has an adult focus and offers such facilities as the Marina Village Club and picnic area, barbecue pit, heated adult swimming pool, Jacuzzi wading pool, sun patio, shuffleboard court, table tennis, croquet, and horseshoe pit. The community center building is also the setting for year-round social activities including square dances, barbecues, bingo, and card parties. At the activities center, which is more youth-oriented, are a preteen room, crafts patio, play lot, barbecue pit and picnic area, family pool, children's wading pool, and areas and equipment for tetherball, volleyball, and basketball. Near this area is an open air chapel in which Sunday services are held. In the marina area, which is shared with residents of Westwood Shores, are the general store and tackle shop, game room with electronic skill games, pool and pinball games, snack bar, bait house, boat launches, fuel pumps, laundromat, boat and bicycle rental, and miniature golf. A full-time activi-

2-144 A swimming pool is located at the community center, the focus for year-round social activities at Marina Village.

2-145 A separate activity center is youth-oriented.

ties director coordinates the recreation and social programs.

Members of Marina Village can play golf and tennis at the neighboring Westwood Shores Country Club when space is available by paying a guest fee. They can become members of Westwood Shores Country Club by paying the initiation fee and dues.

Marketing

The project has been marketed primarily through direct mail to campers in the Houston area, specifically those within 3 hours or 125 miles of the project—a total market area of some 3.5 million people. Any campers are welcome to become members and use the park, but the amenity package and improved nature of the project are aimed at owners of large RVs as the primary market. RV owners who have purchased in Marina Village are typically over 50 years old, with no children, or are in their mid-30s and have children who are generally over 8. The few tent campers who have purchased in the project are under 30 years old.

Mailing lists for the direct mail campaign were obtained from RV dealers and associations and camping supply dealers. The lists were then screened for people from census tracts with median family incomes of more than $15,000. The sales season parallels the camping season, running from March to October and peaking in July and August. During this peak period, 10,000 pieces were mailed per week, at a cost of about $2,500. Prizes (such as sleeping bags) were usually given to couples who visited the project and took the sales tour. Sometimes a cash voucher for travel expenses was included in the mailing to increase lagging sales. At the site, additional prizes were sometimes offered through games of chance. Responses to mailings averaged half to three-quarters percent. Twelve percent of all visitors from the direct mail program actually bought a timeshare.

The developer also used a marketing program based on referrals from Marina Village members. If a friend registered, took the tour, and met other qualifications, the member received certificates which could be used to buy merchandise from a catalog or to pay the monthly maintenance costs. This program produced an average of 21 visitors per month, about 20 percent of whom ultimately purchased a timeshare. The total marketing costs ran at 35 percent of project income, slightly more than the projected 32 percent. The sales staff numbered seven to 12 people, depending on the season.

Experience Gained

- Camping is usually done impulsively. Regardless of the timeshare program set up for a campground, provisions should be made for accommodating campers on short notice.
- The greatest potential for timesharing campgrounds is probably on 50- to 80-acre tracts within 80 to 100 miles of major metropolitan areas. How far a camper will travel to his timeshare campsite will depend on the travel habits of the market area population, the type of roads leading to and from the campsites, the natural and manmade amenities of the site, and other factors.
- Provision for RV storage is a critical element for a park serving a metro area with predominantly repeat or timeshare business. Even after expansions, demand for storage sites at Marina Village has exceeded supply and has proved quite profitable.
- The timeshare purchaser prefers to use his timeshare several times during the year instead of all at once. An overall calendar of use varies with the particular market and camping season.
- Because there is some confusion about the rules among new members, the management staff meets with them on their first camping trips to review the rules and answer any questions. A

2-146 Four comfort stations serve about 60 campsites each and have showers, toilets, washbasins, and dressing areas.

quarterly newsletter and calendar of activities is sent to all campers, and a weekly activity sheet given at the gate helps to keep other campers informed about events and changes in rules.

- In planning for a timeshare campground, it is advisable to anticipate that some financed memberships will need to be resold. Stopped payment on timeshare sales at a good project could run 10 percent or more.
- Maintenance of facilities and grounds must be a high priority. Users insist on a clean, well-operated facility. Particular care must be taken to keep the comfort stations clean and to heat or cool them appropriately.
- An ongoing activity program is essential. Weekend activities for families are particularly important and should include separate programs for children and adults.
- The demand for electrical service has been much greater than expected. While all sites have electrical service, only some were developed with the 50-amp service required by larger RVs.
- The common facilities should be designed for maximum flexibility of use and minimum maintenance. A multipurpose structure used as a meeting room, dancing area, game room, and eating area with small kitchen is considerably more practical than a building devoted to a single purpose. The optimum design would be a convertible structure which could be either open to the air or closed, to permit year-round use.
- Marina Village has avoided the management and security problems often associated with extra, income-producing operations by concentrating these facilities in one easily supervised area and limiting their scope.

PROJECT DATA—MARINA VILLAGE

Land Use Information:

Site Area: 57.24 acres
Total Campsites: 252
Gross Density: 4.3 campsites per acre
Parking: 1 recreational vehicle plus 1 other vehicle per campsite

Land Use Plan:

	Acres	Percent
Campsites	34.32	60.0
Open Space	11.42	20.0
Adult Area	2.00	3.5
Activity Center	1.50	2.6
Comfort Stations	0.50	0.9
Marina	2.50	4.4
Roads	5.00	8.6
Total	57.24	100.0

Notes

[1] Includes pads and parking areas.
[2] Equipment such as picnic tables, barbecue pit, and trash bins.
[3] For country store, game room, fishing piers, boat launch, and rental equipment.
[4] Includes games equipment and renovation of existing facilities.
[5] For the owner's timeshare of the campsite and his right to use the campgrounds at least 42 days per year.
[6] Covers such items as campground activities and newsletter, utilities, common area maintenance, amenity operation losses, and campsite cleanup.

Economic Information:

Site: $57,000 (1975)
Site Improvements:

Sewer Lines	$162,000
Temporary Sewage Treatment Plant	15,000
Water Lines	55,000
Electrical System	140,000
Paving[1]	400,000
Cleaning and Filling	15,000
Land Planning	12,000
Survey	20,000
Other Consultants	15,000
Campsite Equipment[2]	36,000
Total	$870,000

Amenities:

Community Center	$204,500
Comfort Stations (3)	160,000
Security Office	20,000
Tram System	20,000
Recreational Vehicle Storage (500)	86,000
Marina Additions[3]	88,000
Teen Center Equipment[4]	15,000
Tot Lot Equipment	25,000
Total	$618,500

Timeshare Membership: $3,550[5] (1978); 4,250 (1980)
Timeshare Association: $12.50 per month[6]

Developer/Management:
Belin & Associates, Inc.
1900 St. James Place, Suite 120
Houston, Texas 77056

Planning:
Murphey, Pulice & Associates
San Francisco, California

Architecture:
McDonnell/Kuykendahl
Houston, Texas

Workouts

The Lakeland Village Workout, South Lake Tahoe, California

Lakeland Village is a 19-acre, 260-unit, beachfront condominium resort on the south shore of Lake Tahoe. The project consists of 164 townhouses, ranging from one to four bedrooms, all with additional sleeping lofts. There is also a lodge comprised of 96 studio suites, some with lofts.

The project was developed by Grubb and Ellis, a large, western, diversified real estate firm, under a Securities and Exchange Commission (SEC) registration. The first of five phases was begun in 1972.

The project is very favorably situated on a 1,000-foot sand beach, 1 mile from Heavenly Valley, a major ski resort, and 1.5 miles from the Nevada state line casinos on U.S. Highway 50.

The metro market of the San Francisco Bay Area is within 3 to 4 hours' driving distance, while the Los Angeles metro market is approximately a 7- to 8-hour drive. Air service is available between both markets and the South Lake Tahoe Airport, while air service from other regions of the country is provided via Reno, some 45 minutes from the project.
project.

A Troubled Project, 1975

Like many similar projects in 1975, Lakeland Village was deep in the throws of a recession when buyer financing was scarce and the cost high. This was further compounded by several other factors. With construction costs about to escalate in 1973, the fateful decision was made to build out phases III, IV, and V ahead of schedule. This left 155 unsold units, and a \$9 million balance on the construction loan that was in default.

Each year the SEC required that the registration be updated, during which time the project had to be taken off the market, which, unfortunately, was during the prime, summer sales season. Buyer enthusiasm was dampened still further by the 1974 gasoline scare, and the uncertainty of whether or not there would be enough gasoline at the pumps for an owner to make a round trip to his condominium. The rental program, as structured in the SEC registration, was a textbook model as far as the commission was concerned, but a complete failure for the owners who were experiencing low occupancies, high costs, and a return of approximately 10 percent on the rental dollar. Both the owners' association and the rental program were managed by a subsidiary of the developer.

Finally, the developer was in financial difficulty on several fronts simultaneously, and the primary corporate lender had forced a reorganization of the company's top management.

During the preceding 12 months, a wide range of sales and marketing techniques had been employed, including force-feeding prospective buyers from the developer's many brokerage offices throughout the state of California; boiler room telephone operations; media advertising; changes in on-site sales management; and many other strategies. Sales were made at the rate of two units a month.

2-147 Winter view of Lakeland Village.

The Turnaround Management Program

In an effort to reorganize the company and restructure the project simultaneously, Grubb and Ellis divested itself of all nonbrokerage activities, including its resort management division. This division was sold to a group headed by the division president, with several conditions relating to the workout. The developer would curtail virtually all off-site sales and promotion efforts and rely on a well-capitalized, management program to provide a high-quality, on-site program, as well as an aggressive rental marketing program aimed at markets with good buyer profiles. The theory was that after having had a pleasant vacation experience, a guest would be more receptive to an on-site purchase of a unit.

In 1975, the new management company, Village Resorts, introduced a rental marketing plan which disregarded standard condominium marketing practices in favor of the more diverse, proven techniques of resort hotels. Accordingly, an initial promotional budget of $250,000 was targeted for the organized travel industry as well as the consumer, through the use of selected media. Hundreds of travel agents were brought to the property to acquaint them with it while many others received audiovisual presentations in their own market areas. Aggressive lobbying was done at the state Public Utilities Commission on behalf of two interstate airlines trying to service South Lake Tahoe Airport from both the San Francisco and Los Angeles metro markets. These routes were subsequently approved. In order to reach more distant markets, management organized the South Lake Tahoe Visitors' Bureau, a cooperative which pooled promotion funds from government and competing properties to sell the virtues of the entire south Tahoe destination area. This effort soon developed into an "umbrella" campaign of some $400,000, of which Lakeland Village's contribution was $2,400. Management established a Rental Management Advisory Board—whose members were elected by the owners—to advise on rental matters periodically.

2-148 Townhouse units at Lakeland Village.

The developer decided to de-register the project with the SEC. This necessitated a careful working relationship between the broker and the managing agent, which complied strictly with SEC guidelines. The broker was not permitted to talk about the rental program and the financial results from it, and the managing agent portrayed conservatively the benefits of the rental program, while exhibiting the kind of professionalism that gave a prospective buyer confidence.

Results

By September 21, 1977, after 26 months, the project was sold out ahead of schedule, with a sales rate reaching seven units per month at the end. During this time, the developer had reduced off-site sales costs to virtually nothing, while earning a net cash flow from the rental of inventory of more than $400,000. The increased sales demand, plus the high level of guest services, supported significant increases in sales prices over the 26-month period.

The broker in charge credited the on-site management program with 90 percent of the sales made. The majority of the sales were made to renters, and all sales were heavily influenced by the presence of a professional, on-site management program.

In the final analysis, the developer had escaped from a situation which threatened the survival of the project as well as the company. Instead of taking a substantial loss, a worthwhile profit was earned from the final sales. The buyers who purchased both before and during the workout acquired a healthy respect for the developer, which was important to the company's reputation as a brokerage firm throughout the West.

The 5 years succeeding the workout created substantial increases and values for the owners. For 1979/1980, the net cash return to the owners in the rental program was $1,106,000, an increase of 218 percent over 5 years. Asset appreciation for the owners increased to 213 percent during that period, while annual association costs only increased 68 percent and the total impact of inflation over the 5 years was 56.1 percent.

A Workout Strategy for a Troubled Resort Condominium Project

A condominium project can experience difficulty for a variety of reasons. However, under certain circumstances, there has been some demonstrated success in the workout strategy set forth below.

A workout strategy for a resort condominium project like Lakeland Village will be effective where the following conditions exist:

- -The condominium product that has been created is, intrinsically, a good product.
- -A significant number of units have been completed and are in marketable condition.
- -The project is designed to accommodate a rental operation, preferably on-site.
- -The project contains sufficient amenities, both on-site and nearby, to assure a pleasant vacation experience.

In other words, the causes of a slow sales rate will necessarily be due to external factors such as:

- -Difficulties in buyer financing—high rates, availability of mortgages, buyer qualifications, and others.
- -National and regional economic conditions that retard demand, such as recession, inflation, and unemployment.
- -Fuel scarcity or cost that might affect a buyer's ability either to use or rent his condominium.
- -A tourism slump in the area that would have a negative effect on potential rental occupancy.
- -A glut of competitive products on the market.

These conditions affected many projects during the recessions of 1974–1975 and 1979–1980. During both periods, many developers recognized the critical need to expose their products to qualified buyers but did not always know how to go about it successfully.

Professional, On-Site Management

One workout strategy which has proven successful is to bring in a professional, resort management company with a good track record in handling similar situations. If members of the company are properly selected and directed, they should be able to provide buyers for the developer by:

- -First attracting qualified potential buyers to the property through vacation rentals, using an aggressive, broad-based rental marketing program.
- -Operating a high-quality, on-site rental program, including guest activities, which assures a memorable vacation experience.
- -Working closely with the sales program to solicit rental guests.
- -Defining the management program to potential buyers in such a way that it reassures them about the maintenance and security of their prospective investments; it should also define realistically a worthwhile cash flow from rentals and a quality management program that will clearly enhance real estate values.

The Guidelines

Guidelines to developing a successful program of this nature should include:

- -The management company's strong identification with the developer's goals.
- -A significant commitment by the management company, in terms of analysis of the problem, development of a formal plan, top management time, and sufficient capital to assure a successful program. Preferably, the management company will have a track record of having helped other developers achieve similar goals. If the company operates other resorts, it should be encouraged to use those owners as a source for prospective buyers.
- -A formal system of periodic communication between all levels of the development company and the management company.
- -A financial incentive for the management company, geared to the measurable success of the workout.
- -The cultivation of satisfied owners as referrals for future sales.
- -If not enough units are sold to constitute a viable rental program to attract buyers, the developer should be prepared to arrange for some of the unsold units to be furnished to help generate traffic.

Expected Results

If the preceding guidelines are implemented, it is reasonable to expect the following results:

- -The developer will realize a significant cash flow from the rental of his own units to offset some of his carrying costs.
- -Sales costs will be reduced, with the job of getting the prospect to the site now resting largely with the management company.
- -Sales will increase, primarily to renters whose sales resistance has been minimized by a positive vacation experience.
- -Property values will increase due to the cash flow from rentals and the first-class, full-service, professional management program.

The foregoing workout strategy has been successful in supporting the objectives of developers in distress, as well as those of the banks who have acquired properties through foreclosure. In both cases, substantial, predicted losses have been converted into profits and reputations have been restored.

The Mariner Sands Turnaround, Stuart, Florida

Mariner Sands began as a 1,600-acre recreational residential community on the southeast Florida coast. Conceived in the early 1970s, it faltered before the construction of any dwelling units. A restructured development strategy led to the project's successful return as a viable 720-acre PUD, planned to include 980 mixed dwelling units, 36 holes of golf, and other recreational amenities.

Because of the original owner's bankruptcy, a careful strategy was needed to pump new life into Mariner Sands. Although the internal arterial roads and unused golf course were already in place, the absence of proper zoning, permits, and water or sewer systems posed numerous obstacles. A first step was to gain zoning for a PUD, a measure the local government agreed was necessary to improve the abandoned property. Initial financing needs were dealt with in two stages. First, the sale of 900 acres generated cash and reduced the scope of the project to a more manageable size. Second, the new developer was granted a $1.2 million loan to work on the 350-acre first phase of Mariner Sands.

New Development

The opportunities to improve the project were aided by the fact that buildings had not been constructed at Mariner Sands but hampered by the fact that the golf course had been poorly laid out with respect to maximizing property values. The strategy for gradually transforming Mariner Sands involved a number of key elements. An attractive entrance to the project was carefully orchestrated and has proved to be the project's best advertisement. Security was added to an entry gate, a temporary clubhouse was moved to become an attractive sales information center, landscaping and signage were added, and discounts to local custom builders helped spur construction. A deal was negotiated with a local water and sewer utility, and construction began with a phased golf clubhouse, which opened in December 1979. Unimproved waterways were included in special views.

Complemented by a noticeable improvement in the physical setting, mixed multifamily residential units were constructed and have been very well received (see discussion of Foxcross case study). The targeted market for the reborn Mariner Sands is the retired southern Florida purchaser interested in a private country club atmosphere. The upgraded golf course and club were initially marketed to nonproperty owners to guarantee a nucleus of supporters who could be converted to property-owning members or phased out as the number of property owners grew.

2-149 Mariner Sands Country Club (left) and golf cottages (right).

2-150 Typical single-family home at Mariner Sands.

Lessons

Some overriding lessons from the Mariner Sands success include the need to establish a community, the importance of the developer's commitment at the beginning supplemented by the builder's investment to establish the project's credibility, and the value of gradually increasing and maintaining momentum of construction. Most important, the developer must identify the project's place in the market and stick to it. Not surprisingly, developments such as Mariner Sands require a major equity investor to survive the development period.

The Wintergreen Turnaround, Wintergreen, Virginia

Wintergreen is a 13,000-acre recreational community in the Virginia Blue Ridge Mountains. Its market is the affluent buyer within a 3-hour drive of the project, which includes Richmond, the Virginia Tidewater area, and particularly Washington, D.C. Single-family home sites vary from .5 to 5 acres, 7,000 acres are preserved as a park, and the project's amenities include skiing, golf, swimming, tennis, horseback riding, and a large network of hiking trails. Wintergreen is perhaps best described as a horizontal hotel: the developer rents private condominium units and houses. Room-nights are ultimately projected to be 50,000 to 70,000 annually.

Conceived at the end of the 1960s, Wintergreen was purchased in 1973 by a Boston real estate firm with corporate guarantees and the backing of a real estate investment trust (REIT). Subsequent development misfortunes culminated in the takeover by the major creditor, Bankers Trust, in mid-1976, just after the first ski season, which had numerous technical and weather problems. Most of the infrastructure and many of the amenities were constructed but not finished, leaving the project looking unattractive.

The four unanticipated factors at the project's inception that led to Wintergreen's (and other recreational projects') problems in the 1973–1976 period were the scarcity of gasoline, the high cost of money, more restrictive regulations at all levels of government, and lack of buyers' confidence because of the project's early stage. Much of the early capital investment was in necessary utility infrastructure and roads, not readily perceived by the average buyer.

Business Plan

Bankers Trust financed Wintergreen based not on the property but on the owner's strength as a successful Boston real estate firm. The bank was interested in making 4 to 5 points over the prime rate. Instead, the owner ended up selling property just to pay the interest on the loan. The developer was overextended for the project, and corporate finances were not sufficient to back up the loan. The other guarantee on the loan, the REIT, also was not in a position to help the project. The bank was carrying a $16 million loan on a project only 15 to 20 percent completed. At that point the bank's options were:

- to foreclose and sell, obtaining $3 million to $4 million of its $16 million loan;
- to leave the developer in the project and provide further funds; or
- to take over the project's ownership and defer the developer's guarantees by having it pay some of the debts.

2-151 Wintergreen in winter. Dwelling units front on the upper sections of some ski slopes.

The bank chose the last alternative. At this point, a typical bank loan officer's objective is to make the loan smaller and to put no more money into the project. Therefore, good assets of the project typically are sold to pay operating expenses until the project is on more stable footing. The results could be that eventually the remaining parts of the project have little value and the outstanding loan would have to be written off the bank's books.

After a financial analysis, the bank's decision, however, was to sell single-family lots, realizing a breakeven point in 5 years. (According to federal banking rules, banks cannot hold real estate for more than that length of time.) This action meant that the loan would be converted into lot notes (10 percent down plus 10 years to pay), but it also meant that the bank had to spend an additional $5 million to prepare and market the lots for sale. Success for the bank, then, would be to recover its $21 million invested plus 4 to 5 percent interest. It is now apparent that the project could never have reached the 12 percent yields anticipated when the loan was made.

2-152 Natural materials are used extensively.

During the 10 to 12 months of uncertainty in 1975–1976 that led to the bank's involvement, few people invested in the property. One of the bank's initial actions was to spend money on improvements that had the greatest visual impact to assure the public that the bank was committed to the project and would finance everything if necessary.

Although the bank considered changing the project's management, it stayed with the existing management. A partnership of necessity evolved. The bank could not find any better managers for the complex and diverse activities of the ongoing project (supervise $2 million in costs plus utility infrastructure work necessary to market single-family lots, build and sell 125 condominiums per year, and operate the resort facilities and utility district). The local managers needed a partner with stability, some business planning, and, most importantly, money. A 5-year plan with the following features was set up to manage the project:

- monthly reporting of cash flow;
- quarterly reviews to change any intermediate policies;
- hired, experienced real estate accountants and engineering firms to monitor the ongoing overall costs of the project; and
- an incentive program that pays well but not at all if sales quotas are not met.

The project management formulates an annual business plan, which the bank approves with modifications if necessary. Except for periodic reviews, the bank leaves the management alone. Occasionally, senior bank personnel visit the project as a political gesture to show they have confidence in the project.

As the nation's economy improved and major key improvements were completed, the project's credibility also improved. Skiing finally increased traffic to the project, resulting in more sales. By 1980, gross sales reached $20 million, with some 1,500 property owners.

Lessons

The relationship between a developer and a lender during the period of trying to solve a project's problems is important. If the project can be sold at a price greater than the loan, find a lawyer and sell. If a project needs to be completed, find a lawyer but do not give the lawyer the right to make decisions regarding the project. The developer must manage the political process well; otherwise, an unnecessary bankruptcy can result. Many times the decisions are not readily apparent. Lenders do not want to sue or foreclose. The developer, however, must give the lender alternatives if he wants to continue to manage the project. Besides being responsive, competent, and honestly stating his self-interest, a developer must convince a lender that he is good or better than any alternative management. One way to do so is to prepare some of the detailed work for the lender. Short, neat reports are more likely to receive attention, but if prepared 4- to 5-page proposals for restructuring the project are rejected, alternatives should be prepared. The negotiations between a developer and a lender are not just based on economics; a political process is involved. Continued dialogue is of paramount importance.

2-153 Wintergreen's mountain top location provides a cool setting for a variety of summer activities.

3.
Theme Parks

Theme parks are a relatively recent addition to the recreational field, yet their predecessors date back to earlier times. The ancient Greeks and later the Romans held trading fairs in which merchandise was bartered and exchanged. These fairs drew large crowds, and wherever large crowds gathered, there was entertainment, at first with games, music, and dancing, and later with skilled entertainers.

By the early 1600s, rides in the form of crude carousels and other devices were being added to what were still essentially markets of commerce. However, more elaborate short-term fairs featuring entertainment were proving increasingly successful and soon were followed by amusement parks which offered rides and other attractions on a more permanent basis. Their operating periods coincided with good weather, and their numbers grew throughout Europe. A popular French garden park of note in the mid-1600s was Versailles. In the mid-19th century, these "pleasure gardens" reached America; for example, Vauxhall Gardens was established in 1845 in New York City. Again, as craft skills improved, ride designs became more daring and materials used in the production of thrilling rides more reliable. George W. Gale Ferris invented the famous Ferris wheel for the Columbian Exposition of 1893. Simultaneously, many other amusement parks were being constructed across the United States.

Between 1910 and 1930, the production and operations of amusement rides flourished. As stated earlier, streetcar companies played a significant role in helping create amusement park attractions with the hope of increasing their volume of holiday transit business.

When the Great Depression took its toll in the 1930s, surprisingly, most of the parks survived. But the end of an era was in sight as technology and economic prosperity created change in recreational desires and opportunities. Specifically, the automobile brought greater mobility which increased the range of recreational choices significantly. Technological improvements were also being developed in other areas such as the motion picture industry. Many amusement parks were forced to lessen quality, and the vicious cycle of the loss in attendance followed by economic losses brought one after another to an inglorious end. By the 1950s, relatively few successful parks remained. Most of these had survived through the efforts of the hard-working families who often owned and operated them.

When Walt Disney took his daughter to an amusement park in the early 1950s (so the story goes), he noted that it lacked the qualities he believed important for family entertainment. Resolving to build a park of his own, he succeeded in opening Disneyland in 1955.

Disney combined the charm, color, excitement, entertainment, and thrill of his many movies with the essentials of an amusement park. The rides, shows, entertainment, shops, and food facilities were all successfully combined in an atmosphere of cleanliness, friendliness, safety, and nostalgic good times. The art direction and imagination required for Disney's movies were applied equally well to the park, and the thematic areas (such as Fantasyland and Tomorrowland) became known throughout the world.

Thus, the "theme park" was born.

Form and Use

A theme park is an amusement park operating within a specially created environment and atmosphere. There may be one theme, such as a specific historical setting, or multiple themes. In either case, the meaning results from a synthesis of form and concept.

The form of a theme park is derived from the cultural elements characterizing the theme. Consequently, architecture for a park is appropriately novel. It represents a major difference from most commercial design in that every structure becomes a medium for delivering symbols that reinforce a sense of place.

In the thoughtful design and careful development of the overall environment, traditional rides are somewhat subordinate. More important is how the theme concept sparks the imagination. Clearly, some parks are more successful in this effort than others. Special care is needed to develop a park with a strong identity. For example, in order to replicate the appearance and atmosphere of an earlier period, it is frequently necessary to develop new ways of executing old crafts, or to involve those people who are well informed on the period to be reproduced. Considerable research by the design professionals along with on-site construction management is usually required to produce the desired product.

Generally, people visit theme parks for entertainment and relaxation. By accommodating visitors of all ages, theme parks are family-oriented. As one would expect, all the successful parks have a consistently high volume of attendance during the peak season.

Theme park attendance depends on the seasonal factors of weather and the tourist's and vacationer's travel patterns. The average family vacation usually occurs during the summer months which compose

3-1 The 100-acre Magic Kingdom at Walt Disney World includes six areas whose themes are carried out in costuming, food, architecture, landscaping, music, and over 45 adventures. (Walt Disney Productions photograph.)

the peak season for theme parks. It is sound policy to design the project for the typical summer day which, in effect, becomes the basic day around which all planning and new development are designed.

Park use is primarily in the form of passive recreation. That is to say, visitors are not required to exert themselves or be physically active. By sitting during rides or shows, guests usually maintain enough energy to stay in the park longer. Secondly, this passive spectator type of entertainment accommodates a greater number of visitors within a given site. The average theme park visitor spends 6 to 7 hours in a park. Within this time, a person typically spends as much money for food and merchandise as for rides.

Types and Locations

As of 1980, there were over two dozen parks—which can truly qualify as theme parks—spread throughout the United States. Several were being considered or are under construction outside the United States. Numerous other parks claim theme status, yet they lack true distinction. Most of these parks concentrate heavily on rides, primarily "thrill" rides. They are often called "ride parks" or "iron parks" within the trade, but are generally considered to be without legitimate themes. Some theme parks provide other major forms of entertainment. Included are marine parks, with their shows and displays of sea animals. Animal parks offer drive-through or ride-through tours of their landscaped facilities. There are also numerous smaller attractions with various themes, including restored villages, historic railroads, specialty museums, botanical gardens, and even specialty shopping centers. The most popular theme parks, however, are ride parks having themes.

With few exceptions (Disneyland in Southern California and Disneyworld in central Florida), each theme park occupies a primary market area alone and without competition. Their preemptive presence discourages development of others of equal magnitude. As a result, most U.S. markets of sufficient population to support such a park are now served, with some exceptions in certain regions. Markets with good demographics in Europe, the Far East, and the Middle East are prime targets for major theme park developers in the 1980s. In North America, smaller-sized theme parks are considered by some in the industry as the future wave and may begin to develop in some mid-size cities such as New Orleans, Birmingham, Indianapolis, and others. One such "mini-park" has been successfully developed in Minneapolis, though a number of undercapitalized and poorly sited small theme parks elsewhere have operated less well.

3-2 Although rides like the carousel and various types of roller coasters are the staple of "ride parks," they are also distinct features of theme parks.

Mini-Theme Parks

A variety of smaller specialty theme attractions has emerged recently. For example, mini-racetracks using race cars which are one-fourth the size of traditional race cars have achieved some success with their grand prix format and setting. One popular theme park has involved water-oriented attractions in which water slides and wave pools are used. Many of these are loosely themed and are highly seasonal.

An important characteristic of these latter attractions is their appeal to a population increasingly interested in active recreation. One severe drawback in developing participatory attractions is the limited number of participatory elements having a broad enough appeal for all ages, and thus a broad enough market to be economically feasible. Another disadvantage is the limited capacity of facilities when individual rather than mass participation must be planned for.

One other category of attraction is thematic—the true specialty entertainment park. The Universal Studios Tour is an example of a successful operation; the Grand Ole Opry is another. Both deal with large numbers of patrons. Unfortunately, neither lends itself easily to replication. Their location and already established uniqueness are key to their success. The Kennedy Space Center is another unique form of entertainment attraction which is successful at handling large crowds but also cannot be duplicated in location and format. While other developments of this nature may have significant limitations, it would seem worthwhile to identify existing environments and facilities which would lend themselves to imaginative recreational packaging.

Theme parks and smaller specialty recreational attractions have had a limited number of recent failures, but in most cases, a major factor in the failure was the selection of a poor location. As in most retail or public service businesses, the facility must be located where the market size and quality are sufficient. Faulty research or logic can readily lead to a park failure. The development of all successful major theme parks, and undoubtedly most successful smaller theme attractions, has been preceded by a thorough and carefully studied market analysis. This analysis is generally conducted by market specialists familiar with both research techniques and the park/attraction field. Detailed studies of population, demographics, weather, competitive factors including existing entertainment facilities, and numerous other factors lead to projections of potential market penetration and probable levels of spending per patron. These revenue projections, when coupled with estimated operating margins for a given type of facility, are essential in determining justifiable levels of investment.

Again, the projects that have failed, or which are marginal, frequently have had inadequate market analysis. In many cases, they were based incorrectly on either the owner's or developer's hopes or on his biased judgment. Local and nonobjective individuals, or even the developer himself, have actually prepared many such feasibility studies which projected what the developer wanted, rather than what he truly needed to know.

Major Park Sites

Compared with other parks, major theme parks generally require a reasonably noncompetitive location. The primary market needs a minimum of 2 million people, with a secondary market of the same number or more. Large tertiary and tourist markets can be helpful, although these markets cannot be counted on due to probable prolonged high transportation costs. The primary market for a major theme park is generally considered to be within a range of 50 miles or a 1-hour drive; the secondary market is within a range of up to 150 miles or a 3-hour drive, which still allows the patron to make a round trip within a day.

Other important factors in site selection include: location on or near a major highway with ample capacity to handle traffic and good interchange access; a secondary road for auxiliary or emergency entrance/exit and other service traffic; a visible site, capable of displaying key elements (towers, major structures, and a sign) to the passing motorists; identification with an existing landmark or area (helpful, but not essential); adequate utilities since parks are heavy users of power, water, and sewage treatment; a favorable governmental climate for both zoning and taxation negotiation; and a limited number, if any, of neighboring residents who might object to the development and its subsequent operation. Adequate acreage is a necessity, with major parks requiring a minimum of 200 acres. The topography or configuration of the site can increase considerably the number of acres needed. Local requirements for buffer zones can also affect the required acreage. The ideal topography would be relatively level or no more than gently rolling. Otherwise, many guests will find it difficult to navigate; steep hills will discourage on-site movement and even reduce the length of stay—which directly affects spending and profits.

An ideal site would be rectangular in shape with sides in a ratio of roughly two to three, and with an

3-3 Coordination of design and operational details is essential to the creation and maintenance of theme facilities. (Sketches used with permission of Louis Wasserman from *Merchandising Architecture*, copyright 1978.)

3-4 A prime 600-acre site with excellent freeway access and government cooperation contributed to the successful development of Marriott Corporation's Great America theme park in Santa Clara, California.

abundance of natural beauty—wooded areas and one or two low spots where ponds or lakes could be constructed. A meadow area for parking would be best if it is situated close to the highway or in another logical location. Existing greenery of a deciduous type would be an asset in that it would reduce landscaping costs, give the facility an "established" appearance, reduce the need for heavily detailed architecture, delineate separate theme areas, and help to provide the feeling of coolness on hot summer days. Construction within such a situation is more difficult, requiring that the specimen trees be identified and protected, but the cost and effort are well worth it.

Sites for Smaller Attractions

In some respects, it is more difficult to specify a site for smaller attractions. Many of these facilities are developed as ancillary attractions in the vicinity of the primary market area of a major park or attraction. Others relate to long-established, tourist-oriented facilities. Natural wonders—such as caves, springs, mountains, lakes—attract profit-oriented developments which relate to them. A site may be chosen based on the specialty of an area, such as Country Western music, Ozark crafts, the space program, a famous racetrack, the movie production industry, and others. Some of these attractions spring up quickly—often growing out of totally unassuming mom-and-pop operations—and many have thrived. Others have been strategically planned and crafted to capitalize on the given market.

Standing alone, small facilities might attract fewer patrons, but when clustered, they offer enough substance and variety to serve as a destination for tourists. In most cases, visitors will stay in smaller facilities 1 to 2 hours, thus enabling them to take in several separate attractions. They may, incidentally, spend considerably more money on a day's activities in several small facilities than they would for a full day of entertainment at a major theme park.

Because small attractions are far less demanding of space, utilities, and superhighway interchanges, they can fit into odd-shaped land configurations and are clearly much less expensive to develop. Often, however, they must be located only where they can exist parasitically with a major attraction, or as a combination in a tourist-oriented location.

The very small attractions, such as skateboard parks, water slides, mini-golf, various racquet facilities, and others of this participatory nature, can, of course, be constructed in any urban area of sufficient size and demographics. They are generally located on secondary real estate sites although high visibility on a fairly major road is important. They are customarily thought of as temporary land uses. As part of a fad—which many of these are—they may be of an even more temporary nature than their developers had intended. In some cases, they have been constructed too close together and with little or no market research or consideration of competitiveness.

Special Issues

Whether a theme park is major or minor in size, its overall quality correlates directly with the degree of success it achieves. Disney set the tone for today's family entertainment business. His company has developed a level of quality that is highly commendable, yet unaffordable for virtually any other developer. The large volume of visitors generated the expected revenues and profits and enabled Disney to afford the highly sophisticated construction which most developers—lacking Disney's already established large movie following—could not possibly equal. There is, however, a given degree of design, construction, and operational quality below which any entertainment enterprise dare not fall if it is to have a reasonable chance of success.

Most of the major theme parks would cost from $80 to $100 million to duplicate in today's construction market. Another Disneyworld would cost far more. Mini-parks would range in price from $10 million to $20 million. A park for children only, Sesame Place in Pennsylvania, which opened in 1980, was built by a major firm, with a multimillion-dollar budget. Specialty attractions can be expensive, ranging from around $100,000 for a simple water slide to many millions of dollars for a special theme facility.

Overdesigned construction is the economic swamp into which developers are often enticed. Trying to emulate Disney or indulging personal ego are the traps to be avoided. Knowledgeable individuals or companies can be employed to restrain such excesses. If the project manager or consultant is truly experienced and has integrity, the controls will result in a finished project well worth the cost of the specialists.

Design Constraints

The design of any type of theme park requires several kinds of specialists. The routine aspects of vehicular traffic handling, utilities design, and similar planning can be done by any competent firm in these fields. The physical facilities should, in most cases, be designed by firms specializing in these areas. The

3-5 Water is the centerpiece of a variety of themes; in this case, a New England fishing village provides the setting for both active (note water slides) and more passive entertainment.

3-6 Sesame Place, Oxford Valley Mall, Bucks County, Pennsylvania.

Sesame Place, Pennsylvania

Opened in July 1980, Sesame Place is an innovative play park for families with children from ages 3 to 13. It offers opportunities for parents to participate in some activities, which include more than 40 outdoor play elements, an enclosed computer gallery, a science studio, and a restaurant based on the concept of a "nutritional learning center." Physical activities and educational games combine to encourage children to use their own skills and imaginations.

Sesame Place is a joint venture of Busch Entertainment Corporation and the Children's Television Workshop, creators of Sesame Street. Built on a 15-acre site that includes 2.5 acres of park area and 750 parking spaces, the project is a 30-minute drive north from Philadelphia and a 20-minute drive west from Trenton, New Jersey. Sesame Place draws its primary audience from the 5 million persons living within a 25-mile radius of the site. It operates all year, with the exception of the outdoor facilities which are closed during the winter. The park reached its capacity of 7,500 visitors on peak days during its first season of operation.

design requires a theatrical approach, coupled with traditional architectural and planning skills. The objective is to transport the patron through his fantasies into another time, place, era, or mood, which in a sense requires dramatization. Imaginative uses of color with theatrical lighting for proper emphasis are needed. Magnifying certain elements, adding architectural gingerbread, and decreasing (or increasing) certain dimensions are all keys to this form of design.

The components of a park can be placed strategically to maximize patron spending and spread the entertainment experience over the length of a visit. The amount of each component, including entertainment, shows, rides, games, participative elements, merchandising, and food facilities should be carefully considered. Still another reason for careful location of all elements is their effect on crowd flows and thus on crowd satisfaction. It is important for comfort, security, and guest satisfaction that patrons "get their money's worth." Cul-de-sac situations, too narrow walkways, and improperly located plantings (even though aesthetically attractive) can become nightmares in an operation.

Based on properly prepared attendance projections, it is possible to predict, with reasonable accuracy, the daily and even hourly attendance patterns. With this information, skilled planners can then project capacity requisites for peak days and "design days"—which are the average peak high days for which most elements of a park must be planned. In a theme ride park, for example, patrons will expect a certain number of rides as proper value for their price of admission. This data will govern the number of ride units which must be installed, and, thus, the required investment level can be calculated. As in any situation involving large crowds—ball park, shopping mall, or others—certain crowd-pleasing amenities along with necessary services must be provided. Again, thoughtful planning related to previous experience can assure that these are present in proper quantities and styles.

Extensive criteria must be developed for a theme park before beginning its design. In fairness to professional designers, they should be shown detailed guidelines and limitations, all basic concepts formulated by the owner/developer, and the proposed budget. The owner's preconceived ideas on design specifics should be set aside, and the architects encouraged to think freely within the budget constraints agreed upon in advance. In general, it is probably true that the more quality which can affordably be constructed into a theme park, the better chance the park will have for a long and successful life.

Local Impact

The developer of a theme park must consider the potential effect the facility might have on adjacent elements. Unlike Disneyland with its surrounding development in the Anaheim, California, area, most theme parks will not spawn heavy ancillary development. Such developments require a year-round market and, unless they can stand on their own, will not be able to survive on the seasonal market associated with theme parks.

It might be a wise and profitable move for the theme park developer to acquire and control acreage on the perimeter of the development. If the attraction is of sufficient size and quality, it could rapidly gain local or even regional attention and benefit the whole area. Land values would increase significantly as a result, and the developer might well offset some of his project costs through the sale of the acquired acreage. By doing so, he would also be able to control the use of that land. High-quality office parks, hotels, and commercial uses have accompanied recent park developments, all within complementary covenants determined by the theme park developers. Recorded examples have shown that land values associated with park development have appreciated as much as 300 to 400 percent over a short time.

An implicit responsibility of a theme park developer is that he make his project compatible with other developments in the immediate vicinity. Problems with traffic, noise, and light are the most commonly occurring, but can be handled through proper foresight. With good planning, even a residential area can be located immediately adjacent to a theme park.

From the standpoint of government, a theme park can create new problems. A large park project can momentarily inundate a planning department with checks on unique structures, products, and construction techniques. Longer-range concerns, traffic control, and security problems relating to most gatherings of large crowds also cause problems for the local police. Local government, however, often considers these problems offset by the major new tax base and increased employment which the project presents.

Marketing Strategy

Theme parks offer family-oriented entertainment that is generally accessible and affordable. Experience indicates that it is advisable to continually add new family attractions which are both entertaining and educational to a theme park or peripheral area. Visitors then have an incentive to return each year and the new attractions expand the overall market appeal of the facility.

3-7 Modern technology provides many opportunities for offering interesting and highly participatory amusements. Sustained dependability of facilities relies on designing for heavy-use loads and implementing strict management standards.

It is important to maintain a constant program of advertising, promotion, and public relations in the core marketing area—generally defined by a 50-mile radius extending from the park. Also, attempts should be made each year to add new markets which would have the greatest growth potential.

In many cases, theme park managers have joined forces with major corporations in highly successful promotional programs which allow the parks to capitalize on an established identity and audience, often centering around a special product or event. An extension of this approach involves group rentals of theme parks, which are usually very profitable and often renewed annually.

Financial Aspects

New theme parks are unquestionably difficult to finance. The unfortunate failure of a few (Freedomland, Old Chicago, the World of Sid and Marty Kroft) has caused traditional financial sources to consider such enterprises risky, at best. Clearly, they have limited convertibility to other uses in the event of failure. In essence, they are extremely inflexible and expensive users of large quantities of land. Even great sums of money cannot convert a park to an office building, without first bringing in the wrecker's ball.

The best way to prepare for financing a park project is to develop the strongest possible rationale for it. Use of well-qualified experts in market analysis, economic feasibility, land planning, specialty architecture, and operational planning is essential. Coordination of these specialists, with an articulate final presentation, is equally important. The funding sources must be convinced that thorough analysis, devoid of speculation or biased interpretation, is being presented to them.

Short-term construction funds may be obtainable from banks or consortiums of banks, but long-term money is much more difficult to obtain. Insurance companies may be persuaded to make such loans, depending on the stature of the developer and the amount of his equity. At least a 25 percent equity position is demanded, and higher levels will make the loan easier to obtain. Numerous sources outside the United States have recently become more readily available for entertainment-oriented projects which are to be located both within the United States and abroad.

Smaller projects such as mini-parks, specialty parks, and single-subject attractions cost less and traditional sources are far more willing to finance them. In such cases, the developers generally are able to guarantee the loans.

The Bottom Line

A majority of theme parks are owned by large corporations who clearly expect to earn a good net profit. Most do. The net after taxes can range from 5 to 15 percent, depending on numerous factors. A few parks, generally in somewhat marginal market areas, do not return an adequate amount on their investment, most likely as a result of inadequate market re-

Canada's Wonderland, Toronto, Ontario

When the Taft Broadcasting Company (owner of three major theme parks in the United States) proposed in 1972 the first large-scale privately owned theme park in Canada, several locations were considered. The Toronto area was finally selected because of its large population base and easy accessibility. The 370-acre site chosen is just east of a major divided highway and is approximately 18 miles northwest of Toronto's City Hall. Another company, Great West Life, joined Taft in the venture after the site was selected.

Following lengthy negotiations for public approval and the completion of the design work, construction began in April 1979. Great care was taken to preserve the existing wood lots; approximately $12 million was spent on landscaping and site development. Unlike many theme parks, instead of asphalt walkways, 15 acres of interlocking pavers were used.

The focal point of Canada's Wonderland is a 150-foot-high manmade mountain covering 2.5 acres and built at a cost of over $5 million. The

3-8 A sketch of International Street at Canada's Wonderland, a new $115 million theme park located outside of Toronto, Ontario.

search, overbuilding, or unwise forcing of the development by the misguided exuberance of the developer.

The park business deals strictly in cash. A family of four can easily spend $75 during one day in a park. As a result, large quantities of money are exchanged and a well-managed park can enjoy an excellent cash flow, even in its first year. Investment tax credit and locally negotiated tax abatement arrangements can also be highly beneficial to the owner.

Properly located, properly sized to the available market, and properly managed, a theme park can be an excellent investment. None of these criteria are easy to meet in this day of a comparatively crowded entertainment market, but if it works, a theme park can be an exceedingly exciting and profitable business to be in.[1]

[1] This discussion of theme parks was based on an article originally published in the February 1980 issue of *Urban Land*, entitled "Thinking of a Theme Park?" by David L. Brown.

mountain serves a practical use with its 60-foot-high waterfall which acts as a cooling tower for the park's air conditioning system. For entertainment, Acapulco-style high divers plunge from the waterfall while yodelers rappel down the mountainside. From a plateau 90 feet above the park, visitors have a panoramic view of the park's five theme areas. The mountain dominates the International Festival theme area which features various rides and a theater with 3,500 seats.

At the base of the mountain a reflecting pool, 300 feet by 80 feet, is highlighted by computerized fountain and lighting systems. Flanking the pool are four buildings which represent architectural styles from Latin American, Mediterranean, Scandinavian and Alpine countries. Together these facilities make up International Street, where the visitor can shop and sample native foods.

The three other theme areas at Canada's Wonderland include the Grande World Exposition of 1890, with 19th century buildings, amusements, and decor; the Medieval Faire, featuring a castle complete with lake, giant pub, and period theater; and The Happyland of Hanna-Barbera offering an aquatic show, rides designed for younger visitors, and encounters with famous cartoon characters.

3-9 Landscaping was added as early as possible to provide a more established appearance at the park's opening. Canada's Wonderland is shown here a year before its 1981 debut.

Projects

Kings Island, Cincinnati, Ohio

Kings Island is a 1,600-acre family entertainment center developed in the early 1970s by the Taft Broadcasting Company. Located north of Cincinnati, Ohio, the center consists of a theme park, a wildlife preserve, the College Football Hall of Fame, the Kings Island Inn, a campground, and the Jack Nicklaus Golf Center.

Planning was initiated in 1969 when Taft Broadcasting acquired Coney Island—an 85-year old amusement park located in Cincinnati along the Ohio River—as part of a plan to construct a new theme park. The existing site, however, proved unsuitable for a theme park because of flooding each year. A new site was sought which would be outside of the city in an attractive setting and large enough to allow for expansion and control of the area. Taft selected a site consisting of approximately 1,000 acres adjacent to Interstate Highway 71 some 20 miles north of downtown Cincinnati. The key parcel of land was supplemented by acquiring adjacent parcels to form a site of roughly 1,600 acres east of I-71.

Taft developed the theme park and opened it in 1972. In conjunction, a motel and two golf courses were developed west of I-71. In 1975, Taft began a joint project to develop 700 to 800 residential units on land adjacent to the golf courses. The College Football Hall of Fame was constructed 1 mile north of the theme park, adjacent to the campground, and opened in 1978. Of the 1,600 acres purchased by Taft, 870 acres remain undeveloped. By 1979, the total investment was approximately $100 million.

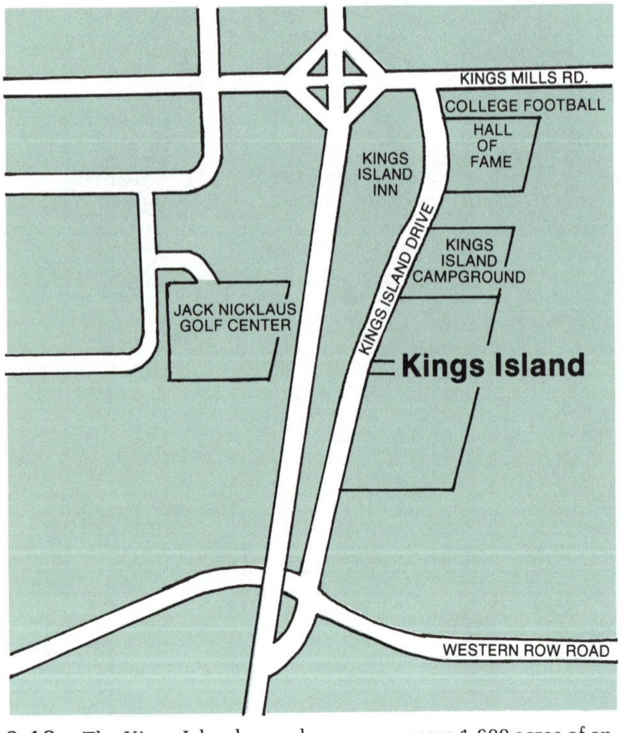

3-10 The Kings Island complex encompasses 1,600 acres of entertainment facilities promoted as a one-stop family vacation resort.

The Site

Kings Island is situated within the I-71 highway corridor on gently rolling open land. The surrounding area is mostly farmland with some interspersed residential development. The vicinity is rural in character with commercial facilities clustered near the highway interchanges.

Most of the Kings Island facilities including the theme park, wildlife preserve, parking lot, motel, campground, and College Football Hall of Fame are located east of Interstate-71. The Jack Nicklaus Golf Center is located on the west side of I-71 across from the theme park. Interstate-71 is a four-lane divided highway, providing excellent visibility of and vehicular access to the site. Two highway interchanges serve Kings Island—one just south of the theme park connecting directly to Kings Island Drive, and one at the north end of the site near the intersection of Kings Island Drive and Kings Mill Road. Kings Island Drive is a four-lane undivided highway providing internal circulation through the site. Shuttle bus service is available for visitors. The southern I-71 interchange was constructed specifically to serve Kings Island.

The 215-acre theme park is the primary attraction of the entertainment center and is divided into six major areas: International Street, Rivertown, Happyland of Hanna-Barbera, Coney Island, Wild Animal Safari, and Oktoberfest. The 100-acre Wild Animal Safari, a wildlife preserve, occupies almost as much land as the other five areas combined.

The theme park offers various rides, food service facilities, retail shops, and live shows. The rides can accommodate 45,000 people per hour, and the food facilities can service 20,000 people per hour. A 150-acre parking lot serves the park.

Kings Island opens for preview weekends in early April and officially opens on Memorial Day. Thereafter, the park is open daily through Labor Day. It continues to operate on weekends until mid-October. After Labor Day the park is occasionally sold out to private parties and closed to the public for the day.

The 300-room Kings Island Inn, located on a 16-acre site just north and across from the theme park, has convention and meeting rooms and is open all year. Motels in the vicinity of Kings Island provide 1,000 rooms within 10 minutes of the park. The

3-11 Kings Island at night becomes a different attraction from that during the day.

campground has 300 sites and is located on 10 acres 1 mile from the theme park. It is also open all year.

On the west side of Interstate-71, the Jack Nicklaus Golf Center occupies 400 acres with two championship golf courses, a clubhouse, pro shop, and tennis stadium. The facility features both professional golf and tennis events during the summer.

The final component of the project is a residential community development of detached condominium houses, townhouses, and homes located near the golf center.

Project Development

Kings Island's short- and long-term strategy is to continue to add new family-oriented attractions which are both entertaining and educational to the theme park and peripheral area. For example, in 1977 a new amphitheater, a major ride, and a games building were added to the complex. The College Football Hall of Fame was opened in 1978, and a new coaster as well as live shows were introduced in 1979, thus providing continual incentives for former visitors to return each year to Kings Island while expanding its market appeal to new visitors. Taft is presently considering the development of several new attractions including a conference center, sports complex, restaurants, and a thematic shopping center.

Taft Broadcasting employs an in-house development team skilled in all phases of land development. The planning, design, and engineering of each theme park project is coordinated by Taft within a management structure that is efficient and experienced. The company is building a new park near Toronto, Canada.

Some 290 full-time, year-round employees manage the Kings Island operation. During the summer months approximately 2,000 young people are employed as seasonal staff. Managing the seasonal staff tends to be a problem because of the high turnover

3-12 A tunnel was added to give a new dimension to this roller coaster.

3-13 Adventurous rides are the mainstay of Kings Island's business.

rates typically associated with temporary positions. New construction and major repairs are done during the winter months when the park is closed.

Because Taft Broadcasting is oriented toward marketing and promotion, Kings Island has an aggressive marketing program. The basic strategy has two goals to achieve:

- To maintain a constant program of advertising, promotion, and public relations support in the park's core marketing area; and
- To add new markets each year based on the greatest growth potential.

While the park concentrates most of its advertising in television,all forms of the media are used, including radio, outdoor signage, direct mail, newspapers, magazines, and brochures. Promotion techniques using celebrities are highly effective.

The marketing program involves advertising, group sales, market research, public relations, and sales promotion. Kings Island is associated with numerous major corporations in diverse promotional programs. Its joint venture arrangements with Jack Nicklaus and the Football Foundation have been highly successful. Both the Golf Center and the College Football Hall of Fame have expanded the market appeal of the park significantly.

The primary market is within a 150-mile radius of Kings Island and is the major focus of advertising. In 1978, almost 80 percent of the visitors came from this area, and in 1979, the percentage was even higher. This trend reflects the increasing cost of gasoline and changing travel patterns.

Although the market extends 250 miles from the facility, only 7.4 percent of the park's visitors come from beyond this distance, and studies show this figure should decline in the future. The total number of visitors in 1979 was 2,747,209—with most of them being from young families. The statistics show that 94 percent of the visitors are under 50 years of age, and 76 percent are less than 35 years of age. In addition, patrons tend to have above-average household incomes, and the adults have achieved relatively high levels of education.

A significant effort is being made to promote group rentals of the park. This use of the park has proven highly successful in the past, with many groups returning each year.

Experience Gained

- Facilities are developed to accommodate rapid turnover and high volumes. Thus, passive recreational experiences are emphasized rather than rides and activities requiring active participation.

3-15 Golf tournaments help attract attention to Kings Island. The Ladies Professional Golf Association Championship traditionally is held there each June.

- New attractions are needed each year as well as new rides during the first 5 years of operation, depending on the availability of land and investment capital. After 5 years, attractions were added in the form of new shows due to the escalating development costs for new rides each year.
- Even though residential development has proven to be compatible with theme park operation, Taft does not expect to continue that small part of its operation.

3-14 An aerial view of Kings Island. Larger rides needing substantial space can make use of sloping terrain less suitable for intensive pedestrian or parking use.

- Having an in-house experienced development team is crucial. Taft maintains control through all phases of development, thus making the process efficient and profitable and the product of high quality.
- The goal behind the marketing strategy is to change the image of Kings Island from that of a day trip to that of a destination where a visitor stays several days.
- Adults indicate that the physical cleanliness of the facilities is Kings Island's main attribute.
- A significant factor was the initial land acquisition. Taft purchased enough land so that more than half of it could be held for future development. In this way, Taft could control development in the area as well as benefit from escalating property values resulting from the success of Kings Island.
- The undeveloped land is leased as farmland so that Taft not only receives rentals but also a reduction in property taxes because the land is under a farmland use value taxation program.

PROJECT DATA—KINGS ISLAND

Land Use Information:

Component	Acres
Theme Park	215
Animal Safari Wildlife Preserve	100
Theme Park Parking Lot	150
Kings Island Inn Motel	16
Campground	10
College Football Hall of Fame	10
Jack Nicklaus Golf Center	400

Economic Information:

Original Development Budget for Theme Park (1972)

Major Categories	Cost
Preopening	$2,300,000
Fees and Overhead	2,900,000
Underground	2,201,000
Landscape	1,368,500
Paving and Walks	2,078,500
Major Buildings	3,535,500
Rides	8,035,500
Food and Refreshment	2,563,000
Merchandise and Games	1,743,000
Live Shows	494,000
Other	1,424,000
	28,643,000
Additional Items	2,369,000
Total	$31,012,000

Development Investment for Theme Park

Year	Investment
1972	$35,000,000*
1973	$5,247,000
1974	$5,542,000**
1975	$4,712,000
1976	$2,630,000
1977	$4,414,000
1978	$3,455,000
1979	$6,250,000
Total	$63,050,000

*Includes land value.
**Includes $4,210,000 cost of wildlife preserve.

Operations Information 1979

Operating Season: Memorial Day to Labor Day, 9:00 A.M. to 11:00 P.M.; April/May and September/October Weekends, 9:00 A.M. to 8:00 P.M.

Annual Attendance: 2,748,000

Employment: Permanent, 290; Temporary, 2,000

Ticket Price: $9.50, Single Admission

Developer:

Taft Broadcasting Company
Amusement Park Group
1718 Young Street
Cincinnati, Ohio 45210

Architecture:

Darrell Daniel Associates
John Grier
5225 Creek Road
Cincinnati, Ohio 45243

Operating Performance

Fiscal Year Ended	3/31/73	3/31/74	3/31/75	3/31/76	3/31/77	3/31/78	3/31/79	3/31/80
Operating Season	1972	1973	1974	1975	1976	1977	1978	1979
Attendance (Thousands)	2.012	2.382	2.574	2.490	2.601	2.580	2.622	2.748
Per Capita Spending	$8.47	$9.25	$10.82	$11.56	$12.33	$13.66	$14.97	$16.37
Net Revenues (Thousands)	$17.349	$22.346	$28.035	$28.070	$30.892	$33.873	$37.592	$43.449

Engineering:

Cliff Schulte
5225 Creek Road
Cincinnati, Ohio 45242

Curt Summers
7800 Laurel Avenue
Cincinnati, Ohio 45243

The Old Country, Virginia

The Old Country is one of a number of Busch Gardens theme parks under development by Anheuser-Busch, Inc. It reflects an evolution in corporate thinking concerning this development type and was the first Busch Gardens location designated from the beginning as a site for a family entertainment center. The 365-acre site is large enough to accommodate future projected growth, and the park itself was carefully laid out to provide for expansion in a phased development program. An earlier facility, adjacent to the company's Tampa breweries, has evolved incrementally in response to market demand and was not part of the original development program. Anheuser-Busch's involvement in the entertainment business derived from the Anheuser-Busch Hospitality Center in its St. Louis Brewery and its St. Louis County estate, Grant's Farm, which is open to the public. The rationale for developing theme parks was twofold: first, to promote sales of company products and enhance their national reputation; second,to incorporate diversification into areas holding the potential of long-term profitability.

The Old Country was developed concurrently with the brewery. Project conception and design took 2 years beginning in April 1971. Construction was initiated in mid-1973 and the park opened in May 1975. During its first operating season, attendance was 1,587,000, or 16.4 percent more than the 1.26 million persons originally projected. During the 1979 operating season, attendance approached 2 million. Acceptance of the project has been sufficient to justify three major expansions since the park's opening.

The Site

In 1969, Anheuser-Busch purchased 3,600 acres just east of Williamsburg, Virginia, from the Colonial Williamsburg Foundation and several other landowners. The property is bounded on the east and west by additional holdings of the foundation, including Carter's Grove Plantation. On the north and south, the property is bounded by U.S. Route 60 and the James River, which is several miles wide at that point. The site is heavily wooded, cut by steep ravines, and contains several archaeological sites associated with colonial era development in the Virginia tidewater area.

Among the reasons Colonial Williamsburg made the property available was to expand the tax base of largely rural James City County. The conveyance was made with a number of provisions as safeguards, including the provision that a parklike roadway be built in the future, linking Colonial Williamsburg with Carter's Grove, and a requirement that the master

3-16 A drawbridge gateway leads into a Norman-inspired village at The Old Country. The winding streets are lined with shops and medieval theme attractions.

plan be approved by a review committee consisting of three persons of national prominence in land use planning—one appointed by Colonial Williamsburg, one by Anheuser-Busch, and the third by both Colonial Williamsburg and Anheuser-Busch.

The company acquired the site as the location of a brewery to serve the southeastern U.S. market, but also wanted enough land to permit the adjacent development of a variety of compatible uses, including a Busch Gardens.

Concept Planning

The development concept sought to complement the historic character of the Williamsburg area by focusing upon the European antecedents of the original settlers and supplementing Colonial Williamsburg as a tourist attraction. The project designers also sought to create a theme park reflecting the corporate identification of the developer with wildlife preservation and environmental conservation. Active amusements such as rides and games are balanced with more passively oriented amenities such as paths through the wooded terrain, wildlife observation points, theatricals, and animal shows. The park creates a European atmosphere through its architectural design, food service, merchandise, and entertainments reminiscent of "the old country."

The development is organized into 17th century English, Scottish, French, Italian, and German Villages—high-intensity nodes of activity—separated by wooded open space and the arms of a 48-acre lake.

Each village contains a variety of shops, entertainments, theaters, rides, and restaurants combined in an irregular streetscape of clustered buildings, varied setbacks, and irregular rooflines suggestive of the intimate scales and dimensions of European architecture. Each has a bell tower, fountain, or other visual amenity as a central focus. These high-intensity "islands" are the scene of crowded activities which sustain an atmosphere of fun and enjoyment. The open spaces between villages present a quiet contrast to the bustle of the activity areas.Wildlife runs free, and benches and curb seating are provided along curving pathways. The overall effect of being removed from the everyday world in these areas is heightened by the heavily wooded and irregular terrain which creates a variety of intricate vistas and panoramas. Through skillful design and coordination within the landscape, spatial relationships among villages are difficult to ascertain, and the visitor is apt to be unaware of previously viewed activities only a few hundred feet away.

The modular design permits orderly and incremental expansion of the park. The first major expansion was the Oktoberfest, which was added to the German Village for the 1976 season, featuring a 1,200-seat, Munich-style hall. The addition of a "thriller" coaster ride in 1978 was another major development. In 1980, the Village of Italy opened, a $6 million development simulating an Italian hillside village on a 9-acre site in the park. A 300-foot bridge which spans the park's Rhine River leads visitors from the Oktoberfest into a tiered plaza in the Italian Village.

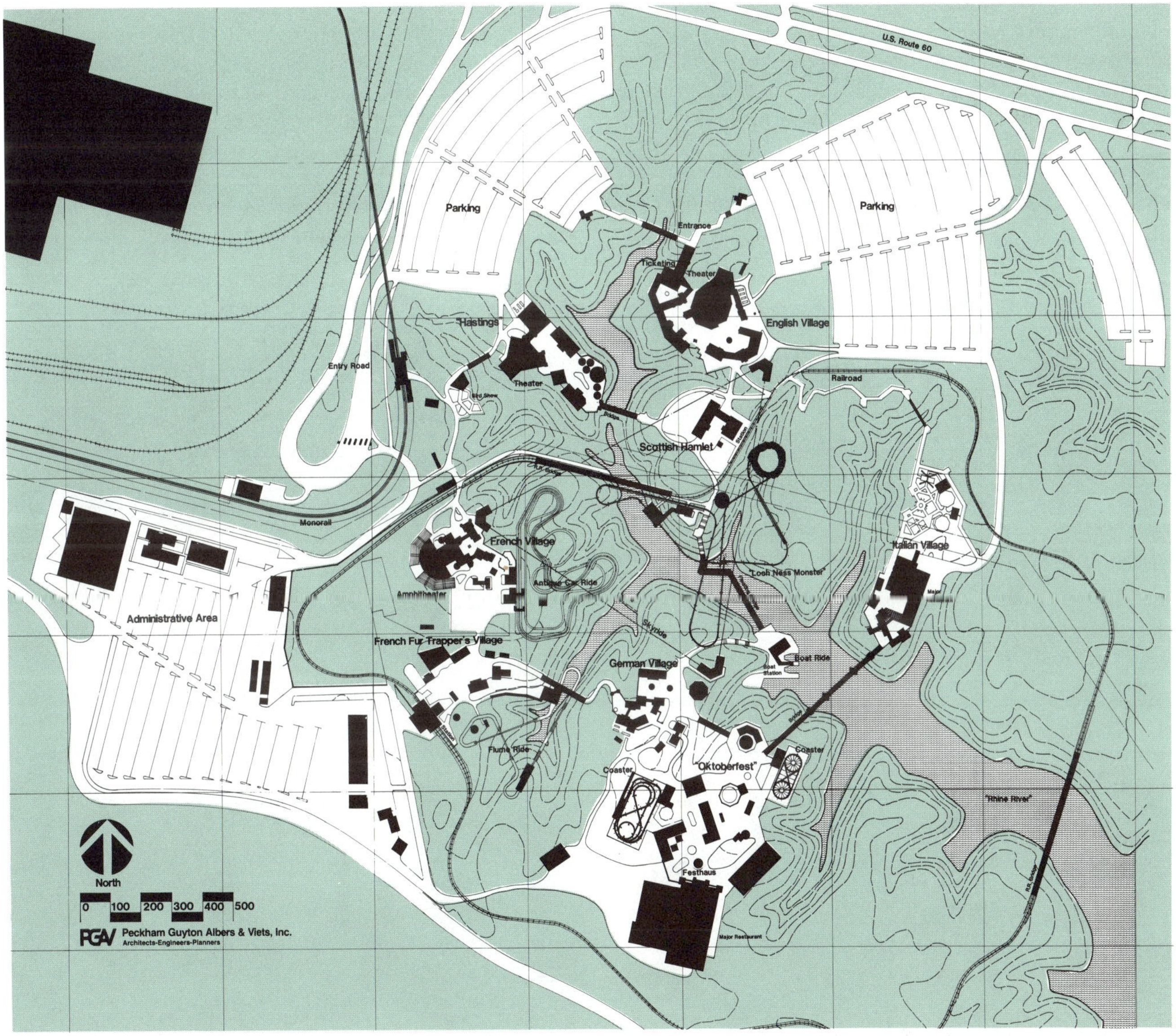

3-17 Site plan of the 365-acre Old Country, adjacent to the Anheuser-Busch brewery. The project's success has justified three expansions since opening in 1975.

In addition to a system of pedestrian pathways, there are three modes of transportation—a monorail which runs from the brewery hospitality center to the edge of the park, 2.5 miles of European gauge railroad which serves both transportation and entertainment functions, and a ski lift cable car system with stations at each village. In addition, there is a "Rhine River Cruise" on the lake. Parking for 5,800 vehicles has been provided adjacent to U.S. Route 60, with trains to transport visitors to the park from the farthest lots. Peak capacity of the park is approximately 25,000 persons per day, with ultimate expansion projected to raise that figure to 30,000.

Engineering and Architecture

Because of its unique character, The Old Country required pragmatic and imaginative approaches to engineering and architectural design. This challenge was compounded by the irregular terrain having some slopes of more than 20 percent and ravines as deep as 90 feet. The railroad was designed from scratch including the rolling stock and two trestles spanning a ravine which was dammed up to form the "Rhine River." Topographic and soil conditions required special footings for village buildings and other structures. Preservation of natural settings wherever possible was a primary part of the design, which meant limiting construction operations to areas slated for intense activity and endeavoring to preserve specimen vegetation within the village areas.

The project was virtually custom designed in its entirety, from village streetscapes to light fixtures. Architectural styles and building groups are meant to be representative of their European counterparts, but not necessarily exact replicas. The 1,000-seat Globe Theater, for example, is more than twice the size of the Shakespearean original. On the other hand, the bridge connecting "France" and "Germany" duplicates an original found in Schwaebish Hall, Germany. The objective was to create perceptions of authentic European character. Building materials included wood, brick, and stucco for walls; slate, cedar shakes, and tile for roofs; and stain glass and lead panes for windows. Special precast concrete was used to create the appearance of rubble and cut stone. These materials form facades for the building groups, all of which were constructed of concrete block. Decorations and interior furnishings are a combination of genuine items and modern replicas.

3-18 Steam locomotive replicas provide visitors with close-up views of animals and nature, which have been carefully integrated with the European theme attractions.

Operation

A critical part of the park operation is to incorporate changes regularly, including both physical expansions or modifications, and programming changes. In this way, a theme park can evolve over time in line with changes in public taste and also draw patrons back for repeated visits.

Experience Gained

- For its first year, The Old Country operated on a somewhat experimental basis while management gained a feel for the nature of the market and the relative popularity of various components of the theme park. Refinements which have been incorporated include more food service facilities and rides.
- The physical design has been quite successful although specific problems have been identified. Visitors tend to bunch up in the high-intensity village areas; therefore, additional activities have been located adjacent to these areas in order to distribute attendees more broadly.
- Training and managing the large temporary staff is the major management responsibility in operating a theme park.
- The number of toilets required for a development accommodating as many as 25,000 persons daily was seriously underestimated. This deficiency was remedied by adding new restrooms and expanding those which were provided at the beginning of the 1975 season.

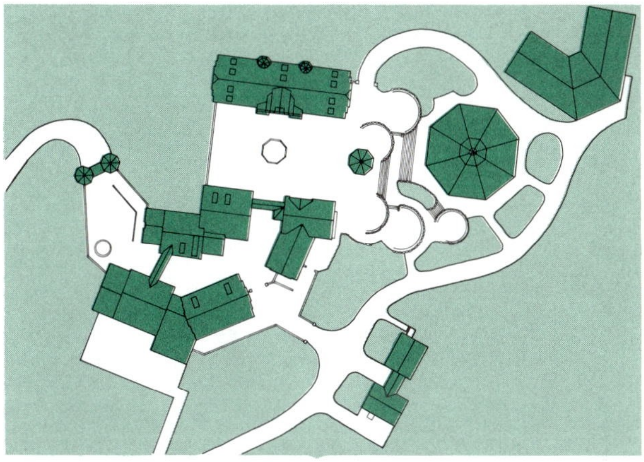

3-19 The original German Village site plan.

PROJECT DATA—THE OLD COUNTRY

Land Use Plan:

The Old Country/Busch Gardens:	Acres	Percent
Theme Development Area	170.5	46.7
Service Area	20.7	5.7
Entrance and Parking (5,800 spaces)	48.0	13.2
Water Area	47.6	13.0
Open Area	78.2	21.4
Total	365.0	100.0

Operational Information 1980:

Operating Season: Memorial Day to Labor Day, 10:00 A.M. to 10:00 P.M.; April/May and September/October Weekends, 10:00 A.M. to 7:00 P.M.
Attendance: 2,140,000
Employment: Permanent, 54; Temporary, 2,200
Ticket Price:[1] $9.95, Single Admission
Theme Park Facilities: Food Service (24), Amusements (7),[2] Rides (25),[3] Shops (29), Theaters (8), Animal Facilities (3), Restrooms (10), Other (10).[4]

Economic Information:

Project Cost-Phase I (1975)	$30,000,000
Oktoberfest Addition (1976)	$11,000,000
Loch Ness Monster Coaster Ride (1978)	$ 4,000,000
Italian Village (1980)	$ 6,000,000
Total	$51,000,000

Developer:

Busch Entertainment Corporation
12555 Manchester Road
St. Louis, Missouri 63131

Architecture/Planning/Engineering:

Peckham Guyton Albers and Viets, Inc.
522 Olive Street
St. Louis, Missouri 63101

Notes

[1]Entitles purchaser to view spectator amusements and take all rides without additional charge. Children 2 years and under, free.
[2]Includes arcades, shooting galleries, fun house.
[3]Includes train stations, skyride stations, flume ride, miniature car ride, roller coaster, merry-go-round, river cruise, catapult ride.
[4]Includes entrance facilities, stroller rentals, bank, picnic areas, etc.

3-20 Attractively placed food services, such as this one located behind a pool at Walt Disney World's River Country, are profitable adjuncts to aquatic facilities.

3-21 Maintaining cleanliness is fundamental to any park operation.

Wet 'n Wild, Orlando, Florida

Aquatic Parks: General Description

In recent years, small-scale specialty theme parks have become popular recreational attractions, partly because of the saturation of major parks and as a lower investment alternative. One successful form of this type of theme development is a facility totally dedicated to water activities. As is the case with many theme park innovations, the Walt Disney organization helped originate the aquatic trend with its highly successful $6 million River Country at Disneyworld.

New water-oriented attractions have been built in several states. Most of the projects include either pools with wave machines or water slides, both popular for the excitement they add to water activity. Wave machines have existed for some years in Europe where over 100 are in operation, including indoor pools. In the United States, wave pools have been popular enough to be included as self-supporting public recreational facilities. The water slide concept began in Gatlinburg, Tennessee, in the early 1970s. At present, dozens of slides are operating in the nation, most of them concentrated in the sunbelt states. A typical four-flume water slide layout could be developed in 1979 for $200,000 to $300,000, with an hourly capacity of about 200 riders and an anticipated annual attendance of 50,000 or more at $2.50 to $3 per hour for each rider.[2]

The true aquatic park with a variety of attractions generally offers good value for the patron fee. Some single-facility operations such as a lone water slide have failed because of the lack of attractions or the poor quality of the facility. The multifaceted aquatic park, with alternative attractions and concessions, provides an incentive for frequent and prolonged attendance.

Project Description

Located in Orlando, Florida, Wet 'n Wild is a specialty park offering a variety of water-oriented activities. Conceived by George Millay of Leisure Marine Corporation, Wet 'n Wild has four body flumes, a 300-foot "Kamikaze" slide, a large pool with a wave machine that creates 3- to 4-foot waves, a children's play area with water squirters and sprays, a pool with a rope trolley, a lake with a beach, and boat rentals.

Project Development

Wet 'n Wild is built on 15-acres amid hotels along International Drive between Orlando and Dis-

[2] Data are drawn from a 1980 unpublished report by Economic Research Associates in Los Angeles.

3-22 Wet 'n Wild benefits from the huge tourist traffic focusing on nearby Walt Disney World as well as from repeat visits from local Orlando patrons.

neyworld. Construction was completed in 8 months and the project opened in March 1977. The total investment was approximately $3.5 million.

Wet 'n Wild is essentially a giant water playground with facilities accommodating both children and adults. Each attraction has been given a name to establish its identity within the complex.

Surf Lagoon is a 570,000-gallon pool ranging in depth from 8 feet to 2 inches and offering more than 17,000 square feet of water surface and giant man-made waves. Cresting at 4 feet in the deep end of the pool, the waves become more docile in the shallow area. Astroturf surrounds the perimeter of the pool providing comfort for sunbathers.

The White Water Slideway is a thrill ride consisting of four body flumes. Dropping from an elevation of three-and-one-half stories, a rider zooms down the straightaway, then slides through the turns of a 400-foot-long flume. Carried by the rush of 2,000 gallons of water per minute, the rider eventually is dunked into the 20,000-gallon pool at the bottom of the flumes.

The Canadian Water Caper is an aquatic playground. Over an acre in size, this attraction features innovative water games that are situated in and around pools ranging from 12 inches to 18 inches in depth. The games are geared for young children with a shaded observation area close by.

Another attraction is the Puddle Jumper Pool. Designed primarily for teenagers, the pool, which is 80 feet in diameter, has several features such as a trolley cable and a diving platform. The pool contains more than 160,000 gallons of water.

Activity also centers around a lake where sailboats and paddleboats are available for rent. A white sand beach provides an area for volleyball, frisbee, and sunbathing. Wet 'n Wild's professional lifeguards are on duty throughout the park.

In the park's third season, a 65-foot-high, $300,000 Kamikaze water slide was added. This popular new attraction also increased the park's visibility from the street. Two more water slides with themes were added in 1981, part of a continuing program of expansion and recreation.

Although water activities dominate the park, other facilities are important to the project. These include a gift shop, restaurant, snack bars, and tree-shaded rest areas.

Marketing/Operation

Location cannot be overestimated as a factor in Wet 'n Wild's success. Disneyworld focused attention on central Florida as a tourist destination, and smaller attractions like Wet 'n Wild have benefited from the exposure. A ready market is provided by tourists who have queued up for hours at nearby Disneyworld and Sea World attractions and are then ready to spend time and money cooling down at Wet 'n Wild. It has attracted group tour business and local patrons are important as well. Thousands of hotel and motel rooms in the immediate vicinity of Wet 'n Wild complement its location at the intersection of major highways and afford the project excellent market access.

The 1980 entry price was $6 for adults and $4.50 for children between the ages of 3 and 12 years. Wet 'n Wild can accommodate 6,000 visitors per day with the average visitor staying approximately 5 hours. Market analysis projects that Wet 'n Wild can anticipate at least 600,000 visitors annually and given an initial breakeven requirement of 300,000 visitors per year, the financial future of the project appears secure.

Experience Gained

- Providing an active recreational experience to people of all ages can be highly marketable.
- In particular, a water-oriented theme has wide-ranging appeal.
- Smaller-scale theme development should be consistent with theme concept, market demand, and investment risk.
- Location of a theme park near a major large-scale tourist destination is highly desirable.
- New attractions, facilities, and periodic remodeling help to bring patrons back for repeated visits.

3-23 A six-story-tall water slide was added to Wet 'n Wild in 1979. Continued growth in attendance and the need to add new attractions led to a $2 million expansion in 1981, including a water roller coaster and a corkscrew/tunnel water slide.

4.
Commercial Recreation

A study of recreational development would not be complete without a section on commercial recreation—the private sector's response to urban and suburban leisure demand. Commercial recreational projects are of two basic types: participatory projects and spectator projects. Participatory recreational facilities include skating rinks, racquet sport clubs, miniature and full golf courses, bowling centers, and others in which patrons are actively involved. Spectator entertainment projects such as movie and dinner theaters, sports arenas, and racetracks provide passive recreation.

Projects involving participatory recreation have proliferated in recent years in response to the growing demand for physical fitness and active sports. The retail sales of sporting goods and equipment in 1980 approached over $20 billion according to manufacturers' estimates.[1] Projects focusing on active recreation combine the attractions of physical exercise and competition with entertainment and sociability.

Attendances at spectator sports and cultural events have been continually increasing; it is estimated that well over 250 million visitors spent over $2 billion at major sports facilities in 1980. Although spectator projects are designed for passive entertainment, the audience in the stands can actively participate in a number of ways. Sociologists have attributed the popularity of spectator and participatory sports to man's desire to return to primitive sensations. Discussing spectators, Andrea Fontana, professor of sociology at the University of Nevada, wrote:

> It would seem that the modern wonders of the technological era have somehow failed society as the American Dream. People become bored and jaded in their sterilized, plasticized, mechanized, soundproofed houses. Their lives have become strictly organized by charts, routines, and clocks, their individuality has been stunted by the prescriptions and proscriptions of their job descriptions, and their upward mobility has been limited by an increasingly complex network of bureaucratic requirements.
>
> They become fans. In the jungle of anonymity afforded them by the other forty-thousand faces, they let loose. If the home team wins or their Sunday hero performs superbly, they can vicariously identify with him; it is a return to mimicry in which the fan takes on the identity of the team or the player and can finally be a winner, although only through simulation.[2]

---

[1] This information was reported in September 1980 by the Sporting Goods Manufacturers Association, 200 Castlewood Road, North Palm Beach, Florida 33408.

[2] Andrea Fontana, "Over the Edge," *Urban Life*, Vol. 7, No. 2 (July 1978), p. 225.

4-1 Professional baseball is a prominent example of a spectator sport in the United States and Canada, with the American and National Leagues drawing over 43 million persons in 1980.

Locational Characteristics

As with all types of real estate ventures, location is essential in achieving success. The locational characteristics of commercial recreational projects will depend on the market that is to be served. Some projects focus on a particular age group or income level; thus, their locations are in part determined by the locations of their consumers. For most recreational projects, proximity to the target market is considered essential; primary users should be within a radius of 15 minutes travel time from the site. In urban areas, sites offering access to public transportation are preferable while in suburban locales sites with highway or freeway exposure and adequate parking are sought. Many recreational projects appeal to such a small percentage of the general community that locations in highly populated areas are necessary to be sure of adequate patronage. Preliminary to any site selection, a thorough market study should be made to determine the target market and the optimal location.

Special Issues

Risks

Commercial recreation of any type is a highly competitive and risky business. Many issues contribute to its success or failure: the economic cycle, the trends in consumer demand, the timing and judgment of the developer, the management of the facility, and the competition with other recreational projects. In general, commercial recreation is risky because it is a cash-oriented business which is both capital- and management-intensive.

4-2 Roller skating is an example of an active form of recreation, particularly popular among younger persons.

4-3 Commercial recreational operations can be freestanding or grouped with other facilities that generate traffic, such as a shopping center.

The following discussion of the various commercial recreational projects points out the constantly changing economic climate for a particular kind of recreation. The economic cycles present in all business ventures are usually telescoped into a much shorter time frame in commercial recreation. Thus, the entire spectrum from boom to bust can be observed at any time. Commercial projects can invent, stimulate, or follow trends in consumer demand, but it is at that point in the cycle when an investment is made which will determine the potential for return. The risk, of course, is in deciding what the trends are, how long the cycle will last, and whether a new idea will be a trend setter or a disaster.

The Business Cycle

Like other economic enterprises, commercial recreational developments have a common pattern of overbuilding and shake-out. Someone has a new idea and develops it—whether it be a trampoline park, water slide, or Disneyland. If it appears to be profitable, others try to duplicate it and repeat the success. Copies of the original spring up everywhere, from right next door to across the country.

As the idea succeeds, consumer demand grows. A restricted number of projects will result in high prices and the early developers can earn a windfall profit while the concept is still a fad. (During the early stages, however, the developers must also cover the high costs of promoting and introducing the new facility to the public.) If and when the novelty wears off, poor replicas may sour the experience for the public and demand may diminish. It may be of major or minor proportions and can shut down the entire industry, or merely eliminate the weakest businesses. As growth slows, the industry changes from an entrepreneurial style of management to one which is more conservative and sophisticated.

If the industry survives the period of being a mere fad, it matures, depending a great deal on returning customers. Therefore, it must improve and enhance the experience for patrons. During this period, others can still compete by adding frills or "professionalism" to the enterprise, but the quick profits are no longer available. Increased costs, overhead, and advertising allow a more modest return to the developer. Profits for the first developers are also reduced as the competitive pressures force reinvestment and upgrading of the facilities. Eventually, the industry stabilizes at a point where the returns are similar to those of other economic ventures, and the incentive others might have to enter the business is dampened.

This pattern seems to be especially prevalent in commercial recreational developments because they are inherently faddish, catering to the imagination and fantasies of the public. Recreation deals with fantasy, image, and fads—not what is commonly seen on a balance sheet.

Conservative Forecasting

Because of the risks involved, commercial recreational projects must be approached cautiously and financial projections must be conservative. More often than not, however, recreational centers are conceived by daring entrepreneurs who are willing to take large risks in order to reap large returns. This contradiction can produce both great wealth and, in many cases, great debt. Some observers characterize the entrepreneurs of recreational investments as egotistical and thus prone to misjudgments. The temptation is strong to be overly optimistic toward one's own idea and to ignore the possible risks. For the developer who is cautious, the financial evaluation of an investment in a recreational project should include an estimate of the life of the project to determine if the investment can be recouped should the market shift.

Lenders, who avoid risks, often are wary of loans to single-use recreational projects. They look for strong proposals with demonstrated value which will compare favorably with standards for conventional loans. They prefer projects having a number of profit centers and the potential for alternative uses since a variety of uses helps level out total revenues during cyclical changes in the industry.

4-4 Skateboard parks flourished in the late 1970s, only to see interest fall off again in a very short time. (Photograph by Bill Golding, courtesy of *Action Now* magazine.)

4-5 Recreational centers with multiple facilities are less vulnerable to market fluctuations than single-use operations. Urban-oriented recreational development often can be located on a variety of sites which would be marginal for other land uses.

Management

Once a project is established, maintaining it successfully and profitably will depend a great deal on the management. Establishing controls on the cash operations, personnel management, physical maintenance, promotion, and public relations is key to management's responsibility. A recurring theme in discussions with developers of all types of recreational projects is the need for a process involving personalized service, program development, and concern for the public. The process must be unceasing. Developers in any project cannot merely open the door, then sit back and count the money. Those projects which have been initiated expressly to capture a projected financial return and are not mindful of the consumers are not successful in the long run.

4-6 Provision for management, the key to effective and efficient operations, is essential at the earliest stages of development.

Competition

As part of the market survey that should be a prerequisite to any recreational development, a developer must identify the competition. With commercial projects, the scope of the competition goes far beyond the other centers in the area offering the same services. A commercial recreational project competes for every leisure dollar with a whole range of alternatives. The competition includes home entertainment involving television, stereos, and books, and privately owned outdoor recreational equipment such as boats, swimming pools, and tennis courts.

Public facilities also compete with commercial recreational projects. The price of recreational services at public facilities will affect the fees which can be charged at similar privately owned projects. A private enterprise may have to justify its higher fees by offering greater convenience and more luxurious surroundings and services than a public facility.

Commercial recreational projects compete with all other for-profit recreational projects as well. For example, miniature golf competes with roller rinks and bowling alleys. Thus, it is important to define and target the market for a particular facility. It may be important to offer instruction to increase the number of people interested in an activity. As stated earlier, recreational developers strive to encourage repeat business and to nurture a regular consumer base.

For some participatory projects, establishing a consumer base might involve joining a national organization to keep abreast of current practices and expand management expertise. Associations work to professionalize the sport they represent, developing tours for professional players and tournaments for prize money. Professionalism adds incentive and excitement to amateur play. Young players can hope to qualify as pros, and older enthusiasts have a standard by which to judge their own play.

Another way to build patronage at a commercial project is by developing leagues and encouraging local organizations, school teams, or clubs to use the facility. The operator of a golf practice range who introduces young people to the sport will help develop an ongoing market for his facility. Sports drawing primarily children and teenagers could also be made attractive to adults and thus expand the market.

Because a visitor to a recreational project often goes there on impulse, facilities must always be inviting and highly visible in their locations and through promotion. A rule frequently cited in planning recreational facilities is:

"availability + accessibility = popularity."[3]

Flexibility is another element that should be added to that equation for long-term success. Developers must always be aware of the trends in public demand for recreation. They must understand and adapt to new ideas. Commercial recreation is a constantly changing and evolving industry. Managing those changes so that they are profitable is the primary challenge of such projects.

4-7 League play—long a primary source of revenue for bowling centers—and other special promotional activities are valuable marketing devices.

Development Types: Facts and Strategies

Some typical types of commercial recreational development are described in the following pages. This information on randomly selected but popular types of commercial developments is provided to characterize the issues and conditions relevant to the general area of recreational development. The data pertinent to these reports were drawn from a variety of industry sources and have been referenced where convenient. Sample pro forma data have been included for a bowling center, roller skating rink, and racquetball club to show the type of expenses to evaluate in planning such commercial operations. Persons considering developing one of these project types are advised to consult with an experienced industry analyst when studying specific business opportunities.

[3] C. Ray Smith, *The American Endless Weekend* (Washington: American Institute of Architects, 1973), p. 29.

Bowling

Bowling reportedly is the single most popular indoor sport in the United States with over 72 million participants in 1980.[4] In the early bowling alleys the pins were set by hand, but the game became automated in the 1950s and its popularity soared. In the 1960s, the prospect of high financial return and easy credit terms for equipment from manufacturers led to considerable overbuilding. The oversupply caused a shake-out which led to the consolidation of the industry and little further growth. From 1972 to 1976, however, a 12.2 percent growth in the amount of bowling was reported, which may indicate a renewed growth trend.[5]

Bowling is a relatively inexpensive form of recreation, allowing it to succeed even during periods of recession. In 1980, a game typically cost from $1 to $1.35. Early bowling centers were rough and noisy compared to the modern centers that are now popular. New bowling centers are larger with better equipment; they are carpeted for sound control and offer other services and more attractive landscaping.

Market Factors

Bowling's popularity is widespread; 35 percent of all families have at least one bowler and 19 percent of the national population bowl regularly. Unlike many participatory sports, bowling is primarily an adult activity. Eighty-six percent of the players are between the ages of 18 and 49. This is mainly due to organized league play with 72 to 80 percent of bowling done in leagues, according to the Bowling Proprietors' Association of America.[6] Bowling is equally popular with men and women. There are coed leagues as well as separate ones for men and women, and frequently centers have daytime leagues for women and offer baby-sitting for their children.

Although bowling has been known as a blue-collar activity, studies show that participation increases with income levels in spite of the fact that those with higher incomes have more alternatives open to them.

A bowling center should be located within a 15- to 20-minute drive from the identified trade area. Because the site should have good access and visibility, locations in shopping centers, commercial districts, or on a freeway are recommended. Bowling continues to have a strong neighborhood orientation although there are also work-related leagues. Industrial parks are generally unsuccessful locations for bowling. Land costs vary, but in 1979, they typically ranged from $2 to $5 per square foot.

[4] These data were reported on October 20, 1980, by the Brunswick Corporation, One Brunswick Plaza, Skokie, Illinois 60077.

[5] See Ronald Ames, "Appraisal and Feasibility Analysis of Bowling Centers," *The Real Estate Appraiser* (April 1978), pp. 15–18.

[6] For further information, contact Bowling Proprietors' Association of America, Box 5802, Arlington, Texas 76011; and the National Bowling Council, 1660 K Street, N.W., Suite 611, Washington, D.C. 20006.

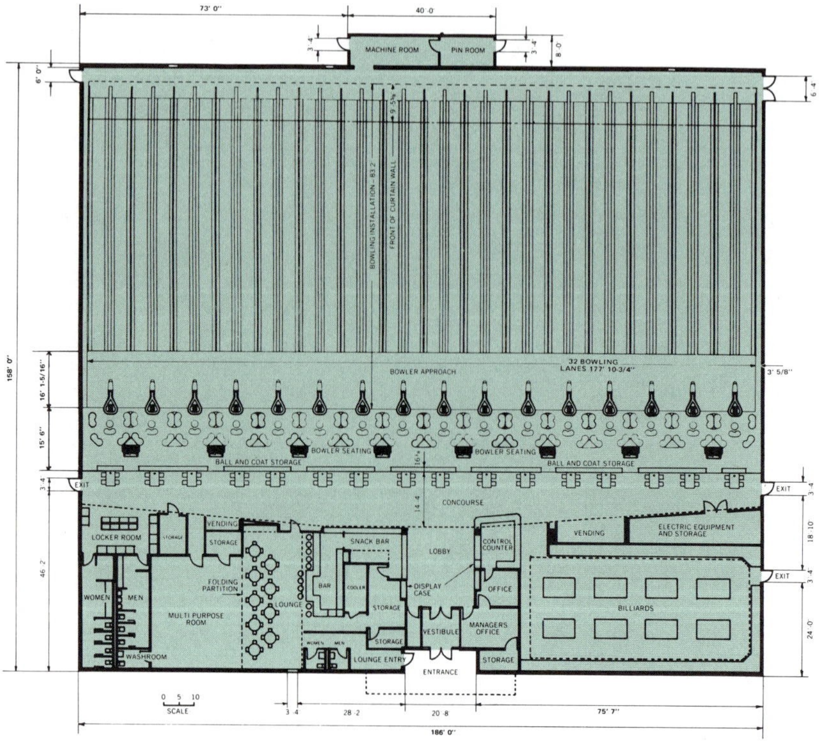

4-8 Typical 32-lane bowling center.

Development

Bowling centers can have from 12 to 72 lanes but newly constructed centers most often have at least 32 lanes. Analysts suggest that centers can accommodate 100 to 110 league bowlers per week per lane, and that a local population of 800 to 2,000 per lane is required to support a center.

In addition to the lanes, modern centers include a restaurant, lounge, pro shop, nursery, game arcade, vending machines, rental shop, and office and maintenance rooms. For planning purposes, 1,000 square feet per lane could include everything. Parking for seven cars per lane is recommended, which would mean a 32-lane center would need about 3 acres of land.

Building costs ranged from $30 to $45 per square foot in 1980. The alleys, electric pin spotting and scoring equipment, and furnishings cost from $25,000 to $30,000 per lane. Equipment can be either leased or purchased from the major manufacturers. Electric games for an arcade are usually owned by an outside operator and the gross is split 50/50 with the center owner; thus, no initial cost is incurred for this equipment. The site development requirements for a bowling center are similar to those for shopping center developments. With land costs of $2 to $5 per square foot, the total development cost of a bowling center can run from $1 million to well over $5 million.

Along with the maintenance foreman, the key staff position in the management of a bowling center is that of the league coordinator. This person must negotiate league contracts and develop new leagues. In addition, a repair/maintenance crew is needed to keep the equipment in good working order, and the restaurant and retail counters must be staffed. Flexible staffing is necessary to deal with seasonal usage.

Bowling centers operate 7 days a week with long hours—9:00 A.M. to midnight on weekdays, and until 1:00 or 2:00 A.M. on weekends. The prime hours of play are scheduled for leagues in shifts—from 6:00 to 9:00 P.M. and from 9:00 P.M. to midnight, with daytime leagues scheduled from 9:00 A.M. to noon and from noon to 3 P.M. Industry sources estimate that 60 to 70 percent of the revenue comes from the prime evening hours.

Financing

A rough breakdown of the revenues of a bowling center shows that approximately 56 percent comes from bowling fees, 30 percent from food and drink, 3 percent from shoe rental, and 11 percent from a game arcade. The average breakeven point requires bowling 9,000 to 10,000 lines per lane per year. Better centers are reported to average 15,000 lines per lane per year. Controllable expenses are estimated to be 40 to 60 percent of the gross, with payroll expenditures accounting for approximately half of this percentage.

The return on investment for bowling centers varies from center to center, of course, but many centers average 12 to 15 percent depending on the management and the costs incurred. A point of caution made by an article in *Forbes* magazine in 1976 is still noteworthy, however. "The people raking in most of the $3 billion in bowling center revenues today are knowledgeable hands who had been in the business years before the first boom."[7]

Bowling centers are recognized real estate developments and usually can obtain loans equal to 65 percent of the mortgage value. Lenders look for sound project feasibility, long-life equipment, and a development concept that provides a number of profit centers.

[7]See "Striking It Rich—Again," *Forbes* (June 15, 1976), p. 68.

Pro Forma Statement for a 32-Lane Bowling Center (1980)

Development Costs	
Building (32,000 sq. ft. @ $32)	$1,024,000
Bowling Equipment ($25,000 per lane)	800,000
Site ($3 per sq. ft. for 3 acres)	390,000
Bar and Restaurant Equipment	160,000
	$2,374,000
Revenue	
Bowling (480,000 lines @ $1.10)	$528,000
Shoe Rental (5% of bowling)	26,000
Bar and Restaurant (55% of bowling)	291,000
Electric Games, Equipment Sales (20% of bowling)	105,000
	$950,000
Expenses (54.5% of sales)	
Payroll (24% of sales)	$228,000
Maintenance/Repairs (18% of sales)	171,000
Restaurant/Bar (40% of food and beverage sales)	118,000
	$517,000
Net Operating Income	$433,000
Return on Investment	18.2%

Roller Skating Rinks

In the 1970s, roller skating made a comeback. After its decline in the late 1950s, roller skating has been increasing steadily and over the last few years its popularity has become infectious. Photographs of celebrities roller skating can be seen in magazines and on record covers, rental skates are available in city parks, and people are even skating to work to save gas and time. Roller skating is inexpensive and good exercise while also providing entertainment. Its renewed popularity is also demonstrated by the fact that roller skating has become a competitive sport.

During its early decades, the roller skating rink passed through several phases—from its ballroom image in the 1920s, to the tough, embroiled, roller derby of the 1930s and 1940s, to the noisy, dusty, teenage hangout of the 1950s, with its incessant organ music. Today, "new concept" roller skating rinks have changed the negative image. Recently, disco has provided both the theme and the music, along with some pop music and "golden oldies." The rinks have incorporated such disco features as fancy lighting, sound systems, and plastic floors. The skates have also changed and now have polyethylene wheels which are quiet and smooth-rolling. Some have soft nylon shoes that resemble jogging shoes. Better management has made roller skating rinks cleaner, more attractive, and more colorful. The industry would like roller rinks to be attractive as family entertainment centers and has increased its promotion to draw new skaters.

Market Factors

In 1979, the Roller Skating Rink Operators Association (RSROA) estimated there were 21.5 million skaters in the United States. It is primarily a youth sport with 73 percent of its participants under 18, but it is becoming more popular with adults, particularly those in their late 20s and early 30s.

Roller skating is no longer thought of strictly as a lower-income sport. One-third of roller skate enthusiasts in this country live in the north central states and the sport is most popular in small- to medium-sized cities, according to the RSROA.[8]

Like bowling and racquetball, roller skating is a "location oriented" industry, which means the site for a roller rink must be located near the intended market although primary commercial locations are not necessary. A successful roller rink in most cases requires a metropolitan area of 50,000 to 75,000 people within a 3-mile radius and 100,000 people within a 5-mile radius with no other rinks competing to dilute the market.[9] A strict number count is not sufficient, however, since rinks can be successful in rural areas with 15,000 to 20,000 people if there is no competition and the rink is used by community and church groups. Wherever the market is located, it should have a large percentage of children in the 10- to 18-year-old age bracket.

Development

A roller rink requires a site of 1.5 to 2 acres. The parking requirements are generally one space per 200 square feet of building and even fewer spaces are needed if the rink does not cater heavily to adults. Many zoning codes require one space per 100 square feet for this general commercial building type but for roller rinks this requirement is excessive.[10]

Rinks are categorized according to size: small (under 11,000 square feet), medium (11,000 to 18,000 square feet), and large (over 18,000 square feet). Most new concept rinks are from 20,000 to 26,000 square feet with a skating surface of 12,000 to 16,000 square feet. Building space is usually divided between skating and service areas in a 60/40 or 50/50 ratio. The service area includes a lobby with box office, a skate rental area, snack bar, lockers, restrooms, and a lounge or area for socializing that overlooks the rink. New rink designs stress colorful, modern decor and surfaces which cost little to maintain. Many new rinks also have a game arcade, private party room, pro shop, sound and lighting control booth, and bandstand/stage area for live music. The RSROA recommends that the building entry be designed with easy access for loading and unloading cars.

To allow for the clear span needed, a pre-engineered metal building is generally used. The exterior surface can be faced with wood, brick, or stone. The skating surface is the most important part of the facility. Traditionally, maple hardwood flooring was used because of its durability and smoothness but it causes noise and becomes slippery without frequent powdering. It is the powder that gives the dusty appearance and poor air quality in some rinks. New floors are made of durable plastic. They are quieter, cleaner, and less expensive. A concrete base is covered with particle board which is then coated with layers of epoxy. The epoxy needs only regular washing and a new coating twice a year. It comes in colors and can be matched to the interior decor. The 1979 cost of the epoxy was 30 to 50 percent less than hardwood at $1.10 to $2 per square foot, with resurfacing costing about $200 per coat.

---

[8] Roller Skating Rink Operators Association of America (RSROA), 7700 A Street, Lincoln, Nebraska 68510.

[9] Philip Stukin, *Factors Influencing Roller Rink Development*, unpublished report (Los Angeles: Urban Projects, Inc., 1979).

[10] See "Investing in Roller Skating Rinks," *Mortgage and Real Estate Executives Report* (June 15, 1979), pp. 2–4.

Building costs in 1979 ranged from $15 to $35 per square foot and fixtures (including rental skates, food equipment, and sound system) ran $2 to $10 per square foot. Thus, a roller rink in 1979 cost from $250,000 to well over $1 million, excluding land costs.

Management of a roller rink has many responsibilities that are crucial to the success of the facility. Management should provide trained skaters to give lessons and to patrol the rink. Rink security also seems to be a concern of roller rink management. It is important that the family entertainment atmosphere be maintained to ensure repeat business. Lining one wall of the rink with mirrors will expand the space and help management keep an eye on the skaters. Carpeting the service areas cuts down the noise and, by extending the carpet up the walls, vandalism can be reduced. In some rinks a separate beginners' rink keeps the main rink open and moving.

Promotions are an important management responsibility—in order to attract new skaters and to sell off-peak hours. Special midweek events, private parties, and reduced admissions fees for community, church, and school groups are frequently used. In some eastern cities, rinks have liquor licenses and adult nights with later hours. Skating exhibitions and disco lessons demonstrate new techniques to skaters and enliven continual skating around the rink that could become monotonous.

The operation of a roller skating rink has weekly cycles that peak on weekends. Sessions after school and weekend matinees are also popular. The peak season is November through April. Rinks normally have two 2.5- to 3-hour sessions on weekdays, from 3:00 to 6:00 P.M. and from 7:00 to 10:00 P.M. A third session—from 1:00 to 3:00 P.M.—is added on weekends. Skating classes are frequently offered on Saturday morning and one afternoon each week.

Financing

The revenues from a roller rink derive primarily from admission fees with other profit centers contributing to the gross. Although the breakdown of revenue will depend on the particular rink, the following is typical: admissions, 45 percent; rentals, 20 percent; sales (of skates), 8 percent; food, 19 percent; lockers, 3 percent; games, 3 percent; and miscellaneous, 2 percent. In 1979, admission fees ranged from $0.75 to $3.50 depending on the day of the week and the time, with skate rentals usually costing $0.75 a pair.

Expenses are calculated to be 40 to 50 percent of the gross excluding debt service. Generally, labor is 20 to 25 percent of the gross; supplies, 12 to 13 percent; taxes and licenses, 2 to 6 percent; utilities, 3 percent; and insurance, 3 percent. In addition, occupancy costs which would include either rent or debt service and property tax usually add another 15 percent. Thus, a well-operated rink can clear 35 to 45 percent before taxes and many new concept rink operators expect to do better.

The financing of a roller skating rink is usually made by a 10-year loan. If a longer-term loan is available, the debt service could be reduced.

Clearly the key to a profitable operation is in the number of admissions and in building up repeat business. A 1979 study for Southern California estimated annual attendances between 188,000 and 344,000 with a median of 265,000 skaters for a large new concept rink. However, as recently as 1976, studies for the same area estimated annual rink attendance of less than 55,000. These figures demonstrate the renewed popularity of the sport but also point out its up-and-down trend.

Pro Forma Statement for a New Concept Rink of 25,000 Square Feet (1979)

Revenue		
Admissions (265,000 @ $1.20)	$318,350	45%
Rentals	141,400	20%
Sales	56,560	8%
Food	134,330	19%
Lockers	21,210	3%
Games	21,210	3%
Miscellaneous	14,140	2%
	$707,200	100%
Expenses (50% of sales)		
Labor	$177,000	25%
Supplies	91,910	13%
Taxes, Licenses	42,420	6%
Utilities	21,210	3%
Insurance	21,210	3%
Net Operating Income	$353,750	50% of sales

Gross	$353,750
Less Occupancy* (15%)	116,050
Net Income	$237,700
Development Costs	
Building ($32 per sq. ft. x 25,000)	$800,000
Fixtures ($8 per sq. ft. x 25,000)	200,000
Land (2 acres @ $3 per sq. ft.)	260,000
	$1,260,000

Return on Investment 18.9%

*Mortgage or rent payments

Racquetball Courts

Racquetball has been one of America's fastest growing sports. Since it was created in the 1950s by Joe Sobek, a Connecticut tennis and squash pro, the number of players has multiplied—50,000 in 1970 to an estimated 6 to 8 million enthusiasts in 1979. Racquetball and handball can be played on the same court, but racquetball is distinct from other racquet sports such as squash and platform or paddle tennis, which have different court dimensions, equipment, and rules.

The popularity of racquetball is attributed to three factors. First, it is easy to play: with only a few lessons one can start playing and men and women are fairly equally matched. Second, racquetball is physically strenuous: it uses up 600 calories per hour and has an aerobic rating of 9 (tennis has a rating of 4.5). Thus, it gives a better workout for people concerned with physical fitness. Third, it is relatively inexpensive compared to other racquet sports, both as far as equipment and court time are concerned. An hour's play is about half the cost of that for tennis.

In response to the burgeoning demand, racquetball clubs are springing up around the country. In 1979, there were over 1,200 clubs with the numbers increasing. They have often been built in conjunction with indoor tennis facilities. However, because a racquetball court is only 40 by 20 feet—one-ninth the size of a tennis court—a club can be built with much less land than that required for tennis. Racquetball courts are ideal for urban settings and increasingly are being developed independently.

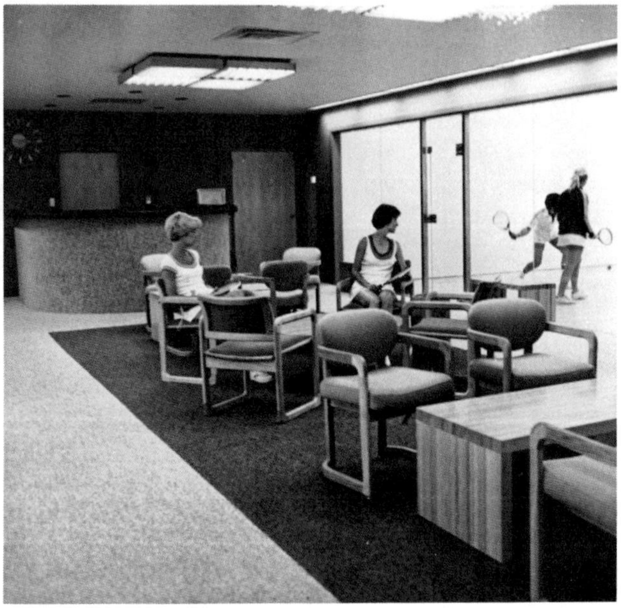

4-9 Comfortable lounge areas are appreciated, if not necessary, extras at sports facilities. (Photograph: Marty Hublitz.)

Market Factors

Racquetball players are young, 20 to 40 years of age, and 30 to 40 percent are women. Although people from all income brackets play the game, it has been found that those who join clubs generally have disposable incomes above average.[11] The usual measure of demand is by the number of players per court. To determine the area market, an estimate of the population available for membership and the number of memberships necessary per court must be figured. For example, approximately 2 percent of the national population play racquetball and 40 percent of them will join a club. To reach a level of 125 members per court, an area population of 15,000 per court would be required.

Location, of course, is important. Convenience is the key to a successful racquetball club. Players rarely develop loyalty to a club; therefore, a location should be selected as close as possible to the market area, preferably within a 15-minute drive. Although a club must have good access, it need not be located on prime commercial land. Several possible sites have been suggested as suitable for racquetball while having little other value: the L-shaped parcel surrounding a gas station; the apron of a shopping center; frontage in an industrial park; narrow plots with depth but limited frontage; and city, county, or state land where favorable leases or purchases can be made. Racquetball clubs have been developed on top of urban buildings, in vacant shopping center spaces, and in other existing structures suitable for conversion. The safety and security of players and staff must also be considered in selecting a location.

Finally, the availability of other courts in the area must be determined, including YMCA, municipal, and school courts; courts included in residential amenities; and courts in existing or planned private clubs. The existence of an adequate number of clubs does not necessarily mean that demand has been satisfied. If courts are poorly constructed, badly managed, or inconveniently located, they can deter players.

Development

The trend today is toward providing a full complement of comfortable amenities. A typical club will provide a lounge, pro shop, lessons, men's and women's locker and exercise rooms, whirlpool, sauna, nursery, and snack bar.

With complete services and parking for four to six

[11] Arthur E. Gimmy, *Tennis Clubs and Racquet Sports Projects* (Chicago: American Institute of Real Estate Appraisers, 1978).

4-10 Instruction can increase user interest and stimulate social exchange, benefiting club activity. (Photograph: Marty Hublitz.)

cars per court, developers plan for 6,000 to 7,500 square feet of site per court. Clubs with 10 courts usually require 1 to 1.5 acres of land but a site should also allow for future expansion. Local requirements for parking, setbacks, and landscaping may add to the land requirements. The price of land will vary with the area but fall in the less expensive end of the local land market.

Zoning for racquetball clubs is usually commercial or light industrial and the approval process should be the same as for any commercial development. Variances have allowed clubs to locate on sites zoned for residential and multifamily neighborhoods although some areas may object to the increased traffic and noise caused by the clubs.

Various plans have been used in designing and constructing the building. Clubs range in size from four courts to over 30, with an average facility having 10 courts. A smaller club cannot take advantage of the additional income which is possible from services such as the pro shop, provision of lessons, and others. These separate profit centers can produce 10 to 12 percent of the gross revenue.

Developers suggest that top quality materials be used to extend the life cycle of the facility. With inflation causing the price of all materials to rise, a court built today will have a cost advantage over one built in a few years. This translates into a lower rate of use needed to break even. In construction, attention must be paid to proper lighting, ventilation, and surface finishes. Constructing one level below ground may help to reduce heating and air conditioning costs. At least one court should have glass walls for tournament observation and viewing sections for all courts are recommended.

Because racquetball clubs are single-use buildings, lenders tend to be wary of them. Designing in elements to facilitate conversion to other uses such as office space may be an important factor in securing the financing commitment. Steel overhead door lintels with knock-out panels, structural systems with nonbearing court walls that can be removed, and mercury vapor lighting will make conversion to other commercial uses possible.

Estimates of construction costs in 1979 for racquetball courts ranged from $50,000 to well over $100,000 per court with the lowest estimates providing only a spare facility lacking in ancillary services. An average of $75,000 per court allowed construction of an adequate building and the typical amenities. Based on this estimate, $600,000 should be budgeted for an eight-court facility; $200,000 for 60,000 square feet of land; and $200,000 for contingencies, furnishings, inventory, and start-up capital for salaries, marketing, and promotion—adding up to a total budget of $1 million.

Developers and analysts agree that successful racquetball clubs require good management who can control cash operations, work well with people, and maintain the enthusiasm and efficiency of the staff. Some developers even offer their staffs continuing training programs in marketing, personnel, and budgeting, and their teachers instruction in how to teach. Marketing and promotion are vital to the success of a club—to increase membership and to sell court time. The initial promotion budget should be substantial (4 to 5 percent of the gross) and then reduced 2 percent in the following years.[12] League play, tournaments, and special drives to attract nonpeak hour players during the day from 9:00 to 5:00 and late at night should be ongoing activities. Presales of court time and membership discount coupons can help generate cash advances. Racquetball can generate more revenue than tennis because more courts can be provided for an equivalent amount of space and year-round play is more common than with tennis. There are no outdoor racquetball courts to compete.

Financing

There are various types of membership fee arrangements. A typical schedule of charges in the late 1970s included a low initial membership fee of $50 to $100, a monthly fee of $10 to $25, and reduced member court fees of $2 to $6 per hour. Nonmember court fees ranged from $3.50 to $12 per hour. Racquetball clubs operate 7 days a week and 16 to 18 hours a day. Developers warn not to overestimate the user rate initially. Fifty-five percent is recommended as an estimated rate until a club is established although many clubs will do better. Reduced use by 25 to 40 percent should be expected during the summer. Depending on the level of expenses and the financing, some clubs have been able to break even with 23 percent utilization although 50 to 60 percent is more common.

Expenses include salaries, heat, light, and property taxes. Based on the experience of existing clubs, expenses have generally run from 50 to 55 percent of the gross. Salaries represent one-third of the expenses. A staff is needed to give instruction, to buy and market sportswear, and to operate food services, a nursery, and, often, a full health club.

It is difficult to obtain financing for single-use recreational projects. Lenders have been hesitant because racquetball has been perceived as a fad with an uncertain market. As a result, lenders offer lower loan-to-value ratios. A standard 75 percent loan can usually be obtained only with personal guarantees, higher interest rates, and a shorter term (15 years is common). Developers recommend reducing the initial loan-to-equity ratio. The lower debt service will allow a lower breakeven point and the club can be refinanced after that point has been reached. Clubs have been financed through tax-exempt bonds and in partnership with city governments. Racquetball clubs have also been built and then leased or sold to a commercial chain operator.

Once established, racquetball can provide a very good return—in some cases, over 30 percent on investment.[13] But there are risks. A developer should be aware of the requirements for marketing and managerial talent to ensure that return. Furthermore, a strong industry trend toward building combined sports/health/social clubs should be recognized as the major competition for a simple athletic facility in the future.

[12] Ibid.

[13] Craig Hall, "Why I'm Riding the Racquetball Boom," *Builder* (January 15, 1979), pp. 189–193. See also Ed Doherty, "Racquetball: A Whole New Ball Game for Builders," *Housing* (February 1980), pp. 49–53.

Pro Forma Statement for a 10-Court Racquetball Club (1979)

Revenue	**1st Year**	**2nd Year**
1,000 Members@ $75[1]	$5,000	$5,000
Monthly Fee @ $10	120,000	120,000
Court Fees		
Members (24,000 hours) @ $3	72,000	108,000
Nonmembers (7,680 hours) @ $6	46,080	43,200
	$243,080	$276,200
Other	40,000	40,000
Gross	$283,080	$316,200
Expenses—at 50%	141,540	158,100
Net Operating Income	$141,540	$158,100
Development Costs		
Building (10 courts @ $60,000)	$600,000	
Land (60,000 sq.ft. @ $1.50 per sq. ft.)	90,000	
Soft Costs (25% of building)	150,000	
	$840,000	
Return on Investment	16.8%	18.8%

[1] Amortized at $5 per year.

Health Clubs

During the mid-1950s, Vic Tanny health facilities were organized as a franchise operation and were heavily promoted with hard-sell techniques. This resulted in considerable overexpansion, and the ensuing financial collapse of most of the gyms gave health clubs a bad public reputation. Increased interest in weight control and exercise since then has enabled health clubs to make a comeback, although on a more realistic scale. Numerous other organizations including handball and racquetball clubs are making major inroads into the health club market. Although there is a definite trend toward combining the functions of a club, such a club would depend on a large number of members who are willing to pay substantial annual membership fees for the privilege of belonging to a private club with multiple top-quality facilities. This would still leave a market for the less expensive average health club.

A small health club can operate with only a few thousand square feet of space and a minimal staff. The basic requirements are gymnasium space, locker rooms, showers, and preferably a sauna bath. Clubs oriented toward neighborhood business usually operate with alternating schedules for men and women with one set of facilities used by both. Clubs located where there is greater drawing power are often organized with separate facilities for men and women in adjoining suites. An indoor swimming pool is highly desirable in attracting members, but it increases the space requirement, operating cost, and maintenance expense so that many neighborhood-oriented clubs do without one.

Most health clubs are operated on a relatively inexpensive budget, with a small staff and minimal operating expenses aside from the overhead costs of rent, personnel, laundry, and administrative items. Marketing costs are often high, however, particularly for chain operators. The typical chain health club must be heavily marketed and must constantly sell new memberships due to the fast turnover of members.

Annual costs generally are no more than 35 percent of the gross revenue, exclusive of space rental. Rent, including percentage rent (for example, 6 percent of gross revenue), ranged in 1980 from $5 to $8 per square foot. Membership costs usually were from $25 to $45 for each member. With an estimated average revenue of $600 from each member, including revenue from additional programs, food and beverage operations, and pro shop sales, a club operating with these costs would require 600 to 700 members to break even.

4-11 Built on a small sloping lot, the Courts Royal raquetball club in Arlington, Virginia, has a parking lot under the rear of the building. Solar collection panels can be seen on the roof.

Dinner Theaters

Dinner theaters are a relatively recent trend in theater production, springing up in the late 1950s as a gimmick to boost food sales. The early dinner theaters were in converted barns and shows were added as entertainment with the actors serving as waiters between scenes. The concept caught on and such establishments became more professional and widespread. Today's dinner theaters serve dinner before the performance and actors no longer function as waiters.

The Actors' Equity Association, the performers' union, saw the employment potential for its members and signed contracts with many dinner theaters across the United States. The American Dinner Theater Institute was established in 1972 to represent dinner theater management in negotiating with Actors' Equity.[14]

The dynamic growth of dinner theaters occurred in the late 1960s and early 1970s with the peak of development from 1973 through 1974. Some theaters have since closed but new ones continue to open, with over 150 theaters throughout the United States as of 1979. Marvin Poons, Executive Director of the American Dinner Theater Institute, commented in an interview in June 1979 that the industry has stablized with slight growth, after having recovered from the rapid growth before 1975. "You can make a decent return," Poons said, "but the windfall profits of a few years ago are no more."

The goal of a dinner theater is to offer a pleasant one-stop evening out that leaves its audience feeling happy and satisfied. The plays performed are generally popular musicals, comedies, and occasionally thrillers. Serious drama is not part of the repertoire and rarely does a theater give the premier performance of a play. Dinner theaters try to emulate the glamor of Broadway without the expense or the hassle. They offer the convenience and safety of on-site, lighted parking and a complete evening's entertainment in one place. The food and entertainment are equally important. As a producer noted, "The show's the draw but they come back for good food. It's 50/50 and the quality has to be maintained for both."

Market Factors

Dinner theaters are primarily adult entertainment—which is not to say R- or X-rated. They have been referred to as a middle-aged, middle-class, middle-America invention. The dinner theater audience is generally made up of professional people, college educated or beyond, who are in the middle- or higher-income brackets. Wives frequently purchase the tickets; therefore, marketing is often directed toward women. Theater managements also make serious efforts to attract multiple sales from corporations and other groups.

Dinner theaters have been most successful on the fringe of metropolitan areas or in suburban locations within 100 miles of an urban center. Their audiences are drawn from those who want entertainment near their residences without having to travel into the city. According to the Foundation for the Extension and Development of the American Professional Theater (FEDAPT), dinner theater audiences are generally drawn from 1 to 4 percent of the community population.[15]

Dinner theaters compete with the whole range of leisure activities, not the least of which is television. The operators of dinner theaters must entice people out of their homes and often have to educate their communities as to what dinner theaters offer, dispelling sometimes incorrect notions. It is best to build an audience from those who have been to some form of theater before, and their numbers are increasing. A 1978 Harris survey found that 62 million Americans attended at least one live theater performance that year.[16]

Development

The American Dinner Theater Institute recognizes four different classifications of dinner theaters based on audience capacity: petite, accommodating up to 229 patrons; small, accommodating from 230 to 349 patrons; medium, from 350 to 549; and large, from 550 to 900. The site needs will depend on the size of the theater developed. Rules for physical standards or building size vary, depending on local fire codes and building requirements. Dinner theaters have been accommodated both in new construction and converted older buildings.

Several elements must be considered in planning the design: the stage, seating, food service, kitchen, lobby, box office, rehearsal area, and storage space. A professional experienced in stage and restaurant design should be consulted early in developing a dinner theater.

In addition to the artistic considerations, the choice of a stage type will dictate the layout of seating and traffic patterns. A stage design can be proscenium,

[14] American Dinner Theater Institute, P.O. Box 2531, Sarasota, Florida 33578.

[15] For more information, contact the Foundation for the Extension and Development of the American Professional Theater, 165 W. 46th Street, Suite 310, New York, New York 10036.

[16] See "Leisure Where No Recession Is in Sight," *U.S. News and World Report* (January 15, 1979).

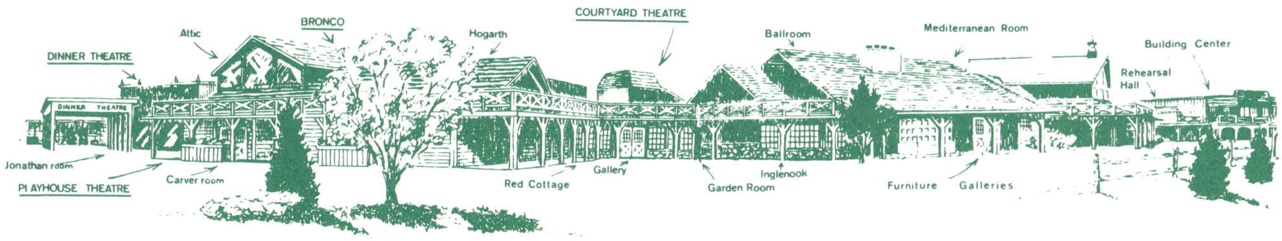

4-12 Chanhassen Dinner Theaters, Chanhassen, Minnesota, containing three dinner theaters and numerous guest conveniences.

thrust, or in-the-round. The majority of dinner theaters use the thrust stage. A stage in-the-round is more difficult to maintain, more expensive to operate, and requires more lighting than the thrust stage. Only a few dinner theaters use the proscenium stage. Adequate space backstage must be provided for performers, musicians, technical crew, and scenery storage. Actors' Equity Association has recommended specifications for backstage facilities.

The seating at dinner theaters at tables for two, four, or six, is usually tiered for best visibility, and ample space must be allowed for comfort and to speed traffic flow. Most seating areas are carpeted to reduce noise.

Food is generally served buffet style. Design for the service area must consider efficient traffic patterns to avoid the appearance of a cafeteria and maintain the desired image of elegance. The kitchen design should include direct service entries and be insulated for noise which might intrude on the performance.

As the first impression made on the audience, the lobby of the dinner theater should set the tone. FEDAPT suggests a standard allowance of 4 square feet of lobby standing space per person exclusive of ticket booths, cloakrooms, and other areas. There should be a covered entrance with a drive-through to allow for passengers to unload.

The costs of a dinner theater can vary substantially—from $100,000 for the conversion of a suitable structure to over $2 million for a large, new facility. The size of the investment must be geared to the size of the potential market and also must allow the theater to compete with surrounding community activities.

The planning and operation of a dinner theater require the best of management versatility because of the multifaceted demands of the business. FEDAPT urges developers to put together a management team which includes professionals in food service management, food purchase, menu planning, and supervision of personnel; a public relations/box office manager for promotion and sales; an artistic director and production manager responsible for program selection, casting, and budgets; and an overall financial manager. Management control is an essential factor in successful operations. It is recommended that weekly financial accounting information be distributed to all management sectors who are then held accountable for their respective financial performances. Weekly reports make it possible for problem areas to receive immediate attention.

Dinner theaters have extensive personnel needs. A Virginia theater, seating 350, employs 80 to 85 people. Steps can be taken to economize, however. Talent agents franchised by Actors' Equity can draw on a large pool of talent for casting, theater "packages" can be brought from other theaters to relieve the need for a full-time production staff, and theaters can coproduce shows to share costumes and offset expenses.

Dinner theaters usually operate throughout the year, with seven to eight productions in a season, each running 6 to 8 weeks. Tickets are priced from $12 to $20 per person (as of 1979), depending on the night of the week and the size of the production. The ticket price must reflect the breakdown of expenses for both food and theater with an adequate profit margin for each sector. The ticket price includes the cost of the meal and the performance; cocktails and gratuities are extra. Liquor sales provide important profits, with drinks averaging 2.5 a person. Performances usually have three acts to allow two intermissions in which to sell drinks.

Financing

A dinner theater operation generally breaks even when 65 to 70 percent of its capacity is filled. Most theater operators project their profits at 7 to 15 percent of the gross revenues. The production costs for each show are fixed regardless of how large the audience, but food and labor costs can be adjusted with proper planning. Advance sales and season tickets provide cash advances as well as an indication of the size of the audience.

Financing of dinner theaters is most frequently done by limited partnership. Unlike standard theater productions which own no real property, the real estate and equipment of a dinner theater represent tangible value which can be mortgaged.

Golf Driving Ranges

In a 1976 study, the A.C. Neilsen Company found that 8 percent of the population participates in the sport of golf, placing it third behind tennis and bowling in popularity. Driving ranges are popular with new golfers and help regular golfers improve their skills. Today, there are about 7,200 ranges in the United States. A continuing need for driving ranges is expected, especially in urban areas where there are too few golf courses for the number of players.

Market Factors

Golf is primarily an adult sport due to the pace of the game and the expense of the equipment and facilities. Since the number of alternatives for active exercise and recreation has increased, players tend to start golf later in life during middle age. Driving range patrons are generally new golfers practicing their techniques although, depending on the facility developed, teenagers and others looking for entertainment can also be attracted.

Driving ranges cannot support competitive pressures and require a large, uncontested market to be successful. Some analysts suggest a local population of 200,000 is needed. However, the success or profitability of a driving range depends on more than population. Since driving ranges complement local golf courses, the number of courses in the area and the degree of their success will either encourage players to improve their skills, or discourage them from practicing. When local courses sponsor tournaments, they provide incentives for both old and new players to practice. The best gauge of the market potential for a driving range would seem to relate to the number of golfers in a given area, reflected in the number of annual golf rounds at local courses. A Maryland golf consultant noted that an area's potential income from a driving range is estimated at $1 per round of golf, with perhaps 150,000 rounds needed to support adequately a commercial driving range.[17]

The actual siting of a driving range is not as critical as it is for other recreational centers. Location will be determined by the cost and availability of land. Ranges are frequently located along highways and sometimes near shopping centers if land costs are not prohibitive. Sites adjacent to an established golf course or public park are of course best and help to enhance the golf club image that operators seek.

Development

The average driving range has 35 tees. The area needed for the range measures 230 to 240 yards wide by 300 yards deep, or about 12.5 acres. Smaller sites are possible but require high fencing to contain the golf balls. Fifty parking spaces are recommended for a 35-tee range, which may add another half acre to the site requirements.

Ideally, the land should be open and gently rolling, sloping up at the far end for better illumination and visibility. Minimal grading is needed to remove low points which are hard to mow and collect water. The ground should support turf grass to reinforce the golf "fairway" image which helps simulate a golf course experience. Sprinklers may be necessary in some climates.

Driving ranges are frequently developed in conjunction with other facilities such as miniature golf, batting ranges, or go-cart tracks. They are also developed by some public recreation departments.

The tees are generally 10 feet by 10 feet in size and are arranged in a gentle arc with each tee aimed at a central point 160 yards from the center tee. A central target helps concentrate the golf balls for easier collection. Tee mats with nylon brush insets commonly are fixed on concrete platforms. Although golfers prefer grass tees, grass is much harder to maintain. A grass tee area must be 20 feet wide, or twice as wide as a mat, so that the tee can be moved about to prevent excessive wear. Automatic tees are also available and reduce playing time and ball theft. Tees are generally sheltered to allow play in poor weather, and, in some northern areas, are equipped with coin-operated infrared heaters to extend the season.

Since many players are inexperienced golfers, safety is a major concern at driving ranges. The tees may be separated by fencing or netting to avoid wild shots which might injure other players. Drainage channels in front of the tee line can also provide obstacles to prevent players from running out to retrieve short hits. Multiple level tees are not recommended although they have been used successfully in some areas.

Fairways are enhanced by target greens spaced at 100, 150, 200, and 250 yards to give golfers a marker to aim at. Circular greens should be sloped toward the tees for good visibility and be about 60 feet in diameter. Green flags make more attractive range markers than metal yardage signs.

Outdoor lighting is also recommended. The National Golf Foundation recommends six floodlights per pole directed toward the center at varying distances.[18] Poles should be 25 to 30 feet high and spaced 50 feet apart.

---

[17] This information was reported by Gus Novotny Associates, Box 246, Glen Burnie, Maryland 21061.

[18] Data reported in the *Golf Driving Range Manual*, published in 1978 by the National Golf Foundation, 200 Castlewood Drive, North Palm Beach, Florida 33408.

4-13 All-season driving range in Maryland.

A building for range equipment and restrooms requires a minimum of 400 square feet. If a pro shop and snack bar are included, the building must be larger.

Driving ranges require golf maintenance equipment such as ball washers, mowing tractors, and equipment to pick up balls. The latter comes in a choice of sizes from models which can be pulled by hand to larger models that are towed by truck. A minimum of 200 balls per tee is recommended to eliminate the need to collect balls during the hours of play.

A bucket of balls comes in two sizes: small with 25 to 40 balls and large with 45 to 75 balls. Golfers demand balls of good quality; damaged or dead balls should be removed and designated for use in sand traps or traded in for new ones. A selection of clubs should also be available, including drivers, and number 2-, 3-, and 4-woods.

Financing and Operation

The costs of constructing a driving range will vary considerably with the location and land costs. The National Golf Foundation suggests that minimal ground improvements can be made and equipment purchased for $20,000 at the lowest, with an additional $30,000 for lighting. This estimate does not include the land or buildings. Recreational consultants estimate that construction of a 12.5-acre range and equipment for it, a parking lot, and clubhouse can cost from $150,000 to $700,000. Because of the large amount of land required, land costs must be low. No more than a dollar per square foot or lease payments of 10 percent of the gross can be supported. With an extra acre or so of land, tees can be placed at both ends of the "fairway," thus, doubling the potential use of the range while only slightly increasing the cost.

Driving ranges cater to the golfer. They are open from early morning to late evening to accommodate golfers who practice before and/or after work. The prime times are evenings and weekends. Fees in 1979 ran from $0.75 to $2 for a bucket of balls or $0.03 to $0.04 per ball. Operators note that up to 15 percent of the gross can be spent replacing lost, damaged, or stolen balls. The average expenditure is about $2.25 per golfer unless the range is built in conjunction with other recreational activities which encourage larger expenditures. A range averages four players per tee per day. In climates allowing year-round play, this means an annual attendance of about 55,000 persons. In seasonal climates, a driving range operation will follow the local golf course season. Practice ranges may open earlier in the spring to allow golfers to get into shape, but only the diehards continue operating after the last tournaments of the summer. With development costs high and attendance limited, management must be sharp to turn a profit.

Developing a driving range is a difficult venture. To be successful, a range should be located near a large population but land costs and site availability in dense areas are prohibitive. Thus, a driving range is often considered an interim use for a parcel if the land is easily adaptable to the layout of a range.

Minature Golf

Miniature golf courses were first developed in the 1920s and spread quickly around the country. "Tom Thumb Golf" courses were located in urban areas and in 1930 there were as many as 30,000 courses worth $125 million. During the first years of the Depression, miniature golf remained a popular, inexpensive leisure pastime, but as the Depression deepened most courses were forced to close. It was not until after World War II that miniature golf again became popular, with courses being developed in the newly growing suburbs. The National Golf Foundation (NGF) estimates there are over 8,000 miniature golf courses operating in the United States.[19]

Miniature golf courses vary widely in their design and size. The "fairyland" image uses exaggerated and comical obstacles to entertain players. Newer courses require more skills and challenge the amateur putter's ability.

Market Factors

Even though a variety of people play miniature golf, the largest group is among those from ages 16 to 35. The game appeals to families and to young, dating couples.

Miniature golf courses are frequently located in resort areas where they depend primarily on large numbers of tourists. Some courses are located near other recreational attractions, shopping centers, motels, and restaurants. They are frequently built in conjunction with golf facilities such as par-3 courses or driving ranges.

To be successful today, a traditional course in a heavily populated area requires that at least 50,000 to 75,000 residents live within easy distance of the facility. However, a course can also be successful in a location with many fewer permanent residents if it is in a highly traveled resort area. A much larger population base may be needed to support a miniature golf course where there are numerous recreational alternatives.[20] As with many recreational attractions, attendance tends to drop at miniature golf centers after the first years of operation.

Development

Traditionally, a miniature golf project has one course with 18 holes, but recently, larger projects with three to six 18-hole courses have been developed. Multiple course installations spread the fixed costs over a larger base and therefore have the potential for greater returns. But they also require a high level of patronage to justify the investment.

The average 18-hole course will need 10,000 to 15,000 square feet of space for adequate landscaping and smooth play, though a course can be designed on as little as 5,000 square feet. The NGF recommends that a parking area be provided for 40 cars per course, or approximately 17,500 square feet. A building for the cashier is necessary but the size can range any-

[19] Vincent Pastena, "Miniature Golf—Alive and Well," *Miniature Putting Course Manual*, National Golf Foundation Information Sheet MN-Z (North Palm Beach: National Golf Foundation, 1978).

[20] "Miniature Golf Courses," *Irvine Ranch Study*, unpublished report (Los Angeles: Economic Research Associates, 1976).

4-14 Miniature golf courses can be ideal for irregularly shaped lots and as a relatively temporary land use. Most often, a course is part of a combined facility which includes a driving range, a regular golf course, or other attractions.

where from a minimum of 100 square feet up to 1,000 square feet and include restrooms, vending machines, and, in some cases, a game arcade.

The fairways of a miniature golf course are usually 30 to 48 inches wide with the most common straightaway 36 inches wide. The standard golf hole, which is 4.5 inches wide and 4 inches deep, is used, although some miniature golf courses use a 5-inch hole to speed play. Fairways should be short enough to discourage wild swings that might threaten players on other tees.

Fairways and greens are generally constructed of concrete which is 3 to 4 inches deep, reinforced with wire mesh, and laid on a 6-inch foundation of crushed stone. Deeper foundations and drainage are necessary to prevent surface cracking and settling in areas where freezing and thawing occur. A pitch of 1 inch per 6 feet provides for drainage. The concrete is finished with either indoor/outdoor carpeting or astroturf. Thin rubber mats recessed into the concrete are used for tees. Greens can be funneled around the hole for faster play but some players might resent this factor.

Miniature golf courses should be imaginative in design. Changing obstacles from season to season helps to maintain variety and interest and bring back customers. Other design factors which should be included are fencing, lighting, and insect control. Fences are necessary to control access to the course and prevent vandalism. An 8-foot, plastic-coated, chain-link fence is recommended to allow visibility from the street or sidewalk. Evening and night hours are the prime time for playing miniature golf; therefore, adequate lighting is essential. Outdoor florescent fixtures spaced so they deliver 10 footcandles at the putting surface are sufficient. Some courses have waterfalls and brooks incorporated into the landscaping, which function as obstacles for certain holes. Water will draw insects, however, in which case electric insect killers are recommended.

Because of the variety of courses, the cost of installing a miniature golf course ranges widely. In 1980, golf suppliers offered concrete courses ranging in cost from $40,000 to $70,000, which included concrete installation, carpet, putters, and balls, but no fencing, landscaping, obstacles, lighting, or buildings. While a minimal course that functions as an auxiliary to another attraction could be built in 1980 for under $20,000, the costs for a modern, competitive, and appropriately elaborate 18-hole course could range up to $300,000, excluding land costs.

A miniature golf course generally cannot support expensive land. Land is often leased to avoid high capital costs; the operation can usually support lease payments of about 10 percent of the gross.

Some indoor miniature golf courses have also been developed. They eliminate the problems caused by inclement weather and can draw a market for as much as 70 percent of the year. The initial investment for an indoor course is much less, and several companies offer a complete 18-hole indoor course starting at $11,000. Indoor courses also require much less space: 3,400 square feet are sufficient. Indoor courses have been set up in barns, basements, and on top of buildings as well as in conjunction with an existing outdoor course. They can provide profitable interim uses for vacant stores in shopping centers. A portable course needs no fixtures other than basic lights. However, a major attraction of miniature golf is being outside and the indoor course removes this important element.

Outdoor courses operate 10 to 14 hours per day with the peak use in the evenings and on weekends in the summer. In warm climates, courses operate all year, but in seasonal climates the season lasts only about 6 months. Nevertheless, the Mid-Atlantic region is reported to have the most successful courses in spite of their seasonal closings. Some operators feel a course in a seasonal climate has greater potential because people associate playing golf with spring and summer and will play more often when the season is limited. Each course can accommodate 18 foursomes at a time with the average time to play the course taking 30 to 45 minutes. The effective capacity is 80 to 100 players per hour for an 18-hole course. The fees may vary according to the time of day or the day of the week. In 1979, the average fee was $1.50 per game.

The play area of the course requires frequent cleaning and the landscaping should be well maintained to keep the facility attractive and encourage return visits. Maintenance help and a cashier are needed although their functions can sometimes be performed by one person.

Financing

Again, the diversity of miniature golf courses makes it impossible to find a standard for financial return. For simple courses, general admission fees account for most if not all income. Annual revenues for a typical 36-hole miniature golf center of good quality, including an arcade and snack bar, would run from $100,000 to $400,000 and higher, with golf revenues representing just under 50 percent of the total. Expenses can range from 50 to over 75 percent of the gross income and are primarily for labor, 25 to 62 percent; insurance, utilities, and advertising, 4 percent; and land costs, 10 percent. Miniature golf can be a good family business because the investment is relatively low and can be returned in 3 to 7 years if the operating costs are kept down.

Arcades

Arcades featuring assortments of electronic video and machine games as well as snack bars are components of virtually all recreational centers. They are often so successful that many developers view them as their key profit center, developing other recreational elements to generate attendance for the arcade. Arcades have also been developed as independent business enterprises in locations with a high ratio of pedestrian traffic such as regional shopping centers and tourist destinations. As developers and operators recognize the profitability of arcades, they are making facilities increasingly elaborate with novel themes and more games and equipment.

Market

Market support is derived from patrons of adjacent attractions; however, the arcade itself generates a significant demand, particularly among the teenage and young adult market. Popular games and attractions should also draw enough customers to make a fast food operation a good source of revenue and profit. New machines must be introduced regularly to ensure the continuing return of patrons.

Development

The space housing the arcade, snack bar, restrooms, offices, and merchandise sales should range in size from 1,000 to 10,000 square feet with 5,000 to 7,000 square feet typical of newer, diversified centers. An arcade of this size would contain 70 to more than 100 machines. The snack bar is generally a small though profitable operation requiring a 10- to 20-foot counter and 100 to 200 square feet.

Arcade buildings range from modest to elaborate. The more elaborate facilities at larger recreational centers will often incorporate exterior and interior themes—for example, castles or riverboats. Development costs for these buildings range from $30 to $50 per square foot. Arcade machines are either leased or owned by the developer. Smaller facilities typically lease machines for 50 percent of the net return. At the larger arcades most operators purchase rather than lease machines. Operators with multiple locations rotate machines. If revenues from a machine decline substantially, it is usually removed for resale. The use of tokens rather than coins is becoming more widespread.

Costs

Development costs in 1979 for a typical 5,000- to 6,000-square-foot arcade/snack bar facility ranged from $500,000 to $800,000 depending on finish, fixtures, and equipment. A typical lease might be for 10 percent of the gross plus a common area charge. Revenues for a 5,000- to 6,000-square-foot arcade/snack bar operation, which is part of a diversified recreational center, could range from $300,000 to $500,000 per year, with a high profit margin. The area occupied by game machines should generate well over $100 per square foot, or more than $100 a week for each machine.

Family Recreational Centers

A strong new trend in commercial recreation is the development of the family recreational center. This center can be defined as a grouping of two or more commercial recreational attractions with an arcade and snack bar into one complete facility. Major components which could be incorporated into such a group include miniature golf, water slides, scale grand prix track, go-carts, batting cages, bumper rides, and the like. In many respects, a family recreational center is like a mini-theme park, although perhaps without a theme.

Southern California has led the nation in the development of family recreational centers, particularly in the use of elaborate miniature golf courses as the key attraction of the center. The development of family centers in Southern California has evolved in one of two ways: (1) recreational elements have been added to existing miniature golf centers by miniature golf developers to stimulate repeat visits and revenue or (2) other developers have added separate recreational components on property adjacent to existing attractions. Thus, most of the larger centers developed to date had not been planned originally as complete operations.

The centers are usually situated adjacent to freeways, providing visibility and accessibility to passing motorists. Many sites are part of strip commercial or industrial park developments and generally are close to residential areas. Several sites contain undeveloped acreage which could provide space for the addition of future recreational elements. Major centers are located on sites ranging in size from 4 to 12 acres—including 2 or more acres for parking—with the average size approximately 10 acres.

Scale Grand Prix Tracks

Scale grand prix tracks offer patrons a chance to drive a scaled-down grand prix car timed against a clock around a bending racetrack which is typically one-half mile long. As many as 10 cars may run on a track simultaneously, released sequentially from the starting line (there is no head-to-head racing) by a timing device. At peak operating hours—typically weekend evenings—cars are started at 6-second intervals, at a minimum. Average lap time, electronically displayed to one-hundredth of a second, is in the range of 60 seconds, and the average participant drives between five and 10 laps per visit. Grand prix tracks have a high number of participants who return repeatedly, attributed in large measure to the appeal of the time clock and the fact that the cars race at speeds faster than the track with its numerous curves will safely allow.

Market Factors

Grand prix tracks are generally open daily throughout the year, from 11:00 A.M. to 11:00 P.M. on weekdays and until midnight on Fridays and Saturdays. Peak hours occur on summer weekend evenings. The track can effectively accommodate approximately 300 laps per hour. With each driver averaging five laps per visit, the track's capacity would allow 60 drivers per hour. The annual attendance ranges from 80,000 to over 120,000 drivers. Young adults make up the primary market. Valid drivers' licenses are required. This type of attraction also draws a large number of spectators and arcade players—from two to three times that of the number of drivers.

Development and Costs

A one-half mile track with space for parking, an arcade, and maintenance buildings would require from 4 to 6 acres of land. Costs in 1979 for a standard grand prix attraction, excluding land, ranged from $400,000 to $500,000 for site preparation, parking,

4-15 Malibu Grand Prix racetrack, Northridge, California.

lighting, track, and buildings, and from $115,000 to $150,000 for equipment and 12 to 15 cars.

Based on 1979 figures, revenues for a freestanding scale grand prix operation can approximate $750,000 per year including income from sales of laps, licenses, and merchandise, and net revenues from an arcade and snack bar. Operating expenses can be fairly high due to the sophisticated nature of the cars. In this era of concern about energy, it should be noted that Malibu cars get about 20 to 25 laps per gallon of gas, which amounts to a nominal cost per lap.

Major developer/operators—Malibu Grand Prix being the largest—are pursuing the development of freestanding grand prix attractions as well as complete recreational centers with a grand prix track as the major element.

Go-Cart Tracks

Go-cart tracks are geared toward the local market, primarily comprised of families, children over 8 years old, and teenagers. For purposes of safety, age and height restrictions are imposed at most go-cart facilities. Typically, a participant must be at least 8 years of age and 4 feet tall.

For a freestanding operation with a 700-foot to one-quarter mile track and a parking area, 1 or 2 acres are needed. Less than 1 acre is required for a track which is part of a recreational center. Tracks can be oval in shape or have a series of turns. Most tracks operate with 12 to 20 carts although some have as many as 25 carts. Based on 20 carts being available and rides being 5 minutes long, the top capacity of a track is estimated at 150 riders per hour. Attendance ranges from 75,000 to 150,000 riders per year at a typical operation. Larger operations having double tracks could attract over 200,000 riders. The peak season is summer, with tracks operating all year in warmer climates.

Either as a freestanding attraction or as part of a recreational center, development costs for a go-cart operation are relatively low. Costs for the track, landscaping, lighting, maintenance building, and carts (20 carts for $1,500 each) for a basic operation ranged from $75,000 to $160,000 in 1979, excluding land and parking. Revenues for a typical go-cart operation can range from $100,000 to $300,000. Operating expenses can be high, and a reliable all-purpose mechanic is essential.

Go-carts can be operated profitably in a good location. For this reason, it is expected that go-cart tracks will be increasingly developed as part of family recreational centers. It is interesting to note that go-carts have done well in conjunction with a scale grand prix track.

5. Supplemental Recreation

Recreational amenities which are subordinate to the primary function of a development are identified as supplemental facilities in this handbook. Recreational facilities which supplement other uses are most commonly associated with first-home development, particularly since the advent of the planned community. In recent years, however, these amenities have also been used to supplement commercial, industrial, business, and mixed-use developments.[1]

The reason for providing recreational attractions in real estate development is to add value to the primary product. Key to a project is that the developer identify and select facilities which complement primary uses. It is important that the recreational attractions, while serving as marketing devices for the project, not obscure or contradict the primary use. Moreover, the prestige, aesthetics, and good intentions associated with recreational components are intangibles which must be translated into an economic return.

A notable difficulty in providing recreational facilities relates to the phasing of construction. For marketing purposes, the facilities should be completed before or simultaneously with the primary product. But to do so may be too costly to finance at the front end, a problem the developer must carefully balance against the benefits of the facilities as a marketing tool.

Selecting recreational facilities and determining where to locate them obviously must reflect the local market interest and the intended function. Attractions provided for prestige value or to generate commercial traffic will be top candidates for highly visible locations. A common use of recreational space is as a buffer between abutting land uses. Whether to centralize or disperse facilities within a residential development will depend on what is wanted. If amenities which are private and convenient are preferred, they may best be provided throughout the development. On the other hand, consolidating the facilities will result in a more efficient and easily maintained operation.

[1] See Urban Land Institute, *Downtown Development Handbook* (Washington: ULI–the Urban Land Institute, 1980) and other volumes in the Community Builders Handbook Series for discussion of strategies for incorporating recreational components into other types of development.

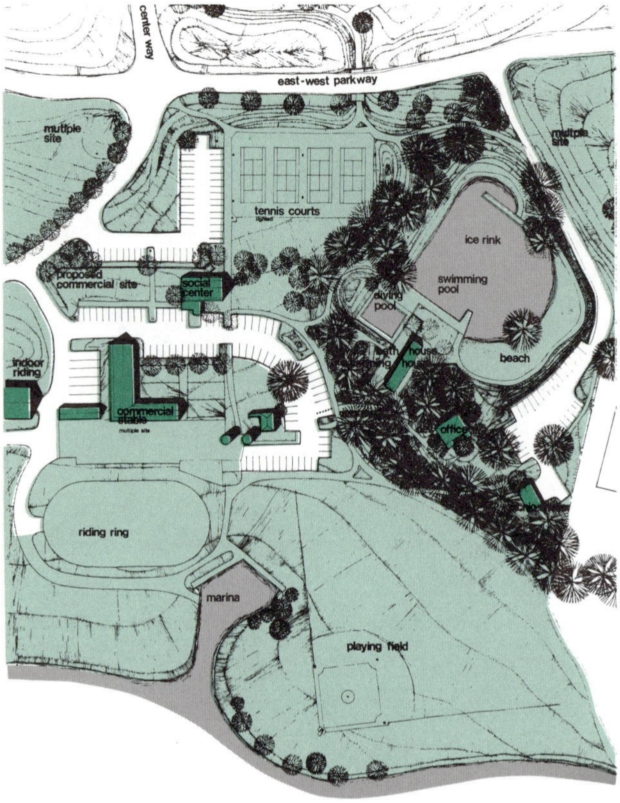

5-1 When associated with larger projects, supplemental recreational facilities may best be clustered in a convenient and manageable location.

5-2 In site planning, amenities can provide attractive view orientations.

An important consideration is whether the recreational facility will occupy land which would be more valuable in another use such as that of a golf course. At the same time, a particular recreational function might permit the use of a portion of a development, which either because of location, shape, or topography would otherwise be useless.

As with a second-home community, the ownership, management, and maintenance of supplemental recreational facilities are crucial issues in structuring a development.[2] User fees, from both within and outside the project, constitute a substantial resource with which to support the operation and service the development cost of facilities. The unique circumstances of each situation will define the alternative facilities which would be compatible with a particular primary land use.

The end result of providing extensive amenities as adjuncts to a residential, commercial, or business real estate venture may in fact be to make recreational opportunities primary attractions. This handbook has focused on development created specifically for leisure time use, recognizing, however, that extensive recreational amenities directly associated with general urban or suburban development, particularly high amenity PUDs, present considerable competition for recreation which is at a distance from one's home or job.

Primary Residential

Recreational facilities typically provided within residential developments include tennis courts, swimming pools, play areas, jogging trails, putting greens, clubhouses, exercise rooms, racquetball courts, activity rooms, and, as a major commitment, golf courses.[3] With the exception of golf courses, the facilities are usually viewed as secondary in importance and are essentially ancillary elements of an overall site plan. Nevertheless, they play important and respected roles in development planning. The fact must also be noted that local development codes may require the provision of some kind of recreational elements, in which case the codes will probably stipulate a need for open space.

A residential project must select those recreational amenities suited to its target market.[4] A young, active consumer often demands and is willing to pay for substantial facilities, including a comfortable clubroom. A golf course is appropriate for a market with a natural affinity for golf, both socially and economically.[5]

[2] For a discussion of these issues, see C. James Dowden, *Creating a Community Association: The Developer's Role in Condominium and Homeowner Associations* (Washington: ULI–the Urban Land Institute and CAI–the Community Associations Institute, 1976).

[3] Urban Land Institute, *Residential Development Handbook* (Washington: ULI–the Urban Land Institute, 1978), pp. 206–242.

[4] See Robert Engstrom and Marc Putman, *Planning and Design of Townhouses and Condominiums* (Washington: ULI–the Urban Land Institute, 1979) for a review of amenity design considerations.

[5] For a full discussion of developing golf courses to add value to a real estate venture, see Rees L. Jones and Guy L. Rando, *Golf Course Developments* (Washington: ULI–the Urban Land Institute, 1974).

5-3 Open space represents important recreational opportunities, though seldom can a residential development offer open space in such dramatic magnitude as seen here in Portola Valley, California.

5-4 Tennis court shelter and play lot.

5-5 Indoor lounge facilities within residential projects provide popular settings for a variety of social recreational functions.

Heritage Hills, Somers, New York

The 1,100-acre Heritage Hills is one of a series of adult-oriented projects in the suburban New York and southern Connecticut area built by the Heritage Development Group of Southbury, Connecticut. The project is designed for the mature and active person who desires a new home in a country setting which offers freedom from exterior maintenance and numerous recreational facilities. One adult in the family must be at least 40 years old and children must be over 18 to be permanent residents in the community. When completed in the late 1980s, the project will contain approximately 3,100 homes with one, two, and three bedrooms and a variety of adult recreational facilities.

Amenities

The first phase in the development of the 16-acre activities area in East Hills includes a health club in a 5,892-square-foot building, designed and equipped with a gym, whirlpool bath, saunas, showers, and locker rooms. Outside this recreation building is a heated swimming pool 40 feet by 65 feet, two tennis courts, and two paddle tennis courts. An adjacent golf pro shop and snack bar serve a 3,000-yard, 9-hole golf course, the first and shortest of two golf courses planned.

The second phase of the recreation center in East Hills will include a building or buildings containing a men's club with billiards, table tennis, games, cards, and reading; a women's club for bridge, tea, and group meetings; an arts and crafts center for woodworking, painting, ceramics, and sculpture; and facilities for meetings, social gatherings, and resident parties.

Located throughout the project will be four neighborhood recreational facilities, each serving 600 units, and each with a swimming pool and tennis or paddle tennis court.

An 18-hole championship golf course with club facilities is planned as part of the development of West Hills. As with the 9-hole course, this will be owned and operated by the developer. During development, nonresidents will be encouraged to become members of the golf club. With increased membership, the developer's initial expenses will be cut with the added benefit that local residents may become more interested in the project.

5-6 A multipurpose clubhouse area is a recreational focal point in the first phase of development at Heritage Hills.

The Heritage Hills Society, a nonprofit corporation, owns and operates all the recreational and activity facilities, with the exception of golf. The society has been operated by the developer but will ultimately be governed by a board of directors composed of one representative from each condominium association within the project.

Market

Heritage Hills is a community for the mature or maturing family catering to active adults who are seeking a sense of freedom from child-rearing responsibilities. It is a community for the working individual as well as for those seeking retirement. More than 85 percent of the residents work full-time, and many of them earned an income of $35,000 or more in 1979. Approximately 70 percent of the residents moved from larger homes in the Westchester County area and 21 percent had apartments in Manhattan or the tri-states—New York, New Jersey, Connecticut—before moving to the project.

5-7 Where topography is steep at Heritage Hills, homes are clustered along walkways.

5-8 When the terrain is relatively flat, homes are grouped around a paved court.

PROJECT DATA—HERITAGE HILLS

Land Use Information:

Site Area: 1,100 acres
Total Dwelling Units: 3,100
Density:
Gross . . . . . . 2.82 d.u. per acre
Net . . . . 5.00 d.u. per acre

Land Use Plan:

	Acres	Percent
Residential	635	57.7
Commercial	102	9.3
Nature Areas	109	9.3
Golf Course: 18-Hole	146	13.3
9-Hole	62	5.6
Activities Area	16	1.5
Model Area and Visitors Center	16	1.5
Maintenance Areas	7	0.6
Utility Service Area	7	0.6
Total	1,000	100.0

Unit Information:

1– 3 bedroom: $68,000–$120,000 (1979)

Amenities (1975):[1]

9-Hole Golf Course	$570,000
Pro Shop	70,000
Maintenance Building	60,000
Recreation Building	290,000
Swimming Pool	58,000
Two Platform Tennis Courts	20,500
Two Tennis Courts	18,000
Total	$1,086,500
Annual Golf Club Dues (optional):	$455 family
	$375 single
Monthly Society Fee:[2]	$18

Developer/Planning:

Heritage Development Group, Inc.
Heritage Village
Southbury, Connecticut 06488

Architecture:

Walz & MacLeod
50 Green Street
San Francisco, California 94111

Surveying:

Alexander Bunney
20 Woodsbridge Road
Katonah, New York

Engineering:

Bibbo Associates, Consulting Engineers
Routes 138 & 22
Goldens Bridge, New York 10526

Notes

[1]Current amenity costs are: golf, $70,000 per hole; swimming, $40,000 (25-foot by 50-foot pool); tennis, $17,000 per court (unlighted); and paddle tennis, $17,000 per court.

[2]Includes operating costs for all recreational facilities except golf. The capital costs for the recreational facilities are included in the purchase price of each home.

The Rotonda, McLean, Virginia

The Rotonda is a 1,168-unit, high-rise condominium project located on a 34-acre site in McLean, Virginia, a suburb of Washington, D.C. Five 10-story buildings surround an interior plaza which contains formal gardens, fountains, and landscaped multicolored parking areas. The condominium units range from one-bedroom apartments of approximately 900 square feet to three-bedroom apartments of approximately 2,000 square feet. Attractive landscaping, abundant open space, and a full complement of indoor and outdoor recreational amenities provide a relaxed resort atmosphere. The site is completely enclosed and has private entrances with attended gatehouses. The buildings also feature security systems.

The project has been designed to reflect the atmosphere of a European villa of the Renaissance period. A circular formal plaza occupies the center of the site. It contains formal gardens with carefully planned floral and topiary arrangements, fountains, promenades, sitting areas, large grassy vistas, swimming pools in a variety of curving shapes, and multicolored decks surrounding the pool areas. The focal point of the central plaza is a circular platform of approximately 300 feet in diameter which contains the outdoor pool complex and the glass-domed community center.

Amenities

The project contains a full range of outdoor and indoor recreational and social amenities which contribute to the relaxed, resort atmosphere. A wooded natural park runs along the site's northern and western borders. It includes a 48,000-square-foot lake, lighted walkways, a gazebo, decks, picnic groves, barbecue areas, a playground, and a walking and jogging trail. Six tennis courts are located adjacent to the lake with four lighted for evening use. An 18-hole putting green has also been provided.

The glass-domed community center is the focus for indoor recreational and social activities. Adjacent to the center is the outdoor swimming pool complex. Inside the center are a lounge and club rooms, a snack bar, a card room, a television room, Ping-Pong tables, billiard tables, a swimming pool and a whirlpool, a health spa, four bowling alleys, a golf driving range, a bank, a convenience shop, and rooms for parties and hobbies.

Market

The project's 1,168 units were sold over a period of 3 years—1.5 years less than was projected at the outset—with the last sales occurring in October 1979. A sophisticated marketing program was used. Purchas-

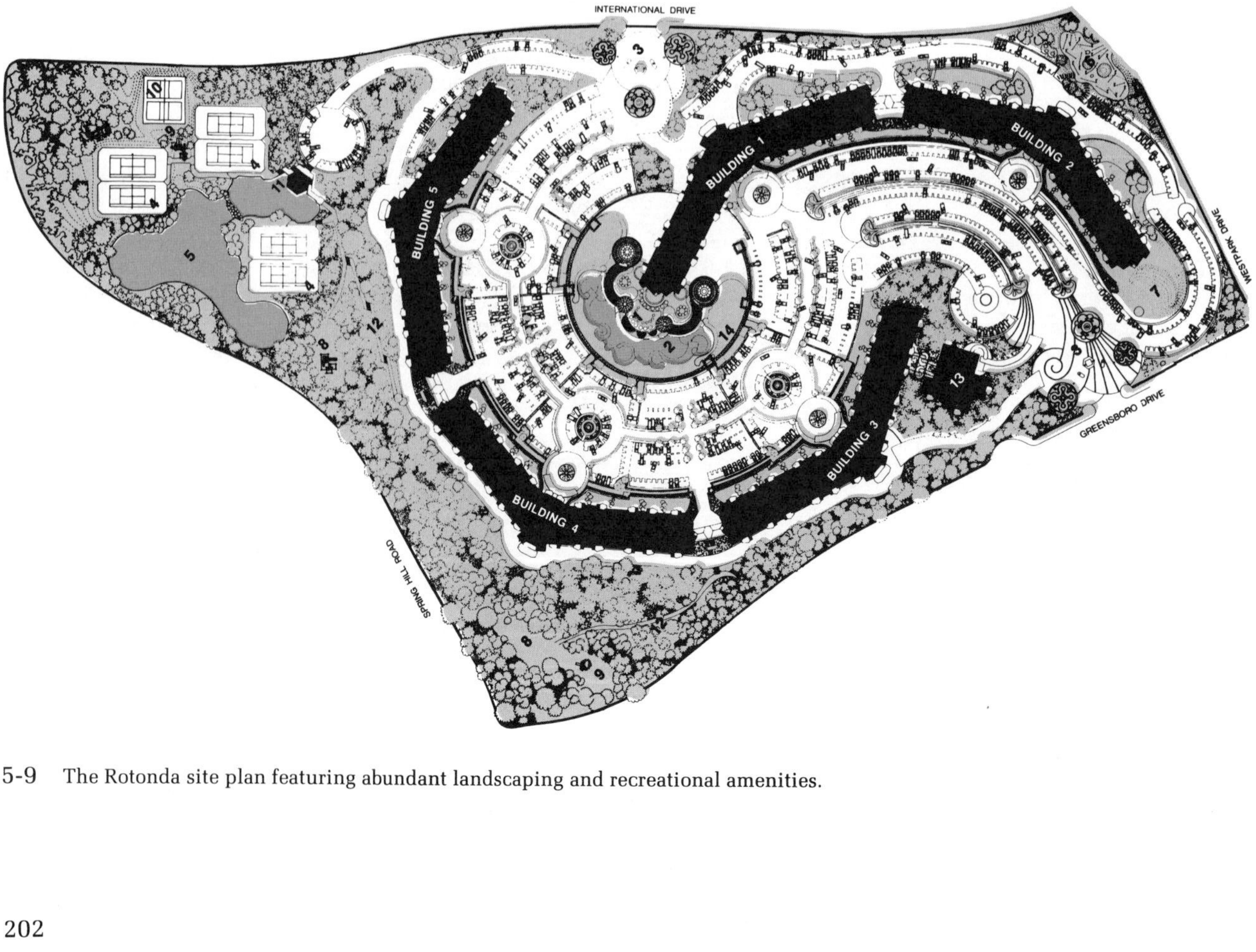

5-9 The Rotonda site plan featuring abundant landscaping and recreational amenities.

5-10 An elaborate outdoor swimming pool complex is attached to a community center.

ers of the units consist primarily of affluent, well-educated, "empty nesters," and young, single professionals. Eighty percent of the buyers have no children and more than 50 percent had annual incomes in 1980 in excess of $40,000. More than half have moved from single-family homes.

The completion of amenities in the initial phases of the project was an important factor in establishing the credibility of the developer and confidence in the project in the minds of potential buyers and was therefore a significant factor in the marketing program. However, as emphasized in earlier discussions, to complete such facilities in the beginning stages of development also generates increased front-end costs and requires a substantially higher initial capital investment than the incremental construction of amenities.

PROJECT DATA—THE ROTONDA

Land Use Information:

Site Area: 33.90 acres
Gross Density: 34.45 d.u./acre
Total Dwelling Units: 1.168

Land Use Plan:

	Acres	Percent
Buildings	4.05	11.95
Paved Area	7.47	22.04
Open Space and Recreation	22.38	66.01
Total	33.90	100.00

Unit Information:

Size: From 902 to 2,097 sq. ft.
Price: From $57,650 to $130,700

Economic Information:

Site Cost (1976):	$2,385,000
Site Improvement Cost:	$3,450,000
Construction Cost:	$44,750,000
Amenities Cost:	
Outdoor Facilities	$400,000
Community Center	$1,450,000

Condominium Association Dues: $0.105 per sq. ft. per month. The association operates with an annual budget of slightly less than $2 million and is responsible for maintenance of the common elements, management, and security.

Developer:

International Developers, Inc.
1700 North Moore Street
Suite 1900
Rosslyn, Virginia 22209

Architecture:

Holle and Graff, Architects
5125 MacArthur Boulevard, N.W.
Washington, D.C. 20016

Planning:

Smith and Williams
1414 Fair Oaks Avenue
South Pasadena, California 91030

Landscape Architecture:

Dewberry, Nealon, and Davis
8411 Arlington Boulevard
Fairfax, Virginia 22030

Sunpointe, Tucson, Arizona

Sunpointe Apartments is a rental apartment complex of 164 furnished units on a 4.45-acre site 3 miles north of downtown Tucson, Arizona. Construction began in October 1977 with the last building completed in August 1978.

The unit mix consists of 56 studio apartments and 108 one-bedroom units distributed in seven one-story buildings containing between 16 and 36 units each. The buildings are oriented inward around a linear-shaped area which includes a laundry, two tennis courts, sand volleyball court, basketball court, Ping-Pong tables, heated swimming pool with piped-in music around the pool, a gazebo with gas barbecue equipment, and a car wash area. In retrospect, the developer feels that rather than having two tennis courts, a more economical trade-off would have been to build one tennis court and a jogging track with exercise stations.

The purpose of Sunpointe is to provide a highly livable environment for the average-income, outdoor-oriented resident. The initial feasibility study had divided the market into two groups: the nonfamily working household and students from the University of Arizona and Pima Community College.

A recent survey of the residents at Sunpointe indicates that the average number of persons per unit is 1.21. Seventy-five percent of the residents are between the ages of 21 and 30. The tenants were willing to give up some square footage in the apartments in order to enjoy amenities at reasonable rents. The project has been well received and in its appeal to average income residents is an example of the value of packaging recreational amenities, rather than adding living space.

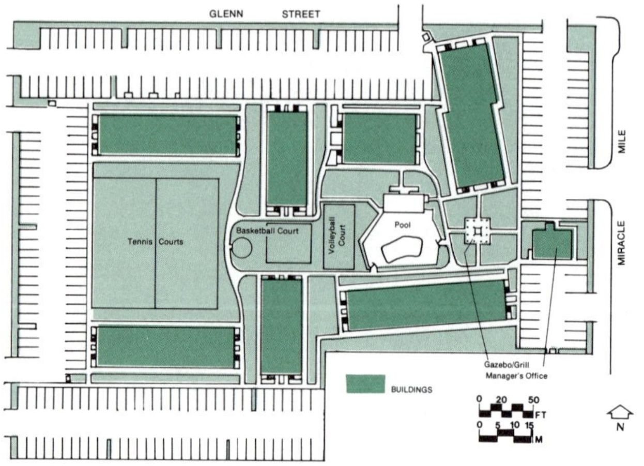

5-11 Providing a range of recreational facilities while keeping overall project costs down may require maximum use of available land, as shown here in Sunpointe's site plan.

PROJECT DATA—SUNPOINTE

Land Use Information:

Site Area: 4.455 acres
Total Dwelling Units: 164
Gross Density: 36.81 d.u. per acre

Land Use Plan:

	Square Feet	Percent
Buildings	34,350	17.70
Amenities and Open Space	70,837	36.50
Parking and Circulation	88,875	45.80
	194,062	100.00

Unit Information:

Type	Square Feet	Rental Range[1]
Studio	327	$155
One-Bedroom	418	$185

Economic Information:

Site Cost: $205,000 (1977)
Construction: $21.46 per sq. ft. (1978)[2]
Amenities (1978):

Swimming Pool	$13,000
Tennis Courts	17,000
Volleyball Court	2,000
Barbecue Islands and Gazebo	10,000
Basketball Court	3,000
Total Project Cost:	**$1.7 million**

Notes

[1]Does not include utilities which average $14 to $17 per month. Includes free use of all amenities.

[2]Includes all hard and soft costs including finance costs, points, and interest.

Developers:

Jerry Sonenblick/Cary Marmis
Empire West Companies
655 N. Alvernon, Suite 124
Tucson, Arizona 85711

Architecture/Planning:

Howard Peck
Howard Peck & Associates
4001 E. Pima
Tucson, Arizona 85712

Landscape Architecture:

Warren Jones
4665 N. Country Club Road
Tucson, Arizona 85718

Management:

Empire West Realty & Management, Inc.
Tucson, Arizona

Commercial/Retail

Similar to the use of recreational facilities as a marketing tool in residential development, such facilities serve to draw various retail tenants into a commercial development project. The most typical entertainment activities are provided by arcades, theaters, and eating establishments. Additional recreational facilities, however, have been incorporated in shopping centers, such as skating rinks and areas which can be used for theatrical performances and other activities.[6]

People shop not only out of necessity, but also to occupy leisure time. They visit commercial centers to be entertained, to watch people, and otherwise to spend time. Shopping centers can take advantage of this situation by offering entertainment to potential customers. For instance, some observers feel that amusement parks can complement department stores by acting as major shopping center anchors, each drawing traffic for the other. Among an array of special attractions, the prospering 1-million-square-foot Omni International shopping center in Miami features a 23,000-square-foot amusement park called Treasure Island.

5-12 Leisure environments are increasingly recognized as major attractions in shopping facilities. Pictured here is an interior view of the first phase of Eaton Centre in downtown Toronto.

Although some entertainment facilities may generate less revenue per square foot than a retail use, alternative recreational uses may provide a better tenant mix and ultimately better combined gross sales. The key, again, is in achieving a complementary mix. An amusement arcade with a furrier adjacent would not likely be complementing tenants.

The most appropriate recreational amenities will, of course, be determined by the characteristics of other retail tenants and the market which is attracted. For example, arcades, fast food areas, and active recreational facilities such as ice rinks will appeal to a young, energetic clientele. On the other hand, art fairs, theaters, sit-down restaurants, and related recreational activities would tend to attract the older or middle-aged shopper.

The addition of a recreational facility in a shopping mall can serve a variety of purposes. For example, a racquetball court can contribute to a shopping center both by generating traffic for retail business as well as by functioning as a tenant for less desirable retail space. From the standpoint of the racquetball operator, the mall location may offer additional market exposure, proximity to other consumer attractions, and security for its patrons.

A mall can also use more visible activities to generate the traffic flow. In 1979, the 1.35-million-square-foot, 4-year-old Countryside Mall in Clearwater, Florida, put a 15,000-square-foot ice skating operation in its central court. The $360,000 project was undertaken in order to draw a younger crowd and compete with incoming competition. Moreover, it helped transform the common area into productive leasable space.[7]

Specialty Shopping Centers

The specialty center has been a rapidly expanding concept in shopping center development.[8] (In many respects, specialty shopping centers offer a recreational service, in which spending leisure time and disposable income on discretionary consumer items is itself perceived as a recreation.) By appealing to recreational and entertainment needs as well as to consumer needs, the specialty center has demonstrated a capacity to outperform the traditional shopping center both in terms of sales per square foot and

[6] See Urban Land Institute, *Shopping Center Development Handbook* (Washington: ULI–the Urban Land Institute, 1977) for examples of recreational elements included in retail facilities.

[7] See "Ice Rink Solidifies Mall's Drawing Power," *Chain Store Age Executive* (December 1979), p. 50.

[8] Nina Gruen, "Gestalt Magnetism . . . or, What Is Special About Specialty Shopping Centers?" *Urban Land* (January 1978), pp. 3–10.

in operating profit. Annual sales can run well over $300 per square foot. The specialty shopping center differs from the traditional center in a number of important characteristics:

- Its consistency of design and merchandise offerings carry out a unifying theme.
- Recreation and entertainment attract the tourist and sightseer as well as the shopper.
- A wide selection of unusual merchandise not typically available at one location is offered by a relatively large number of tenants.
- A variety of restaurants and bars function as key tenants and help to create a social ambience for the center as a whole.
- The specialty shopping center provides a continuing program of special activities designed to entertain, inform, or amuse.

Because of its strong focus on entertainment and recreation and its atypical merchandise, the specialty center is essentially noncompetitive with conventional shopping facilities and generally has broad regional pull. Although specialty centers have been developed successfully in numerous kinds of locations, most sites likely will have one or more of the following characteristics: proximity to a harbor or sea coast; easy access to a large resident or tourist population; orientation toward high-income patrons; and proximity to existing attractions such as a tourist area or regional shopping center.

Specialty centers typically range in size from 40,000 to 175,000 square feet. While exceptions do exist, they often experience problems. Those centers smaller than 40,000 square feet may not offer enough to encourage a reasonable length of stay, and those larger than 175,000 square feet tend to outgrow their intimate specialty appeal, becoming more like a traditional community or regional center.

Restaurants and drinking establishments are the mainstay of the specialty center and normally account for 30 to 60 percent of the gross leasable area. Shops are typically small, averaging less than 1,000 square feet which allows for a relatively large number of retail tenants offering unusual specialty merchandise or services not commonly found in the traditional shopping center.

In addition to the shops and restaurants, many specialty centers have one or more motion picture theaters. The movie theaters add a dimension of entertainment to the specialty center while the theater audiences provide additional support for the restaurants and shops during nonpeak shopping hours. Finally, the theater space can be used to accommodate special entertainment programs as well as cultural or social events in the community.

The enormous success of specialty shopping centers such as Ghirardelli Square in San Francisco and Quincy Market in Boston is attributable to powerful markets, matchless locations, easy accessibility, fine restaurants and mix of tenants, integrated parking, and unique design and attention to detail.[9] Specialty centers over 200,000 square feet may be too large for a specialty operation, and without a first-class restaurant anchor, imaginative architecture, and strong local markets, a so-called specialty center may not be distinguished as such and thus would be placed in direct competition with conventional shopping centers. Although the specialty shopping center usually requires dealing with many small tenants without strong financial staying power or management, and a shake-out period of 1 to 2 years must be anticipated, the high rents which can be charged can compensate for the risks involved.

[9] See Urban Land Institute, *Adaptive Use: Development Economics, Process, and Profiles* (Washington: ULI–the Urban Land Institute, 1978) for case studies of development opportunities for reusing existing facilities and the potential for theme attractions.

5-13 Developments which encourage window shopping tend to ring up much higher average sales per square foot than those without attractions aimed at pedestrians.

5-14 Food service helps draw volume traffic to specialty centers.

The Cascades, Ocala, Florida

The Cascades is a small, theme shopping center (79,580 square feet of gross leasable area, or GLA) that responds to a growing customer preference for leisure shopping in a pleasant, social shopping environment. The project is located in a growing, affluent regional market in the area of Ocala, Florida, and has fashion-oriented shopping, good restaurants, and financial services. The concept of The Cascades, with its created amenity of waterfalls and floral gardens, along with some 30 specialty shops, is directed at pleasing, exciting, and entertaining the shopper. The center's anchor tenant is a 17,430-square-foot restaurant and club lounge which looks out over a lagoon through water cascading from another lagoon on the club's roof.

The project was largely preleased before construction began in January 1976, enabling it to open in late 1976. A second phase is scheduled to include a five-story office tower with 27,000 square feet of gross building area (GBA) and an additional 35,000 square feet of retail space for another restaurant.

Project Planning

Located approximately 1 mile east of downtown Ocala, the site was wooded and had a lime rock depression, created by the undercutting action of the natural drainage and considered a liability for development. The center's plan, however, turned the site's lime rock depression into an asset. The depression was enlarged to accommodate one story of the two-story project, resulting in a lower profile from the street as well as reduced energy costs made possible by the earth which surrounded and insulated some of the exterior walls. The space above grade was further insulated by earth berms created with fill from the excavation. The berms are landscaped and buffer the facilities facing inward from the noise and congestion of the parking areas and surrounding streets. The office and retail components of the second phase, when finished, will complete the enclosure of the waterfalls and garden.

The two-level core, with its natural appearance and the sound of cascading water, contrasts with the streetscape on the outside of the core. Wide, covered walkways with sitting areas and a bridge over the lower lagoon permit a special view of the waterfalls and connect the shops and offices of the project. The structural system using heavy timber gives the project a rustic look and was chosen because of the fact that it is a natural insulator and can be easily obtained. The 20-foot spans contribute to the human scale of the center. Concrete, where used, was left exposed. The outer sides of the buildings have mansard roofs finished in hand-split cedar shake shingles and descending to the 8-foot-high, sod-covered berms. These facades are broken at intervals with skylight windows.

Market

The Cascades has no department store anchor and must rely on a combination of the specialty shop mix, the restaurant, and the themes of waterfalls and landscaping to attract and hold the customer. In typical centers, small retailers must depend on the drawing

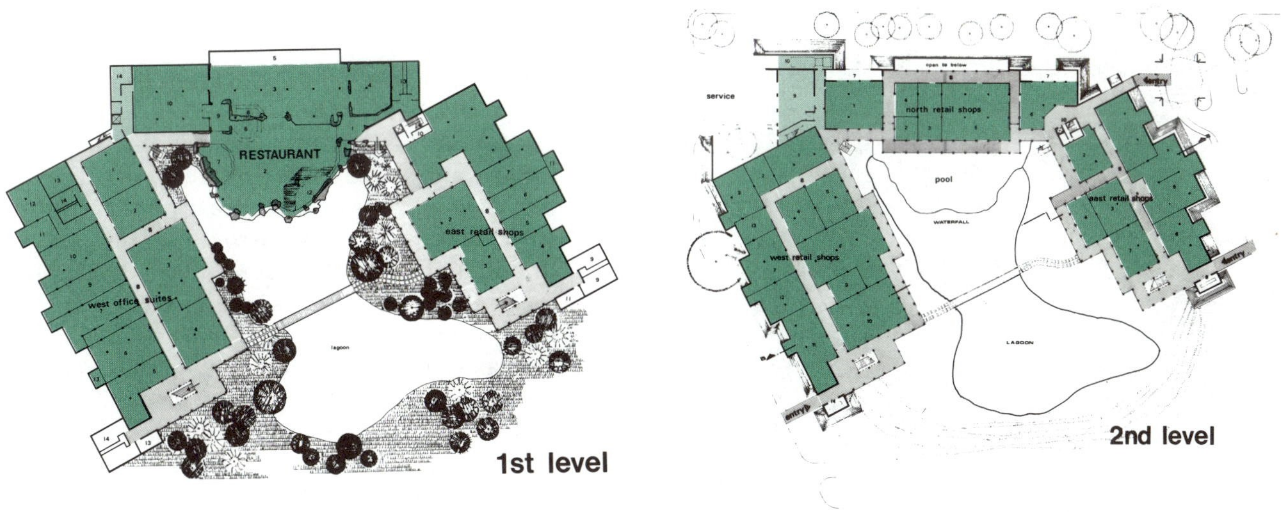

5-15 The Cascades features two levels oriented towards an interior space.

5-16 A floral garden . . .

5-17 . . . and a waterfall create the special setting at The Cascades.

ability of large competitive department stores, and these anchor stores in turn impose a greater financial burden on the small retailer. Rents in The Cascades are generally $3 to $6 lower per square foot than comparable area centers with major tenant anchors. Leases at The Cascades generally run from 5 to 10 years. Tenants have an allowance of $15 per linear foot for exterior walls. When space is leased to tenants, the floors have no covering. The restaurant, as the anchor tenant, has a 25-year lease with an option to renew for another 25 years.

The project's primary trade area is the city of Ocala and Marion County which together have a population of 119,000, according to 1977 figures. Studies show that before quality specialty stores were located in Ocala, many of the people in the area traveled to Jacksonville or Orlando to purchase luxury goods. It is estimated that tourists make up 40 percent of The Cascade's shoppers.

Experience Gained

- The day of the lackluster shopping strip is gone even for retailing medium-quality merchandise. People want shopping centers which are interesting, pleasing, and relaxing places in which to shop and dine.
- A developer of a specialty center should pass all operating expenses to the tenants.
- It is important to secure in writing, if possible, what the tax assessments will be after development. The project's predevelopment assessment, which was the figure given to obtain financing, actually doubled after development.
- Without a well-known department store of quality, high initial advertising expenditures will be required to establish the center's image in the market. The project's advertising expenses during the first year were $50,000 instead of an estimated $15,000.
- To enforce the sign restrictions prohibiting backlighted and neon signs, the developer built all the signs as part of the lease. They are constructed of cedar and were routed or sandblasted.
- Important to the design concept was the input of the architect, the landscape architect, and the marketing consultant as a project team.
- To make it easier to replace a marginal tenant, the developer recommends a lease of 1 to 2 years instead of the 5 to 10 years required by banks for financing.

5-18 Section elevation.

PROJECT DATA—THE CASCADES

Land Use Information:

Site Area: 12.5 acres
Gross Building Area (GBA): 104,000 sq. ft.
Gross Leasable Area (GLA): 79,580 sq. ft.
Percent Rentable: 77
Floor Area Ratio (FAR):[1] 0.19
Parking:
Spaces: 400 at present
Index: 5 spaces per 1,000 sq. ft. GLA

Land Use Plan:

	Square Feet	Acres	Percent
Buildings	104,000	2.61	19.1
Parking	237,946	5.24	43.7
Waterfalls and Gardens	98,010	2.25	18.0
Future Parking	43.560	1.00	8.0
Satellite Site	60,984	1.40	11.2
Total	544,500	12.50	100.0

Economic Information:

Site (1973): $566,845
Site Improvements: $280,000[3]
Construction (1976): $3,120,000
Amenities: $45,000[4]
Sales and Rent Information (1980):
Total Sales: $120 per sq. ft. GLA
Lease Rates:
Retail: $6 per sq. ft. GLA, plus 2 to 9 percent over gross sales
Office: $8 per sq. ft. net rentable area
Merchants Association: $0.20 per sq. ft. GLA, plus developer's contribution of $0.075 per sq. ft. GLA
Common Area Charges: $2 per sq. ft. GLA[5]

Tenant Information:

Classification	No. of Stores	GLA Sq. Ft.	Percent of GLA	Average Percent of GLA in Regional Centers[2]
General Merchandise	—	—	—	19.3
Food	2	1,400	1.8	7.3
Food Services	2	19,380	24.4	5.8
Clothing	7	11,430	14.4	23.0
Shoes	1	830	1.0	6.2
Home Furnishings	1	975	1.2	2.4
Home Appliances/ Music	2	2,780	3.5	3.2
Building Materials/ Garden	1	1,055	1.3	0.8
Automotive Supplies/ Service Station	—	—	—	1.2
Hobby/Special Interest	2	2,000	2.5	3.1
Gifts/Specialty	7	11,900	15.0	4.0
Jewelry and Cosmetics	1	1,400	1.8	2.1
Liquor	—	—	—	0.3
Drugs	1	2,700	3.4	3.6
Other Retail (Vacancies)	3	4,619	5.8	3.6
Personal Services	3	2,305	2.9	2.1
Recreation/ Community	1	540	0.7	4.1
Financial	1	1,923	2.4	2.6
Offices (other than Financial)	16	12,643	15.8	1.6
Other	1	1,700	2.1	3.7
Total	52	79,580	100.0	100.0

Developer/Management:
A.M. Collins, Jr.
1515 East Silver Springs Boulevard,
Suite 104-W
Ocala, Florida 32670

Architecture:
Hal Thomas Reid
206 Southeast 14th Avenue
Ocala, Florida 32670

Landscape Architecture:
Robert L. Dell'orso
1920 Northeast 50th Avenue
Ocala, Florida 32670

Notes

[1]FAR—gross building area divided by total site area.
[2]*Dollars & Cents of Shopping Centers: 1978* (Urban Land Institute) p. 275.
[3]Includes paving only.
[4]Includes waterfalls, floral garden, and other courtyard landscaping.
[5]Includes taxes, insurance, and maintenance of mall, landscaping, and parking lots.

Trolley Square, Salt Lake City, Utah

Trolley Square is a novel entertainment and specialty shopping center located in a 13-acre complex of car barns and maintenance shops—once the home of Salt Lake City's trolley car system.

Its four freestanding masonry buildings incorporate an intricate network of internalized pedestrian shopping streets, courtyards, and common open areas interconnected by landscaped walkways. The project features a turn-of-the-century design theme and architectural artifacts and antiques have been used for both functional and decorative purposes throughout. These elements give Trolley Square an ambience that strongly differentiates it from the suburban shopping centers which are its primary market competition. The project has been designed to make shopping a recreational and leasure-time experience. Its focus on small, intimate boutique shops, and a varied and stimulating physical environment places Trolley Square in the forefront of commercial design innovation. It has become one of the city's major attractions and the developer believes the carefully devised nostalgic atmosphere in large measure explains the success of the project.

Trolley Square is situated in an aging low-density residential section of Salt Lake City approximately nine blocks southeast of downtown. The development contains a total of 120 tenants including 15 restaurants, six movie theaters, 19 apparel shops, a farmer's market, and a variety of other tenants with an emphasis on arts and crafts, gifts, and boutique items.

Renovation got under way in 1970, following 12 months of project planning and design. The first components of the complex opened in June 1972. Since then, development has been phased and expansion is continuing as additional sections of the vacant industrial buildings are converted to commercial use. A total of 250,000 square feet of gross leasable area had been developed and leased by 1978.

Perhaps the most noteworthy aspect of the Trolley Square project was the assumption that a development of this type could succeed in a community the size of Salt Lake City. Although this assumption has proven to be correct, it represented a major gamble at the time the project was initiated since developments of the type planned had previously been attempted only in the largest and most sophisticated metropolitan areas.

Project Planning

From the outset, Trolley Square was planned as a pedestrian-oriented shopping and entertainment complex modeled after similar successful developments on the West Coast. The "turn-of-the-century" design theme was an integral part of the concept. Likewise, the developer planned to place a far heavier emphasis on entertainment functions than is customary in shopping center development. Only limited provision was made for office space.

5-19 Period artifacts help establish Trolley Square's unique theme.

The gradual phasing of new space was essential to developing the more than 250,000 square feet of GLA to be rented. The first uses to open were the theaters and restaurants since it was felt that the entertainment components could stand on their own while the success of the commercial uses would depend on a sufficiently large scale of operation to generate pedestrian traffic.

Market

Trolley Square was devised as an alternative to the conventional shopping center, from which it differs in several important respects. A heavy emphasis has been placed upon entertainment activities including theaters and restaurants. This orientation heightens the festive atmosphere suggested by the design scheme and extends heavy usage of the complex into the evening hours. Most tenants are local merchants rather than national franchise outlets, and the understanding of local interests and tastes which they have brought to Trolley Square constitutes an invaluable marketing asset.

A full range of retail outlets is provided, but the tenant list also includes a number of stores selected because they would help to generate additional vitality and interest. Among these are a farmers' market, a flower shop, and craftsmen workshops.

Visitors number up to 70,000 or more per week, of whom an estimated 60 percent come from the Salt Lake City area, 25 percent from other parts of Utah, and 15 percent from elsewhere. One objective of the tenant mix was to stimulate return traffic on a daily or weekly basis, thereby establishing Trolley Square as a major shopping location. To a considerable degree, this objective has been accomplished.

Trolley Square is operated like a conventional shopping center, with the developer leasing space to individual tenants and assuming responsibility for overall project management and control. Minimum retail leases generally ranged from \$8 to \$15 per square foot in 1980. Office space is priced from \$6 to \$8.50 a square foot. Most leases run for 3 to 5 years.

Experience Gained

- Opening the entertainment component as the initial feature of Trolley Square was essential to its success. It was also important to convey the fact to the public at the outset that Trolley Square would contain many activities having more than a tourist orientation.
- The original cost was projected at \$5 million. Market response, however, has been sufficient to justify enlarging the scope of the project. Actual costs as of 1980 stood at \$12 million with additional elements remaining to be completed.
- In order to create a self-contained shopping center of this type, a minimum of 150,000 to 200,000 square feet of space is needed. Where less space is available, it may be necessary to rely on adjacent commercial activities in order to attract the market scale required.
- Important savings were made by using recycled building materials. The value of these items when imaginatively reused is frequently unrecognized.
- The unusual design of the buildings and the materials used give Trolley Square a uniqueness that is unachievable in new construction. Although new construction for the activities contained in Trolley Square might have been provided at a competitive cost, the character of the new construction would have been entirely different, and most likely not as appealing.

Industrial/Business Parks

Recreational amenities in industrial/business parks are often outdoor facilities which provide a contrast to the employees' indoor setting as well as an attractive, pleasant, recreational environment. Such facilities are appealing both to prospective tenants or purchasers and to employees. Where the total environment is emphasized in a project, the amenities generally make it possible to obtain significantly higher rents than in comparable developments not having such facilities.[10]

Typical outdoor recreational facilities in office/industrial parks include golf courses, softball fields, tennis courts, jogging trails, and open areas conducive to other recreation, such as picnicking. Of course, decisions regarding the type of facilities to be provided will be directly related to the image of the project which is desired.[11] An office park development might find golf courses or tennis courts most appropriate, while the employees of an industrial project might prefer softball fields. In any case, it is imperative that the recreational components be carefully maintained in order to assure an attractive setting.

An indoor fitness facility and clubhouse may also be a desirable amenity. A full athletic or other recreational facility can complement an industrial or business project by providing an amenity to both management and employees, thus adding an extra dimension to the project. Such a facility also has a potential for outside use and support from the community.

[10] Urban Land Institute, *Industrial Development Handbook* (Washington: ULI–the Urban Land Institute, 1975).

[11] John C. Melaniphy, Jr., *Commercial and Industrial Condominiums* (Washington: ULI–the Urban Land Institute, 1979).

5-20 The golf course at the Arvida Park of Commerce, Boca Raton, Florida. Country club facilities are sought after amenities in a corporate business setting.

Inverness, Englewood, Colorado

Occupying 845.6 acres, Inverness is a business park of mixed uses, including office, warehouse, light industrial, recreational, and commercial uses. A 142-acre, private golf course weaves through the park serving as a well-maintained greenbelt. The golf course, land features, and project covenants allow a mixture of diverse uses. The project, 25 minutes on Interstate 25 southeast of downtown Denver, is adjacent to the Arapahoe County Airport. As well as selling 1- to 80-acre parcels of land and constructing multiple tenant buildings on speculation, the developers provide a full program of designing, building, and leasing facilities.

Site improvements and construction of the golf course began in 1972. The project's acreage was enlarged in 1977 with the addition of 171 acres to the south and 50 acres to the north. The original acreage was developed in six phases, including that of the golf course and five other phases. The first building constructed in the first of eight phases of development was occupied in 1973, and the golf course was opened in 1974. By 1979, road and utility improvements had been completed for four of the development stages, leaving the remaining sections of land unplatted. When each stage of development is filed for a plat with the county, the mix of uses is designed to meet the marketing considerations at that time. Planned uses include a 400-room hotel-conference center with banquet rooms, restaurants, shops, health club, and recreational facilities. Also planned is a separate commercial area for related services such as banks and convenience stores. Current market projections indicate the project will be fully developed some time in the early 1990s.

Market

Image-conscious companies are attracted to the project. In general, they are industries technically oriented toward energy, electro-medical, and information systems. The office market is composed primarily of companies which do not need a downtown location and are interested in a prestigious building and location.

Project Planning

A prime objective of the project has been to preserve the rolling terrain and natural features of the landscape by adapting the roads and buildings with a minimum amount of site grading and retaining walls. Although there are distant views of the Rocky Mountains to the west, most of the sites in Inverness also have views of the golf course, which are reinforced from a looped collector road within the park. The curvilinear streets throughout the project have rights-of-way of at least 50 feet. Extensive landscaping and the golf course, coupled with the low-rise structures and the design covenants, establish a campus environment. All parking is offstreet and the setbacks—50 feet from public rights-of-way for buildings and parking, 50 feet from the golf course for buildings, and 25 feet from the golf course for parking—exceed those required by zoning. Freeway frontage and prominent golf course sites are reserved for principal offices. Many of the warehousing and assembly uses are backed up to the airport or to each other.

Treated effluent is pumped to a reservoir (155-acre-foot) where the water is stored during the winter months and used to irrigate the golf course during the summer months.

5-21 Preserving the natural features of the rolling terrain is an important objective at Inverness.

5-22 The golf course at Inverness is zoned as private open space.

The buildings at Inverness vary greatly in size, shape, and architectural treatment. Design continuity, however, is achieved through covenant requirements for landscaping, structural types (no double tee or metal buildings), materials (nonreflective), colors (earth tones), signage, and lighting. No improvements are allowed until approval is obtained from the Inverness Planning and Architectural Control Committee, which also carefully reviews such items as utility locations, driveways, traffic, and views from other buildings. The committee is composed of five members including a licensed architect, a landscape architect, a land planner, a person with building construction experience, and a representative of the developer.

The private 18-hole, championship golf course and club are open to those in the project as well as to those in surrounding communities. The number of memberships is unlimited, with two types of membership offered—one with preferred starting times and no greens fees, and another with greens fees. Although only a temporary pro shop now exists, when the 400-room, hotel-conference center is complete, there will be indoor and outdoor tennis courts, swimming pools, and a health club.

Experience Gained

- Although in size the project greatly exceeds the current market demand, it has been successful because of the quality of the development, the long-term control, and a master plan with amenities.
- For a project such as this, a developer cannot be involved in the land sale business alone but must also be involved in the design and construction of buildings.
- A project having a large front-end investment, (which today, would be at least $10 million), takes a long-term commitment, in this case, 25 years. Such a commitment is difficult, not necessarily because costs must be projected over time but because the absorption rates cannot be determined over such a long period. Until the project is well established, it is particularly vulnerable in its ability to recover any return on the large investment.
- Aesthetics has an economic value even in an industrial setting. Although the major part of the golf course is on buildable land, its location, generally along the project's natural drainage ways, has proved to be the best and highest use of the land at no maintenance cost to tenants, while contributing materially to the overall appearance of the park. Although the golf course in itself could not be justified economically, it has provided a marketing identity and will have increased value when the hotel-conference center is developed.
- A tree and plant nursery is a good interim use for a phased development which has extensive landscaping needs. For nursery purposes, the property had the further advantage of having both well and flow rights, based on its established history of water consumption—an important legal factor in an arid region.
- The mix of uses within the park has been successful, attributable to the high architectural and master planning standards required.
- The successful marketing of building sites three-quarters of a mile from the freeway at freeway frontage prices illustrates the strong appeal of the golf course.

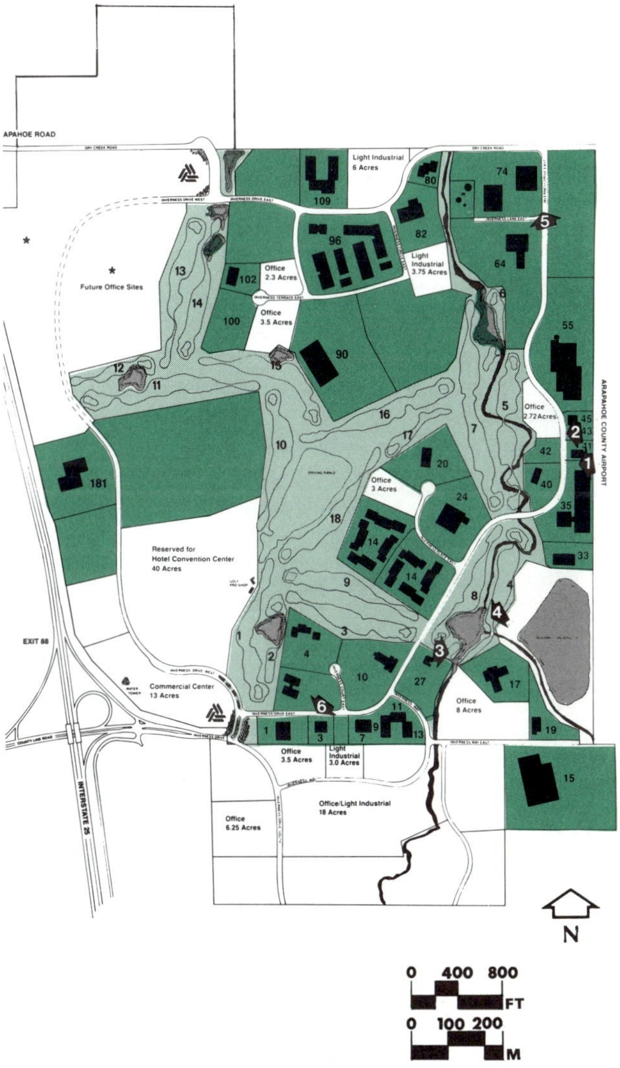

5-23 Inverness site plan.

5-24 Stormwater is controlled by retention ponds located throughout the golf course which generally follows the drainage ways.

5-25 Integrating the size and placement of signs into the overall development plan was important in gaining approval from the Planning and Architectural Control Committee at Inverness.

PROJECT DATA—INVERNESS

Land Use Information:

Parcel size: 1 to 80 acres (average 4 to 6 acres)
Absorption Rate: 25 to 35 acres per year (planned)

Land Use Plan:

	Acres	Percent
Office	40.339	7.4
Office/Light Assembly	125.315	23.0
Roads	25.054	4.6
Water and Sewer District Reserve	22.089	4.0
Golf Course	142.010	26.0
Unsold Land[1]	190.782	35.0
Total Platted	545.589	100.0
Unplatted (1979)	300.000	
Total	845.589	

Developer/Management:

Central Development Group
2505 18th Street
Denver, Colorado 80211

Planning and Landscaping:

Denton, Harper, Marshall & Assoc.
Denver, Colorado 80202

Engineering:

KKBNA (civil)
Denver, Colorado 80226

C.H_2M Hill (water/sewer)
Corvallis, Oregon

Golf Course Architect:

J. Press Maxwell
Morrison, Colorado

Economic Information:

Site Costs (1979):

Office:	$3.25 to $3.75 per sq. ft.
Light Assembly:	$2.95 to $3.25 per sq. ft.
Commercial:	$4.25 per sq. ft.

Site Improvement Cost: $0.49 per sq. ft. of building parcel[2]

Amenities:

Building Parcels $0.06 per sq. ft. of building parcel budgeted[3]

Golf Course: $1.2 million initial (1974)
$0.3 million in improvements (since 1974)
$50,000 to $60,000 per year capital improvement budget and $140,000 maintenance per year

Maintenance: $0.10 per sq. ft. of building parcel;[4] $90 per acre per year for common area maintenance.

Notes

[1]The plan includes sites for a hotel-convention center (42.2 acres) and a commercial center (10.0 acres).

[2]Roads, entries, curbs, gutters, and utilities to each building parcel are included.

[3]For landscaping, entries, and signs.

[4]Maintenance figure included labor, irrigation, replanting, reserve fund, some maintenance, general trash removal, common area property tax, and liability insurance.

Mixed-Use Development

Another type of real estate project for which supplemental recreation can play an important role is in mixed-use development (MXD). MXDs have three or more types of significant income-generating uses—typically office, retail, and hotel or residential—functionally integrated in one physical entity.[12] Recreational amenities appropriate to these development types can enhance market values, and the facilities may enjoy the fuller use associated with the multiple consumer markets of a mixed-use development.

Since MXDs are highly urban in character, indoor amenities are most common. These include health clubs, indoor racquet clubs, skating rinks, theaters, and restaurants. Several MXDs also contain sports arenas.

The Galleria, Houston, Texas

As a highly successful office/retail/hotel MXD in Houston, The Galleria features significant recreational facilities. An ice rink running almost the full length of the shopping mall serves both recreational and visual functions, drawing patrons to The Galleria and encouraging pedestrian circulation. The ice rink is most popular during the evening and attracts some 3,000 users on Saturdays.

The University Club, a 104,000-square-foot social/recreational center, is located above The Galleria mall. The facilities include 10 indoor tennis courts, exercise equipment, a track, and a social club. With the introduction of numerous recreational and other after-hours activities, The Galleria is able to maximize use of costly parking facilities and other common elements of the project.

[12]See Robert E. Witherspoon, Jon P. Abbett, and Robert M. Gladstone, *Mixed-Use Developments: New Ways of Land Use*, Technical Bulletin 71 (Washington: ULI–the Urban Land Institute, 1976).

5-27 Skating rink and shopping concourse at The Galleria.

5-26 The Galleria office/retail/hotel complex in Houston, Texas.

6. Emerging Trends

Considering the implications of present conditions on the future of recreational development helps both to prepare for the future and to understand better where development is today. The flexible application of the general development practices and the interpretation of the opportunities described in this handbook should point to how modern recreational development can best be structured through the 1980s.

The specific vision of what lies ahead in 1990 and beyond varies. Among numerous uncertainties as to the nature of the conditions which will influence future recreational development, one unquestioned fact is that recreation has become a necessity for most people. In the United States, tourism is ranked as the third largest industry, after food and automobile manufacture.[1] Receipts from tourism totaled $214 billion in 1979, up from $189 billion in 1978, and do not include many close-to-home recreational expenditures. The economic ills experienced in the latter 1970s, that may or may not be expected to continue into the future, failed to alter seriously the recent pattern of spending for recreation rising more rapidly than consumer spending as a whole.[2] Nonetheless, while continued growth in overall recreational interest can be anticipated, many interceding variables make its future form unpredictable, including considerations of demand, energy, financing, marketing, and public issues.

---

[1] Jeanne V. Beekhuis, "Tourism as a Tool for Economic Development," *Environmental Comment* (January 1981), p. 8.

[2] For a comprehensive discussion, see U.S. Heritage Conservation and Recreation Service, *The Third Nationwide Outdoor Recreation Plan* (Washington: U.S. Department of the Interior, December 1979).

Demand

North American society is growing older. The median age of the U.S. population was 30 in 1980 and is projected to increase to over 35 by the year 2000.[3] The population of the 1980s will be characterized by more single and working adults, small families, and retirees or those nearing retirement. Today's maturing population is generally better educated and more physically fit than its predecessor, requiring more specialized and sophisticated recreational projects.

Younger consumers are having smaller families (or none at all) than in the past, are likely to be relatively more affluent and mobile, and can be expected to seek more distinct experiences in recreation, whether through a fully equipped sports spa, a wilderness adventure, or a highly sophisticated resort. The demand for traditional, family-oriented recreational activities will probably expand more slowly, yet by no means should it be overlooked.

The retirement segment should undoubtedly continue to affect second-home development most heavily. Often having sold a vastly appreciated primary home, a purchaser in this group is frequently in a position to pay cash for a recreation-oriented residence. Smaller homes are needed for this market; high-priced products with substantial amenities are in particularly strong demand. As retiring second-home owners make more permanent use of their vacation homes, fewer units will be available for rental, and move-up units may be in greater demand. Existing and new development will be expected to upgrade units to full-time use, underlining the importance of planning certain recreational projects in anticipation of this demand and of mitigating possible adverse environmental impacts which might result from heavier use. As with any form of development, long-range plans should project and plan the life cycle of a project.

Future investments by the recreational industry will be dictated by the following consumer dispositions:

- increasing preoccupation with health and general well-being;
- advances in technology and communications;
- demands for dynamic, quality experiences (based in part on increasingly sophisticated past experiences);
- an ecological ethic; and
- greater wealth for some persons primarily attributable to dual-income families and highly appreciated assets.[4]

Prospects for shorter hours of work, as discussed at the beginning of this handbook, remain unclear although the advent of limited practices such as alternating 3-day weekends should have some influence on recreational patterns. More predictable is the emerging role of recreation in lifestyles. One example is that of urban apartment/condominium living which reduces time needed to maintain primary homes, making regular weekend and evening recreation a more common pastime, often readily available in high-amenity, primary-home projects. In this scenario, recreational property offers an escape from the city as well as the opportunity for real property ownership, particularly if shortages and price pressures on primary homes continue and people turn to second-home ownership as an alternative.

6-1 People in or approaching retirement compose the most rapidly growing market for second-home developments.

Another example of recreation emerging as part of a lifestyle can be seen in retail commercial operations which serve essentially as leisure time attractions. The interest in specialty themes in packaging retail facilities has probably only just begun to be tapped and will be reflected increasingly in future development that incorporates typical recreational elements into other types of facilities.

A further important factor in speculations on emerging trends is discretionary income available for recreation. Although projections of real growth seem to have a common bond in their uncertainty, some preview is still practical. With the need for recreation firmly entrenched, its purchase is dependent on money available and expenses incurred. If inflation remains high and real economic growth goes nowhere, value will be increasingly stressed. This

[3] "It's All Downhill from Here," *American Demographics* (January 1981), p. 7.

[4] Weiner, Edrich, Brown, Inc., *The Coming New Environment for Marketing Leisure Goods and Services in the U.S.* (New York: Weiner, Edrich, Brown, Inc., 1979.)

should not imply that cheap recreation will prevail, but that getting one's money's worth will be most important. It points to the potential for profit from providing recreational opportunities of quality for middle-income consumers, without excluding the importance of luxury. Regardless of the immediate economic prospects, one Florida developer anticipates an unprecedented boom in conspicuous but calculated consumption of wealth, spurred by the coming of age of empty nesters.

Location

Regional recreational development can be expected to follow demographic patterns to a large extent, related to natural attractions, and augmented by political, economic, and transportation factors. In the United States, the South and West should continue to experience the strongest expansion, based on their wealth of natural attributes and on their rapidly growing local populations. At the same time, increased travel costs present opportunities for recreation suppliers in the North and Midwest as large local populations stay nearer home during vacations.

Nonetheless, retirees and more affluent consumers will still be drawn to the sunbelt regions and areas with outstanding natural amenities. The trend toward specialized recreation not based on the use of automobiles will be evident at more exotic destinations while attractions near major urban areas will become more popular, especially with auto-dependent consumers who have less money for recreation.

6-2 Pyramid Place, a family entertainment center in Niagara Falls, Ontario, featuring a large screen movie theater, a free form playground and an array of other attractions, shops, and restaurants. This type of facility serves on a small scale the demand which falls somewhere between a theme park and conventional retail commercial operations. Because such developments can have major impacts on land use, it is important that they be compatible with public interests.

The 20 million annual visitors to the United States from foreign countries are also generally more affluent, having spent an estimated $10 billion in 1979. In the years leading up to 1981, the United States has increasingly come to be viewed as a vacation and investment bargain—with associated jumps in the number of visitors—though this situation continues to be subject to fluctuating exchange rates and inflationary cycles. Major urban centers such as New York, Miami, and San Francisco typically form the backbone of the most favored itineraries for visitors from outside North America. Resort areas are also attracting growing numbers of foreign visitors.

A twist in the locational question involves the political environment. Domestically, locations are distinguished by regulatory and tax differences, as well as by general economic and social values. For example, casino development could become increasingly influential as a form of recreational development. States considering the legalization of gambling during the 1980s will be tempted by the wish to attract and retain investment, preventing consumer dollars from shifting to states where gambling is permitted.[5]

The overall stability of the political system as it affects development in the United States is generally taken for granted. Internationally, politics can play a more significant role especially as it affects second-home purchases by nonnationals. The need for stability, investment incentives, convenience, and security are all critical in the context of real estate development in other countries. The record from country to country is mixed. Where political uncertainties persist, developers must exercise special caution in considering recreational development schemes targeted at nonlocal consumers. These risks may be offset by the availability of prime sites, lower relative wage scales, fewer regulatory restrictions, and government incentives.

6-3 An urban area can itself provide built-in manmade attractions and natural amenities. Pictured here is San Diego.

The U.S location offering the least risk for new resort/recreational development would be a stable, established, and growing area of high natural appeal. Local labor forces must also be considered. Given ideal social and political circumstances, a developer must still determine if the importance of natural amenities mandates avoiding the congestion of more intensive development, or if a more developed location is better in that the developer then does not need to supply an abundance of amenities. While both approaches are valid and will be followed in future development, the option involving the least risk—that of not being responsible for community amenities—will dominate.

Energy and Mobility

One pronounced change caused by the energy crisis of the 1970s has been the reevaluation of the long distance automobile vacation trip. Although stabilized gasoline supplies and more energy-efficient automobiles are helping auto travel maintain its popularity, the energy crisis has reportedly helped boost regional attractions as a focus of family recreation. One-stop destinations affiliated with major hotel chains offering a wide variety of amenity choices are becoming very popular. Moreover, a notable shift has occurred toward the use of local parks, movies, and other community-based recreation.[6] This may signal a greater emphasis being placed on fully equipped primary residences which are closely affiliated with neighborhood recreational amenities, thus reducing the need for travel and giving the primary home an additional dimension.

The limited resurgence of some older city areas, with more development, transit improvements, and population increases, may encourage additional investment in higher-quality recreation in downtown areas. Certain resort type facilities offering swimming, racquet sports, elegant settings, and access to cultural amenities could become increasingly popular attractions at many urban hotels that are typically underused on weekends. The movement to upgrade metropolitan parks and encourage their use, combined with improved public transportation, could strengthen the ability of urban centers to offer recreation and thus keep people at home.

[5] Urban Land Institute, "Meeting Report: Casinos Across America," *Urban Land* (January 1981), p. 24.

[6] Lawrence Maloney, "Goodbye to Our Good Life," *U.S. News & World Report* (August 4, 1980), p. 49.

6-4 One-stop destinations, varying from the dense type of development at Waikiki Beach to remote but full-amenity locations are highly marketable vacation settings.

Energy issues are affecting location preferences for recreation in at least two ways. Isolated auto-dependent destinations have already suffered. At the same time, the increased efficiency and convenience of air travel are contributing to greater reliance on air transportation, even with the rapid escalation in fares between 1979 and 1981. Total U.S. domestic commercial passenger trips grew from 246.7 million in 1978 (with an average distance of 717 miles) to an estimated 278.1 million in 1980 (average distance, 730 miles). Early 1981 projections estimate over 500 million passenger trips a year by 1993, with an average distance of 759 miles.[7] As vacationers become accustomed to traveling by air to recreational destinations and if air travel continues to be affordable, it will become less necessary for second homes to be within driving distance of primary residences. An apparent anomaly of the 1980s is that, despite high costs, transportation systems will permit access to secluded destinations as never before. Combination air/auto travel will probably offer the greatest growth potential for travel by both reducing energy consumption and increasing mobility. Marketing and advertising in the coming years will necessarily reflect the public's increasing consciousness of energy-related problems.

While encouraging visitors to stay longer at a destination, the cost of travel may also discourage the marginal visitor who is most often seen in the off-season and at the budget end of the market. Nevertheless, losses in one market may be compensated for by gains in another. For example, as higher costs discourage the marginal visitor from taking a Florida vacation, the regular visitor to a Caribbean destination may opt for Florida, while the exclusive or exotic Caribbean resort still maintains its attraction for the occasional vacationer seeking a unique experience. One effect of higher transportation costs is to put greater importance on the value of a destination, requiring it to justify the expense by offering a special recreational experience. The need to travel when one is on vacation is still strong; the vacationer will more likely trim his budget in other areas, such as in the amount of money spent at restaurants, rather than forgo a trip altogether.

The tremendous popularity of ship cruises represents the trend toward vacations which offer a full complement of diversions and minimal transportation concerns. Cruises reduce individual travel costs by pooling the expenses of energy use and distributing the cost over a large number of consumers.

Project design in the 1980s will require close attention to energy issues, such as consolidating transportation and providing less energy-dependent activities. Clearly, the physical plant will need to be efficient, emphasizing modern technology, solid construction, compactness, and site sensitivity. Refreshing climates will enjoy a natural advantage, as will one-stop destinations. With longer stays many amusements are often needed. Highly accessible urban attractions and multi-use facilities should serve as ready alternatives and will compete with facilities in more isolated locations.

6-5 While sophisticated condominium communities will thrive at specific destinations, the modest independently built second home should continue to be the typical type of recreational dwelling unit found within a convenient driving distance of primary urban centers.

[7] Data provided in February 1981 by the Federal Aviation Administration, U.S. Department of Transportation.

6-6 Ocean cruises characterize many of the attributes of the popular vacation package: an exotic environment, a range of amenities, familiar conveniences, pooled expenses, and single pricing.

Finance and Management

The money available for recreational development will continue to be tied to many variables, among them general economic conditions, the stability of credit markets, yields on alternative investments, and developer equity. In a word, it is probably reasonable to expect financiers through the foreseeable future to be "cautious." The fiascos of the mid-1970s are still recent reminders of the folly of reckless expansion. Interest rates at a few points above the inflation rate are not likely to drop substantially; the signs point to the increasing importance of substantial and stable equity financing and possible structural change in the traditional developer/investor/lender roles.

An evident victim of high risk capital, high interest, and economic uncertainty is large-scale recreational development, making it unlikely that many new projects of the magnitude of Sea Pines Plantation will be created in the early 1980s in the United States. Continued development and infilling at existing projects may cover the overall demand for a number of years; new development probably cannot compete with these approaches because of the escalated costs of construction. This situation may change toward the end of the decade as prices rise and existing space is consumed.

Many factors point toward new recreational development continuing predominantly as a spin-off from existing attractions, whether it be a subdevelopment on Hilton Head Island, an addition to an aquatic park near Disneyworld, or a new hotel at the Kaanapali Beach Resort in Hawaii. Most new recreational development is likely to occur on smaller sites, with a completion span of 2 to 4 years. An alternative to new development is the redevelopment or restructuring of earlier projects which have been less successful, usually because of financial difficulties. With the first and perhaps second owners writing away the development losses, a new owner may inject smaller but highly effective targeted capital and achieve notable results.

The high cost and risk of development have made it increasingly important for developers to consider contracting out their services to projects, leaving ownership of the project to other financial entities. Developer equity investment alone may not provide sufficient leverage to see a project through, although, as past experience has shown, investment institutions not depending on the experienced developer tied to the project through some equity participation are ill equipped to do the job themselves. Development success depends on management skilled in marketing and operation as well as in land use planning and construction. All indications are that in the future more sophisticated management techniques will be applied to recreational development.

The evolution of recreational development management is partly a response to consumer sophistication, but is more immediately attributable to trained business managers prominently assuming the authority for making decisions. With success or failure depending increasingly on such highly skilled management—particularly during economic downturns—fewer marginal developers will be able to operate on any kind of scale, which will make a marked difference in the traditional independence of recreational development.

As more management expertise is needed, development teams, composed of specialized consultants, will be increasingly brought in. Consultants, while often more expensive than in-house persons, may be preferred by the flexible developer, who can quickly add or drop such support as needed. It is this flexibility which further defines the successful recreational developer when dealing with market changes and related financial uncertainties.

Despite the seeming contradiction, the inspired developer must be prepared to provide diverse recreational opportunities as well as to offer a carefully tailored product for a specific market. The product must be responsive to market changes and ideally be capable of a transition to meet other demands. This product flexibility will in turn influence the amount of financing made available. The future should see development offering a balance between distinctive specialized facilities and a range of more average facilities having broad appeal.

Consumer financing has a direct impact on recreational development. Such financing is immediately responsive to current economic conditions. Although developers and financiers will be making commitments years in advance, consumer decisions will always define and react to present conditions.

Apart from economic conditions, consumer investment will be affected by tastes and value. Through the 1980s, value may be severely threatened by inflation and various shortages, including the availability of financing at interest rates low enough to encourage second-home purchases and other major consumer recreational investments. A safe prediction is that timesharing will become a more important segment of the recreation industry as it is increasingly recognized as a vacation investment alternative. Timesharing offers the buyer guaranteed facilities at relatively affordable costs that are, with the exception of maintenance fees, protected from inflation. It offers the developer important and potentially lucrative early sales. And it offers the operator the opportunity to mix rentals with owned units and to predict occupancies more accurately. Although interval ownership has its share of management, financing, and regulatory problems, its potential to provide enjoyment and creative use marks it with continued promise. Whether timesharing, with its explosive growth, will cut seriously into other markets and succeed in the resale market is still being determined.

Marketing

Most recreational ventures of major size must merchandise their facilities, which includes not only the marketing of recreational operations such as theme parks or resort hotels but also the sales of individual recreational properties. This may involve promoting the frontier spirit associated with individually owned, minimally controlled land, or promoting a highly differentiated and controlled built product.

Successful merchandising helps give distinction to a recreational attraction. As previously discussed, foreign vacationers to the United States are increasingly drawn to well-known cities and coastal areas, especially when accessible through all inclusive tours. In the future, domestic and international marketing can be expected to exploit new markets and sustain old ones. With a good product, a cooperative economy, and a well-implemented plan, recreational developers are in a position to create demand, as is true in other areas of merchandising.

6-7 Value, represented in all aspects from good planning to maintenance, is a critical consumer interest.

The days of high pressure sales of single undeveloped lots appear numbered. Outside of those on the strongest and most expensive markets, countless single lots have been largely undersold, leaving a substantial surplus. Where aggressive salesmen of the 1960s and 1970s were busy at the forefront of lot sales activity, today's real estate sales are best conducted in a more low key, subtle, and ultimately convincing style. Often the high price of the developed product is such that heavy sales pressure would only frighten away an interested purchaser. Therefore, a sound marketing program will depend on the actual quality of the facilities to promote real estate sales.

As air travel replaces some auto-dependent vacation travel, particularly to unfamiliar destinations, packaged promotions become more significant. Cooperative marketing of a vacation destination among competing businesses is often a highly effective way to spread visibility and increase demand. Vacation packaging for groups or individuals is an obvious way to cut travel costs, and the industry is becoming much more sensitive to the need for providing these services to each individual. The implication is that competitors in the industry will work together increasingly to coordinate particular overall travel strategies in order to meet the changing needs of the public.

6-8 Marketing recreational opportunities can require merchandising a full lifestyle.

Environment

Unique natural amenities and special urban settings will continue to monopolize the interest of the resort market. No matter what the level of amenities enjoyed in everyday life, most people have an innate desire for a change of scene. Many of the prime recreational destinations, however, are already spoken for and are becoming prohibitively expensive. New sites for recreational development are often restricted by competing land uses, public opposition, and prohibitive development costs, and are at a disadvantage when it comes to competing with other recreational projects that are already established.

Although their significance and form will vary from place to place, powerful environmental forces are acting to preserve the environment that comprises and defines recreational appeal. Environmental regulations and practices have been adopted, sometimes with unfortunate consequences where development is diverted to less restricted but also less appropriate areas. A developer must often have patience and substantial financing to see an environmentally sensitive proposal through planning and approval although the result usually proves well worth it in the long run. Since environmental interests have been thoroughly institutionalized and integrated into consumer demand and the regulatory process, the best development strategy turns the requirements into advantages through a well-planned, environmentally sensitive development. Such planning can help preserve a unique recreational attraction and protect an investment from the ravages of nature, whether on a sea coast, mountain slope, or in a river valley.

Government's Role

Public actions affect recreational development in many ways. Regulation and approval procedures provide a means for reacting to private initiatives. These influences are expected to continue growing as local governments, particularly in rural areas, become more sophisticated in their capacities to deal with development questions. Local governments have recognized the need to upgrade local land development practices, in part a response to past abuses and to the greater availability of technical expertise. Recreational developers must be prepared to allocate sufficient time and money and to structure proposals flexibly in working under regulatory conditions. In highly regulated communities, however, such as certain localities in California and Colorado, controls may ease somewhat as serious economic consequences surface and the developer's need for efficient and speedy regulatory review is recognized. Growth regulations are

6-9 Most recreational attractions originate from unique environmental factors. While development can make it possible for people to more fully enjoy the environment, it is essential that any development preserve such resources.

notedly biased in their tendency to favor existing development by limiting the opportunities for new development, allowing the price of recreational properties in such locations to be bid up to very high levels.

The public's direct role in recreational development has other implications. Government traditionally is responsible for providing open park space—with ongoing consideration of the addition of national, state, and local parks—and for encouraging private inholders in public parks to vacate. In general, however, government is finding its assignment to preserve space for outdoor recreation frustrated by limited and strained facilities and resources and is leaving the private sector, in many cases, to service the demand at a market price.

In the United States, government participation in capital-intensive recreational development of the sort discussed in this handbook has been minimal, with the exception of substantial investments in transportation networks and similar indirect support systems. Yet certain trends may indicate a shift in this stance. Tourism is recognized as a primary component of public economic policy; in recent decades, it has been among the fastest growing industries. The economic benefits from it can be quickly identified, but in some settings the risks in undertaking a recreational project are too great to attract private commitments. Mexico is a good example of government underwriting the development of major projects. In the United States and Canada, the risks of certain large-scale projects could mandate similar action in order to support policies on tourism. Further, if private development fails to provide for the needs of those with only average incomes, government underwriting could become a necessity.

The federal government has shown concern for recreational opportunities by cooperating with the private sector in developing such projects. For example, public land is commonly leased for approved privately operated recreation. Cooperative relationships could well expand into other arrangements as the need presents itself and the parties involved recognize the advantages. One community issue which involves this relationship increasingly respects the need for employee housing in expensive and isolated resort areas such as Vail and Snowmass in Colorado. History and current practice are full of examples of partnerships; the obstacle lies as much in steadfast notions of the adversary roles business and government are thought to play as in the actual differing interests of the two sectors.

6-10 Technology and innovation will help supply new opportunities for exciting recreational experiences.

6-11 Expanding on new concepts will broaden the market and increase competition for leisure time opportunities. Pictured here is Jackson Court, an urban timeshare conversion in San Francisco.

6-12 Artist's rendering of Epcot Center, an $800 million addition to Walt Disney World encompassing two main themes: nations of today, and technology of the future. (Walt Disney Productions photograph.)

The Recreational Development Industry

The challenge to the recreational development industry is to provide enjoyable settings to a growing and demanding market. Competing with many forms of consumer expenditures as well as with various types of capital investments, recreational development must operate like any other business. Although numerous implied costs and accrued benefits will be involved, the major test of the success of private recreational development will be its cost effectiveness. Appropriate pricing of the products becomes an important goal, although it is often difficult to determine optimum price levels in tight and fast-changing markets.

Sophisticated skills need to be applied in all phases of development to maximize the potential benefits and efficiency of the product. By facing the realities of government regulation and public interests and producing a product worthy of a good merchandising program, the developer is in a strong position to participate in facility operations or resale activities which will provide a valuable income source years after development is completed.

As a recognized necessity, recreational facilities are increasingly appreciated as desirable components of a community. The fact that newly planned communities include close-to-home recreational amenities attests to their importance. Multiregional and international vacation markets in which advancing communications and transportation are allowing consumers to be more selective and demanding are also of significance.

Competing recreational types must often employ innovations to respond to, and in many ways, control demand. The electronics industry continues to influence leisure tastes through new home entertainment devices. The most important innovations likely to affect recreation will be those which intensify the recreational experience and help to provide it efficiently. New exotic resorts and full amenity cruise ships will characterize many successful recreation packages in the early 1980s. Vacation marketing, such as that used in the promotion for "Club Med" operations, stresses lifestyles in offering specialized recreational packages. Numerous hybrids of existing project types are likely to appear as markets are combined and facility use is enhanced. Technology should offer a more diverse choice of amenities, made economical through certain standardized procedures, which also encourage the use of local and unique aesthetics and service. Various hotel and restaurant chains are pursuing this strategy. In the future, multiple themes and special recreational attractions will be increasingly adopted to complement retail functions. A variety of period themes, with subjects ranging from early industrialization to old movie sets, may be readily exploited as "new" attractions.

Innovative operating practices can help in the use of a project's facilities by accommodating peak periods more smoothly and reducing user conflicts. Flexible application of the axiom that quality can compensate for quantity in generating profit should result in a multitude of product variations and choices. Effective innovative practices can encourage more efficient use of facilities and produce adequate returns for the investor and relatively lower costs for the user.

The recreational developer is in the position to respond to the challenges of providing reasonably priced and rewarding recreational experiences by employing solid economic practices, supporting concepts with foresight which will offer the consumer an effective and efficient product, and doing the utmost to preserve and improve resources essential to the enjoyment of recreation.

APPENDICES*
AND
INDEX

*The Appendix material is meant to be illustrative and is no substitute for qualified counsel. If legal advice is required, the services of a competent professional should be sought.

APPENDIX A
Selected References and Information Services

Publications

Resort/Residential Communities

American National Standards Institute. *Standard for Recreational Vehicle Parks* (NFPA 501D). Boston: National Fire Protection Association, 1977, 30 pp. Available from Recreation Vehicle Industry Association.

Baud-Bovy, Manuel, and Lawson, Fred. *Tourism and Recreation Development: A Handbook of Physical Planning*. Boston: CBI Publishing Company, 1977, 210 pp.

Bloch, Stuart Marshall, and Ingersoll, William B., eds. *Timesharing*. Washington: ULI–the Urban Land Institute, 1977, 136 pp.

Campground Management (monthly). Highland Park, Illinois: Woodall Publishing Company.

Carestio, Ralph M., Jr., and Tischler, Paul S. "Developing Vacation Camprgrounds." *Urban Land*, November 1971, pp. 12–18.

Cornell Hotel and Restaurant Administration Quarterly. Ithaca, New York: Cornell University, School of Hotel Administration.

Crim, Sarah K. "Resort Community Industry Suffers Serious Blows From Economic Downturns." *Mortgage Banker*, January 1976, pp. 8–15.

Crosson, Stephen T., and Dannis, Charles G. "Time-Sharing Ownership in Resort Development." *The Appraisal Journal*, April 1977, pp. 165–172.

Davern, Jeanne M., ed. *Places for People*. New York: McGraw-Hill, 1976, 244 pp. (Articles from *Architectural Record* on restaurants, hotels, resorts, and conference centers.)

Fraser, Charles E. "Sea Pines Communities in an Energy-Short Society." *Urban Land*, June 1974, pp. 10–15.

"The Getaway Market." *Professional Builder*, November 1974, pp. 72–83.

Haimes, Jim, and Rose, Marvin. "The Second-Home Condominium Boom in Ocean City, Maryland: A Case Study of Overbuilding." *Urban Land*, December 1974, pp. 10–17.

Jacobus, George H. "A Strategy for Success in Recreation Home Developments." *Real Estate Review*, summer 1973, pp. 21–25.

Urban Land Institute. *Land: Recreation & Leisure*. Washington: ULI–the Urban Land Institute, 1970, 97 pp.

Lawson, Fred R. *Hotels, Motels, and Condominiums: Design, Planning, and Maintenance*. Boston: CBI Publishing Company, 1976.

Lykes, Ira B. *Recreational Vehicle Park Design and Management*. Grass Valley, California: Rajo Holding Company, 1977. Available from Recreation Vehicle Industry Association.

Manheim, Uriel. "Condotels: Promise Versus Performance." *Real Estate Review*, fall 1977, pp. 23–29.

Martin, Wendell H. "Remote Land: Development or Exploitation?" *Urban Land*, February 1971, pp. 3–10. (Recreational land sale developments—extent, developers' approaches, examples, regulatory issues.)

"New Tactics To Sell the Changing Resort Market." *Housing*, December 1978, pp. 70–79.

Pearson, David; Sandor, Gary; and Schock, Fred. "Resort Conversion: A New Response to a Developer's Dilemma." *Urban Land*, September 1975, pp. 3–12.

Poeschl, William H. "The Right Way To Market Vacation Homes: How a Professional Marketing Program Can Upgrade the Image of the Land Development Industry and Still Sell the Product." *Real Estate Review*, summer 1973, pp. 31–35.

Ragatz, Richard L. "The Expanding Market for Vacation Homes." *Real Estate Review*, summer 1973, pp. 15–19.

———. *The Resort Timesharing Industry: A Socio-Economic Impact Analysis of Resort Timesharing*. Washington: American Land Development Association, 1980, 2 vols.

———. "Vacation Housing: A Missing Component in Urban and Regional Theory." *Land Economics*, May 1970, pp. 118–126.

Reardon, Tim. "The Expanding Market for Recreation Condominiums: The Corporation and Vacation-Second Home Developments." *Real Estate Report*, fall 1973, pp. 1, 8.

"The Resort Market: Surviving Despite the Crunch." *House & Home*, November 1974, pp. 59–71.

Resort Timesharing Today (monthly). Los Altos, California: The CHB Company.

Richard L. Ragatz Associates. *Recreational Properties: An Analysis of the Markets for Privately Owned Recreational Lots and Leisure Homes*. Washington: U.S. Council on Environmental Quality, 1974, 508 pp. Available from National Technical Information Service, Springfield, Virginia. Order No.: PB-233 148/6 WU.

"The Road Is Open for Profits in RV Parks: Financial Prospects Are Favorable for the Investor in Recreational Vehicle Parks and Campgrounds." *Realtors Review*, October 1978, pp. 24–27, 33.

RV Campground Business (eight issues per year). Agoura, California: Trailer Life Publishing Company.

"The Second Home Market: Building for Fun." *Professional Builder*, February 1973, pp. 94–106.

Smith, William C. "A Lender Looks at Second-Home Financing: Guidelines to Sources and Cost of Funds for the Five Major Types of Vacation Home Loans." *Real Estate Review*, summer 1973, pp. 27–30.

U.S. Department of Health, Education, and Welfare. *Environmental Health Practice in Recreational Areas*. 1977, 84 pp. Available from Recreation Vehicles Industries Association.

U.S. Lodging Industry (annual). Philadelphia: Laventhol & Horwath. (Data on income, occupancy, expenses, and restaurant operations.)

"Vacation Homes." *Professional Builder*, April 1972, pp. 194–197.

Zoning for Recreational Vehicle Parks. Planning Advisory Service Report No. 326. Chicago: American Society of Planning Officials. 1977, 26 pp.

Theme and Amusement Parks

"Can Disney Still Grow on Its Founder's Dream? (Why the Theme Parks Must Turn to Thrills)." *Business Week*, July 31, 1978, pp. 58–62, 67.

Griffin, Al. *Step Right Up Folks!* Chicago: Henry Regnery Company, 1974, 274 pp.

Hellman, Hal. "Those Incredible New Amusement Parks: A Taste of Thrills to Come." *The Futurist*, August 1980, pp. 38–43.

Kyriazi, Gary. *The Great American Amusement Parks: A Pictorial History*. Secaucus, New Jersey: Citadel Press, 1976, 240 pp.

Managing the Leisure Facility (quarterly). Nashville: Billboard Publications, Amusement Business Division.

Pastier, John. "The Architecture of Escapism: Disney World and Las Vegas." *AIA Journal*, December 1978, pp. 26–37.

Wasserman, Louis. *Merchandising Architecture: Architectural Implications & Applications of Amusement Themeparks*, 1978, var. pag. Available from Louis Wasserman, P.O. Box 526, Sheboygan, Wisconsin 53081.

Zoos and Aquariums in America (biennial). Wheeling, West Virginia: American Association of Zoological Parks and Aquariums.

Commercial Recreation

Adie, Donald W. *Marinas: A Working Guide to Their Development and Design*, 2d ed. New York: Nichols Publishing Company, 1977, 352 pp.

Ames, Ronald, "Appraisal and Feasibility Analysis of Bowling Centers." *The Real Estate Appraiser*, March/April 1978, pp. 15–18.

Darrow, Lawrence P., and Daly, Patrick F. "Handball/Racquetball Clubs: The Recreational Boom Continues." *The Appraisal Journal*, April 1976, pp. 201–216.

Doherty, Ed. "Racquetball: A Whole New Ball Game for Developers." *Housing*, February 1980, pp. 48–53.

Epperson, Arlin F. *Private and Commercial Recreation: A Text and Reference*. New York: John Wiley & Sons, 1977, 385 pp.

Gimmy, Arthur E. "A New Racquet—The Indoor Tennis Club." *The Appraisal Journal*, October 1973, pp. 513–525.

———. *Tennis Clubs and Racquet Sport Projects*. Chicago: American Institute of Real Estate Appraisers, 1978, 94 pp.

Hall, Craig. "Why I'm Riding the Racquetball Boom." *Builder*, January 15, 1977, pp. 189, 191, 193.

Hever, Karla L., and McKay, Cecil, Jr. *Golf Courses: A Guide to Analysis and Valuation*. Chicago: American Institute of Real Estate Appraisers, 1980, 128 pp.

McGrath, John Williams, and Mulligan, Patrick S. "The Golf Course of the Future: Economic Realities." *Urban Land*, December 1975, pp. 3–16.

"Riding the Concrete Waves to Sound Financial Investment: Skateboard Parks, Like Indoor Tennis and Racquetball Courts, Promise To Be a Lucrative Area for Speculators in America's Thriving Recreation Economy." *Realtor's Review*, December 1977, pp. 10–14.

"Special Report: Investment Analysis of Tennis and Racquetball Courts." *Mortgage and Real Estate Executives Report*, October 15, 1978, pp. 4–6.

Steele, Robert L. "Racquetball." *Builder*, July 1, 1980, pp. 78–83.

"Tennis. Try It as a Non-Res Investment Opportunity. Use It To Help Spur Residential Sales." *Professional Builder*, April 1977, pp. 132–143.

Supplemental Recreation

Barasch, Stephen B. *Recreational Planning for New Communities*. New York: Exposition Press, 1974, 54 pp.

"Center Carnivals—Pitfalls or Profits." *Shopping Center World*, October 1978, pp. 22–24.

"The Dollars and Cents of Recreation." *House & Home*, February 1973, pp. 75–97. (Explores the cost element in creating recreational packages—swimming, tennis, golf, skiing—for primary housing and for resorts/second homes. Provides examples of projects including amenities.)

Fream, Ronald W. "Great Green Monster or Jolly Green Giant?" *Urban Land*, March 1978, pp. 5–9. (Golf as a residential amenity.)

Hanson, William A., and Bigelow, Frans. *Lake Management Case Study: Westlake Village, California*. Technical Bulletin 73. Washington: ULI–the Urban Land Institute, 1977, 113 pp. (History and discussion of the management of a comunity-owned lake.)

Jones, Rees L., and Rando, Guy L. *Golf Course Developments*. Washington: ULI–the Urban Land Institute, 1973, 105 pp.

"New Opportunities in Shopping Centers." *Mortgage and Real Estate Executives Report*, October 1, 1978, pp. 1–2. (Phenomenon of racquetball courts in shopping centers.)

Tourbier, Joachim, and Westmacott, Richard. *Lakes and Ponds*. Technical Bulletin 72. Washington: ULI–the Urban Land Institute, 1976, 73 pp. (Problems, functions, engineering criteria, maintenance, and legal and financial considerations of lakes and ponds—natural and manmade.)

Walker, Charles. "Amusement Centers: Still Problems, But Their Early Image Is Changing." *Shopping Center World*, April 1978, pp. 22–25. Reprinted in *The Real Estate Appraiser*, May/June 1978, pp. 29–31.

General References and Regulatory Issues

American Society of Planning Officials. *Subdividing Rural America: Impacts of Recreational Lot and Second Home Development*. Washington: U.S. Government Printing Office, 1976, 139 pp. Stock No. 040-000-00374-6.

Alan, Leslie; Kuder, Beryl; Oakes, Sarah L; and Simko, Patricia A. *Promised Lands*. Edited by Jean M. Halloran. New York: Inform, 1976–1978, 3 Vols. Vol. 1—*Subdivisions in Deserts and Mountains*; Vol. 2—*Subdivisions in Florida's Wetlands*; Vol. 3—*Subdivisions and the Law*.

Browning, Peter. "Mickey Mouse in the Mountains: The Folks Who Brought You Disneyland Yearn To Turn California's Mineral King Valley into a Mammoth Ski Resort." *Harper's Magazine*, March 1972, pp. 65–71.

Bosselman, Fred T. *In the Wake of the Tourist: Managing Special Places in Eight Countries*. Washington: The Conservation Foundation, 1978, 278 pp.

Dinger, Julius J. "Recreational Real Estate." *Urban Land*, May 1970, pp. 3–12. Reprinted in *The Real Estate Appraiser*, November/December 1970, pp. 26–34.

Gunn, Clare A. *Tourism Planning*. New York: Crane Russak, 1979, 378 pp.

Hall, Sam L., and Rogers, Michael P. "Reexamining the Federal Role in Meeting Urban Recreation and Open Space Needs." *Urban Land*, December 1978, pp. 7–13.

Heritage Conservation and Recreation Service, U.S. Department of the Interior. *National Urban Recreation Study* (Executive Report). Washington: U.S. Government Printing Office, 1978, 184 pp. Stock No. 024-016-00090-1. (Describes and assesses the current condition of urban recreation and identifies possible public and private actions to improve urban recreation.)

———. *The Third Nationwide Outdoor Recreation Plan*. Washington: U.S. Government Printing Office, 1979.

Hudson Research Institute. *Energy and Recreation*. Washington: American Recreation Coalition, 1980, 53 pp.

Jensen, Clayne R. *Leisure and Recreation: Introduction and Overview*. Philadelphia: Lee & Febiger, 1977, 295 pp.

Journal of Leisure Research (quarterly). Arlington, Virginia: National Recreation and Park Association.

Journal of Travel Research (quarterly). Boulder: University of Colorado, Graduate School of Business Administration, Business Research Division.

Leisure Sciences (quarterly). New York: Crane, Russak & Company, Inc.

Lustek, Joseph A., and Mann, Jack K. "The Feasibility of Recreational Land Development." *The Appraisal Journal*, January 1978, pp. 7–19.

Parks and Recreation (monthly). Arlington, Virginia: National Recreation and Park Association.

Ragatz, Richard L. "Future Demand for Recreational Properties." *Urban Land*, November 1974, pp. 10–16.

Robson, Arthur J., and Scheffman, David T. "The Crunch, the Boom, and the Recreational Land Market." *Canadian Journal of Economics*, February 1978, pp. 38–55.

Rosenow, John E., and Pulsipher, Gerreld L. *Tourism: The Good, The Bad, and The Ugly*. Lincoln, Nebraska: Century Three Press, 1979, 264 pp.

Rosenthal, Murray. "Playground-Building Battleground: The Santa Monica Mountains as a Microcosm." *Cry California*, winter 1977–1978, pp. 14–18. (Conservation/recreation/economic resource use conflicts.)

Stockwell, Sherman. "Balancing Private and Public Interests: Conservation and Development at Lake Tahoe." *Urban Land*, March 1976, pp. 3–12.

Stroud, Hubert B. "The Land Development Corporation: A System for Selling Rural Real Estate." *Journal of the American Real Estate and Urban Economics Association*, fall 1978, pp. 271–286.

Urban Land, July/August 1974. (Issue devoted to articles on federal regulation of the sale of raw land.)

Vaux, H. J. "Rural Land Subdividing: A Lesson from the Southern California Desert." *Journal of the American Institute of Planners*, July 1977, pp. 271–278.

Organizations

American Alliance for Health, Physical Education, and Recreation
1201 16th Street, N.W.
Washington, D.C. 20036

American Association of Zoological Parks and Aquariums
Oglebay Park
Wheeling, West Virginia 26003

American Dinner Theater Institute
P.O. Box 2531
Sarasota, Florida 33578

American Land Development Association
604 Solar Building
1000 16th Street, N.W.
Washington, D.C. 20036

American Planning Association
1313 East 60th Street
Chicago, Illinois 60637

American Recreation Coalition
P.O. Box 204
Chantilly, Virginia 22021

American Society of Golf Course Architects
221 North LaSalle Street
Chicago, Illinois 60601

Amusement and Music Operators Association
Suite 1940
35 East Wacker Drive
Chicago, Illinois, 60601

Association of Physical Fitness Centers
5272 River Road
Washington, D.C. 20016

Bowling Proprietors' Association of America
P.O. Box 5802
Arlington, Texas 76011

Camp Coast to Coast
1000 16th Street, N.W.
Washington, D.C. 20036

The Conservation Foundation
1717 Massachusetts Avenue, N.W.
Washington, D.C. 20036

Foundation for the Extension and Development of the American Professional Theater
165 W. 46th Street
Suite 310
New York, New York 10036

Ice Skating Institute of America
1000 Skokie Boulevard
Wilmette, Illinois 60091

Marina Owners, Developers, and Operators Council
American Land Development Association
1000 16th Street, N.W.
Washington, D.C. 20036

National Bowling Council
1919 Pennsylvania Avenue, N.W.
Washington, D.C. 20006

National Golf Foundation
200 Castlewood Drive
North Palm Beach, Florida 33408

National Industrial Recreation Association
20 North Wacker Drive
Chicago, Illinois 60606

National Ski Areas Association
P.O. Box 83
20 Maple Street
Springfield, Massachusetts 01101

National Swimming Pool Institute
2000 K Street, N.W.
Washington, D.C. 20006

Recreational Vehicle Industry Association
P.O. Box 204
14650 Lee Road
Chantilly, Virginia 22021

Roller Skating Rink Operators Association
7700 A Street, P.O. Box 81846
Lincoln, Nebraska 68510

United States Racquetball Association
4101 Dempster Street
Skokie, Illinois 60076

United States Tennis Association
51 East 42nd Street
New York, New York, 10017

U.S. Tennis Court and Track Builders Association
1201 Waukegan Road
Glenview, Illinois 60023

APPENDIX B

Lakeridge Regulations Torrington, Connecticut

I. GENERAL REGULATIONS

A. Use of Lots

1. Residence lots shall be used for residential purposes only.

2. No industry, business, trade, or commercial activities except for home professional pursuits without regular visits from the public shall be conducted, maintained, or permitted on any lot.

3. No "For Sale," "For Rent," or "For Lease" signs or other window displays or advertising shall be maintained or permitted on any part of the properties or in any lot therein, nor shall any lot be used or rented for transient, hotel, or motel purposes, except with the prior written consent of the Board of Directors.

4. Each garage lot may be used only for the storage of a motor vehicle, boat, or trailer and the neat and clean storage of domestic material related to its use as an accessory to a residence.

5. The Board of Directors or its designated agent may retain a pass key to the premises for use in emergency situations only. No owner shall alter any lock or install a new lock on any door of the premises without the written consent of such Board of Directors. In case such consent is given, the owner shall provide the Board of Directors or its agent with an additional key pursuant to its right of access to the demised premises.

6. No electrical device creating unusual electrical loading may be used on the lots without prior written permission from the Board of Directors.

7. No alteration or remodeling involving the exterior of a building on a lot may be done without written permission from the Architectural Review Committee.

8. Misuse or abuse of appliances or fixtures within the lot is prohibited; any damage resulting from such misuse shall be the responsibility of the owner in whose lot it shall have occurred.

9. On those lots on which buildings are constructed on piers, the area under the building shall be kept free of unsightly material and no storage of materials or animals will be permitted on any lots except in such manner as to prohibit the spread or encouragement of fire or vermin, and except in specific structures or structural additions to the buildings, which have been approved in writing by the Architectural Review Committee for health, safety, and architectural fitness.

10. Owners shall not cause or permit anything to be hung or displayed on the outside of windows, with the exception of the American flag on holidays, or placed on the outside walls or doors of a building and no awning, canopy, shutter, or radio or television antenna shall be affixed to or placed upon the exterior walls or doors, roof, balconies, or patios, or any part thereof without the written consent of the Architectural Review Committee.

11. No terrace, balcony, or patio shall be enclosed or covered by anything or otherwise enclosed without the written consent of the Architectural Review Committee.

12. Nothing shall be hung, with the exception of the American flag on holidays, from the windows, terraces, balconies, or patios, or placed upon the window sills, nor shall any rugs or mops be shaken or hung from or on any of the windows, doors, balconies, patios, or terraces. No clothes, sheets, blankets, laundry, or any other kind of articles shall be hung out of a building or exposed on the Common Properties. No clothes shall be hung or dried outside of the buildings on the lots.

13. Owners shall not paint, stain, or otherwise change the color of any exterior portion of any building.

14. Each owner shall keep all buildings and structures on his lot in a clean and sightly condition.

B. Use of Common Properties

1. The Common Properties shall be used only for the purposes for which they are intended.

2. There shall be no obstruction of the Common Properties, nor shall anything be stored in the Common Properties without the prior written consent of the Board of Directors except as hereinafter expressly provided.

3. No garbage cans, trash barrels, or other obstructing personal property shall be placed on the Common Properties by the owners.

4. No accumulation of rubbish, debris, or unsightly material will be permitted in Common Properties, except in designated trash storage areas, nor shall Common Properties be used for the general storage of personal property.

5. Storage of materials in Common Properties or other areas designated by the Board of Directors shall be at the risk of the person storing the materials. Buildings used for storage shall be kept neat, clean, and free of vermin.

6. The Developer may make such use of the unsold lots and Common Properties as may facilitate completion and sale of the property including, but not limited to, maintenance of a sales office, the showing of the Common Properties, and the display of signs.

7. From time to time the Board will promulgate policy resolutions to provide for the safety, protection of equipment, and good order of the use of the Common Properties. Common Properties will be used in accordance with the policy resolutions as posted at the applicable facility.

C. Insurance

1. Nothing shall be done or kept which will increase the rate of insurance of any of the buildings or contents thereof applicable for residential use without the prior written consent of the Board of Directors.

2. No owner shall permit anything to be done or kept in his lot or in the Common Properties which will result in the cancellation of insurance on any of the buildings or contents thereof or which would be in violation of any law. No waste shall be committed in the Common Properties.

3. An owner shall comply with the Rules and Regulations of the New England Fire Rating Association and with the rules and regulations contained in any fire insurance policy upon said building or the property contained therein.

4. Damage by fire or accident affecting the Common Properties or the liability of the members will be promptly reported to the Board of Directors or the Manager immediately following the occurrence thereof.

D. Actions of Members

1. No noxious or offensive activity shall be carried on in any lot or in the Common Properties, nor shall anything be done therein either willfully or negligently which may be or become an annoyance or nuisance to the other members or occupants. No member or occupant shall make or permit any disturbing noises in the buildings by himself, his family, servants, employees, agents, invitees, and licensees, nor do or permit anything by such persons that will interfere with the rights, comforts, or convenience of other members or occupants. No member or occupant shall play upon, or suffer to be played upon, any musical instrument or operate or suffer to be operated a phonograph, television set, or radio in the premises at such volumes or times so as to cause a disturbance to other members or occupants.

2. No immoral, improper, offensive, or unlawful use shall be made of the Property or of any part thereof, and members and occupants shall comply with and conform to all applicable laws and regulations of the United States and of the State of Connecticut, and all ordinances, rules, and regulations of the City of Torrington, and shall save the Association or other members harmless from all fines, penalties, costs, and prosecutions for the violation thereof or noncompliance therewith.

3. No animals or reptiles of any kind shall be raised, bred, or kept in any lot or in the Common Properties, except that a dog or cat that is not kept, bred, or maintained for any commercial purpose may be kept inside residences. Also, any other household pet that is not kept, bred, or maintained for any commercial purpose may, with the prior written approval of the Board of Directors or Manager, be kept inside residences. Any such dog, cat, or other approved household pet may also be kept in a specified area on a lot outside of the residence which has been approved in writing by the Board of Directors or Manager.

4. Any pet causing or creating a nuisance or unreasonable disturbance or noise shall be permanently removed from the Properties upon three (3) days' written notice from the Board of Directors or Manager.

5. In no event shall any dog be permitted in any portion of the Common Properties unless carried or on a leash or be curbed in any courtyard or close to any building or patio.

6. Members and occupants shall be responsible for any damage or injury caused by any pets owned by them, their families, servants, employees, agents, guests, or tenants.

7. Members shall be responsible for the actions of their children, tenants, guests, and pets, and shall hold the Association harmless for the actions of their children, tenants, guests, pets, servants, employees, or agents.

E. All Motorized Vehicles

1. Connecticut State laws and Motor Vehicle Bureau regulations will prevail on Lakeridge roadways.

2. All vehicles must also be registered with the Manager and must be operated by licensed drivers only. NOTE: Non-registered construction vehicles will be identified as such.

3. No vehicle shall be parked in such manner as to impede or prevent ready access to any other parking space.

4. Vehicles belonging to owners or their families are to be parked only in designated parking areas or in garages.

5. The parking area shall not be used for any purposes other than to park vehicles excluding specifically trucks, commercial vehicles, trailers, and boats, which may be parked in specially designated areas only.

6. Except where special arrangements have been made, visitor parking spaces are only for the temporary use of guests and invitees of owners or of the Association. Employees are to park only where specifically designated. The parking area near the Sports Field is designated as visitor parking between December 1 and April 1. The Ski Lodge parking area is designated for visitor parking from April 1 until December 1.

7. The speed limit on Lakeridge roadways is established at 20 M.P.H.

8. The operation of snowmobiles is prohibited on the Common Properties.

TOWING

1. Vehicles blocking direct access to another owner's garage or legally parked vehicle:

Upon receipt of a complaint from an owner or designated occupant of a lot that a car is blocking access to the owner's garage or vehicle legally parked, Management will immediately contact the approved towing company who shall remove the offending vehicle to the towing company's premises or such place as the Manager will direct.

2. Emergency Access:

If a vehicle is parked in an area where parking is not permitted, in such manner as to obstruct access for service or emergency purposes, the vehicle shall be immediately towed away as above upon complaint by an owner or security personnel.

3. No Parking Zones:

Parking is restricted to those areas laid out by lines specifically designated for permitted parking. No parking is permitted anywhere else on the Common Properties or where signs are posted. In the event vehicles are parked in such a manner as to not block access as in paragraphs 1 or 2 above but located in those areas not designated for parking, the vehicle will be ticketed by Management, the owner of the vehicle traced, and the complaint registered with the Management Office.

Parking in a no parking zone will subject the owner following notice from Management, an opportunity to be heard and give a reason before a designee of the Management Company, and thereafter, if no suitable reason is given for such parking, a $5 per day charge levied pursuant to Article XII, Section 3(d) of the Bylaws. In the event violation continues for more than eight (8) days after ticketing-offense is repeated, the vehicle will be towed. In the event the offending vehicle is not owned by a member but owned by a guest of a member, and the vehicle owner refuses to pay the charge, the host member shall be responsible for payment following notice and hearing as above.

4. Approved Towing Agency:

English Shell, Winsted, Connecticut, shall be designated as the approved towing company for Lakeridge Association, Inc., and the president is authorized to enter into an agreement with English Shell guaranteeing payment of towing charges in the event that an owner does not or will not pay for any reason. Towing charges shall be the responsibility of the owner of offending vehicle. In the event the owner of the offending vehicle does not pay the towing changes, and the Association pays, the member who is host to the vehicle owner or is the vehicle owner, shall pay the charge as a special fee pursuant to Article IV, Section 3(d) of the Declaration for additional expenses which shall be added to the monthly assessment and common charges bill for the subsequent month, which shall become a lien and personal obligation of the member under Article V of the Declaration.

F. Trash Removal

1. Trash pickup containers will be located by Management at each village. Pickup will be from those containers only. Occupants will be solely responsible for removal of trash from their lots to the pickup containers.

2. Trash is to be sealed or tied within plastic bags reasonably strong enough to prevent bursting and the bags deposited in the containers. Loose trash or trash cans will not be permitted within the trash containers, nor will such trash be picked up.

G. Payment of Services

1. All services are charged to the owner's account. Owners must give written permission to the Management Office for guests to be allowed to charge on the owner's account. All tenants must charge to the owner's account.

II. LODGE REGULATIONS

1. Invited guests to the lodges shall be limited to a maximum of ten per lot.

2. The lodges shall be used in accordance with the Policy Resolutions posted therein.

3. No pets will be allowed in the lodges.

4. The Association shall not be responsible for personal property left in the lodges.

5. The lodges shall not be used for events that are concerned with interests of sales or business, politics, or religion, or where a fee or contribution is required of an attendee.

6. Management personnel have the responsibility and authority under the Bylaws to expel or recommend suspension or charge any individual whose actions are sufficiently hazardous or potentially damaging to the property. Responsibility for behavior of any individual, regardless of age, lies with himself, or in the case of a minor, the parents or guardians.

7. The East Lodge is closed during the week during the winter months. The key to the Crafts Room, however, is made available to adults through the Recreation Office.

8. The Ski Lodge, in the off-season, may be reserved subject to a fee of $____ for parties to a maximum of 50 people. In the event this lodge is to be reserved for a party, the Manager shall be notified at least one (1) week in advance and a reservation requested. Any group having a party shall see that the party facilities are provided, that provision is made for ample parking, that the conduct of the party is such as to minimize the disturbance of members, and that the lodge is cleaned and straightened up within twelve (12) hours from the end of the party. A $____ damage deposit is also required, returnable upon inspection of the lodge by Management.

9. Any persons using lodges shall be responsible for keeping it clean and presentable.

III. RECREATION

A. Swimming Areas

1. Except by prior arrangement with Management, the number of guests in one group in the pools at any one time will not exceed four (4) per lot.

2. Swimming areas will be used in accordance with the Policy Resolutions as posted.

3. No pets are allowed in the swimming pools or pool areas or at the Ridge Pond beach area.

4. Management will store personal articles found at the swimming areas until the end of the current swimming season and will dispose of these unclaimed articles remaining at that time. It will assume no responsibility for personal property left at the pool.

B. Boats and Canoes

1. Boaters must reserve each craft through the Recreation Office or East Lodge attendant.

2. Boaters under the age of 18 MUST have a signed permission slip on file in the Recreation Office or be accompanied by a responsible adult.

3. Boaters must use ONLY the authorized trail to the launch site and crafts must be launched from the designated site ONLY.

NOTE: Lakeridge's launch site is limited to crafts rented by Lakeridge Association, Inc. Private boats must be launched from the State's boat launch ramp on Burr Mountain Road. Lakeridge agreed to limit the number of boats to a maximum of 20; motors are not permitted on any Lakeridge craft except an emergency vessel.

4. Boaters must return craft if a storm approaches. Diving from boats on the lake is not permitted.

C. Horseback Riding

1. Reservations are made through the Recreation Office ONLY. No reservation can be taken at the Stables.

2. All rides will be accompanied by the Horseback Riding Instructor and are normally for one hour. Late arrivals' riding time will be cut short by the amount of time the party is late. There must be more than one rider at a time.

3. The stable area shall be used in accordance with the Policy Resolutions as posted.

D. Ski Slopes

1. The ski slope may be operated by the Association either directly or on a concession basis. The slope manager will be responsible for all operations and activities on the ski slope. Users of the ski slope will comply with his directions and with the safety regulations posted at the entrance.

2. A reasonable fee for skiing will be charged for the use, maintenance, and operation of the skiing facilities in accordance with a schedule of fees posted at the ski slope.

3. Ski schools may be operated on a fee basis by arrangement with the slope manager.

4. No schussing, boisterous, or rough play will be permitted on the slope. Courteous trail behavior will be required. Lift lines will be respected and there will be no cutting ahead, skiing through, pushing, or shoving. Sitzmarks will be filled and tamped down by the persons causing them.

5. Skiers must maintain control at all times and will be responsible for skiing on the slopes which are commensurate with their abilities and experience.

6. Consumption of alcoholic beverages and food, use of glassware, pets, discarding of trash and debris, sleds, toboggans, walking or climbing without skis are prohibited.

E. Tennis

1. All tennis courts shall be used in accordance with the Policy Resolutions posted.

2. Players must wear smooth sole tennis shoes on the courts. The playing surface will be respected and hard objects will not be placed or struck on the court.

3. Good manners are expected and conduct shall be such as to minimize interference with the play of others. Do not chase balls across courts while play is in progress.

4. Pets, food, beverages, breakable containers, trash, or debris are not permitted in courts.

5. The last group to leave will lower nets.

F. Sports Field Area

1. The Sports Field area will be used for active sports, including baseball, football, and similar games. Rough, dangerous behavior is forbidden.

2. The Sports Field area may be reserved for organized games on a first-come basis upon request to Management.

3. Persons using facilities will be responsible for cleanliness and their activities. . . .

IX. ADMINISTRATION

1. Right is specifically reserved to the Board of Directors to rescind, change, or amend the foregoing Rules and to adopt such other rules and regulations as from time to time the Board of Directors may deem necessary or appropriate.

2. No member shall send any employee of the Manager out of the project on any private business of the member, nor shall any such employee be used for the individual benefit of any member, unless in the pursuit of the mutual benefit of all members.

3. Management personnel are authorized to detain persons who are violating provision of the Declaration of Covenants and Restrictions, Bylaws, Regulations, and Policy Resolutions in the Common Properties for purposes of commencing an investigation and determination of the responsible person. Detention shall be only for such time as is necessary to identify the violator and, if necessary, contact his or her parent, guardian, host, or host member.

4. Management personnel who are sworn in as special police officers in the City of Torrington are directed to arrest persons who are found committing crimes within the properties of Lakeridge and commence undertaking the arrest pursuant to procedures established by the Police Department of the City of Torrington.

5. Any complaint regarding the management of the Properties or regarding actions of other members shall be made in writing to the Manager or the Board of Directors or the appropriate committee.

6. No recreational facilities of Lakeridge may be used by any person who has not registered with Management. Management personnel may ask for the display of Lakeridge identification of a member, tenant, guest, or employee using a facility, and ask any person not so displaying or otherwise satisfying the personnel of his bona fides to leave the facility immediately.

7. Any consent or approval required by these Regulations must be obtained in writing prior to undertaking the action to which it refers and may be added to, amended, or revoked at any time by resolution of the Board of Directors, subject to notice and comment or notice and hearing, at the option of the Board.

8. All members, guests, tenants, employees, and other visitors are required to become a part of the Lakeridge Identification System.

PROCEDURES

A. Enforcement Resolutions Affecting Single Individual

1. A report for a recommended enforcement procedure shall be received by the Board in writing in the form of a complaint of property owner, staff, governmental official. Tenants or property owners must forward complaints through their owner.

2. Complaint will be referred to the appropriate staff member or committee for investigation and recommendation.

3. A date and time for a hearing on the complaint will be established. The appropriate staff or committee will be designated to receive information at the hearing and investigate the details of the complaint.

4. Notice of the complaint including the date and time for the hearing including the notice of the opportunity to be heard will be sent to the accused.

5. The designated agency will hold the hearing, accept communications, make investigations, and obtain such other evidence as it deems necessary.

6. The hearing agency will make the report in writing to the Board of Directors including the resolution in a form to be adopted by the Board.

7. The Board will receive a report, discuss the resolution and accept, reject, or modify the resolution as it deems necessary, sending a copy of the conclusion to all affected parties.

B. The following procedure with respect to the adoption of permanent resolutions affecting all unit owners interpreting or amending rules or regulations to be adopted.

1. Communication, staff recommendation, or Board of Directors proposes an administrative resolution or topic of discussion to the Board of Directors.

2. If the Board determines that the rules and regulations are to be amended, the Board will refer the topic to the appropriate committee or staff for investigation and drafting of the proposed regulation or amendment and set a date and time for a hearing before the Board of Directors for adoption.

3. If the Board determines that the topic can be handled by an interpretative or a policy resolution, the topic will be referred to staff or a committee for review, informal hearing, and report including a draft in a form suitable for passage by a committee.

4. If the topic can be the subject of an internal operating policy which does not directly affect the members as a whole, but merely governs Board or staff procedures, the topic will be referred to a committee or staff for drafting in the form of an administrative resolution suitable for adoption without hearing.

5. Draft resolutions are to be published in the Bulletin prior to adoption, and if a hearing is then needed, prior to hearing.

6. The hearing will be conducted with an opportunity given to all interested parties to be heard or communicated with the hearing agency in writing.

7. Resolution will be drafted and submitted to the Board of Directors meeting within the time set and referred to the Board with a report.

8. Upon passage, the Board will publish a copy of the proposed resolution in the Bulletin and record resolutions in the Board of Resolutions maintained by the Secretary.

C. Form of Resolutions

1. Resolutions adopted by the Board shall include introductory paragraphs wherein reference is given the appropriate Declaration, Bylaws, or other legal basis for the passage of the resolution. The purpose of the resolution is described and the intent of the Board is summarized.

2. Policy and administrative resolutions will be maintained in a Book of Resolutions by the Secretary and a table of contents including the subject of the resolution and the date of preparation will be included in the book. The book will be available at the Management Office at all times during business hours for examination by members. From time to time, but no less than once a year, the Secretary will review current resolutions and recommend to the Board with suggestions to the appropriate committee any amendments or deletions determined necessary by passage of time, change, or practice or determination of the need for the resolution.

D. Home Owner Attendance at Meetings/Copies of Minutes

In the interests of time and due to the multitude of matters discussed, the meetings of the Board are closed to residents unless a specific matter is to be brought before them and a prior request for an appointment is submitted in writing to the Board. However, the minutes of all meetings are available to the residents at the Management Company and may be read there, or photocopied at a cost of 25¢ per page.

X. IDENTIFICATION SYSTEM

1. Each owner shall state those whom he/she wishes to be a part of the photo I.D. system. Any other person who visits an owner's unit will be classified as a tenant or guest. Every owner must be a part of the photo I.D. system.

2. Every guest of an owner who will remain at Lakeridge for MORE THAN 10 days is required to become part of the photo I.D. system.

3. Every tenant is required to become part of the photo I.D. system.

4. Every guest of an owner who will remain at Lakeridge for LESS THAN 10 days shall be issued a guest pass by Security at the time of arrival. These passes shall be carried to the lodges if the guests wish to enter.

XI. TENANTS, GUESTS, AND TRANSIENT OCCUPANCY

1. Guest permits will be issued to guests as defined in this section to as many guests as requested by a Member, on a week to week basis, who by acceptance, agree to be bound by these Regulations and the requirements of the Declaration and Bylaws and acknowledge that they are paying no consideration for occupancy of the host Member's lot.

2. Tenant membership licenses will be issued to as many tenants as defined here as a Member may request, to tenants occupying his Lot under a lease of no less than two weeks in duration, for the duration of said lease. The issuance of said permit shall follow the granting of a revocable license by the Board of Directors pursuant to Article IV, Section 3(j) of the Declaration and Article VIII, Section 2(j) of the Bylaws. The Board can delegate to any officer of the Association the power to issue such licenses.

3. Application for such license for a Tenant shall be on the form established by the Board (see sample copy). The application shall be accompanied by a copy of an executed lease, and shall be filed with Management at least seven days before commencement of the lease.

4. A $25 (twenty-five) fee will be assessed to the Member for each lease on his/her lot. This fee is to be charged to the Member's account at the initiation of the lease period.

5. The lease must provide:

a. That the Tenants have received copies of, understand, and agree to be bound by these Regulations and the requirements of the Declaration and Bylaws.

b. A minimum $200 security deposit, subject to law.

c. The Landlord grants, and the Tenant attorns to, the Association, acting through its president, an irrevocable power of attorney for the Landlord for the term of the lease, and holdover periods, to act on behalf of the Landlord, to terminate the lease and commence summary process and other legal action against the tenant, to abate actions or recover damages, in the event that the Tenant or his guests or invitees shall violate the Regulations, Policy Resolutions, Declaration, or Bylaws of this Association.

d. All actions of the Association hereunder shall be undertaken at the cost of said Landlord, including reasonable attorney's fees of the Association, *provided* before any action is commenced, Landlord Member is notified by certified mail at least five days before commencement of such action, with a copy by ordinary mail to Tenant, and Landlord fails to commence such action itself or abate the violation prior to the date set for commencement in said notice.

e. The Landlord or the Tenant may in a timely manner, request a hearing before the Board, to be held prior to said date, to protest the action, or indicate reasons for the violation. After opportunity to be heard, the Board may either agree to proceed, agree to delay, or terminate the action.

f. Use restrictions of Article IX will be reprinted in the lease.

g. The lease may not be modified, amended, extended, or assigned without prior written consent of the Board of Directors (Article XIV, Section 11, Bylaws).

h. The tenant shall not sublet or let out for temporary use, with or without payment, the demised premises, or any part thereof, without the prior written consent of the Board of Directors (Article XIV, Section 11, Bylaws).

6. Acceptable leases shall be for a period of not less than fourteen days, and a Member shall not be permitted to lease his Lot for more than twelve separate rental periods per year.

7. The following definitions shall interpret the terms of this Regulation and the Declaration and Bylaws:

a. Guest—shall be a person who is an invitee of a Member or Tenant occupying a lot who pays no consideration for his occupancy. Corporate occupancy pursuant to corporate purposes permitted by Article IX, Section 2 of the Declaration, shall be permitted by corporate guests, provided that such occupants pay no rental for such occupancy, and such occupancy is only incidental to the corporation activites of the Member. Occupancy for investment purposes may not be on a transient basis as defined herein.

b. Tenant—shall be an invitee of a Member, occupying his lot in return for rental or other consideration.

c. Transient—as restricted in Article IX, Section 1 of the Declaration, which is a prohibited purpose, is defined as occupancy by a tenant or tenants under leases or agreements of less than fouteen days duration.

APPENDIX C

Sunriver Design Committee Rules, Sunriver, Oregon

1.0 DEVELOPMENT OBJECTIVES

Sunriver is a unique environment, blessed with those natural attributes rarely found in any development. Meadowlands, pine forests, abundant water, natural rock outcroppings, mountainous horizons, sunshine and clean air, all form the ingredients of that environment. It is of prime importance to the continued aesthetic and ecological quality of Sunriver that all structures and landscaping are compatible with one another, and insofar as possible, are in harmony with the natural surroundings.

1.1 Objectives

Under Section 8 of the Plan of Sunriver, the "Design Committee" was established, not to inhibit freedom of individual expression, but to encourage design excellence through stringent but reasonable architectural and landscape standards. Contrary to the usual "economic" standards, which are the rule in other communities and developments throughout the country, no arbitrary square footage or cost minimums are required at Sunriver. Each project will be reviewed by the Design Committee and judged on the basis of its quality of design and compatibility with the site and overall environment.

1.2 Duties and Rules

The Sunriver Plan, Section 8 states in part:

"The Design Committee may from time to time and in its sole discretion, adopt, amend, and repeal rules and regulations to be known as the 'Design Committee Rules,' establishing its operating procedures and interpreting, detailing, and implementing the provisions of the instruments pursuant to which it is charged with responsibility."

1.3 Procedures

The Design Committee will establish and announce to property owners of Sunriver its administrative procedures. In general, these principles will be followed:

1.3.1 Interested property owners may submit comments on any plan, and plans can be inspected by making arrangements with the Secretary of the Committee.

1.3.2 Property owners within 250′ will be routinely notified when a plan is submitted and their comments are invited.

1.3.3 The Design Committee will meet regularly, a quorum of four members will be mandatory, a majority vote will be required for design approval, and two signatures required of the majority to be affixed on the plans.

2.0 SUBMITTAL AND APPROVAL PROCEDURE

Assurance of conformity to the Sunriver Design Committee Rules requires that all proposed new buildings, remodeling, and additions, landscaping, and other improvements of private areas be approved by the Sunriver Design Committee before commencing work of any kind. The procedure shall be as follows:

2.1 Submittals

Drawings and specifications for any proposed project shall be submitted in duplicate to the Design Committee through the Secretary for presentation to the Committee.

2.2 Preliminary Design

In order that an Owner who so desires may ascertain the probability of Design Committee acceptance of the proposed work before proceeding with the preparation of final plans, the Design Committee welcomes preliminary design submittals for review and evaluation. This procedure will often save the Owner expense and delay.

2.3 Final Design

Upon review of final design submittals the Owner will be notified in writing of Design Committee action.

2.4 Permits

Upon approval of final submittals and payment of the required fees to Sunriver Properties, Inc., and to Deschutes County, building permits will be issued and the Owner may commence construction. Deschutes County has adopted the Uniform Building Code. Following Sunriver Design Committee final approval, all plans must be submitted to Deschutes County for a detailed plans review. This review generally takes two to three weeks.

2.5 Inspections

Up to three "field" inspections may be made by representatives of the Design Committee. The first shall in all cases be an inspection and approval of building "stake-out," which shall be required prior to issuance of a building permit, within 24 hours after requested by the Owner or Contractor. Additional inspections will be "as required" due to participation of Deschutes County.

2.6 Preliminary Design Submittals (Optional)

Review of preliminary submittals by the Design Committee shall be of an advisory nature; therefore, such submittals may consist of informal presentations. In order, however, that the Design Committee may give just consideration to the proposed work, it is recommended that preliminary submittals adequately describe the site plan, floor plans, and exterior character of the proposed structure. (Drawings may be of any scale, however, drawing sheet sizes shall be multiples of 9″ x 12″.) Preliminary submittals shall be in duplicate. Favorable review of preliminary submittals by the Design Committee shall neither imply nor guarantee acceptance of final design submittals.

2.7 Final Design Submittals

The final design submittals will constitute the only basis of conclusive action by the Design Committee, and must adequately reflect to the Committee the true design quality of the proposed work as it relates to the innate "Design Philosophy" of Sunriver. It is recommended that submittals be prepared by a competent professional. Final plans shall be submitted in duplicate. A tear out check list is included in this manual.

2.8 Site Plan

In lieu of arbitrary setbacks, each lot at Sunriver will be considered individually by the Design Committee. No improvement shall be less than five feet from an adjacent lot property line and the Site Plan shall be developed to define the relationship of structure to site. However, every unit shall conform to the applicable setback provisions of Deschutes County. This plan should be produced at a scale not less than 1″ = 20′. (Drawing sheet size shall be multiples of 9″ x 12″.) In addition to the principal structures, the following information must be provided.

- direction of primary view
- natural site topography
- field stake out with necessary datum points
- proposed finish grades and site drainage
- existing trees, shrubs, and other natural features, such as rock outcroppings
- proposed removal of trees
- location of existing structures on adjoining lots
- proposed off-street parking, drives, walks, patios, and decks
- proposed fences, screens, earth berms
- proposed landscaping plan and description of plant materials to be added
- line of proposed roof overhangs
- proposed exterior lighting location and description

2.9 Construction Plans and Specifications

Construction documents for the proposed project shall be completed in sufficient detail to fully explain the intent of the structural, architectural, mechanical, and electrical systems as well as the materials and finishes involved. Drawings shall be at a scale of not less than ¼″ = 1′. (Drawing sheet size shall be multiples of 9″ x 12″.) The inclusion of the following information is required:

- footing and foundation plan
- floor plans
- building elevations showing all views
- building section showing building height
- specifications (description of materials and finishes)
- proposed exterior stain and paint colors

Although review and approval by the Design Committee is for appearance and design compatibility only, all proposed construction systems shall be in accordance with the requirements of state and local codes (Uniform Building Code, latest edition), and appropriately designed for local climatic conditions. The Design Committee shall assume no responsibility for the structural or mechanical soundness of approved designs.

2.10 Deschutes County Requirements

Deschutes County requires that a Building Permit be obtained prior to beginning construction on any structure or making any additions or changes to an existing structure. The County requires two sets of drawings as described in paragraphs 2.8 and 2.9; (1) one set must have the Sunriver Design Committee stamp affixed to it indicating that it has received Design Committee final approval.

Deschutes County has adopted the Unified Building Code (UBC). Key elements in this code are. . . .

2.11 Procedure for Application for Deschutes County Building Permit

You or your contractor can make application for a Building Permit at the Building Inspection Department (Room 104, Courthouse Annex). After the clerk makes out the application, you will be directed to the Planning Department for an address and site approval. The application is then brought back to the Building Inspection Department, where the fee is paid. The Plans Examiner will then expedite the Plans Review, after which the actual Building Permit is issued. The Permit and Plans may then be picked up here. No work other than excavation may be done before the Permit is actually issued. The Permit and sign-off card must be conspicuously posted at the site.

(1) If the structure has more than one width or incorporates a unique design, more than one cross-section may be necessary.

2.12 County Building Department Inspections

In addition to Sunriver's inspections, Deschutes County will inspect the structure at four points in its construction sequence:

- Footings: After staking and excavation but before any concrete is poured.
- Framing and rough plumbing: After the walls are up, and roofing, siding, and windows, etc. are installed.
- Sheetrock nailing: After all sheetrock has been hung but before it is taped.
- Final: Upon completion of the structure.

It is the responsibility of your contractor to notify the Building Department when he is ready for each inspection. No building may be occupied until final inspection has been made and a Certificate of Final Inspection has been affixed to the electric panel.

(1) The set of Plans bearing the Plans Examiners approval stamp must be on the job site at all times during the course of construction and be available to the Building Inspector.

2.13 Example

The sample site plan and working drawings which follow represent the minimum levels of quality and content which will be accepted by the Design Committee for final approval.

3.0 ARCHITECTURAL GUIDELINES

The climatic environment of Sunriver is widely varying; and, as such, experience suggests that certain construction methodology is prudent. For your convenience and enjoyment, we recommend these practices [concerning:]

3.1 Temperatures. . . .

3.2 Precipitation. . . .

3.3 Soil Conditions. . . .

3.4 Prevailing Winds. . . .

3.5 Heating. . . .

3.6 Insulation. . . .

3.7 Garages, Carports, or Other Accessory Buildings. . . .

3.8 Roofs. . . .

3.9 Exterior Walls, Fences, and Trim

Material shall be wood of any regionally appropriate species, such as cedar, redwood, Douglas fir, or pine treated with one of the many available semitransparent wood stains, or, if approved by the Design Committee, finished naturally to allow it to "weather." Paint, other than on entrance doors, sash, or other incidental trim is not desirable. The Design Committee will accept for review other materials and finishes and will consider them on an individual basis.

3.10 Masonry

Exposed masonry surfaces shall be limited to normally local stone. Concrete, concrete block, stucco, and brick will be acceptable where appropriate, subject to specific approval by the Design Committee.

3.11 Sash and Sliding Glass Doors

Frames must be stained, painted, or color anodized in a manner, which, in the opinion of the Design Committee, is acceptable. Mill finish aluminum frames and screens shall not be permitted.

3.12 Exposed Metals*

All exposed metal surfaces such as roofing, flue pipes, fireplace chimneys and caps, plumbing stacks, miscellaneous flashings, etc., shall be painted flat black or colors, which, in the opinion of the Design Committee, are acceptable.

3.13 Service Areas*

Proposed plans must provide for fencing or screening of clotheslines, wood and outdoor storage, bicycle racks, garbage cans and trash areas, service meters, and air conditioner condensing units from the view of adjacent property, golf course, roads, and paths. Such fencing or screening shall be of materials and finish consistent with the principal structures on the site or plantings of suitable plant materials whose growth patterns will screen both in height and density. No plan will be considered without location of garbage/trash enclosure being shown.

3.14 Off-Street Parking*

The location of each single-family residential structure shall allow for the off-street parking of at least two automobiles.

If a carport or garage is provided, that structure will fulfill the requirement for one space. In any event, at least one additional open, off-street parking space must be provided.

3.15 Building Height

Height limit restriction may be imposed by the Design Committee primarily to preserve the views from adjacent homes and areas. At present a 26′ ridgeline is used as a guideline maximum.

3.16 Exterior Lighting*

Type and placement of exterior lighting devices must be approved by the Design Committee. The concern is to eliminate glare and annoyance to adjacent property owners and passersby.

3.17 Fences*

It is intended that fences will be used for screening and privacy purposes only. Under no circumstances will fences be permitted to be built along property lines for the purpose of dividing one lot from another. The basic concept of Sunriver land planning is that common land surrounding the property blends into each private lot. To install fences between lots would defeat this. Please refer to Section 3.13 which describes types and uses of fencing that are acceptable.

3.18 Spark Arrestors*

Appropriate fire spark arrestors must be provided on all chimneys designed for homes built in Sunriver.

3.19 House Numbers*

House must have lot number clearly posted and visible from cul-de-sac.

*Required by the Sunriver Design Committee.

4.0 LANDSCAPE GUIDELINES

It is the desire of the Design Committee that structures built in Sunriver be in harmony with the forest, so also is it the Committee's desire that any landscaping be in harmony not only with the forest, but with the meadow environment. The attached list of plants and trees indigenous to the Sunriver area has been found to grow well here.

4.1 Grasses and Ground Covers

Seeding of buildable and open areas with meadow fescue, native grasses, and wildflowers will be encouraged. Lawns planted close to homes in enclosed, screened areas are acceptable. The normal city-type or suburban manicured grass lawn is discouraged.

4.2 Paths and Walkways

Paths and walkways made of bark chips, lava cinders, gravel, or log sections are effective and fit well into the natural environment. Surfacing material, which is reflective such as white stone chips, is prohibited.

4.3 Removal of Trees, Rocks, Shrubs, or Other Natural Forms to Private Property

No tree, major shrub, major rock, or other prominent vegetation shall be removed from private property without the consent of the Design Committee whose decisions will be based upon aesthetic considerations, common sense and judgment.

4.4 Outdoor Furniture and Accessories

Location of permanently placed outdoor furniture such as swings, picnic tables, barbecues, arbors, jungle gyms, and tree houses must be approved by the Design Committee.

4.5 Execution of Landscape Plan

It shall be the responsibility of the lot owner, when landscaping his property, to follow the plan submitted to the Design Committee with the initial construction drawings. If a landscaping plan has not been previously approved, or if changes are contemplated, a plan must be submitted for approval prior to commencing landscape work. The plan must show location of all features—trees, shrubs, rocks, grasses, berms, structures, and any other additions.

5.0 GENERAL REQUIREMENTS

5.1 Building Permits

Upon approval of "final plans," it is required that a building permit be obtained prior to commencing any construction activity whatsoever. Permit fees currently are as follows:

Initial building permit is $_____, payable to Sunriver Properties, Inc. Although there is no fee for a subsequent addition to the structure, permission must be granted prior to execution of the work. Building permits must be affixed to the project in a prominent location.

Contractor will also deposit $_____ as a "Contractors Damage Deposit" when obtaining building permit. This is refundable after final inspection and approval of finished building, along with interest earned while on deposit.

5.2 Excavation

Extreme care must be taken during excavation to assure that trees not authorized for removal are not damaged. Also that brush, surplus soil, and other excavated debris are promptly removed from the building site.

5.3 Protection of Property

All construction activity shall be contained on the lot for which a building permit has been issued. Access to the lot shall be only from the road abutting the site. Any common ground, adjacent lots, or roads damaged during construction shall be promptly restored to their original condition to the satisfaction of the Design Committee or required repairs will be performed by Sunriver Properties, Inc., with all costs thereof charged to the person in whose name the building permit was issued.

5.4 Garbage and Trash

5.4.1 Owners are responsible for their own garbage and trash removal during and after construction. Collection service may be obtained by calling disposal companies.

5.4.2 Burning or dumping of garbage or trash anywhere at Sunriver is strictly prohibited, except by written consent of the Sunriver Operations Department.

5.4.3 During construction, (or after, if you wish) trash may be disposed of at the LaPine Dump (approximately 7 miles south of Sunriver just off Highway 97).

5.5 Temporary Structures

Temporary structures or construction trailers which have been approved by the Design Committee shall be permitted on a unit during the period of construction of a building. However, any such temporary structure shall be removed within 30 days after completion of the building or within a year after the date upon which the temporary structure was erected, whichever period first expires.

5.6 Signs

No sign shall be placed or kept on any private dwelling unit or private home site other than signs stating the name of the occupant, the address of the unit, and any name given by the unit owner to the unit, except that in the event that the unit owner wishes to advertise his unit for sale or lease he may do so provided that he shall use for the purpose a sign approved by the Design Committee. "For Sale" signs are available at the sales office for a nominal charge. No For Sale sign, owner name, or unit signs shall exceed dimensions of 18" x 12". Contractors' signs shall not exceed dimensions of 18" x 24". Colors of all signs must consist of yellow background with dark brown lettering or dark brown background with yellow lettering unless otherwise approved by the Design Committee. Signs may be posted as follows:

a. No more than two signs if the cul-de-sac is directly accessible from a main road, in which case one sign may be located at the cul-de-sac intersection and the other at the home or lot being sold.

b. If two culs-de-sac share a common entry street, then three signs may be used with one being posted at the main intersection, one at the cul-de-sac entrance and the third at the home or lot being shown.

c. Open House signs shall be blue on white and shall be no larger than 18" x 24" and will read as shown:

d. Signs shall be removed when the home is not being shown.

5.7 Mailboxes and Newspaper Receptacles

As the community grows, should it become necessary to provide mailboxes and/or newspaper receptacles, such conveniences shall be of uniform design and placement as determined by the Design Committee.

6.0 THE DESIGN COMMITTEE
(PERTINENT EXCERPTS FROM THE PLAN OF SUNRIVER)

Section 8.1: Function of Design Committee

"Generally, the Design Committee will be responsible for the approval of plans and specifications for the development of private areas and for the promulgation and enforcement of rules and regulations governing the use and maintenance of private areas and the improvement thereon."

Section 8.8: Liabilities

"Neither the Design Committee nor any member thereof shall be liable to any unit owner or the Administrator of Sunriver for any damage, loss, or prejudice suffered or claimed on account of any action or failure of the Committee or a member thereof, provided only that the member, in accordance with actual knowledge possessed by him, has acted in good faith."

7.0 SUNRIVER LAND USE
(PERTINENT EXCERPTS FROM THE PLAN OF SUNRIVER)

Section 4.2: Private Areas

"By accepting a deed or lease to a private area within a village the grantee shall be deemed to have convenanted that he will use and permit the use of the property only in accordance with, and that he will abide by the restrictions, covenants, and conditions contained in the Plan of Sunriver and in the Sunriver Declaration creating the village . . . in which his unit is located."

Section 4.4: Common Areas

"Each resident of Sunriver is hereby granted a nonexclusive easement to use common areas for such recreational purposes as may be permitted by the Sunriver Rules and Regulations and in the manner permitted therein . . . the Administrator in its discretion may dedicate common areas to the public for park purposes and may use common areas for the purpose of location of utilities thereon . . ."

7.1 Stop Work Order

Awareness of the Design Committee to any of the above-described violations or nonconformance to any of the provisions of this document may result in issuance of an immediate STOP WORK ORDER to be affixed to the project until such violations are remedied.

Section 11.1: Enforcement of Sunriver Rules and Regulations

"It will be important to the residents of Sunriver that the Sunriver Rules and Regulations be enforced in as impartial and uniform manner as practicable. In most cases it will not be desirable to resort to the public authorities for the enforcement of these rules and regulations. Therefore, the Administrator of Sunriver may impose penalties for the violation of the Sunriver Rules and Regulations within the following limits:

(a) The Administrator may impose a fine upon the resident of Sunriver who has violated or whose guest has violated a rule or regulation in an amount not to exceed the sum of $_____ for any one violation. If such fine is not paid by the person upon whom it is imposed it shall be paid by the unit owner who by virtue of his ownership of a unit caused the person upon whom the fine was imposed to be a resident of Sunriver.

(b) The Administrator may provide that a person who has violated a rule or regulation shall be deprived of his right to use the common areas, semipublic recreational or service areas, or any specified parts of either for a period of not to exceed one year on account of any one violation. Such penalty shall become effective ten days after delivery by the Administrator of notice thereof to the person upon whom it is imposed."

Section 11.2: Violation of Sunriver declaration by non-qualifying improvement

"In the event any unit owner constructs or permits to be constructed on his unit an improvement contrary to the provisions of a Sunriver declaration or in the event that a unit owner maintains or permits any improvement, condition, or other thing on his unit contrary to the provisions of a Sunriver declaration, the administrator of Sunriver may no sooner than 60 days after delivery to such unit owner of written notice of the violation enter upon the offending unit and remove the cause of such violation, or alter, repair, or change the item which is in violation of such declaration in such manner as to make it conform thereto. The Administrator may charge such unit owner for the entire cost of the work done by it pursuant to this section. Such amount shall become payable upon delivery by the Administrator to the unit owner of notice of the amount due, and shall be paid into the maintenance fund to the extent that the costs being reimbursed were paid out of the maintenance fund."

Section 11.3: Violation of Sunriver declaration relating to landscaping

"In the event that any unit owner fails to comply with the provisions of a Sunriver declaration limiting the removal of trees and shrubs, the Administrator of Sunriver may impose on such unit owner a fine in an amount not to exceed $_____ for each shrub removed in violation of such declaration and not to exceed $_____ per inch of the diameter of the stump of each tree removed in violation of such declaration. The Administrator may also restore the original landscaping insofar as is reasonably possible and charge the unit owner for the entire cost involved in such restoration. Such costs shall become payable upon delivery by the Administrator to the unit owner of notice of the amount thereof and shall be paid into the maintenance fund to the extent that amounts being reimbursed were paid out of the maintenance fund."

7.2

The Sunriver Plan, the appropriate village declaration, and, in the case of multi-unit projects, the condominium declarations or other basic recorded documents, should be examined for special restrictions or uses in certain villages or projects. Periodic review of these documents is advisable before and during the course of construction or remodeling.

8.0 UTILITIES CONSTRUCTION GUIDELINES

Following are utility guidelines for Owners and Contractors, which will apply during construction of homes in Sunriver. These instructions are designed to clarify policies and to protect all parties thereto, and supersede all previously published guidelines.

Please note the division of responsibility. Sunriver has responsibility for some items; the Contractor and Owner must insure that their obligations are met in the proper sequence, before, during, and after construction. No building permits shall be issued on a lot until underground utilities are completed to that lot.

8.1 Sewer and Water Hook-up

8.1.1 It is Sunriver's responsibility to bring sewer and water lines to each property owner's lot line.

8.1.2 Construction of sewer and water lines from the lot line to the home is the Owner's responsibility.

8.1.3 Location of sewer and water hook-ups must be determined prior to start of construction.

8.1.4 Please follow the procedures for construction of sewer and water lines exactly in the following sequence. . . .

8.2 Electrical

8.2.1 Sunriver will provide underground power lines to the lot line of each Owner's property. There is no charge to the Owner for the underground installation.

8.2.2 Lot Line to Home. . . . Service rates will vary for full-time residency or seasonal use. Underground power lines should be coordinated for installation when the water and sewer trenches are open.

8.2.3 Electrical Wiring—During the construction phase, the Contractor or Owner is responsible for obtaining an electrical permit from the State of Oregon. . . .

8.2.4 When power turn-on is required, call ________.

8.3 Telephone

8.3.1 Underground telephone lines to the pedestal in each block of home sites will be provided without charge to the lot owner.

8.3.2 Owner and Contractor should request underground telephone wire installation from the pedestal to the home to be installed at the same time as other underground lines. . . .

8.4 Television

8.4.1 TV cable should be installed underground from the pedestal to the home at the same time as the water, power, and telephone line. . . .

8.5 Garbage and Trash

8.5.1 Owners are responsible for their own garbage and trash removal during and after construction.

8.5.2 Burning or dumping of garbage or trash anywhere at Sunriver is prohibited.

8.5.3 During construction (or after, if you wish) trash may be disposed of at the LaPine Dump. . . .

APPENDIX D

Bylaws for Amelia Island Plantation Club, Amelia Island, Florida

Article I—Name and Purpose

The name of this Club shall be the Amelia Island Plantation Club. The Club is owned and operated by the Amelia Plantation Company, an Ohio corporation (hereinafter known as the Company). Subject to the provisions of these Bylaws, members shall be entitled to use the Club's facilities but shall have no vested interest therein.

Article II—Membership

SECTION I: Classes and Privileges

Each membership shall include husbands, wives, and unmarried dependents under 21 years of age. A dependent is one who is living at home or away at school but dependent on family support. There shall be four classes of membership:

A. Full Membership:

Full membership shall allow full use of all Club facilities at no charge other than monthly dues. The member shall be responsible for all charges incurred for golf cart rental, food and beverages, and personal incidentals. The members's immediate relatives not included within the membership, as provided above, shall be allowed to use the recreational facilities when authorized by the member, provided that such relatives shall be charged and pay the then current rate for such use as charged associate members. For purposes hereof, "immediate relatives" shall be defined as sons and daughters 21 years of age or more, sons-in-law and daughters-in-law, parents, grandparents, and grandchildren.

B. Tennis Membership:

Tennis members shall have full use of all Club facilities except golf at no charge other than monthly dues. A tennis member may use the golf facilities upon payment of the current rate for such use as charged associate members. The member shall be responsible for all charges incurred for golf, food and beverage, and personal incidentals. The member's immediate relatives not included within the membership, as provided above, shall be allowed to use the Club facilities when authorized by the member, provided that such relatives shall be charged and pay the then current rate for such use as charged associate members. For purposes hereof, "immediate relatives" shall be defined as sons and daughters 21 years of age or more, sons-in-law and daughters-in-law, parents, grandparents, and grandchildren.

C. Associate Membership:

Associate members shall have full use of all Club facilities at a reduced user rate. An associate member shall be responsible for all charges incurred for golf, tennis, spa, food and beverage, and personal incidentals in addition to monthly dues.

D. Corporate Membership:

Corporate memberships shall be identical to the aforementioned classes of membership in privileges, initiation deposits and dues. These memberships are issued in the name of a firm or corporation and shall be assigned to a designated employee. Each corporate membership shall have only one designee, such person to be approved by the Membership Committee. There shall be no limit to the number of memberships a corporation may have. The designee and the corporation shall be jointly and severally liable for charges and dues incurred by the corporate memberships. The designee may be changed by the corporation from time to time subject only to approval of that designee by the Membership Committee and the payment of a corporate transfer fee.

The Board of Directors of the Company, upon advice and counsel of the Board of Governors, shall have absolute power and authority to establish additional categories of membership, determine the number of members to be allocated in each category, the terms of admission, privileges, and facilities to be extended.

SECTION II: Initiation Fee, Dues, and Assessments

Each member, whether individual or corporate, shall pay an initiation fee and monthly dues in such amounts as fixed from time to time. There shall be no assessments of any kind or character ever levied against the membership.

SECTION III: Screening of Roster of Invitees

A. The evaluation of the roster of membership invitees shall be conducted with the intent and purpose of securing the optimum number of members with compatible social, economic, and professional backgrounds.

B. Invitations to be extended and applications will be evaluated on the basis of the following criteria:

1. Interest of the invitee or applicant in the use of the Club membership for business and/or social purposes.
2. Financial responsibility either as an individual or a corporate entity.
3. Compatibility with Club members in respect to social setting.

A qualified applicant shall be approved for membership invitation unless there are specific reasons for rejection in which case the prospect may be rejected without giving reasons or explanations.

SECTION IV: Applications

A. All applications for and acceptances of membership shall be made on the required form supplied by the Club. Each application shall include the name of the applicant, address, required family and business information, club memberships, if any, and sponsors' names.

B. All applications for membership shall be accompanied by an initiation fee as fixed by the Board of Directors. Such fee shall be immediately refunded to the applicant if the application for membership is disapproved by the Club.

SECTION V: Termination of Membership

Termination of membership shall result in the loss of the right to use the Club's facilities. The termination shall not release the member from payment of dues or other obligations to the Club which occurred before he or she ceased to be a member.

A. Resignation

Members may resign from the Club at any time by giving thirty (30) days advance notice to the Club and paying all dues and charges, for which they are liable, up to the date the Club receives such notice of resignation. Upon such resignation, they shall not be thereafter subject to any dues or other charges. A member may be reinstated following resignation upon payment of the appropriate initiation fee.

B. Death

In the event of a member's death, the surviving spouse shall thereupon automatically succeed to all the rights and privileges of such membership without payment of any charge or other fee by reason of such transfer.

C. Delinquency of Account or Misconduct

In accordance with Article IV, Section II, and Article VIII, Section I, of the Bylaws, a member may be expelled from the Club for delinquency of account or misconduct.

d. Disposition of Property

When a person sells or otherwise disposes of his Amelia Island Plantation property, his membership shall terminate at the end of the month in which he sells his property unless he requests an extension of up to 6 months.

SECTION VI: Transfer of Classification of Membership

Any member approved by the Membership Committee for transfer to a different classification of membership shall, at the time of such transfer, pay the initiation fee currently applicable to the classification to which the transfer is made, less, however, the amount the member previously paid as initiation fees in his present classification, provided, however, that no refund of initiation fees will be made to a member who transfers to a classification having a smaller initiation fee than that previously paid by such a member in his present memberships classification.

Article III—Board of Governors

SECTION I: Number, Qualifications, and Terms of Office

The Board of Governors of the Amelia Island Plantation Club shall be composed of not more than sixteen (16) members.

A. Twelve (12) members shall be elected by a majority of the Club's members to serve a 2-year term. Such a member may serve two consecutive terms if so elected.

B. Four (4) members shall serve on the board by virtue of holding the following positions:

1. Current President of the Amelia Island Plantation Ladies Golf Association.
2. Current President of the Amelia Island Plantation Women's Tennis Association.
3. Current President of the Amelia Island Rental Property Owners' Association.
4. Appointed representative of the Amelia Island Plantation Community Association, Inc.

C. Serving in an advisory capacity, the immediate Past President of the Board shall be an ex-officio member for a period of 1 year.

A member of the Board shall be a member in good standing of the Club. Terms of office will commence on August 1.

SECTION II: Duties

The Board of Governors for the Club shall advise and counsel with the Board of Directors and the Club management on any and all items relating to the conduct of Club affairs including, but not limited to, the following areas:

A. Membership admission policies.

B. Design and functional arrangement of Club facilities.

C. Initiation fees and levels of dues for all categories of membership.

D. House rules and regulations, guest policy, and normal operating hours of the Club.

E. Menu prices and all items related to charges incurred by members.

F. All policies having to do with delinquent accounts of members, questions of conduct, expulsion of members, mode of dress and other related disciplinary matters.

G. The eligibility and fitness of senior technical personnel in staff positions charged with the responsibility of serving members directly or indirectly in accordance with high-quality standards preferred by the members.

H. All plans for renovating, remodeling, or modernizing on the Club premises.

SECTION III: President, Vice President, Secretary

The Board of Governors shall elect a President, Vice President, and Secretary from within the membership of the Board.

SECTION IV: Committees

The President may, from time to time, establish from members of the Board of Governors such committees as he may deem reasonable for the orderly conduct of the Club. Other members of the Club, in addition to members of the Board, may also be appointed to such committees. The function, tenure, and number of such committee members shall be determined at the discretion of the President of the Board of Governors.

Article IV—Club Management

SECTION I: Rules and Regulations

The operation of the Club and the management of the Club property shall be vested in the Amelia Plantation Company acting through the officers, directors, and appointed staff. The Directors, working with the Manager of the Club and the Board, are authorized and empowered to adopt, promulgate, and enforce rules and regulations governing the use of the clubrooms and other Club facilities and every member is subject thereto and shall abide thereby.

SECTION II: In Settlement of Account

Because failure of a member to pay promptly all dues and charges is to the detriment of his fellow members, each member's club account shall be due and payable upon receipt of his monthly statement. Members' accounts unpaid 30 days after the billing date are considered delinquent and a one-time late charge equal to 5 percent of the past due amount (not to exceed $5) may be added to the member's next statement. If any member's acount shall remain unpaid for a period of 70 days from the date of the first billing, the member shall be suspended from all Club privileges. If payment is not received within ten (10) days of posting and suspension, appropriate action will be taken which may include expulsion and legal action.

Article V—Definition of Terms

SECTION I:

"Directors" shall mean and refer to the Board of Directors of the Amelia Plantation Company.

SECTION II:

"Governors of the Board" shall mean and refer to the Board of Governors.

SECTION III:

"President" shall mean and refer to the President of the Board of Governors.

Article VI—Membership Meeting

SECTION I: Notices
Special meetings of the Club membership may be called at any time by the President. The call for the meetings shall set forth the purpose of the meeting and a notice thereof shall be mailed to each member at least 20 days prior to the time of such meeting.

SECTION II: Quorum
Fifty (50) members shall constitute a quorum at all meetings of the membership of the Club, and all matters shall be decided by a majority vote of the members present and voting. If less than a quorum (50 members) are present, the meeting may nevertheless proceed to conduct business unless the question of a quorum is raised by motion and vote of one-third or more of those present, in which event the meeting shall be recessed until such time as a quorum may be obtained. Use of proxies shall never be permitted at meetings of the Club membership.

Article VII—Committees: Their Duties and Powers

SECTION I: General
A. The standing committees of the Amelia Island Plantation Club shall include those committees described in Section II through V of this Article VII. The object and purpose of each committee shall be to consult with the management and with other members of the Board of Governors with respect to each committee's particular area of interest. All committee actions shall be subject to the approval of the Board of Governors.

B. Each committee shall have at least two members chosen by its Chairman or Chairwoman.

C. The President may from time to time authorize special committees. All committees shall have the power to enact and enforce rules governing Club activities and facilities within their respective jurisdiction but these must first be approved by the Board of Governors.

SECTION II: Social Committee
This Committee shall oversee the social activities of the Club. This may include, but not be limited to, types of social events, types of entertainment at social events, determination of the menu, special inter- and intra-club activities and overseeing of teen functions.

SECTION III: Membership Committee
This Committee shall, in conjunction with the management and the Board of Governors, establish all classifications of membership, establish membership qualification, and approve applications for admission to the Club.

SECTION IV: Golf Committee
This Committee shall assist the Golf Professional and the Golf Course Superintendent in the performance of their duties. They shall also organize play on the courses for the overall benefit of the members.
They shall:

A. Assist in the enhancement and the protection of the quality of the courses.

B. Assist the Board of Governors in recommending course expenditures for capital improvements pertaining to golf.

C. Promote U.S.G.A. regulations in regard to play and etiquette.

D. Enact and enforce rules as they affect golf carts.

E. Oversee the administration of the handicapping system.

F. Keep members current with golf affairs.

G. Provide members with committee representatives interested in their individual questions and problems regarding the courses or any aspect of the play.

H. Schedule, supervise, and promote tournaments, special events, and the administration of prizes.

SECTION V: Tennis Committee
The Committee shall assist the Tennis Professional in all phases of tennis activities. This shall consist of, but not be limited to, the establishment and conduction of a tournament schedule, the administration of prizes, the establishment and enforcement of rules and regulations governing play, the development of a Junior Tennis program, and all other activities which will be of a beneficial nature to the tennis-playing members of the Club.

Article VIII—Discipline

SECTION I: Reprimands, Suspension, or Expulsion
Any member who is consistently delinquent in payment of his or her Club account, or is guilty of any violation of the Bylaws or Rules of the Club, or who displays conduct unbecoming of a gentleman or a lady, or conduct which tends to be against the best interest of good government of the Club may be temporarily suspended or expelled from the Club by the affirmative vote of not less than a majority of the Board of Governors. On behalf of the Board of Governors, the Club Manager shall initiate such suspension or expulsion procedures as he deems necessary in the best interest of the Club.

SECTION II: Due Process
With the exception of the instances involving the failure of a member to pay his or her Club account, a member charged with the conduct giving rise to suspension or expulsion may be afforded the right of appearance before the Board of Governors within a reasonable time prior to the enforcement of such sanctions.

Article IX—Amendment of Bylaws

These Bylaws may be amended at any time by a two-thirds vote of the Directors of the Company after consultation with the Board of Governors.

APPENDIX E

Master Deed
Loggers Run Condominium Project
The Homestead, Glen Arbor, Michigan

This Master Deed is made and executed on the 19th day of June, 1979, by Crystal River Associates, a Michigan co-partnership, hereinafter referred to as "Developer," whose office is situated at The Homestead, Glen Arbor, Michigan 49636, represented herein by The Homestead Inn of Michgan, Inc., a Massachusetts corporation, and Kuras & Co., Inc., a Massachusetts corporation, its partners which are fully empowered and qualified to act on behalf of said partnership, in pursuance of the provisions of the Michigan Condominium Act (being Act 59 of the Public Acts of 1978), hereinafter referred to as the "Act." . . .

ARTICLE I
TITLE AND NATURE

The Condominium Project shall be known as Loggers Run, Leelanau County Condominium Subdivision Plan No. 14. The architectural plans for the Condominium Project were approved by the Building Department of Leelanau County, Michigan. The Condominium Project is established in accordance with the Act. The Buildings and units contained in the Condominium, including the number, boundaries, dimensions, area, and volume of each unit therein are set forth completely in the Condominium Subdivision Plan attached as Exhibit "B" hereto. Each building contains individual units for residential purposes and each unit is capable of individual utilization on account of having its own entrance from and exit to a common element of the Condominium Project. Each co-owner in the Condominium Project shall have an exclusive right to his unit and shall have undivided and inseparable rights to share with other co-owners the common elements of the Condominium Project as are designated by the Master Deed.

ARTICLE II
LEGAL DESCRIPTION

The land which is submitted to the Condominium Project established by this Master Deed is particularly described as follows.

ARTICLE III
DEFINITIONS. . . .

ARTICLE IV
COMMON ELEMENTS

The common elements of the Condominium Project . . . and the respective responsibilities for maintenance, decoration, repair, or replacement thereof are as follows:

A. The general common elements are:

(1) The land described in Article II hereof, including driveways, roads, sidewalks, and unassigned parking spaces;

(2) The electrical wiring network throughout the Condominium Project, including that contained within unit walls, up to the point of connection with electrical fixtures within any unit (it being the purpose hereof to include wiring as a general common element but to exclude therefrom all switches, outlets, circuit breaker boxes, and fixtures of any sort to which such wiring may be connected);

(3) The underground television cable and antenna system throughout the Condominium Project up to the point of connection with, but not including, the outlets therefor;

(4) The telephone wiring network throughout the Condominium Project up to the point of connection with, but not including, all appliances or fixtures relative thereto;

(5) The water distribution and sanitary plumbing network throughout the Condominium Project including that contained within unit walls and including water

meters, up to the point of connection with plumbing fixtures within any unit (it being the purpose hereof to include all pipes and their valves as general common elements but to exclude therefrom all sinks, toilets, drains, drain traps, faucets, and their fixtures and attachments);

(6) The water distribution system and sanitary sewer system throughout the project, including leads from mains to units but exclusive of the water mains and sewer mains the ownership of which is retained by the Developer;

(7) Foundations, supporting columns, unit perimeter walls (including windows and doors therein), roofs, ceiling, floor construction between unit levels, and chimneys;

(8) Trash sheds;

(9) Stairs and entrance decks;

(10) All beneficial easements . . . ;

(11) Such other elements of the Condominium Project not herein designated as general or limited common elements which are not enclosed within the boundaries of a unit, and which are intended for common use or necessary to the existence, upkeep, and safety of the project.

B. The limited common elements are:

(1) Each individual balcony in the Condominium Project is restricted in use to the co-owner of the unit which opens into such balcony ;

(2) Each individual porch in the Condominium Project is restricted in use to the co-owner of the unit which opens into such porch . . . ;

(3) Each individual space within the storage sheds shall be restricted in use to the co-owner of the unit to which the same was assigned by the Association;

(4) Each individual fireplace hearth in the Condominium Project is restricted in use to the co-owner of the unit in which it is located;

(5) The interior surfaces of unit perimeter walls (including windows and doors therein), ceilings, and floors contained within a unit shall be subject to the exclusive use and enjoyment of the co-owner of such unit.

C. The respective responsibilities for the maintenance, decoration, repair, and replacement of the common elements are as follows:

(1) The costs and responsibility of maintenance, decoration, and cleaning of each balcony described in Article IV B(1) above shall be borne by the co-owner of the unit to which such limited common element appertains and the costs of repair and replacement thereof, except in cases of co-owner fault, shall be borne by the Association.

(2) The costs and responsibility of maintenance, decoration, and cleaning of each fireplace hearth described in Article IV B(4) above shall be borne by the co-owner of the unit in which such fireplace hearth is located.

(3) The costs of decoration, cleaning, maintenance, and repair (but not replacement except in cases of co-owner fault) of all surfaces referred to in Article IV B(5) above shall be borne by the co-owner of each unit to which such limited common elements are appurtenant.

(4) The costs of maintenance, repair, and replacement of all general and limited common elements other than as described above shall be borne by the Association.

No co-owner shall use his unit or the common elements in any manner inconsistent with the purpose of the Condominium Project or in any manner which will interfere with or impair the rights of any other co-owner in the use and enjoyment of his unit or the common elements.

ARTICLE V
UNIT DESCRIPTION AND PERCENTAGE OF VALUE

A. Each unit in the project is described in this paragraph with reference to the Subdivision and Site Plan of Loggers Run. . . . Each unit shall include all that space contained within the interior finished unpainted walls and ceilings and from the finished subfloor all as shown on the floor plans and sections. . . . The dimensions shown on basement and foundation plans . . . have been or will be physically measured. . . . In the event that the dimensions on the measured foundation plan of any specific unit differ from the dimensions on the typical foundation plan for such unit. . . , then the typical upper-floor plans for such unit shall be deemed to be automatically changed for such specific unit in the same manner and to the same extent as the measured foundation plan. Building elevations are shown in detail in architectural plans on 35 millimeter microfilm aperture cards on file with the Michigan Department of Commerce.

B. The percentage of value assigned to each unit is set forth in subparagraph C below. The percentages of value were computed on the basis of the relative sizes of the units, with the resulting percentages reasonably adjusted to total precisely one hundred percent (100%). The percentage of value assigned to each unit shall be determinative of the proportionate share of each respective co-owner (i) in the common elements of the Condominium Project, and (ii) in the proceeds and expenses of the administration and the value of such co-owner's vote at meetings of the Association of co-owners. The total value of the Condominium Project is 100. The percentage of value allocated to each unit may be changed only with the prior written approval of each holder of a first mortgage lien on any unit in the project and with the unanimous consent of all of the co-owners expressed in an amendment to this Master Deed, duly approved and recorded.

C. Set forth below are:

(a) Each unit number as it appears on the Condominium Subdivision Plan.

(b) The percentage of value assigned to each unit.

Unit Number	Percentage of Value Assigned
1	25
2	25
3	25
4	25

ARTICLE VI
EXPANSION OF CONDOMINIUM

The Condominium Project established pursuant to the intial Master Deed of Loggers Run and consisting of 4 units is intended to be the first stage of a multi-stage project to contain in its entirety approximately 30 units. Additional units, if any, will be constructed upon all or some portion of the following described land. . . .

ARTICLE VII
EASEMENTS

A. EASEMENT FOR MAINTENANCE OF ENCROACHMENTS

In the event any portion of a unit or common element encroaches upon another unit or common element due to shifting, settling, or moving of a building, or due to survey errors, or construction deviations, reciprocal easements shall exist for the maintenance of such encroachment for so long as such encroachment exists, and for maintenance thereof after rebuilding in the event of any destruction. There shall be easements to, through, and over those portions of the land, structures, buildings, improvements, and walls (including interior unit walls) contained therein for the continuing maintenance and repair of all utilities in the Condominium Project. There shall exist easements of support with respect to any unit interior wall which supports a common element.

B. EASEMENTS RETAINED BY DEVELOPER AND RESTRICTIONS AGAINST CERTAIN ACTIVITIES

1. *Roadway Easements.* Developer reserves for the benefit of itself, its successors and assigns, an easement for the unrestricted use of all roads and walkways in the Condominium Project for the purpose of ingress and egress to and from all or any portion of the parcel described in Article II and any other land contiguous to the Condominium Project which may be owned or hereafter acquired by the Developer or its successors or assigns. All expenses of maintenance, repair, replacement, and resurfacing of any road referred to in this Article shall be shared by this condominium and any developed portions of the contiguous land which may be owned or hereafter acquired by the Developer or its successor or assigns whose closest means of access to a public road is over such road or roads. The co-owners of the Condominium Project shall be responsible from time to time for payment of a proportionate share of said expenses which share shall be determined by multiplying such expenses times a fraction, the numerator of which is the number of dwelling units in this Condominium Project, and the denominator of which is comprised of the number of such units plus all other dwelling units in such contiguous land whose closest means of access to a public road is over such road; provided however, that any adjoining developments sharing such expenses shall do so only in the same proportions as the portion of such roads used hereunder bears to the entire road system in the Condominium Project. Developer shall also have the right to extend the existing roads in the Condominium Project and install and pave connecting roadways thereto in order to service adjoining developments hereafter constructed and perpetual easements for the continuing use of such additional roadways shall exist in the same manner and for the same purposes and upon the same conditions as the easements established over existing roadways in preceding portions of this paragraph.

2. *Utility Easements.* Developer also hereby reserves for the benefit of itself, its successors and assigns, and all future owners of the land described in Article II or any portion or portions thereof, and any other land contiguous to the Condominum Project which may be owned or hereafter acquired by the Developer or its successors or assigns, perpetual easements to construct, modify, repair, maintain, utilize, tap, tie into, extend, and enlarge all utility mains located in the Condominium Project including, but not limited to, water, storm, and sanitary sewer mains. In the event Developer, its successors or assigns, utilizes, taps, ties into, extends, or enlarges any utilities located on the Condominium Premises, it shall be obligated to pay all of the expenses reasonably necessary to restore the Condominium Premises to their state immediately prior to such utilization, tapping, tying-in, extension, or enlargement; and such restoration shall be promptly made.

3. *Hiking Easements.* Developer also reserves for the benefit of itself and its successors, assigns, licensees, and guests, as Developer and/or owner of adjoining and nearby properties, the right to go over and across the Condominium Project from time to time for hiking or cross-country skiing purposes in order to enable free and unobstructed pedestrian access throughout said properties owned and/or developed by Developer or its successor and assigns.

4. *Restrictions Against Certain Activities.* Neither the Association nor any co-owner, without consent of the Developer, shall construct or install or cause to be constructed or installed any paths, roads, stairs, electrical lines, or structures whatsoever or cut any trees in any area of the Condominium Project lying westerly of the units, it being essential for purposes of aesthetics and erosion control to prohibit any such activities without the consent of the Developer.

ARTICLE VIII
AMENDMENT

This Master Deed and the Condominium Subdivision Plan . . . may be amended with the consent of sixty-six and two-thirds percent (66⅔%) of the co-owners and of the unit mortgagees (allowing one vote for each mortgage held) except as hereinafter set forth:

A. No unit dimensions may be modified without the consent of the co-owner of such unit nor may the nature or extent of limited common elements or the responsibility for maintenance, repair, or replacement thereof be modified without the written consent of the co-owner of any unit to which the same are appurtenant.

B. Prior to expiration of one year from the date of the First Annual Meeting of members of the Association, the Developer may, with the approval of the Michigan Department of Commerce (but without the consent of any co-owner or any other person), amend this Master Deed and the Plans . . . in order to correct survey or other errors made in such documents and to make such other amendments to such instruments and to the Bylaws . . . as do not materially affect any rights of any co-owner or mortgagee in the project, including, but not limited to, amendments for the purpose of facilitating conventional mortgage loan financing for existing or prospective co-owners and to enable the purchase of such mortgage loans by the Federal Home Loan Mortgage Corporation, the Federal National Mortgage Association, the Government National Mortgage Association and/or any other agency of the federal government or the State of Michigan. The Developer expressly reserves the right to amend the legal description of the Condominium Project contained in Article II and the Plans . . . to delete and withdraw from the Condominium Project that certain portion thereof, being a rectangular parcel approximately fifty (50) feet on each side, lying directly under the easement located at the Southeast corner of the Project; provided, however, that said easement shall be retained and not terminated by such amendment.

C. The value of the vote of any co-owner and the corresponding proportion of common expenses assessed against such co-owner shall not be modified without the written consent of such co-owner and his mortgagee nor shall the percentage of value assigned to any unit be modified without like consent.

D. Article VI and this Article VIII shall not be amended nor shall the provisions thereof be modified by any other amendment to this Master Deed without the written consent of the Developer so long as the Developer continues to offer any unit in the condominium for sale.

E. The Condominium Project may not be terminated, vacated, revoked, or abandoned without the written consent of ninety-five percent (95%) of all co-owners and all mortgagees (allocating one vote for each mortgage held) . . . .

MASTER DEED DRAFTED BY:
James C. Adams, of
Dykema, Gossett, Spencer, Goodnow & Trigg
35th Floor, 400 Renaissance Center
Detroit, Michigan 48243

APPENDIX F

Lakeridge, Inc., Torrington, Connecticut
PURCHASE AGREEMENT

This Offer to Purchase made this __________ day of __________, 19__________, by

(Buyer's Name)	(Street)
(Buyer's Name)	(Town) (State) (Zip Code)
(Home Telephone)	(Business Telephone)

("Buyer"), to LAKERIDGE, INC., a Connecticut corporation its successors and assigns ("Seller").

(1) *Premises.* Seller agrees to sell and Buyer agrees to purchase from the Seller the following ("premises"):

Residence Building Type: __________ Lot No. __________

Garage Building: __________ together with the improvements now hereon or hereafter constructed thereon located in the Town of Torrington. County of Litchfield and State of Connecticut. shown on a map entitled "Final Subdivision Plan Lakeridge. Inc." Prepared by Storch Engineers. Wethersfield. Connecticut. September. 1974. Scale 1" = 40' Sheet 1. 4-10 of 18" and "Revised Final Subdivision Plan Lakeridge. Inc." Prepared by Storch Engineers. Wethersfield. Connecticut. June. 1974. Scale 1" = 40' revised September. 1974. Sheet 2 and 3 of 18". which maps were revised March 6. 1975. October 14. 1975. December 2. 1975. June 29. 1976. September 7. 1976. January 21. 1977. March 7. 1977. July 1. 1977. and November 4. 1977. as it may be revised to the date of closing. and are on file in the Torrington Town Clerk's Office. subject to the rights reserved in paragraphs 9 and 13 hereof.

Said Lot is to be conveyed together with interests appurtenant thereto. including a non-exclusive easement of enjoyment in the Common Property. and membership in Lakeridge Association. Inc.. all as more particularly set forth in paragraphs 9 and 12 hereof.

(2) *Purchase Price.* To be paid by Buyer is the sum of $__________. payable as follows:

(a) $__________ having been previously paid upon execution of Reservation Agreement or binder.

(b) $__________ upon execution of this instrument by check. receipt of which. subject to collection is hereby acknowledged.

(c) $__________ deposit to be increased to __________ on or before __________.

(d) $__________ in cash by certified check or cashiers check at the time of closing of title.

(3) *Closing of Title and Possession.* Seller will make diligent effort to have the premises ready for closing of title on or before __________.

If the premises are not so ready. the closing will take place within five (5) days after written notice from Seller to Buyer that the premises have been completed on such date and time as are specified in such notice. The closing shall take place at such time and place as may be designated by Seller in such notice. Buyer shall have possession of the premises at and after the time of closing.

(4) *Mortgage Contingency.* This Agreement is conditioned upon the Buyer being able to obtain a commitment for a mortgage of at least $__________, at an annual interest rate not to exceed __________% per annum, providing for monthly amortization of principal and interest over a period of at least __________ years, and if he unsuccessfully used all reasonable efforts to obtain such commitment, and so notified the Seller in writing within 30 days of this Agreement, then the Seller shall have an additional period of thirty (30) days within which to obtain such a commitment for the Buyer, and Buyer shall furnish Seller with fully executed financial statements and applications as necessary at Seller's request. In the event that the Buyer does so notify the Seller within thirty (30) days and the Seller is unable to obtain such commitment within the additional thirty (30) days period, then Seller shall refund all sums theretofore paid on account of the purchase price, and this Agreement shall be void and all rights and liabilities of the parties by reason of this Agreement shall terminate. In the event Buyer does not so notify Seller within said thirty (30) day period, this contingency shall be deemed to have been fully satisfied.

(5) *Improvements.* The Seller shall sell on the premises a building substantially in accordance with the model type identified in paragraph 1 hereof. Furniture and/or decorations located in any model are for display purposes only and shall not be included in a sale to Buyer. If this Agreement includes the sale of a Garage Lot, Seller agrees to sell the Garage substantially similar in size and design to those Garages presently existing at Lakeridge in the same relationship to other garages in similar clusters or in accordance with plans and specifications available at Seller's office. If Seller cannot advantageously procure any of the materials used in said Models because of "freeze orders," priority regulations, allocation orders, labor disputes, the existence of a state of war, shortages or other inability to obtain such materials not due to the fault of the Seller, the Seller may substitute other materials of like value in place thereof, and the Buyer agrees to accept the same, provided that said substitutions comply with the Connecticut Basic Building Code. Depending on location of the building, the floor plan may be the reverse of the layout in the model, and the Buyer agrees to accept such reversal.

Buyer agrees that incompletion with respect to items not necessary for certificate of occupancy from the building inspector, including landscaping, shall not render the premises not ready for closing and shall not operate to delay the closing, nor shall Seller be required to accept less than the full amount required hereunder on account of such incomplete items provided Seller undertakes in writing to complete such items within a reasonable time after closing. The provisions of this paragraph 6 shall survive the closing of title.

(6) *Warranties.* Seller makes no warranty, express or implied, except as specifically provided pursuant to Chapter 827 of the Connecticut General Statutes, provided that to the extent this contract pertains to improvements completed at the time of this agreement, such improvements are considered to be sold "as-is" and no additional implied warranty is given that the improvements are: (1)—free from faulty materials; (2)—constructed according to sound engineering standards; (3)—constructed in a workmanlike manner; and (4)—fit for habitation, except with respect to the statutory express warranty that the building conforms substantially to the applicable model home shown to and inspected by the purchaser, and the implied warranty of Section 52-563a of the Connecticut Statutes that the building was built in accordance with the building code. The purchaser hereby consents to the exclusion of the above additional implied warranties with respect to the premises. The above warranties EXPRESSLY EXCLUDE ANY ADDITIONAL IMPLIED WARRANTY OF MERCHANTABILITY OR FITNESS FOR A PARTICULAR PURPOSE. No written warranty of consumer products included in the premises is given by the Seller under the Moss Magnusen Warranty Act. Any of Seller's rights to the manufacturer's warranties shall be given and assigned to purchaser at closing of title. The provisions of this paragraph shall survive transfer of title.

(7) *Construction Details, Extras.* In the event any building has been painted, carpeted, tiled, etc. at the time of acceptance of this agreement, the premises are sold "as built" and repainting or changing of materials will be at Buyer's request and cost. Extras, choices, and options will be only in accordance with a separate agreement, which may be appended hereto as entered into at a later date. All extras must be paid in full before work commences. Closing shall not be delayed, nor shall any funds be retained because of failure to complete custom extras by the date of closing of title.

In case Buyer shall have the right of a choice or selection of colors or materials or Buyer shall elect to purchase extras from Seller which require that Buyer make a selection of color materials, the right to said choice or selection on the part of the Buyer shall be deemed waived unless such selection or choice is made within two (2) weeks after Buyer's mortgage has been approved or in the event of a cash sale, within three (3) weeks of the date hereof. Seller retains the right to terminate this Agreement and to return any payment made by the Buyer to the Seller if the Buyer becomes unreasonable in his demands or interferes with the workmen and the work in progress, and upon such return of payments, this agreement shall be null and void without further liability to either Buyer or Seller. Buyer shall not take possession nor exercise control or supervision of the premises prior to closing, nor shall Buyer enter the premises of Lakeridge, other than to the Models and sales office unless accompanied by a representative of the Seller. Violation of this provision will entitle Seller to terminate this Agreement at its option.

(8) *Adjustments.* Real estate taxes for the current tax year as assessed, or if not, as estimated by the Seller, will be adjusted in cash as of the date of closing in accordance with the custom of the Litchfield County Bar Association. Common Charges and Assessments for the month in which title closes, which are payable in advance on the first of the month, and all other customary adjustments, will be adjusted in cash as of the date of closing. Special assessments shall be adjusted for the assessment year made. All of the legal costs, escrows and expenses of the Buyer in connection with the purchase or mortgaging of the premises will be the obligation of the Buyer.

(9) *Title.* Title will be conveyed by a warranty deed, subject to current taxes; to a Declaration of Covenants and Restrictions for Lakeridge, Inc.; to the Bylaws, Certificate of Incorporation, and Rules and Regulations of Lakeridge Association, Inc.; to the Management Agreement between Lakeridge, Inc., and Lakeridge Management Company; to easements, and such other agreements and restrictions as of record may appear; to matters shown on the maps referred to herein or in the aforesaid documents; to contracts and agreements of Lakeridge Association, Inc., administering the provisions of the foregoing documents; and to any and all provisions of any Federal, State, or Municipal laws or regulations, none of which, however, will either render the title uninsurable or be violated by occupancy of the premises for the purposes set forth in the Declaration and Bylaws. The Buyer acknowledges that prior to the execution of this Agreement, he has received a copy of the Declaration of Covenants and Restrictions, the Bylaws, Rules and Regulations, Certificate of Incorporation, and Management Agreement and agrees that all are incorporated herein by reference and made a part of this Agreement as though fully set forth herein. Buyer further acknowledges that he or his attorney has examined all of these documents and are satisfied therewith.

(10) *Mergers.* It is specifically understood and agreed that this contract is a single, indivisible contract and that the acceptance of the deed by the Buyer shall be deemed and considered as full compliance by the Seller to the terms of this Agreement, and as a release by the Buyer of any and all rights, obligations, claims, or causes of action against the Seller. The Buyer further agrees that none of the terms of this Agreement, except those provisions which this Agreement expressly states shall survive the transfer of title, shall survive the delivery and acceptance of the deed.

(11) *Default.* In the event of default by the Seller, the Buyer may terminate this Agreement and upon the return to Buyer of all sums paid to Seller hereunder. plus liquidated damages in the amount of $100. this Agreement shall terminate and both parties relieved of any further obligation or liability hereunder. and Buyer shall have no other legal and equitable remedy. The foregoing sentence notwithstanding, the Seller's obligation to erect the building shall be specifically enforceable if the Seller has not erected the building two years from the date of this agreement and if this agreement has not been terminated prior to such time. In the event of default by the Buyer, the Seller may terminate this Agreement and retain any sums paid pursuant to this Agreement: or at the option of the Seller, the Seller may seek any other remedy provided by law or

equity. Buyer will be liable for Seller's reasonable attorney's fees and costs incurred by it by virtue of any proceedings or litigation as to the parties' rights under this agreement.

(12) *Lakeridge Association, Inc.* By acceptance of the deed, Buyer shall become a member of Lakeridge Association, Inc., a nonstock Connecticut corporation, and shall be subject to its Certificate of Incorporation, Bylaws and its Rules and Regulations, and agrees and covenants to maintain membership in said Association as long as Buyer shall retain any interest whatsoever in the aforesaid premises, and to bind his heirs, successors and assigns likewise. Buyer agrees that any mortgage or encumbrance placed on the land and interest being purchased will also attach to his membership in the Association. Effective on closing of title the Buyer hereby consents to and authorizes and ratifies the actions of Seller and the Board of Directors of the Association in adopting the Bylaws of the Association as though the undersigned had affirmatively voted for each Bylaw at a duly called membership meeting; including but not limited to any and all provisions contained in the Bylaws with respect to the Association's right to levy and assess any fines, penalties, dues, Common Charges or assessments as provided therein, and in entering into the Management Agreement as set forth in the documents incorporated herein by reference. Upon request, Buyer will execute a certificate of this consent at closing of title. This consent and ratification shall survive transfer of title.

(13) *Amendments.* The Buyer acknowledges the rights of the Association and the Seller to supplement and amend the Declaration, Bylaws, maps or any other document relating to the establishment or operation of Lakeridge so long as there is no substantial change in any obligation or rights of Buyer. No change in said documents required by any governmental regulatory agency, the New York Attorney General or the regulations of the Federal Home Loan Mortgage Corporation shall be considered to be a substantial change in any obligation or rights of Buyer. Seller reserves the right to control, design and lay out improvements on the Common Property until completion of all construction at Lakeridge. Interference will be deemed trespass. The provisions of this paragraph shall survive transfer of title.

(14) *Recording.* Buyer agrees that he shall not record this Agreement in the Land Records of the Town of Torrington. In the event Buyer violates this provision and does record this Agreement, the act of such recording shall be deemed to be a default hereunder and shall render this contract terminated and null and void at the option of the Seller. Such option to terminate this Agreement shall be exercised and effective by Seller executing a notice of termination and recording the same in the Land Records of the Town of Torrington which notice need be signed only by the Seller to be effective.

(15) *Broker.* Buyer represents that he has not dealt through any real estate agent or broker in this transaction.

(16) *Rights of Mortgagee.* At the option of mortgagee, this Agreement and all terms and provisions thereof may be subordinated to any construction or permanent mortgage now or hereafter on the premises. In the event of foreclosure, or proceedings in lieu of foreclosure, the mortgagee has the right at its option to acquire the rights of Seller under this Agreement to perform the obligations hereunder, and Buyer will recognize and accept such mortgagee as Seller hereunder upon exercise of such option.

(17) *Amendments and Other Agreements.* The Seller is not and will not be bound by any stipulations, representations, obligations, agreements or promises, oral or otherwise, made by or on the part of the Seller, its agents, employees or representatives, not printed, attached to or inserted in this Agreement. This Agreement may not be changed or terminated orally. This provision shall survive the transfer of title.

(18) *Assignment.* This Agreement is binding upon the parties hereto and their heirs, successors and assigns, and may not be assigned by the Buyer without the prior written consent of the Seller.

(19) *Subdivision Approval.* Until the Planning Commission of Torrington has given final subdivision approval to a map on which the Lot identified in paragraph 1 hereof is shown, this Agreement shall be contingent on Seller's obtaining such approval. If Seller fails to obtain such approval on or before one year after the date specified in paragraph 3, Seller shall refund all sums theretofore paid on account of the purchase price and this Agreement shall be void and all rights and liabilities of the parties by reason of this Agreement shall terminate.

PLEASE DO NOT SIGN THIS AGREEMENT BEFORE YOU READ IT, OR IF IT CONTAINS ANY BLANK SPACES OR IF YOU HAVE NOT RECEIVED THE DOCUMENTS LISTED IN PARAGRAPH 9.

________________________(L. S.)
Buyer

________________________(L. S.)
Buyer

Deposit received without acceptance of this offer until signed below.

________________________(L. S.)
Salesman

ACCEPTANCE

This offer to purchase is accepted this ________ of day ________, 19______

Seller:
LAKERIDGE, INC.
By________________________(L. S.)
Its

APPENDIX G

AMELIA ISLAND PLANTATION AMELIA ISLAND, FLORIDA VILLA OWNER'S RENTAL AGREEMENT

THIS AGREEMENT is made as of this ________ day of________________, 19____, by and between AMELIA PLANTATION COMPANY (hereinafter referred to as "Company"), and ________, (hereinafter referred to as "Owner").

WHEREAS, the Owner wishes to engage the services of the Company as the exclusive rental agent to offer the Owner's dwelling (hereinafter referred to as "Premises") for rental under the terms and conditions set forth below; and

WHEREAS, the Company will advertise and promote the rental properties and facilities of Amelia Island Plantation ("Plantation") as a vacation resort community and a group business meeting place to prospective guests consisting of non-group business resort guests ("Vacation Guests") and group business resort guests ("Conference Guests") both of which are sometimes hereinafter referred to as ("Tenants").

WHEREAS, the maintenance of the good will of all Tenants and prospective Tenants, except for those who destroy property or occupy the Premises in violation of the terms and conditions set forth below, shall be considered a paramount objective of both parties.

NOW, THEREFORE, in consideration of the terms, conditions and the mutual covenants herein set forth, the parties agree as follows:

(1) The Company agrees to use its best efforts to secure Tenants to occupy Owner's Premises pursuant to Owner's election set forth at the end of this agreement and in accordance with the terms and conditions set forth herein and the Villa Rental Rates which are attached hereto and marked Exhibit A.

(2) The Owner agrees to make available for rental, and the Company agrees to offer for rental Villa No. ________, located at ________________, subject to the terms and conditions set forth herein.

(3) The Owner agrees that this Rental Agreement is an exclusive agreement and that from the Villa Rental Rate charges rendered in accordance with Exhibit A (hereafter referred to as "Villa Income") the Owner will compensate and pay the Company a commission equal to 40% of the Villa Income for Vacation Guests and 50% of the Villa In-

come for Conference Guests. Monthly Villa Rental Rates will be offered from November 16 through February 28 in an effort to get additional Tenants to provide increased Villa Income to the Owner during the off-season. The Company shall be entitled to a commission equal to 15% of the monthly Villa Income for monthly villa rentals. All Villa Income as it is received by the Company shall be placed in a separate and segregated account for the exclusive benefit of all Owners having entered into a Rental Agreement with Company pursuant to the provisions of this Agreement. As authorized hereinabove, the Company is authorized to disburse and pay to itself a commission equal to 40% of the Villa Income received by the Company from Vacation Guests and 50% of the Villa Income received from Conference Guests in accordance with the Villa Rental Rates. The remaining percentage of the Villa Income paid to the Company in accordance with the Villa Rental Rates will be held and disbursed for the benefit of the Owners as follows:

(a) The Owner agrees from the remaining percentage of the Villa Income held for Owner's benefit that Company is authorized with the concurrence of the Amelia Island Rental Property Owners', Inc., Board of Directors (hereinafter referred to as "AIRPO") if requested by said association, to disburse and pay all amounts due the Villa Association of which Owner is a member, property owner's association fees, the tele-communication expenses of Owner pursuant to paragraph 11 hereof, maintenance and repair fees due and payable pursuant to paragraph 15 hereof, the AIRPO dues as authorized by AIRPO as being due from each member, and resulting balance of funds shall be paid to Owner monthly. The Company will use its best efforts to pay owners 15 days after the end of the month; however, in no event later than 30 days after the end of the month, together with a separate written accounting to Owner for all Villa Income received less disbursements therefrom as authorized in this Agreement.

(b) The Company reserves the right to reject Owner's requests for special restrictions in connection with rentals (other than provided for by this Agreement); in the event it accepts special restrictions, the Company shall receive an additional commission equal to 10% of the Villa Income.

(c) The Owner agrees that all remuneration from the rental of Premises will be collected through the Company's resort accounting office, subject to the commission as specified in this paragraph. Should the Owner collect directly any money or other consideration for use of the Premises, the rental commissions set forth herein shall be paid to Company by the Owner.

(d) The Owner shall receive a commission equal to 10% of the rental rate paid by the guest for booking a reservation. In order to qualify for a commission the Owner must call or write the Reservations Department giving guest name and address as well as arrival and departure dates. This commission does not apply to monthly rates.

(4) In order to provide the rental management services required of Company under this Agreement, Company shall provide the following:

(a) Maintain and operate a housekeeping department to provide the necessary housekeeping services for which Company will be compensated in accordance with the housekeeping fees set forth on Exhibit B attached hereto and made a part hereof.

(b) Maintain and operate an Office of Rental Properties which shall be the Owners' contact point with the Company and which will maintain inventories and conduct inspections.

(c) Maintain and operate a Reservations Office through which all reservations for the Premises shall be processed.

(d) Maintain and operate a Resort Accounting Office to process all charges for guests, collection of guest resort fees, and to process payments to Owners.

(5) The Owner understands that Amelia Island Plantation Club (hereinafter referred to as "Club") is a private club and that to use the facilities of this private club, the Owner must be a member of the club, or in the alternative the Owner must pay the then current Amenity Usage Fee. Tenants renting Owner's unit from the Company shall be granted a limited use of the Club facilities for the duration of tenants' occupancy upon payment to Company of the Amenity Usage Fee as set forth in Exhibit B attached hereto and made a part hereof. The Amenity Usage Fees as set forth in Exhibit B hereto shall be subject to change by the Company without notice to the Owner but with advice to AIRPO. In the event the Amenity Usage Fees, as set forth in Exhibit B, are increased during the term of this Rental Agreement, the Company agrees there will be no increase in the total charges to resort guests rendered in accordance with Exhibits A and B except for increased charges rendered in accordance with paragraphs 19 and 23 of this Agreement.

(6) The Owner agrees not to enter the Premises or to permit any person, whether family member, repairman, or guest, to enter the Premises, other than during confirmed times of occupancy by Owner, without prior notification to, approval of, and coordination by, the Company. Pets shall be prohibited from the Premises when occupied pursuant to a Guest Rental Agreement (which is attached as Exhibit C hereto). The Owner, guests, and tenants of Owner are subject to such restrictions as are set forth in Master Deed (or equivalent document(s)).

(7) The Owner authorizes the Company to accept reservations for the Premises up to 12 months in advance, except for excluded dates submitted in writing by the Owner on Owner's initiative or upon the periodic request of the Office of Rental Properties, and such reservations shall be binding on the Owner. All instructions not to rent the Premises must be submitted in writing by the Owner, and will be acknowledged in writing, subject to existing reservations previously confirmed to Tenants. The Company will confirm reservations for specific villas, if available, when requested by Tenants, and in all cases will specify the location within the resort area of the reserved villa. Both the Owner and the Company shall use their best efforts to avoid reservation conflicts. If, through error a Tenant is occupying the Premises when the error is discovered, and if substitute accommodations are available, such accommodations shall be provided to the Owner at the prevailing rate, less the Company's commission, which will result in no additional charge to the Owner in excess of charges the Owner would have incurred as a result of residing in his rental unit.

(8) The Owner authorizes the Company to rent the Premises for use as a hospitality suite in connection with group business and for which use Owner will receive the normal full rental, in order to enable the Company to meet a requirement for such use in promoting group business. The Company agrees to inspect and when necessary inventory the Premises, and to provide, at the Company's expense, any extraordinary housekeeping and maintenance service as may be required due to such use. The Company shall see that no unit is used more than twice a year as a hospitality suite. As an alternative, a unit may be used as a hospitality unit more than twice a year providing the Owner is paid 200% of the normal full rental rate. A "hospitality suite" is defined as a unit with no intended Tenant.

(9) Should the Owner accept remuneration directly from a Tenant, this contract is subject to cancellation by the Company without prior notice unless Owner remits the rental commissions to Company as provided in Paragraph (3)(c).

(10) The Owner shall be responsible for direct payment to the utility companies of all utility bills for the Premises.

(11) A central communications system has been installed by the Company and Owner agrees to have his unit connected to said system. To effect installation in a rental villa, there will be a deposit of approximately $77 required which will be advanced by the Company and reimbursed by the Owner, who will authorize the Company to deduct from the Owner's portion of Villa Income the reimbursement of the deposit to Company in six equal monthly installments. The Company agrees to refund the deposit and disconnect the service in the event the Owner should sell or terminate this contract. The monthly charge for this system is approximately $17.85 which will be deducted from Owner's portion of the Villa Income each month. Owner understands that upon connection with the central communication system he will no longer be responsible for long distance calls made by guests staying in the unit. The Owner agrees to subscribe and pay for cable television service and installation as directed by the Company.

(12) The Owner agrees to pay to the Company for each Owner-occupancy period the standard departure cleaning and linen fee which will be billed to the Owner's account. Such fee, at rates then in effect, shall also be billed to the Owner's account for each period of occupancy by Guests (not Tenants as the term is used herein) of the Owner.

(13) During periods of Owner-occupancy the Owner and Guests (not Tenants as the term is used herein) of the Owner shall abide by the standard check-in and check-out times required by the Company for Tenants. Failure to do so will result in a late departure fee (one day's Villa rental commission), which will be billed to the Owner's account and paid to Company.

(14) The Owner agrees that writers, travel agents, group planners, support and administration personnel, and participants in any major tournaments sponsored and/or held by Company to promote the Plantation may be offered accommodations at no charge during site inspections and tournaments. The Company will pay the Villa Owners $5 per night for such use. The Company warrants that no villa will be used more than five (5) nights per year under this program. Company agrees that it will make every effort to arrange for utilization of each Villa at such time as it will not otherwise be occupied and no Villa will be used more than three (3) consecutive nights at any one time for such purposes. Company further agrees that the utilization of all Villas subject to Villa Owner's Rental Agreement will be apportioned equally whenever possible. Upon the Board of AIRPO's giving written notice to Company, on or before December 1 of each succeeding year, the number of complimentary nights hereinabove provided for may be reduced to three (3).

(15) The Owner agrees to maintain the Premises in a satisfactory rental condition as follows:

(a) The Company, to assist the Owner in the rental of the Premises, and to maintain written quality standards, (1) shall conduct at least once annually (and as needed, or upon request of the Owner, more frequently) an inventory of all major furnishings and equipment, (2) shall inspect the general condition of the Premises, and (3) shall provide the Owner with the inventory report, a statement as to the condition of the Premises, and written recommendations for improvements. The Company will annually assign one of the following ratings to the Premises: standard or sub-standard.

(b) Owners of "standard" units will be given a list of recommendations to maintain their standard rating. The Owners must notify the Company in writing when recommendations for maintaining the rating have been accomplished. If the above notification is not received within 60 days from the date of Owner's receipt of the recommendations, it will be assumed that the Owner has elected not to comply with the recommendations, and the unit will be rated sub-standard and removed from the rental market. Upon receipt of notification from the Owner that recommendations have been completed, the rental properties office will have the premises inspected for the purpose of assigning a rating so as to return the unit to the rental market.

(c) In the event that an Owner questions the recommendations to maintain a standard rating, he must notify the Rental Properties office within thirty (30) days of receipt of the recommendations. The recommendations will then be reviewed by the President or a Vice President of the Company and the Owner notified accordingly. The Owner's 60-day period as outlined herein will begin upon receipt of the results of the review.

(d) The Owner shall maintain an effective maintenance agreement with a responsible maintenance company approved by Amelia Plantation Company to assure quality of maintenance for the Premises.

(e) The Owner agrees to maintain the Premises, including furnishings, in rental condition, and to maintain a complement of kitchen utensils, glasses, dishes, and flatware and other equipment, as specified in the "Rental Properties Basic Equipment List" (attached hereto as Exhibit D), based on number of rooms. The Owner agrees the Company may replace missing and no longer usable items and charge Owner's account for such costs up to a total replacement cost of $50 without prior approval of the Owner.

(f) The Owner agrees that the Company may have the carpet cleaned, floor waxed, bed spreads and draperies cleaned, and touch-up painting done as is necessary (in Company's sole discretion) to maintain the Premises in rental condition, and that the Company may bill the Owner's account for the cost thereof; provided, however, that such cost may not exceed $100 total for cleaning, waxing, and/or painting without the Owner's prior approval.

(g) The Owner shall undertake an annual general interior house-cleaning of the Premises in addition to the Company's normal housekeeping services.

(16) The Owner agrees that the Company may offer Tenant up to a 20% rebate in the event of a failure of the heating or air conditioning systems, or a major appliance, which cannot be repaired or replaced within 12 hours of notification of failure, and the Owner agrees the Tenant may be transferred to another rental property if such rebate is unacceptable to Tenant. In the event of such a transfer, the Owner shall be credited with a prorated share of the rents earned from such Tenant, the balance being credited to the Owner of the Premises to which said Tenant is transferred.

(17) The Owner agrees to indemnify, and hold harmless, the Company, its employees or agents, from and against all claims, suits, damages, costs, losses, and expenses arising from injury to any person or property occurring on or about the Premises relating to the performance of this Agreement, which result from any defect in the Premises, and the Owner acknowledges that losses from theft, vandalism, acts of God, or the elements, etc., shall be borne by the Owner; however, the Company

agrees on behalf of Owner to use its best efforts to collect from Tenants for any damages to the Premises and to the furnishings and equipment and household items therein, which occur during Tenants' occupancy.

(18) The Company agrees to bear the cost of uncollectible rental fees.

(19) The Company may, from time to time, change the Villa Rental rates to meet prevailing market conditions when, in the Company's opinion, it would increase the occupancy to the Owner for the year to make such a change. The Company will not change its published Villa Rental rates in excess of 10% without receiving written approval of the majority of the Board of AIRPO, except that Company has the permission and option of using the weekly rate set forth in Exhibit A and the proration of it on a daily basis to promote additional occupancy without securing the prior approval of the majority of the Board of AIRPO. The Company shall give the Owner thirty (30) days written notice of general changes in Villa Rental Rates when the rate changes are in excess of 10%. This paragraph will not be construed to prevent the Company from renting a Villa Rental Unit at the next lower bedroom rate in the event the bedroom size requested by a guest is not available for the rental category requested.

(20) The Company and Owner agree that AIRPO is the representative of the Owner. The Company agrees to consult with AIRPO relative to all permanent rental rate changes, and other major rental property matters.

(21) This Agreement shall not affect the terms and conditions of any other contract or agreement between the parties.

(22) The interest of the Company hereunder cannot be assigned or transferred to another without the prior written consent of the Owner, provided, however, Company can assign without prior written consent of the Owner all of its rights, title, and interest in and to this Agreement to any wholly owned subsidiary or related corporation of Company.

(23) This Agreement shall be effective ____________, 19____, and shall continue in full force and effect until a new contract is entered into between the parties or until terminated by either party as provided in paragraph 24 hereof. It is agreed that the Company at its option may decline to accept future reservations and may transfer all existing reservations to other rental properties upon the occurrence of either of the following events:

(1) Listing of the Premises for sale, or

(2) Permanent occupancy of the Owner as a resident in the Premises.

The Parties to this Agreement may modify this Agreement by supplemental agreement or addendum signed by both parties which supplemental agreement or addendum will not invalidate or void this Rental Agreement except as set forth therein. It is understood and agreed that Exhibits A and B to this Agreement may be changed by Company with the written consent and concurrence of a majority of the Board of Directors of AIRPO pursuant to Paragraph 19 hereof and any such changes to Exhibits A and B will not require the written consent or concurrence of the Owner.

(24) This Agreement and the Company's exclusive authority to accept reservations on behalf of the Owner may be terminated upon thirty (30) days written notice by one party to the other party. Such written notice shall be delivered personally or by certified or registered mail. Said 30-day period shall commence on the day such notice is received by the addressee. Cancellation of this Agreement shall terminate the Company's authority to accept future reservations for the Premises, and the Company will use its best efforts to effect occupancy by Tenants during the 30-day notice period; however, the Owner shall be responsible for any expense incurred by the Company as a result of the Owner's failure to honor confirmed reservations beyond the 30-day period.

(25) Notice(s) shall be sent as follows:

If to the Company, to:
Amelia Plantation Company
Amelia Island Plantation
Amelia Island, Florida 32034
Attention:
If to the Owner(s), to:

____

____

____

OWNER'S ELECTION:

Pursuant to paragraph 1 and 3 hereinabove, the Owner makes the following election:

☐ Owner elects to rent the premises to vacation guests and conference guests (on a priority basis), and understands that the Company will receive a 10% higher commission on conference guests business in accordance with paragraph 3.

☐ Owner elects not to receive priority on conference guests business. Owner agrees that Company shall rent the premises to vacation guests, except that in its sole discretion the Company may rent the premises to conference guests for a commission payable to the Company equal to 40% of the villa income.

IN WITNESS WHEREOF, the parties hereto have caused this Agreement to be duly executed as of the date first above written.

AMELIA PLANTATION COMPANY

By ______________________________

*If the Premises are owned by more than one person, all Owners must sign, and one person must be designated as the single point of contact with the office of Rental Properties.

Owner Information (Please Print):

____
Name

____
Street or Postal Box Number

____
City State Zip Code

____
Home Phone Number

____
Business Phone Number

OWNER(S)* ______________________________

____

____

Taxpayer ID Number: ____________________

APPENDIX H

Model Timeshare Ownership Act Prepared by the Resort Timesharing Development Council of the American Land Development Association

ARTICLE 1
GENERAL PROVISIONS

Section 1-101. Short Title. This Act shall be known and may be cited as the ______ Timeshare Act.

Section 1-102. Time of Taking Effect. This Act shall take effect sixty (60) days after its approval as to any Timeshare Program hereafter created or commenced and sixty (60) days after its approval as to any Timeshare Program heretofore created or commenced with respect to the requirements of Articles[s] 3 [and 4].

Section 1-103. Definitions. In this Act and, unless otherwise required by the context or expressly provided in any governing instruments, ordinances, or other governmental regulations:

"Acquisition Agent" means, a person who by means of telephone, mail, advertisement, inducement, solicitation or otherwise attempts directly to encourage any person to attend a sales presentation for a Timeshare Program.

"Agency" means ________________, which is an agency within the meaning of ____________.

"Developer" means, in the case of any given property, any person or entity which is in the business of creating or which is in the business of selling its own Timeshare Intervals in any Timeshare Program. This definition does not include a person acting solely as a Sales Agent.

"Development," "Project," or "Property" means, all of the real property subject to a Project Instrument, and containing more than one Unit.

"Exchange Agent" means, a person who exchanges or offers to exchange Timeshare Intervals in an exchange program with other Timeshare Intervals.

"Managing Agent" means, a person who undertakes the duties, responsibilities and obligations of the management of a Timesharing Program.

"Offering" means, any offer to sell, solicitation, inducement or advertisement whether by radio, television, newspaper, magazine or by mail, whereby a person is given an opportunity to acquire a Timeshare Interval. Any offering of a Timeshare Interval which is not located in this State shall not be an offering if such offer states that the Timeshare Program is in compliance with the law of the jurisdiction in which the Timeshare Interval is located.

"Person" means, one or more natural persons, corporations, partnerships, associations, trusts, other entities, or any combination thereof.

"Project Instrument" means, one or more recordable documents applicable to the whole Project by whatever name denominated, containing restrictions or covenants regulating the use, occupancy or disposition of an entire Project, including any amendments to the document, but, excluding any law, ordinance, or governmental regulation.

"Public Offering Statement" means that statement required by Section 3-101.

"Purchaser" means, any person other than a developer or lender who acquires an interest in a Timeshare Interval.

"Sales Agent" means, a person who sells or offers to sell Timeshare Intervals in a Timeshare Program to a purchaser.

"Timeshare Estate" means, an ownership or leasehold estate in property devoted to a timeshare fee (tenants in common, time span ownership, interval ownership) and a timeshare lease.

"Timeshare Instrument" means, any document by whatever name denominated, creating or regulating Timeshare Programs, but, excluding any law, ordinance or governmental regulation.

"Timeshare Interval" means, a Timeshare Estate or a Timeshare Use.

"Timeshare Program" means, any arrangement for Timeshare Intervals in a Timeshare Project whereby the use, occupancy or possession of real property has been made subject to either a Timeshare Estate or Timeshare Use whereby such use, occupancy or possession circulates among purchasers of the Timeshare Intervals according to a fixed or floating time schedule on a periodic basis occurring annually over any period of time in excess of three (3) years in duration.

"Timeshare Project" means, any real property that is subject to a Timeshare Program.

"Timeshare Use" means, any contractual right of exclusive occupancy which does not fall within the definition of a Timeshare Estate including, without limitation, a vacation license, prepaid hotel reservation, club membership, limited partnership, or vacation bond.

"Unit" means, the real property or real property improvement in a Project which is divided into Timeshare Intervals.

Section 1-104. Status of Timeshare Estates With Respect to Real Property Interests.

A. A "Timeshare Estate" is an estate in real property and has the character and incidents of an estate in fee simple at common law or estate for years, if a leasehold, except as expressly modified by this Act. The foregoing shall supersede any contrary rule at common law.

B. A document transferring or encumbering a Timeshare Estate in real property may not be rejected for recordation because of the nature or duration of that estate or interest.

Section 1-105. Separate Titles. Each Timeshare Estate constitutes for purposes of title a separate estate or interest in property except for real property tax purposes.

Section 1-106. Applicability of Local Ordinances, Regulations, and Building Codes. A zoning, subdivision, or other ordinance or regulation may not discriminate against the creation of Timeshare Intervals or impose any requirement upon a Timeshare Program which it would not impose upon a similar development under a different form of ownership.

Section 1-107. Severability. If any provision of this Act or the application thereof to any person or circumstances is held invalid, the invalidity does not affect other provisions or applications of this Act which can be given effect without the invalid provisions or application, and to this end the provisions of this Act are severable.

ARTICLE 2
CREATION, TERMINATION, AND MANAGEMENT

Section 2-101. Timeshare Intervals in Units. A Timeshare Program may be created in any Unit, unless expressly prohibited by the Project Instruments or local governing laws.

Section 2-102. Instruments for Timeshare Estates. Project Instruments and Timeshare Instruments creating Timeshare Estates must contain the following:

1. The name of the county in which the property is situated.
2. The legal description, street address, or other description sufficient to identify the property.
3. Identification of time periods by letter, name number, or combination thereof.
4. Identification of Timeshare Estates, and, where applicable, the method whereby additional Timeshare Estates may be created.
5. The formula, fraction, or percentage, of the common expenses and any voting rights assigned to each Timeshare Estate, and, where applicable, to each Unit in a Project that is not subject to the Timeshare Program.
6. Any restrictions on the use, occupany, alteration, or alienation of Timeshare Intervals.
7. The ownership interest, if any, in personal property and provisions for care and replacement.
8. Any other matters the Developer deems appropriate.

Section 2-103. Timeshare Estate Management. The Timeshare Instruments for a Timeshare Estate Program shall prescribe reasonable arrangements for management and operation of the Timeshare program and for the maintenance, repair, and furnishing of Units, which shall ordinarily include, but need not be limited to, provisions for the following:

1. Creation of an association of Timeshare Estate owners.
2. Adoption of bylaws for organizing and operating the association.
3. Payment of costs and expenses of operating the Timeshare Program and owning and maintaining the Units.
4. Employment and termination of employment of the Managing Agent for the association.
5. Preparation and dissemination to owners of an annual budget and of operating statements and other financial information concerning the Timeshare Program.
6. Adoption of standards and rules of conduct for the use and occupancy of Units by owners.
7. Collection of assessments from owners to defray the expenses of management of the Timeshare Program and maintenance of the Units.
8. Comprehensive general liability insurance for death, bodily injury, and property damage arising out of, or in connection with, the use of Units by owners, their guests, and other users.
9. Methods for providing compensating use periods or monetary compensation to an owner if a Unit cannot be made available for the period to which the owner is entitled by schedule or by confirmed reservation.
10. Procedures for imposing a monetary penalty or suspension of an owner's rights and privileges in the Timeshare Program for failure of the owner to comply with provisions of the Timeshare Instruments or the rules of the association with respect to the use of the Units. Under these procedures an owner must be given notice and the opportunity to refute or explain the charges against him in person or in writing to the governing body of the association before a decision to impose discipline is rendered.
11. Employment of attorneys, accountants, and other professional persons as necessary to assist in the management of the Timeshare Program and the Units.

Section 2-104. Developer Control.

A. The Timeshare Instruments for a Timeshare Estate Program may provide for a period of time, hereafter referred to as the "developer control period," during which the Developer or a Managing Agent selected by the Developer may manage the Timeshare Program and the Units in the Timeshare Program.

B. If the Timeshare Instruments for a Timeshare Estate Program provide for the establishment of a developer control period, they shall ordinarily include provisions for the following:

1. Termination of the developer control period by action of the association.
2. Termination of contracts for goods and services for the Timeshare Program or for Units in the Timeshare Program entered into during the developer control period.
3. A regular accounting by the Developer to the association as to all matters that significantly affect the interests of owners in the Timeshare Program.

Section 2-105. Instruments For Timeshare Use. Project Instruments and Timeshare Instruments creating Timeshare Uses must contain the following:

1. Identification by name of the Timeshare Project and street address where the Timeshare Project is situated.
2. Identification of the time periods, type of Units and the Units that are in the Timeshare Program, and the length of time that the Units are committed to the Timeshare Program.
3. In case of a Timeshare project, identification of which Units are in the Timeshare Program and the method whereby any other Units may be added, deleted or substituted.
4. Any other matters that the Developer deems appropriate.

Section 2-106. Timeshare Use Management. The Timeshare Instruments for a Timeshare Use Program shall prescribe reasonable arrangements for management and operation of the Timeshare Program and for the maintenance, repair, and furnishing of Units which shall ordinarily include, but need not be limited to, provisions for the following:

1. Standards and procedures for upkeep, repair, and interior furnishing of Units and for providing of maid, cleaning, linen, and similar services to the Units during use periods.
2. Adoption of standards and rules of conduct governing the use and occupancy of Units by owners.
3. Payment of the costs and expenses of operating the Timeshare Program and owning and maintaining the Units.
4. Selection of a Managing Agent to act on behalf of the Developer.
5. Preparation and dissemination to owners of an annual budget and of operating statements and other financial information concerning the Timeshare Program.
6. Procedures for establishing the rights of owners to the use of Units by prearrangement or under a first-reserved, first-served priority system.
7. Organization of a management advisory board consisting of Timeshare Use owners including an enumeration or rights and responsibilities of the board.
8. Procedures for imposing and collecting assessments of use fees from Timeshare Use owners as necessary to defray costs of management of the Timeshare Program and in providing materials and services to the Units.
9. Comprehensive general liability insurance for death, bodily injury, and property damage arising out of, or in connection with, the use of Units by Timeshare Use owners, their guests, and other users.
10. Methods for providing compensating use periods or monetary compensation to an owner if a Unit cannot be made available for the period to which the owner is entitled by schedule or by a confirmed reservation.
11. Procedures for imposing a monetary penalty or suspension of an owner's rights and privileges in the Timeshare Program for failure of the owner to comply with the provisions of the Timeshare Instruments or the rules established by the Developer with respect to the use of the Units. The owner shall be given notice and the opportunity to refute or explain the charges in person or in writing to the management advisory board before a decision to impose discipline is rendered.
12. Annual dissemination to all Timeshare Use owners by the Developer, or by the Managing Agent, of a list of the names and mailing addresses of all current Timeshare Use owners in the Timeshare Program.

Section 2-107. Partition. No action for partition of a Unit may be maintained except as permitted by the Timeshare Instrument.

ARTICLE 3
PROTECTION OF PURCHASERS

Section 3-101. Public Offering Statement: General Provisions.

A. A Public Offering Statement must be provided to each Purchaser of a Timeshare Interval and must contain or fully and accurately disclose:

1. The name of the Developer and the principal address of the Developer and the Timeshare Intervals offered in the Statement.
2. A general description of the Units including, without limitation, the Developer's schedule of commencement and completion of all buildings, Units, and amenities, or if completed, that they have been completed.
3. As to all Units offered by the Developer in the same Timeshare Project.
    (i) the types and number of Units;
    (ii) identification of Units that are subject to Timeshare Intervals; and
    (iii) the estimated number of Units that may become subject to Timeshare Intervals.
4. A brief description of the Project.
5. If applicable, any current budget and a projected budget for the Timeshare Intervals for one (1) year after the date of the first transfer to a Purchaser. The budget must include, without limitation:
    (i) a statement of the amount, or a statement that there is no amount, included in the budget as a reserve for repairs and replacement;
    (ii) the projected common expense liability, if any, by category of expenditures for the Timeshare Intervals;
    (iii) The projected common expense liability for all Timeshare Intervals; and
    (iv) a statement of any services not reflected in the budget that the Developer provides, or expenses that it pays;
6. Any initial or special fee due from the Purchaser at closing, together with a description of the purpose and method of calculating the fee.
7. A description of any liens, defects, or encumbrances on or affecting the title to the Timeshare Intervals.
8. A description of any financing offered by the Developer.
9. A statement that within three (3) days after receipt of a Public Offering Statement a Purchaser may cancel any contract for purchase of a Timeshare Interval from a Developer.
10. A statement of any pending suits material to the Timeshare Intervals of which a Developer has actual knowledge.
11. Any restraints on alienation of any number or portion of any Timeshare Intervals.
12. A description of the insurance coverage, or a statement that there is no insurance coverage, provided for the benefit of Timeshare Interval owners.
13. Any current or expected fees or charges to be paid by Timeshare Interval owners for the use of any facilities related to the property.
14. The extent to which financial arrangements have been provided for completion of all promised improvements.
15. The extent to which a Timeshare Unit may become subject to a tax or other lien arising out of claims against other owners of the same Unit.

B. If the owners of Timeshare Intervals are to be permitted or required to become members of or to participate in any program for the exchange of occupancy rights among themselves or with the owners of Timeshare Intervals of other Timeshare Projects or both, the Public Offering Statement or a supplement delivered therewith must fully and accurately disclose:

1. The identity of the person operating the exchange program and whether that person is an affiliate of the Developer.
2. A general description of the procedures to qualify for and effectuate exchanges, including any stated or practiced priorities and restrictions, and the extent to which changes thereof may be made, whether membership or participation in the exchange program, or both, are volun-

tary or mandatory, and a statement of the disposition, if any, of the unused exchange Timeshare Interval, of the Exchange Agent.

3. The expenses, or ranges of expenses, to the Timeshare Interval owners of membership in the exchange program including the expenses, if any, of exchanging as of a date not more than one (1) year before the Public Offering Statement is delivered to the purchaser, and the person to whom those expenses are payable.

4. Whether and how any of the expenses specified in paragraph 3 may be altered and, if any of them are to be fixed on a case-by-case basis, the manner in which they are to be fixed in each case.

5. With respect to the owners of Timeshare Intervals in the exchange program, the geographical location of each Timeshare Project and the minimum duration of Timeshare Intervals and number of Timeshare Interval Owners in the exchange program at each project during a calendar year ending not more than fifteen (15) months before the Public Offering Statement is delivered to the Purchaser.

6. The percentage of exchanges properly applied for by members of participants in the exchange program that were fulfilled during a calendar year ending not more than fifteen (15) months before the date the Public Offering Statement is delivered to the Purchaser, together with a statement of the criteria used to determine whether an exchange was properly applied for and fulfilled.

7. The number of persons applying for an exchange as a percentage of the number of members in the exchange program as a whole during the calendar year ending not more than fifteen (15) months before the Public Offering Statement is delivered to the Purchaser.

8. In those cases where the Exchange Agent is not an affiliate of the Developer, the Exchange Agent shall provide the Developer with all of the information contained in items 2 through 7 of this subsection B which it shall certify as being true, accurate and complete in all particulars. The Developer shall include the certified information in the Public Offering Statement as replacement for the Developer's disclosures required by this subsection B.

Section 3-102. Escrow of Deposits. Any deposit made in connection with the purchase or reservation of a Timeshare Interval from a Developer must be placed in escrow and held in this State, in an account designated solely for the purpose, [by an independent bonded escrow company, or] in an institution whose accounts are insured by a governmental agency or instrumentality, until (1) delivered to the Developer at the expiration of the time for rescission or any later time specified in any contract or sale, (2) delivered to the Developer because of the Purchaser's default under a contract to purchase the Timeshare Interval, or (3) refunded to the Purchaser.

Section 3-103. Mutual Rights of Cancellation.

A. Before transfer of a Timeshare Interval and no later than the date of any sales contract, the Developer shall provide the intended transferee with a copy of the Public Offering Statement and any amendments and supplements thereto. The contract is voidable by the Purchaser until he has received the Public Offering Statement and for three (3) days thereafter. Cancellation is without penalty, and all payments made by the Purchaser before cancellation must be refunded within thirty (30) days after receipt of the notice of cancellation as provided in subsection C below.

B. Up to three (3) days after the receipt by the Purchaser of the Public Offering Statement, the Developer may cancel the contract of purchase without penalty to either party. The Developer shall return all payments made, and the Purchaser shall return all materials received in good condition, reasonable wear and tear excepted. If such materials are not returned, the Developer may deduct the cost of the same and return the balance to the Purchaser.

C. If either party elects to cancel a contract pursuant to subsection A or B, he may do so by hand-delivering notice thereof to the other party or by mailing notice thereof by prepaid United States mail to the other party or to his agent for service of process.

Section 3-104. Other Filings Not Required.

A. Any Timeshare Program in which a Public Offering Statement has been prepared does not require registration under any of the following:

1. State Securities Act.
2. State Land Sales Act.
3. Any other State Act which requires the preparation of a Public Offering Statement or substantially similar document for distribution to Purchasers.

B. Any Timeshare Program that fails to restrict the price at which an owner may sell or exchange his Timeshare Interval shall not by virtue of such failure cause the Timeshare Interval to become a security under (State Securities Act) nor shall an Exchange Agent offering such a Timeshare Interval for exchange be construed to be offering a security under such Act.

Section 3-105. Exemptions.

A. The Developer shall not be required to prepare and distribute a Public Offering Statement if the Developer has registered and there has been issued a Public Offering Statement or similar disclosure document which is provided to Purchasers under the following:

1. Securities and Exchange Act of 1933.
2. State Securities Act.
3. Applicable State Land Sales Act.
4. Federal Interstate Land Sales Full Disclosure Act in which the Timeshare Program is made a part of the subdivision that is being registered.
5. Any federal or state act which requires a federal or state Public Offering Statement or similar disclosure document to be prepared and provided to Purchasers.

B. A Public Offering Statement need not be prepared or delivered in the case of:

1. Any transfer of a Timeshare Interval by any Timeshare Interval owner other than the Developer and/or his agent.
2. Any disposition pursuant to Court Order.
3. A disposition by a government or governmental agency.
4. A disposition by foreclosure or deed in lieu of foreclosure.
5. A disposition of a Timeshare Interval in a Timeshare Project situated wholly outside this State provided that all solicitations, negotiations, and contacts took place wholly outside this State and the contract was executed wholly outside this State.
6. A gratuitous transfer of a Timeshare Interval.
7. Group reservations made for fifteen (15) or more people as a single transaction between a hotel and travel agent or travel groups for hotel accommodations, where deposits are made and held for more than three years in advance.

Section 3-106. Material Change. The Developer shall amend or supplement the Public Offering Statement to report any material change in the information required by Section 3-101. As to any exchange program, the Developer shall use the current written materials that are supplied to it for distribution to the Timeshare Interval owners as it is received.

Section 3-107. Liens.

A. Unless the Purchaser expressly agrees to take subject to or assume a lien prior to transferring a Timeshare Interval other than by deed in lieu of foreclosure, the Developer shall record or furnish to the Purchaser releases of all liens affecting that Timeshare Interval, or shall provide a surety bond or insurance against the lien, as provided for in liens on real estate in this state.

B. Unless a Timeshare Interval owner or his predecessor in title agree otherwise with the lienor, if a lien other than an underlying mortgage or deed of trust becomes effective against more than one Timeshare Interval in a Timeshare Project, any Timeshare Interval owner is entitled to a release of his Timeshare Interval from the lien upon payment of the amount of the lien attributable to his Timeshare Interval. The amount of the payment must be proportionate to the ratio that the Timeshare Interval owner's liability bears to the liabilities of all Timeshare Interval owners whose interests are subject to the lien. Upon receipt of payment, the lien-holder shall promptly deliver to the Timeshare Interval owner a release of the lien covering that Timeshare Interval. After payment, the managing entity may not assess or have a lien against that Timeshare Interval for any portion of the expenses incurred in connection with that lien.

Section 3-108. Effect of Violations on Rights of Action; Attorneys' Fees and Criminal Penalties. If a Developer or any other person subject to this Act violates any provision thereof or any provision of the Project Instruments, any person or class of persons adversely affected by the violation has a claim for appropriate relief. Punitive damages may be awarded for a willful violation of this Act. The court may also award reasonable attorneys' fees. Any Developer or any other person subject to this Act who offers or disposes of a Timeshare Interval without having complied with this Act or who violates any provision of this Act shall be guilty of a misdemeanor punishable by a fine not exceeding Five Thousand Dollars ($5,000) or by imprisonment in the state prison or in the county jail not exceeding one (1) year, or by both such fine and imprisonment.

Section 3-109. Statute of Limitations. A judicial proceeding where the accuracy of the Public Offering Statement or validity of any contract of purchase is in issue and a rescission of the contract or damages is sought must be commenced within four (4) years after the date of the contract of purchase, notwithstanding that the Purchaser's terms of payments may extend beyond the period of limitation. However, with respect to the enforcement of provisions in the contract of purchase which require the continued furnishing of services and the reciprocal payments to be made by the Purchaser, the period of bringing a judicial proceeding will continue for a period of four (4) years for each breach, but the parties may agree to reduce the period of limitation to not less than two (2) years.

Section 3-110. Class Actions. No Timeshare Owner can bring an action on behalf of other Timeshare Interval owners unless he has received the written authorization to represent the other Timeshare Interval owner or owners.

Section 3-111. Financial Records. The person or entity responsible for making and/or collecting common expense assessments or maintenance assessments shall keep detailed financial records. All financial and other records shall be made reasonably available for examination by any Timeshare Interval owner and his authorized agents.

ARTICLE 4
ADMINISTRATION AND REGISTRATION

Section 4-101. General Powers and Duties of Agency.

A. The Agency may adopt, amend, and repeal [rules] [regulations] and issue orders consistent with, and in furtherance of the objectives of this Act. The Agency may prescribe forms and procedures for submitting information to the Agency.

B. The Agency may accept grants in aid from any governmental source and may contract with agencies charged with similar functions in this or other jurisdictions, in furtherance of the objectives of this Act.

C. The Agency may cooperate with agencies performing similar functions in this and other jurisidictions to develop uniform filing procedures and forms, uniform disclosure standards, and uniform administrative practices, and may develop information that may be useful in the discharge of the Agency's duties.

D. The Agency may initiate private investigations within or outside this state.

E. The Agency after notice and hearing, may issue a Notice of Suspension if any of the following conditions exist:

1. Any representation in any document or information filed with the Agency is false or misleading.
2. Any Developer or agent of Developer has engaged or is engaging in any unlawful act or practice.
3. Any Developer or agent of Developer has disseminated or caused to be disseminated orally, or in writing, any false or misleading promotional materials in connection with a Timeshare Program.
4. Any Developer or agent of Developer has concealed, diverted, or disposed of any funds or assets of any person in a manner impairing rights of Purchasers of Timeshare Intervals in the Timeshare Program.
5. Any Developer or agent of Developer has failed to perform any stipulation or agreement made to induce the Agency to issue an order relating to that Timeshare Program.
6. Any Developer or agent of Developer has otherwise violated any provision of this Act or the Agency's [rules] [regulations] or orders.

F. The Agency may issue a Cease and Desist order if the Developer has not registered the Timeshare Program as required by this Act.

G. The Agency, after notice and hearing, may issue an order revoking the registration of a Timeshare Program upon determination that a Developer or agent of Developer has failed to comply with a Notice of Suspension issued by the Agency affecting the Timeshare Program.

Section 4-102. Registration Required.

A. Unless exempted by Section 4-107, a Developer may not offer or dispose of a Timeshare Interval unless the Timeshare Program is registered with the Agency, provided, however, that a Developer may accept a reservation together with a desposit if the deposit is placed in an escrow account with an institution having trust powers and is refundable at any time at the Purchaser's option. In all cases, a reservation must require a subsequent affirmative act by the Purchaser via a separate instrument to create a binding obligation. A Developer may not dispose of or transfer a Timeshare Interval while an order revoking or suspending the registration of the Timeshare Program is in effect.

B. An Acquisition Agent including the Developer if it is also the Acquisition Agent shall register with the Agency the Timeshare Program or Programs that it is providing prospective purchasers for, its principal office address and telephone number and designate who its responsible managing employee is. The Acquisition Agent shall furnish evidence that a bond of $5,000 has been placed with a surety company or a cash bond with the Agency to cover any violations of any solicitation ordinances, zoning ordinances, building codes, or other regulations governing the use of the premise or premises in which the Timeshare Program is promoted.

C. A Sales Agent including the Developer if it is also the Sales Agent shall register with the Agency the Timeshare Program or Programs that it is selling, its principal office address, and telephone number and designate who its responsible managing employee is and any special escrow accounts set up for the deposit and collection of purchasers' funds. The Sales Agent shall furnish evidence that a bond of $5,000 has been placed with a surety company or a cash bond with the Agency to cover any defalcations of the Sales Agent.

D. A Managing Agent including the Developer if it is also the Managing Agent shall register with the Agency the Timeshare Program or Programs that it is managing, its principal office address, and telephone number and designate who its responsible managing employee is. The Managing Agent shall furnish evidence that a bond of $5,000 has been placed with a surety company or a cash bond with the Agency to cover any default of the Managing Agent in his duties and responsibilities.

E. In the event that the Acquisition Agent, Sales Agent, and Management Agent are under the control of, subsidiary of, or affiliate of the Developer or any person, the bond can be consolidated and reduced to $10,000 provided that there is a disclosure of the affiliation and the disclosure as provided above.

F. An Exchange Agent including the Developer if it is also the Exchange Agent shall file a statement with the Agency containing a list of the Timeshare Program or Programs that it is offering exchange services for, its principal office address, and telephone number and designate who its responsible managing employee is or the person to whom any contact is to be made.

G. The Acquisition Agent and Sales Agent shall maintain their respective records or any independent contractors employed by them, their addresses, and the commissions paid for the immediately preceding two calendar years.

Section 4-103. Application for Registration. An application for registration must contain the Public Offering Statement, a brief description of the property, copies of Timeshare Instruments, and any documents referred to therein (other than tract maps, plats, and plans), and such other information required by the Agency's [rules] and [regulations] and be accompanied by any reasonable fees required by the Agency.

Section 4-104. Agency Regulation of Public Offering Statement.

A. The Agency at any time may require a Developer to alter or supplement the form or substance of a Public Offering Statement to assure adequate and accurate disclosure to prospective Purchasers.

B. The Public Offering Statement may not be used for any promotional purposes before registration and afterwards only if it is used in its entirety. No person may advertise or represent that the Agency has approved or recommended the Timeshare Program, the Disclosure Statement, or any of the documents contained in the application for registration.

Section 4-105. Receipt of Application; Effectiveness of Registration.

A. Except as hereinafter provided, the effective date of the registration, or any amendment thereto, shall be the (45th) day after the filing thereof or such earlier date as the Agency may determine, having due regard of the public interest and the protection of Purchasers. If any amendment to any such registration is filed prior to the effective date, the registration shall be deemed to have been filed when such amendment was filed.

B. If it appears to the Agency that the application for registration, or any amendment thereto, is on its face incomplete or inaccurate in any material respect, the Agency shall so advise the Developer prior to the date the registration would otherwise be effective. Such notification shall serve to suspend the effective date of the filing until the (45th) day after the Developer files such additional information as the Agency shall require. Any Developer, upon receipt of such notice of suspension may request a hearing, and such hearing shall be held within thirty (30) days of receipt of such request.

Section 4-106. Amendment. A Developer shall amend or supplement its registration to report any material change in the information required by Section 4-103.

Section 4-107. Exemptions.

A. No registration with the Agency shall be required if the Developer is registered and there has been issued a Public Offering Statement or similar disclosure document which is provided to Purchasers under the following:

1. Securities and Exchange Act of 1933.
2. State Securities Act.
3. Applicable State Land Sales Act.
4. Federal Interstate Land Sales Full Disclosure Act in which the Timeshare Program is made a part of the subdivision that is being registered.
5. Any federal or state act which requires a federal or state agency to review a Public Offering Statement or similar disclosure document which is required to be distributed to Purchasers.

B. No registration with the Agency shall be required in the case of:

1. Any transfer of a Timeshare Interval by any Timeshare Interval owner other than the Developer and/or his agent.
2. Any disposition pursuant to Court Order.
3. A disposition by a government or governmental agency.
4. A disposition by foreclosure or deed in lieu of foreclosure.
5. A disposition of a Timeshare Interval in a Timeshare Project situated wholly outside this State provided that all solicitations and negotiations took place wholly outside this state and the contract was executed wholly outside this State.
6. A gratuitous transfer of a Timeshare Interval.
7. Group reservations made for fifteen (15) or more people as a single transaction between a hotel and travel agent or travel groups for hotel accommodations, where deposits are made and held for more than three (3) years in advance.

ARTICLE 5
FINANCING

Section 5-101. Financing of Timeshare Programs. In the financing of a Timeshare Program, the Developer shall retain financial records of the schedule of payments required to be made and the payments made to any person or entity which is the holder of an underlying blanket mortgage, deed of trust, contract of sale, or other lien or encumbrance ("lien holder"). Any transfer of the Developer's interest in the Timeshare Program to any third person shall be subject to the obligations of the Developer.

Section 5-102. Rights Under Foreclosure. The Developer whose Project is subject to an underlying blanket lien or encumbrance shall protect nondefaulting Purchasers from foreclosure by the lien holder by obtaining from the lien holder a nondisturbance clause, subordination agreement, or partial release of the lien as the Timeshare Intervals are sold. In the alternative, the Developer may obtain the agreement of the lien holder to take the Project in the event of default by the Developer subject to the rights of the nondefaulting Purchasers by posting a bond equal to 50 percent of the amount owed to the lien holder, making an assignment of receivables equal to 125 percent of the principal amounts due from Purchasers, pledging collateral security equal to 100 percent of the amount owed to the lien holder or entering into any other financing plan or escrow agreement acceptable to the lien holder.

Section 5-103. Protection of Lien Holder. The lien holder in any Timeshare Program shall have the following rights:

1. A lien holder shall have his lien rights preserved as against any Purchaser of Timeshare Interval claiming that the Timeshare Instrument is invalid, void, or voidable, thirty (30) days after written notice by certified mail or personal delivery has been given by the Developer to the Purchaser. Said notice must state that Developer has assigned the receivables to the lien holder and that Purchaser has thirty (30) days within which to object and specify the invalidity or defect contained within such Instrument.
2. Any Purchaser who fails to indicate the invalidity, void, or voidableness as provided in subparagraph I waives or is estopped to raise the same in any subsequent enforcement of the collection of the receivable by the lien holder.

APPENDIX I

Rules and Regulations for Marina Village Camping Club, Inc. Trinity, Texas

INTRODUCTION

The Board of Directors of Marina Village Camping Club, Inc. ("Club"), has adopted the following Rules pertaining to the use of the facilities within Marina Village Camping Club, Inc.

The primary consideration in the adoption of these Rules has been to enable the Owner-Members and their guests to obtain maximum enjoyment from the use of the facilities, while at the same time considering the health, safety, and general welfare of the Owner-Members and their guests in the use thereof. These Rules are subject to change by the Board of Directors of the Club, pursuant to the Bylaws of the Club. The Board has the right to make changes at any time without prior notice.

The Club requests that the Owner-Members make every effort to comply, and cause members of their family and guests to comply with these Rules.

The manager of the Club shall at all times have the authority to see that each of these Rules is carried out and to enforce same by suspension or revocation of the privilege of use.

GENERAL

1. Membership cards will be issued to Owner-Members (Husband and Wife) and unmarried children, under 21 years of age, residing with parents. Cards should be carried on the person for identification purposes when at the Club.

In the event of error, or loss, new cards should be requested in writing from the Club.

2. Windshield decals will be issued to members. Owner-Members' cars and recreational vehicles must bear the decal when on the Club premises. In the event an additional decal is needed for another vehicle of a member of their immediate family, it may be obtained by a request in writing to the Club. Requests must include the following information:

Name of vehicle owner
Address of vehicle owner
Family relationship of vehicle owner to member
Age of vehicle owner
Make, model, and year of vehicle
License number of vehicle

Vehicle decals are to be used only on personal vehicles registered to the Owner-Member or his immediate family as defined above.

3. The recreational facilities operated by the Club shall be kept open in accordance with a schedule determined by the Board of Directors.

4. All facilities of the Club are used by Owner-Members and their guests at their own risk.

5. Employees of the Club shall not be subject to the individual direction or control of Owner-Members. The specific direction and control of Club employees is vested in the Club and its duly authorized agents.

6. Under no circumstances will minors be served or allowed to consume liquor in or on any part of the Club's property.

7. The Club will not be responsible for the loss or damage to any property of the Owner-Member or guests.

8. All Club equipment shall be checked out by using the membership card as a deposit which will be returned when the equipment is returned in good condition. Rental equipment may require a deposit to be refunded on return of equipment. Equipment shall be returned to the space provided for its storage immediately upon the completion of its use.

9. Receptacles are provided in convenient locations throughout the Club area for all trash, garbage, worn out gear, etc. Please use them.

10. Nothing shall be posted on any Club bulletin board except by Officers, Directors, or the Manager of the Club. Bulletin boards are provided for general notices, Club business, and particular announcements of the management. Anything posted on a bulletin board must not be changed or be destroyed by anyone except by the Manager or by order of the Officers or Directors of the Club. Special bulletin boards for the use of Owner-Members shall be maintained in the general area of the Center and all individual notices by Owner-Members shall be placed on them.

11. All Owner-Members and guests shall register at the Club's main office upon arrival and departure.

12. Owner-Members, members of their respective families, visitors, or guests shall conduct themselves with decorum while upon the premises of the Club and shall not indulge in loud or boisterous conduct. Games or sports which may be calculated to bring the Club into disrepute or interrupt the harmony of the community will not be allowed. In the event any Owner-Member or guest is guilty of a breach of the rules of conduct, it shall be the duty of any duly authorized Club agent to immediately require said party or parties to leave the premises.

13. Owner-Members will at all times be fully responsible for the conduct of their children on the Club's premises.

14. Owner-Members entertaining guests shall be responsible for their conduct while on the Club's premises, and shall be responsible for any charges incurred by their guests.

15. Any Owner-Member who willfully or negligently defaces, injures, or destroys property or equipment of the Club shall be held liable for the full value thereof.

16. All Owner-Members will be expected to camp only during their designated time period unless prior arrangements have been made with the manager for nonreserved time. Owner-Members who do not leave the Club when their reserved time has expired will be subject to fine, suspension and/or loss of membership.

In no event will permanent occupancy be permitted. Permanent occupancy shall mean any vehicle, tent, or other encampment that remains on any part, lot, campsite, or other area set aside for Owner-Members, for a period of 30 consecutive days, provided, however, that any interruption of 10 or more consecutive days shall constitute the beginning of a new 30-day period. Physical use of said part, lot, campsite, or other area on normal weekends, holidays, or vacation periods not in conflict with the aforementioned and vacant through the normal work week shall not be construed as permanent occupancy. No person shall use the park as a principal place of residence, and Owner-Members shall maintain a permanent residence outside the park. No occupant shall use a permanent mailing address within the Club facilities, and shall not be entitled to vote using an address within the park as a place of permanent residence.

17. No Owner-Member or guest shall attach any appurtenance, attachment, or accessory building or structure to the trees or other living plants within the Club.

18. During periods of extreme fire or rising water hazard, special precautions or measures may have to be ordered by the management. In the event the fire or rising water hazard is severe, the park may be closed or other precautionary measures ordered by the management. Upon notice from the management all Owner-Members and guests shall immediately comply with orders to take special precautions or evacuate.

19. No trail bikes, motor bikes, motorcycles, dune buggies, sand buggies, off-road vehicles, or other similar powered apparatus are allowed to be operated within the Club.

20. The gathering or cutting of wood or other vegetation within the park is prohibited.

21. Fires are allowed only in designated fireplaces, and the management may prohibit building of fires at any time when such fires may present a fire hazard. Only charcoal or briquets may be used at the individual campsite barbecues. Open fires are not allowed.

22. Pets: Owner-Members may bring family pets, providing such pets are the usual household pets such as dogs, cats, birds. Pets shall be well mannered; dogs shall be kept on leashes at all times. Management reserves the right to request members to remove unruly, loud, and misbehaving animals from the Club area and to restrict roaming pets.

23. No signs, placards, displays, or notices of any type or kind are to be located on a campsite or in the park, except on the bulletin board provided for the use of the Owner-Members at the village center.

24. The possession of firearms and/or other weapons in the park is prohibited.

25. The speed limit on all roads in the area shall be 10 mph, or as posted.

26. Any noise generating equipment such as televisions, radios, record players, and generators shall be restricted in their use and time of operation as the Club shall from time to time direct for the mutual comfort and pleasure of all Owner-Members, and at no time shall the use of said equipment cause a nuisance to other users of the area.

27. Outside clothes drying and/or clothes lines are not permitted within the Camp area.

28. Swimming is not allowed at the marina, boat launch ramps, boat stalls, or fishing docks.

MASTER SCHEDULE

Each Owner-Member will be assigned a permanent designation to his membership. Every eight (8) years, the Board of Directors will adopt a Master Schedule of usage for each group. The Master Schedule applicable to an Owner-Member's guaranteed usage will be provided to the member by the Club. The Board may amend or revise the Master Schedule from time to time. The intent is to provide a variety of times and groupings of camping experiences on a fair and equitable basis.

Any Owner-Member may camp within his designated time schedule or without, providing the Rules regarding Reservations are followed.

RESERVATION SYSTEM

Each Owner-Member must notify the management by phone of each intended camping visit. Notice and reservation confirmation must be accomplished prior to forty-eight (48) hours before arrival. It is intended that Owner-Members will camp according to their membership designation in accordance with the Master Schedule.

An Owner-Member is allowed to camp not in keeping with his group's schedule, providing he requests off-schedule time from Management only during the period twenty-four (24) hours prior to his intended camping arrival. Such unscheduled camping shall be restricted to no more than seven (7) continuous days at any one time. Unscheduled reservations will be based on availability and on first reserved, first served basis. Unscheduled campers will be expected to yield their sites to scheduled campers if necessary to accommodate scheduled campers within the park. Failure to do so can result in fines or loss of membership privileges.

Guests of individual Owner-Members cannot use the facilities of the Club unless accompanied by such Owner-Member and occupying the same campsite as the Owner-Member, provided that:

a. The Owner-Member shall notify the Club at least 48 hours prior to the arrival of any such guest at the facilities and management has agreed to the guest's presence.

b. Any such guest must fill out the registration form provided by the Club.

c. The Owner-Member is fully responsible and liable to the Club for any and all damage, charges, expenses, or liabilities incurred by that guest.

d. The Owner-Member is fully responsible for the conduct of the guest.

e. The guest has not used the Club's facilities previously during that calendar quarter.

f. No more than eight (8) people are in the combined camping unit unless prior permission has been obtained from Management.

g. No more than one (1) camping vehicle and one (1) tent are to occupy the site.

An Owner-Member may request a reservation for an additional campsite for a guest accompanying the Owner-Member, provided that he meet the criteria set forth:

a. The Owner-Member shall not have more than one additional campsite per calendar quarter.

b. Notice and reservation confirmation must follow the normal reservations system and shall be on a space available basis.

c. The Owner-Member pays a guest fee of $____per night.

d. The additional campsite shall be restricted to no more than three (3) continuous days' use during any one quarter.

e. All rules and regulations which apply to a guest occupying the same campsite as the Owner-Member shall apply.

CAMP COAST TO COAST

Manager shall have control over allocation and usage of each Owner-Member's days which have been allocated for Camp Coast to Coast usage. Manager shall insofar as possible use days when the Owner-Member will not be using his membership. Camp Coast to Coast does not apply to Memorial Day, Independence Day, and Labor Day weekends.

RECREATIONAL FACILITIES

1. Any Owner-Member in good standing may obtain, at certain times and under certain conditions, the use of certain recreational facilities for group parties by applying to the Manager of the Club. However, no Owner-Member shall be excluded from the facility or denied the ordinary use of the facilities while such private parties are taking place. The facilities shall not be used for private parties or affairs, unless authorized by the Board of Directors.

2. Any reservation made for a function provided by the Club and not properly cancelled shall be charged to the member regardless of whether he attends or not.

3. Pets are not allowed in the recreational facilities at any time.

4. All rates for services shall be fixed from time to time by the Board of Directors. No Officer, Director, or employees shall have any authority to change, alter, or modify any rate or charge approved by the Board of Directors.

SWIMMING POOL

1. Swimming pool for use of Owner-Members and their guests only.

2. Pool only to be used when lifeguard on duty.

3. Pool will be open in accordance with a schedule to be published by the Club Management. Daily schedule will be posted.

4. On inclement days, Activities Director has authority to close the pool.

5. No children under 12 years of age will be allowed in the Clubhouse pool without their parents.

6. Pool rules will be posted. All Owner-Members and guests are expected to observe the rules. The lifeguard is there for two purposes:
(1) LIFESAVING, and (2) SUPERVISION.

7. Parents will be held responsible for the conduct of their children and it will be their responsibility to see that their children observe the rules.

CAMPGROUND

1. Facilities are available on a first-come, first-served basis. Upon entering, an Owner-Member may use any available site in his selected area.

2. The maintenance and keeping of horses or other livestock at the campsites is prohibited.

3. Charges for camping—none.

4. Number of guests shall be limited as prescribed by Management.

5. The Management shall have the authority to move equipment, vehicles, and belongings of Owner-Members and guests without liability in the event of an emergency; however, the Club shall have no duty or obligation to do so.

6. Fires are allowed only in designated pits or fireplaces. Fires to be totally extinguished when not personally attended.

7. All debris and garbage shall be placed in containers provided.

8. Tents shall be pitched only in areas designated for tents except by express permission of management.

9. Recreational vehicles shall be parked only in areas designated for such use.

10 Vehicular traffic shall only be allowed on designated roadways and parking areas in campground for means of ingress and egress.

11. Barbecue grills to be cleaned upon leaving.

12. Radio, television, and record players to be kept at volume not to disturb others. Public address systems and model airplanes are prohibited.

13. Loud talking, singing, playing of musical instruments, etc., after 10:00 P.M. is not permitted.

14. Cutting or gathering wood destroys natural beauty of the area and is, therefore, not permitted.

15. Self-contained vehicle storage tanks when parked on an unsewered site must have the outlet plugged. . . .

RIDING AND HIKING TRAILS

1. No motorized vehicles.
2. Debris to be placed in containers.
3. Picnicking only at designated locations.
4. All gates to be closed and secured.
5. To lessen the danger of fire, no smoking is allowed on riding or hiking trails or in other areas so designated.

VOLLEYBALL, HORSESHOES, TETHERBALL, ETC.

1. Use of these facilities will be on a first come, first served basis with no reservations permitted.

2. Persons using these facilities must check out the equipment from the Manager by presenting their membership cards and return the equipment to the Manager promptly when finished. Persons damaging, destroying, or failing to return the equipment will be held liable for the full value thereof.

3. Play on any of these facilities will be limited to 45-minute periods when other persons are waiting to use the facility. At the expiration of that time, the players will be expected to relinquish the court.

4. The only footwear allowed on the courts will be rubber soled athletic wear. Cleats, boots, street shoes, etc. will not be allowed.

5. Profanity, loud and abusive language, and other objectionable acts are prohibited.

MARINA AND BOAT USAGE

1. Boats may be launched only at the designated areas within the Club. Wet storage space is available subject to the rules of Westwood Shores Marina. Dry storage is not available.

2. Boats may be stored temporarily at campsites during the Owner-Member's stay at the Club but must be removed from the park when the Owner-Member departs. Boats may be stored only on the paved driveways or pads but may not be stored in any street or thoroughfare.

3. Fish cleaning is allowed only where designated. Fish may not be cleaned at a campsite.

4. Persons using the marina facilities will be expected to observe all of the rules relating to the Marina as established by the Westwood Shores Country Club.

TRAM SYSTEM USAGE

1. The tram system has been provided for the convenience of the Owner-Members to permit them full use of the park without the necessity of using their own vehicles for travel within the park. Therefore private vehicular traffic will be prohibited except as necessary to move recreational vehicles, boats, campers, etc.

2. The tram system can be used at any time by Owner-Members, their families, and guests without charge.

3. Persons using the tram system will be expected to remain seated at all times while the tram is moving and to keep their hands and feet inside the tram except when entering or leaving.

4. Children under 10 cannot use the tram without an adult accompanying them who is responsible for their conduct.

5. All persons using the tram system do so at their own risk.

ELIGIBLE VEHICLES

The Board of Directors reserves the right to determine the suitability of any particular vehicle for use within the Club and to exclude vehicles it deems unsuitable for use within the Club. By way of illustration, converted buses and other makeshift vehicles are not suitable vehicles.

WESTWOOD SHORES COUNTRY CLUB FACILITIES

Each Owner-Member in good standing with Marina Village Camping Club may become a member of Westwood Shores Country Club in accordance with that Club's bylaws and rules.

APPENDIX J

Preparing a Property Report
(Pursuant to the rules and regulations of the
U.S. Office of Interstate Land Sales and Registration)

Developer Documentation Checklist

This checklist has been prepared to aid the registrant in submitting all required documentation in the initial filing. *All unasterisked* documents must be included with each registration. If any unasterisked document cannot be obtained, the Secretary may allow the submission of the best alternate documentation.
(Include items noted with asterisk (*) only where applicable.)

GENERAL DOCUMENTS

[ ] *Copy of the State Property Report.
[ ] *Two copies of subdivision general plan.
[ ] Articles of incorporation, partnership, association, or joint venture.
[ ] Title evidence.
[ ] Copies of all recorded documents creating exceptions or objections to the title.
[ ] *Authorization to develop and sell.
[ ] *Copies of any escrow agreements or other instruments which protect the purchaser in the event of default or bankruptcy of the developer.
[ ] Copies of sales contract or agreement and note forms (must include proper recision language).
[ ] Copy of deeds or leases which will be used to convey title or lease lots.
[ ] Copy of plat map.
[ ] *Summary of environmental study.
[ ] Copy of restrictions or covenants.

ROADS

[ ] *Any financial assurance of completion of access roads.
[ ] *Any financial assurance of completion of interior roads.
[ ] *Letter from public authority as to acceptance and maintenance of interior roads.

WATER

[ ] *Letter from supplier if central system.
[ ] *Hydrological survey.
[ ] *Report on purity.
[ ] *Any financial assurance of completion of central system.
[ ] Copies of permits secured by developer.
[ ] *Membership agreement or contract requiring the use of the central system.

SEWER

[ ] *Letter from local authorities on individual systems.
[ ] *Letter from supplier of service if central system.
[ ] Copies of permits secured by developer.
[ ] *Any financial assurance of completion of central system.
[ ] *Membership agreement or contract requiring the use of the central system.

ELECTRICITY

[ ] *Any financial assurance of completion.

TELEPHONE

[ ] *Any financial assurance of completion.

COSTS AND FINANCING

[ ] *Financing plan for on-site and off-site improvements.
[ ] Copy of financial statement.
[ ] *Synopsis of plans and cost of incomplete facilities.
[ ] *Copy of any financial assurance of completion of recreational facilities.
[ ] *Copy of lease for any leased facilities.

SOIL AND DRAINAGE

[ ] Two copies of geological survey topographic map.
[ ] *Copy of any approval of soil erosion and flooding plan.
[ ] *Synopsis of proposed drainage plan.
[ ] *Copy of any financial assurance of completion of drainage facilities.

PROPERTY OWNERS' ASSOCIATION (POA)

[ ] *Summary of terms of any contracts between POA and developer.
[ ] *Summary of any agreement between POA and developer as to litigation.
[ ] Copies of formation articles and charter.
[ ] *Copy of membership agreement.

PRICE RANGE AND MARKETING

[ ] Price range of lots.
[ ] Description of marketing plans.
[ ] *Copy of advertising or promotional material.

VIOLATIONS AND LITIGATION

[ ] *Copies of any litigation.
[ ] *Copies of any bankruptcy proceedings.
[ ] *Copies of any orders issued on violations.

FOREIGN SUBDIVISIONS

[ ] *Copies (translated into English) of any laws restricting ownership by aliens.

APPENDIX K

Sample Questions To Be Answered in a Second-Home Property Buyers' Guide

Concept
What is the project concept?
Location
Where is the project?
How do you get there?
Environment
What about the climate?
Ecologically, what is the area like?
What fish and wildlife are present?
How is the water quality?
Ownership
Who owns the project?
Finances
What about financial matters
Operating Policies
What are the basic policies regarding planning, design, construction, and management?
Master Plan
What is a master plan?
What is the current master plan for the project?
Existing Facilities
What parts of the project have been completed?
What about the lodge and the reception center?
Recreation
What recreational facilities are available?
How does membership in the "Club" work?
Is there a children's program?
Property Ownership
What types of properties are available?
On what terms may they be purchased?
Are there annual fees associated with property ownership?
What restrictions will protect property owners?
Must the owner of a home site build on his land?
What is the procedure for building, and what costs should be expected?
Will the developer build units?
How does condominium ownership work?
Can a property owner rent his property? What are the terms?
What about warranties?
Will the developer assist in reselling owner's property?
What security provisions have been made to protect owner's property?
Utilities
What fire protection is available?
Will utility lines be underground?
What is the source of water? How is sewage disposed of?
Who pays for road maintenance?
The Local Community
What is the local community like?
How is it governed?
How are the taxes assessed?
What emergency facilities are available?
Is there a school system?
What churches are nearby?
What cultural amenities are offered?
What about general commercial services?
In general, how does the project relate to the community?

APPENDIX L

Town of Snowmass Village Master Plan (July 1979)

Purpose and Goals

With the incorporation of the Town of Snowmass Village in November, 1977, an opportunity was created for local, formal participation in land use decision making for the Brush Creek Valley/Snowmass Village. A long and somewhat convoluted planning history preceded incorporation. While many studies and reports have been prepared for private and governmental entities, no long-range master plan has been adopted for the Town of Snowmass Village and its environs. This plan has been prepared to meet the full requirements of Colorado Law as it pertains to master planning with specific authority cited in Sec. 31-23, Part II CRS, 1973.

In September of 1978 the Town of Snowmass Village adopted the "Master Plan Policy Statement" which set forth community goals and objectives, an historical planning summary and general planning guidelines for transportation, employee housing, land use and community facilities. This document set forth the intention of annexing some 2,800 acres of Snowmass Company lands to the Town of Snowmass Village and in doing so prescribed planning policies for the development of the expanded community.

In conjunction with the annexation process, the Snowmass Company, Benedict Land and Cattle Company, the Aspen Skiing Corporation and the Town agreed to plan cooperatively for the physical development of the Snowmass community with special emphasis on employee housing, land use, transportation and community facilities. In order to effect more detailed plans in these areas and incorporate broader based citizen participation in the planning process, committees were established. These groups monitored the development of the detailed plans which are presented herein.

The purpose of this master plan is to create a policy framework to guide growth in a way that results in harmonious, well-integrated, environmentally sound and fiscally balanced development. In a larger sense the master plan contributes to the establishment of a reliable and rational decision-making process for all matters related to the physical development of the community. The fundamental purpose of this plan is to protect and ensure the "health, safety and welfare" of the resident and tourist population.

It is most important to note that master plans are dynamic designs which can and should be modified and altered over the years in response to changing community needs. The process of planning needs to be a continuous and comprehensive activity and not constrained by assumptions and base data which may no longer be valid.

Specifically for Snowmass Village, the purpose of the master plan is to understand the landscape which surrounds the Town as a sum total of opportunities and constraints for development activity and to use this understanding as a policy basis for locating future development.

The State of Colorado enabling legislative authority Sec. 31-23-207, CRS, 1973, provides: "The plan shall be made with the general purpose of guiding and accomplishing a coordinated, adjusted, and harmonious development of the municipality and its environs which will, in accordance with present and future needs, best promote health, safety, morals, order, convenience, prosperity, and general welfare, as well as efficiency and economy in the process of development, including, among other things, adequate provision for traffic, the promotion of safety from fire, flood waters, and other dangers, adequate provision for light and air, the promotion of healthful and convenient distribution of population, the promotion of good civic design and arrangement, wise and efficient expenditure of public funds, and the adequate provision of public utilities and other public requirements." In order to effectuate the above, the master plan presented here emphasizes: (1) the protection and preservation of the unique natural resources of the Brush Creek Valley, (2) the protection and enhancement of the fiscal resources of the municipality and supporting district governmental functions and (3) the proper provision of public facilities and services. To explain further the above elements mean:

Natural Resources: The identification of key natural hazard and stress areas to include geologic conditions, soils, steep slopes, flood plains, wildlife migration and reproduction areas and unique and natural vegetation, and recreational resources. These areas will be carefully analyzed in locating future development activities.

Fiscal Resources: The development process will be guided in a way that controls adverse financial impact on any operating governmental service so as to minimize local taxation and ensure fiscal capability for the Town.

Public Facilities and Services: Sewer and water, transportation, solid waste disposal, drainage systems, recreational facilities and services, educational services, police and fire protection and other publicly provided systems and facilities.

Traditional community master planning stops with the identification of the physical distribution of land use activities by type. Authority is now provided for phasing development by the State of Colorado via H.B. 1034, which provides, in part, under Article 8, Section 29-20-104, CRS, 1973, "Without limiting or superseding any power or authority presently exercised or previously granted, each local government within its respective jurisdiction has the authority to plan for and regulate the use of land by:

(a) Regulating the location of activities and developments which may result in significant changes in population density.

(b) Providing for phased development of services and facilities."

In addition to the above, a community master plan sets the basic policy framework for the development of all implementing land use regulations. At Snowmass Village, this means that the zoning code and map, subdivision regulations and the planned unit development district in the zoning code must be broadly expressive of the values and goals embodied within the master plan statement. The flow chart below illustrates the interrelatedness of the plan and implementing regulations. In short, the regulations carry out through law what the plan states as a more general intention. In this way, individual development applications may be compared with the community goal statement as embodied in the master plan.

The annexation of Snowmass Company lands has created the opportunity for the Town to achieve a viable, self-contained community identity with independent support services.

GOALS

The following constitutes a generalized statement of local goals and supporting policies for the Snowmass Village community. Eleven major goals are hereby identified:

Goal 1: *Preserve the unique natural resources, scenic quality and ecological balance of the community.*

Snowmass Village provides a rare opportunity, for highest quality tourism in a manner that is consistent with an emerging permanent community. The wilderness, outdoor image in the Snowmass Village environs is essential to the long-range success of the area for both tourist and permanent residents. In order to preserve this image, certain key policy objectives are in order.

Policy Objectives:

(a) Physical development should be located to maximum extent possible so as not to disrupt the prominent scenic features of the valley, and be designed to enhance and maintain the natural environment in order to preserve optimal aesthetic and health standards.

(b) Physical development should be located not to disrupt local wildlife.

(c) Flood plains should be free of manmade improvements and all adjacent vegetation protected.

(d) Avoid the development of excessively steep, unstable slopes with either building sites or roadways.

(e) Avoid the removal of unique natural vegetation for development purposes.

(f) Take positive action to maintain optimum levels of air and water quality.

(g) Initiate policies and programs establishing and maintaining minimal levels of noise.

(h) Develop land use regulations which allow for the sensitive siting and design of all physical improvements.

(i) Encourage the Forest Service to maintain the scenic and recreational qualities of Forest Service lands near the Village for the growing needs of the summer tourist for dispersed recreation.

Goal 2: *Maintain a tourist and permanent residential mix at Snowmass.*

The infrastructure needed to support a healthy tourist economy in the context of a growing and stable permanent residential community should be provided. The land use pattern should evolve in a way that provides for a vital and interesting year-round tourist environment while at the same time preserving the peace and opportunity for quality permanent residential areas. While tourism is an important industry, more will be needed in cultural, educational and other supporting services to allow Snowmass Village to evolve as a community with a sense of permanence, identity and individual character.

Policy Objectives:

(a) Provide expanded commercial support for tourism to include a wider diversity of facilities and activities to encourage a more stable year-round economic base for the community and make Snowmass Village more self-sufficient in providing for the tourist.

(b) Provide a broad range of educational, recreational and cultural programs and facilities adaptable for use by both permanent residents and tourists.

(c) Make adequate provisions for commercial space for goods and services primarily directed to the requirements of the permanent residential community.

(d) Adopt land policies to maintain an appropriate level of tourism and produce a high quality of life in permanent residential areas within the community.

Goal 3: *Encourage a clustered development style for multifamily and commercial development which is easily and economically supportable by governmental facilities and services.*

With the inevitable growth that will occur in the Brush Creek Valley, a number of development styles are possible. This plan expresses the goal of providing for an efficient clustering of multifamily and commercial development in addition to the single-family lots identified in the overall development outlook. The clustering of multifamily and commercial development will allow economies in service costs by public utilities and will require less land and thereby preserve vistas and open space.

Policy Objectives:

(a) Adopt land use policies and regulations that provide incentives for the clustering of development and requirements for the dedication of open space.

(b) Adopt land use policies and regulations that encourage clustered development in locations that are highly serviceable with public facilities to include transportation, sewer and water services, solid waste disposal, fire and police protection, and locations which are in close proximity to commercial support facilities and places of employment.

Goal 4: *Maintain a fiscally healthy community.*

Only private development which provides adequate revenues to cover the anticipated increases in capital and operating costs for local governmental services should be encouraged. Careful design should be applied to each development to ensure public cost efficiencies.

Policy Objectives:

(a) Encourage efficiencies in the design of new development that will minimize public service costs.

(b) Encourage land uses which minimize school and municipal tax burdens.

(c) Coordinate municipal capital budgeting in anticipation of development.

Goal 5: *Develop a reliable, attractive and cost-effective public transportation system to reduce the use of the private automobile as an exclusive transportation system.*

With the growth in population that is anticipated for Snowmass Village, it will be in the best interests of air quality preservation, aesthetically pleasing resort design, and the development of a quality lifestyle in the community for tourists and permanent residents to minimize auto travel and enhance the use of public transportation. It will be necessary also to ensure that development which is typically serviceable by transit is located to take advantage of practical transit routes.

Policy Objectives:

(a) Seek the cooperation of all appropriate public and private entities in the development of a transit system between the Town and the airport, the City of Aspen and down valley destinations. This system should provide frequent and dependable service.

(b) Land use policies and regulations be developed to ensure that new multifamily and commercial development is located in areas that encourage pedestrian movement but in any event are serviceable by public transit.

(c) Develop a system of cross-country ski, pedestrian, equestrian, and bike trails removed from motorized vehicles where feasible, connecting major points of interest, places of employment, commercial centers and recreational sites within the Town. Easements should be acquired by virtue of the development process or purchased when not achievable through land dedication requirements.

(d) Develop an efficient and effective intra-Snowmass transportation service as well as the valley-wide, Aspen Airport–Snowmass Village system.

(e) Establish road systems and standards that will maximize the movement of people, goods and services safely and quickly with minimum impact to the environment.

Goal 6: *Preserve open space and recreational opportunities.*

Development should take place in a manner that preserves significant amounts of active and passive open space lands. The overall integration of public and private open spaces into a larger integrated system shall be encouraged. A wide range of outdoor recreational experiences on public lands shall be encouraged.

Policy Objectives:

(a) Provide incentives for open space preservation and dedication via the development process.

(b) Optimize the utilization of institutional lands for open space purposes.

(c) Develop a mechanism to accept donations of "conservation easements" or less than fee interests in land for the purpose of preserving open space and providing tax advantages to private landowners.

(d) Develop, with time, an open space acquisition program in furtherance of a specific open space plan.

(e) Develop outdoor recreational facilities and programs that take advantage of multiple uses of the land without reducing the quality of open space.

Goal 7: *Study skiing expansion to provide adequate mountain capacity for anticipated skiing demand increases.*

With the projections for growth in tourist visitations and permanent residents, the skiing capacity of the Snowmass Village ski area will have to be analyzed to ensure a skiing experience of the existing quality. Public transportation and services in general will be encouraged to provide a high level of support to sites selected for new lift construction and adjacent residential and commercial development.

Policy Objectives:

(a) Create a constructive and cooperative planning context for evaluating skiing expansion alternatives, including specifically Burnt Mountain.

(b) Develop a cooperative planning process with representatives of the Snowmass Skiing Corporation to harmonize mountain planning requirements with that of real estate development.

(c) Appropriate mountain expansion should be encouraged when required to accommodate increased skiing demand resulting from the long-range development of Snowmass Village.

Goal 8: *To provide a climate for the attraction and retention of quality employees as an integral part of the development of the Snowmass Village community.*

The inevitable inflationary pressure in the cost of all goods created by tourism and the present high cost of residential property are creating an environment which is increasingly less attractive to prospective permanent residents and employees. A critical element is the need to create non-market housing for local employees. Present conditions require employees to live in other areas, creating serious traffic problems on Highway 82, Brush Creek Road and Owl Creek Road. This arrangement has caused some employee dissatisfaction with the community and transience, high turnover and a potential general reduction in the quality of services are largely a result of poor employee housing provisions and related employment conditions. Positive steps must be taken to reverse this situation by affording good working conditions, maximum recreational opportunities and a chance for comfortable, serviceable and affordable housing.

Policy Objectives:

(a) Adopt policies and regulations that recognize the need for affordable employee permanent moderate housing, long-term rental units and seasonal rental housing and reserve such housing for employees on a continuing basis.

(b) The Town should actively encourage the use of federal housing grants via FHA and HUD whenever feasible and appropriate.

(c) The development process itself should contribute a fixed percentage of dwelling units for individuals of low and moderate income.

(d) That mechanisms be pursued to qualify the Town of Snowmass Village for Federal and State housing grants and to continue studying local housing needs and provide recommendations on individual development submissions.

(e) All steps should be taken to provide a season skiing pass opportunity for local employees.

(f) Local employers should be encouraged to provide housing directly for their employees.

(g) Cultural, educational and recreational opportunities should be extended year-round to create a greater sense of permanent community and provide opportunities for greater stability in the working population of the community.

Goal 9: *In the development of the Town of Snowmass Village, all efforts should be directed to the conservation of water.*

The strict application of water conservation measures will provide benefits to the municipality, the water district, local residents and the broader community of Western Colorado. Reduced consumption will ensure adequate supplies for years to come to handle all anticipated demand and will provide for smooth management by the Town and water district. Reduced consumption will result in savings for local water users. Finally, reduced consumption will enhance stream flow and water quality to help area aesthetics and fisheries management.

Policy Objectives:

(a) Support the institution of water metering on all new construction requiring water and the phasing in of meters for existing Snowmass Village water users.

(b) Encourage, where appropriate, the use of indigenous species of vegetation in new construction landscaping to minimize water consumption and discourage and regulate, if necessary, the irrigation of lawns and gardens.

(c) Encourage conservation through an inverted price structure which will provide clear benefits to users of less water.

(d) Encourage innovative architecture, general design solutions and water-saving devices which may depart from traditional design in the attempt to save water.

Goal 10: *Develop a comprehensive, year-round community.*

As development proceeds, attention must be paid to the economic functioning of the community with special emphasis on non-winter activities.

Policy Objectives:

(a) Provision should be made for non-ski related recreational, conference and cultural facilities to keep pace with the development of residential and ski expansion in order to provide a viable year-round economy.

(b) The municipality should provide leadership in a cooperative effort with other appropriate organizations and entities, both public and private, to assure effective promotional and marketing programs for the valley on an equitable basis.

Goal 11: *Encourage conservation of all forms of energy.*

The conservation of energy has become an absolute necessity to preserve and enhance the high quality of living standard that now exists in Snowmass Village and the country as a whole. It is a national crisis that will undoubtedly be with us for many years. The Town should fully exploit every existing as well as new innovative solutions to this major problem in all future development activities.

Policy Objectives:

(a) Formulate design criteria to promote solar energy and all other appropriate forms of self-renewing energy sources.

(b) Establish and enforce building codes to promote conservation and to encourage present energy-saving design standards to be updated.

APPENDIX M

Example of Facility Standards Per Participant
(Will vary in any given situation)

Facility and Standard

Swimming Pool. 27 sq. ft. of surface area for each swimmer with a ratio of 2 sq. ft. of deck area per sq. ft. of water surface; 45 sq. ft. per person for teaching purposes, and 15 sq. ft. of water surface for each bather (water less than 5 ft. deep).

Golf Course. 9-hole: 350 persons or less per day with minimum size of 50 acres.
18-hole: over 350 persons per day with minimum size of 110 acres.

Tennis. Outdoor: 1 court for 60 players if there is a reservation system; more if lighted.
Outdoor: 1 court for 20 to 40 players without a reservation system.

Clubhouse/Lodge. 7 sq. ft. per person.
Community Kitchen. 200 sq. ft. per occupant.
Dance Floor. 7 sq. ft. per occupant.
Lodge Room. 7 sq. ft. per occupant.
Equestrian. 1 horse per mile.

Lake/Boating. 20 acres of surface water per power boat.
Skiing. 1 ski boat per 40 acres of surface water.
Ramp. 1 acre of ground space for 40 boats per day.
Beach. 150 sq. ft. of water for each swimmer in the water. 75 sq. ft. of land for each swimmer not in the water.

Fishing
Boating. 4 acres of water area per boat.

Park/Playground
Playlot. 10 to 20 families.
Playground. 40 to 100 families.

Recreation Building
Locker Room. 50 sq. ft. per occupant.
Assembly Room. 15 sq. ft. per occupant.

Hiking
Nature trail. 50 people per mile of trail.

Sauna/Jacuzzi. 1 person sitting for each 2 ft.; 8 by 10 ft. sauna for 9 people; average time per person is 15 to 20 minutes a day.

Skiing. 1 acre of ski slope for 20 to 30 skiers; parking of 1 acre for each 10 acres of ski slope to accommodate 75 autos.

Ski Lifts. Aerial tramway, 450 persons per hour; Gondola, 500 per hour; Double chair lift, 1,000 per hour; T-bar, 1,000 per hour; Convertible T-bar, 1,000 per hour; Convertible chair lift, 350 per hour; Disc type, 750 per hour; Trainer (traction) lift, 600 per hour; rope tow, 1,000 per hour.

Source:

De Chiara, Joseph, and Koppelmann Lee. *Urban Planning and Design Criteria.* New York: Van Nostrand Reinhold Company, second edition, 1975.

U.S. Tennis Association. *Tennis Courts.* New York: U.S. Tennis Association Facilities Committee.

International Conference of Building Officials. *Uniform Building Code.* Whittier, California: author, 1976 edition.

Cecil Ellis Sauna Corporation, Connecticut, 1978.

APPENDIX N

Recommendations for Developing a Major Ski Project in the Rocky Mountains

Success of a major project will always depend on the quality of the skiing offered. The skiing is not an amenity, but the major reason for the project. The market acceptance of the skiing offered will determine in large part the success or failure of the project.

Criteria for a successful ski mountain must be adhered to as closely as possible. They are:

1. Vertical Drop
3,000 feet or more.
2. Orientation
Magnetic north to northeast. Avoid northwest.
3. Slopes
Average 20 to 24 percent slope grade, top to bottom with interesting terrain.
4. Snow
Must be dependable from November to April.
5. Cover
60 percent or more original tree cover, to protect trails.
6. Surface
Free of rocks, ledges, obstructing features such as cliffs or deep gulches.
7. Wind
Evidence and history of light to medium average wind conditions.
8. Elevation
Base: Colorado, 8,000 feet minimum.
Montana/Wyoming, 7,000 feet minimum.
New Mexico, 9,000 feet minimum.
9. Terrain
Must provide for all classes of skier. Require good beginner location at bottom (14 percent slope).
10. Village/Lodging
Must be as close to skiing as possible; on lower ski slopes is desirable.
11. Water/Sewer
Property must have adequate deeded water rights to support development, or these rights must be acquired. Developer must plan for appropriate sewage treatment facilities. If land is available, lagoon systems with treatment may be possible.
12. Location
Preferably accessible to interstate highways and within reasonable distance of an airline or feeder served airport. Although at present ski customers will arrive primarily by car, major investors will arrive by air.

The locational criteria indicate that the ski mountain will probably be located on federal land, in most cases administered by the U.S. Forest Service.

Forest Service approval of a 30-year permit for skiing facilities will require extensive feasibility studies acceptable to the Service. Current practice such as at Beaver Creek in Vail, Colorado, suggests that it will take 6 to 10 years before the permit is granted, although if the public wants the ski project, this period could be shortened. Attacks by environmentalists could also lengthen the period.

The process of requesting a 30-year permit cannot be started until the developer acquires land adjacent to a ski mountain, thus generating large holding costs, unless land can be acquired with allowances for this problem.

Operated properly, the ski facilities can produce a 30 to 35 percent annual cash flow based on sales. The developer should hire professionals to run the ski operation and should retain the operation after build-out is complete. The Forest Service will renew the term permit indefinitely, under present rules.

The developer will face financing problems due to the ski development's location on federal land. In the past, federal agencies such as the Small Business Administration or Farmers Home Administration have guaranteed some funds. The financing requirements for the skiing development, plus high front-end costs for mountain village development, seem to indicate that the most successful developer would be a large corporate type with diversified interests, several limited partnerships of financially able individuals, or similarly qualified joint ventures.

Construction will be demanding because of the short building season. Experienced people must be used in all phases—mountain and village development, planning, roads, etc. Contractors and builders must also be experienced. Construction schedules will not only be tight, but also sources of materials will be at a distance. Conflicts between various elements of the project during construction must be avoided by accurate scheduling and by retention of overall planning/building control in early phases of project.

The approval process will be very slow. Forest Service planners considering a grant of a 30-year term permit will try to enforce constraints on the developer, having to do with parking, access, densities, and design limitations. Some states such as Colorado require a joint review by Forest Service, state, and county officials before approval of the project. The difficulty in obtaining approvals will be reflected by current development levels in the particular county and state. Some Colorado counties already have downzoning and growth controls. Others, with little or no development, are eager for projects. Because of a project's dependence on the Forest Service, a developer must understand how to negotiate with this particular branch of the U.S. Department of Agriculture.

INDEX

Absorption rates, 86, 111; over long term, 213
Access, in design, 50; and site selection, 37; to theme parks, 157
Access rights, of nonproperty owners, 58
Accounting, dinner theaters, 189
Active recreation: highly marketable, 174; and mini-theme parks, 155
Activities: as key attractions, 26; subsidized, 116
Activities director, 143
Activity center, 76, 111
Activity program, recreational vehicle park, 144
Actors' Equity Association, 188
Aesthetics, and industry, 213
Advertising: direct mail, 143; highlighting recreational activities, 10; institutional, 96; through master program, 139; media and projecting lifestyle, 10; and specialty shopping center expenditures, 208; theme parks, 161. *See also* Marketing.
Ahwahnee Resort Hotel, The, 69
Air travel, 5, 221
Airport, private, 107
Allocating development costs, 104
Amelia Island Plantation, 57, 70–75
Amenities: accustomed to, 9; as adjuncts, 198 (*See also* Supplemental recreation); as advertising focus, 78; centralized, 131, 134; clustered, 110; combination, 3; community responsibility for, 220; and condominium rentals, 36; cost effectiveness, 47; and the cyclical nature of real estate, 36; as essential attractions, 4; and existing consumer traffic, 38; and hotel chains, 220; overbuilding, 59; in permanent home communities, 16; preliminary step, 35; profit from operation, 36; and project phasing, 37; promises of, 38; proximity, 2; with reasonable rents, 204; at recreational vehicle parks, 63; in resort marketing, 56; and retirement communities, 62; self-supporting, 78; social, 202; standards of quality, 36; subsidized for lot sales programs, 36; subsidizing of, 36; and timesharing, 140; turnover agreement, 136
Amenities in real estate development. *See* Supplemental recreation.
Amenity package, 35–36; careful design of, 136; and conference centers, 65; and the surrounding community, 36
American Dinner Theater Institute, 188
American Planning Association, 63
Amfac, 88, 92, 93
Amusement parks, 13. *See also* Theme parks.
Anchor tenants, 207
Anheuser-Busch, 168
Appreciation, and speculators, 16
Approval process, resort/residential communities, 48–49
Aquatic parks, 172
Arcades, 181, 194
Architecture: derived theme, 118; local, 124; variety, 112
Arvida, 123, 126, 127
Arvida Park of Commerce, 211
Aspen Ski Corporation, 115, 116
Associations, in promoting recreation, 179
Athletic facility, and business parks, 211
Attendance projections, theme parks, 160
Attractions, proximity to, 74. *See also* Theme parks.
Automobile vacation, long distance, 220
Average incomes, 204, 225. *See also* Moderate incomes.

Banff Springs Hotel, 11
Bankers Trust, 149
Baseball, professional, 176
Beach attractions, 71
Beaver Creek, 48, 117–119
Bicycle paths, 109
Blue Ridge Real Estate Company, 120, 122
Boca Raton Hotel, 123
Boca West, 123–128
Bowling center, 180–181
Bowling Proprietors' Association of America, 180
Broadmoor, The, 65, 66
Builder/developers: 126; discounts to, 148; land sales to, 40
Building codes, second homes, 29
Building dwelling units, a development strategy, 40
Buildings, pre-engineered metal, 182
Build-out rate, 13
Bulk land sales, 91, 127
Business plan, 149; flexibility, 41
Buyer confidence: from early completion of amenities, 203; lack of, 149
Buyer profile, 117
Buyer skepticism, 113

Campgrounds; advertisement of, 29; private, 29. *See also* Recreational vehicle parks.
Camping, USA, 62
Canada's Wonderland, 162, 163
Capacity studies, 44
Cape May, 11
Capital-intensive recreational development and government role, 225
Carrying costs, 127
Cascades, The, 207–209
Cash flow, 119
Central sewer system, 133
Chain operator, racquetball club, 186
Changing markets, 17
Chanhassen Dinner Theaters, 189
Cleanliness, 167
Climate, in consumer choices, 33
Club atmosphere, in marketing, 148
Club Med, 226
Club membership, 133
Clubhouse, as recreational focal point, 200
Clubs: attraction of comfortable amenities, 184; campground, 30; consumer ownership of, 31; parking at, 184
Clustered facilities, in large projects, 198
Clustering of development, 110
Coastal amenity, 35; and site selection, 37
Coastal sea islands, 83
Commercial facilities, at resort, 81, 86, 92
Commercial hotel, 25–26
Commercial recreation, 175–195; attendance drop after first year, 192; competition, 178; definition, 3; financing, 177; location, 176; management, 178; market, 176; profit centers, 177; risks, 176
Common area, leased for recreational use, 205
Communications, and vacation markets, 226
Community analysis, 48
Community association, 57-60
Community building, 34, 110; versus unimproved lot sales, 20
Community center, focus for activity, 202
Community impacts, 19–20; theme parks, 160
Community preference, 20
Community relations. *See* Public involvement.
Community services, transition from developer responsibility, 58
Competition, 178–179; from high-amenity primary home PUDs, 198
Competitive projects, survey of, 85
Concept: and desired image, 34; matched with site, 36
Concept planning, 33; theme park, 168
Condominium, definition, 30
Condotel, 31
Coney Island, 11
Conference centers and resort/recreational communities, 65–68
Conference facilities, 74
Conferences, 131
Conflict negotiation, 91
Construction: and competition for resources, 87; contracted, 100; cost economics in, 37; using subdeveloper or developer, 40; financing, 46; momentum, 148; of resort/residential communities, 53–54; of theme parks, 170; at an urban scale, 29
Construction costs: escalation of, 22; and rehabilitation, 69; in remote places, 97; and site selection, 37
Construction funds, theme parks, 161
Consultants, 42, 109; team of, 82. *See also* Development team.
Consumer: abuses, 13; demands, 60; and desired image, 22; dispositions, 218; expenditures and competition for, 226; financing, 223; instability, 18; locational preferences, 22; spending in the 1970s, 217; tastes, 57
Contingencies, in a business plan, 68
Contracted management, 58
Convention center, 122
Conversion of buildings to nonrecreational uses, 185
Cooling off period, 14
Cooperative planning, 49
Corporate identification, 168
Cost effectiveness, 226
Cost estimates, 45
Cost of travel, 221
Country clubs, as status symbol, 9
Countryside Mall, 205
Covenants, 77; and enforcement, 58; with ownership, 30
Critical mass, 119

Deed restrictions, 136. *See also* Covenants.
Definition of recreational development as real estate development, 1–3
Demand, 4–11; consumer, 16; for family experience, 9; and forecasts of downtown, 16; and future, 218, 219; growth in, 15; history, 10–11; and mobility, 5; psychological, 8–10; related to free time, 4; related to income, 4; in United States, 11
Demographic patterns, in United States, 219
Demographics, 122; and retirement, 60; U.S. shifts, 32
Density, 110
Dependence on real estate values, 18
Depression, The Great, 12; and theme parks, 153; and miniature golf, 192
Design: consistency, 78; continuity, 213; details, 50, 52, 53; dinner theaters, 188; in the '80s, 221; over irregular terrain, 170; through questionnaires, 113; resort/recreational communities, 43, 44; retirement communities, 62; second homes, 28
Design control, Sunriver Design Committee, 106
Design criteria, establishing, 44
Design days, 160
Design standards, 52
Destination: recreational vehicle parks, 63; value of, 221
Destination resort, 95; theme park, 164
Destinations, creating, 32
Developer: as building contractor, 110; bulk lot, 88; commitment to public involvement, 117; contracting of services, 222; long-term control, 213; patience, 224; transfer of skills, 117; of year-round community, 116
Developer: commitment, 148; promises, 109, 135
Developer role, 34; and financing, 222
Development: momentum of, 127; and need for managerial commitment, 47
Development codes, and provision of recreation, 198
Development costs, and site selection, 37
Development management, 41, 81, 109, 222, 223
Development phasing, 37–38
Development practices, government role in upgrading, 224
Development process: new home tract, 106; resort/recreational communities, 33–60
Development standards: recreational vehicle parks, 63; supporting concept, 34
Development strategies, resort/recreational communities, 40, 41
Development team, 41, 42, 50, 80, 85, 223; in-house, 165; marketing person, 54
Diamondhead Corporation, 133
Dinner theaters, 188–189
Dirt sales, 20. *See also* Consumer abuses.
Disclosure of sales contract, 14
Discretionary income, 218
Discretionary market, 65
Discretionary spending, 4, 22, 205
Disneyland, 154, 160
Disneyworld, 3, 33, 37, 155, 158, 172, 222. *See also* Walt Disney World.
Dispersed facilities, low activity levels, 74
Documentation, 50
Documents, community association, 58
Drainage, 124
Driving ranges, golf, 190–191

Eaton Centre, 205
Ecological ethics, and consumer demand, 218
Ecological planning, 71. *See also* Environmental planning.
Economic change, project vulnerability to, 134
Economic concerns: conference centers, 68; market analysis, 42
Economic conditions, and financing, 222
Economic cycles: and commercial recreation, 177; reality of, 17
Economic downturn, carrying cost of buildings, 40
Economic ills, 1970s, 217
Economic return, and supplemental recreation, 197
Economics, of rehabilitation, 69
Employee housing, 20, 49, 97, 115, 118, 225
Employees, training for resort, 107
Empty nesters, 27, 203. *See also* Retirement.
Energy, fuel availability, 15; and the future, 220, 221; gasoline prices effect, 17; and pooled expenses, 221
Energy shortages, effect on demand, 6
Engineering, 134

Entertainment: provided in commercial projects, 205; theme park, 154
Entertainment market, 163
Environment, 224
Environmental assessment, defined, 14
Environmental concerns, with land sales, 13
Environmental impact assessment, 100
Environmental impact statement, 14
Environmental planning, 101, 111
Environmental standards, market appreciation, 74
Environmentally sensitive planning, 38
Equity, 45, 222; racquetball club, 186
Equity in financing, 18, 19
Equity investor, 148
Escape, theme parks as, 169
Existing facilities, higher use of, 23
Existing resorts, built-in amenities, 32

Facilities: for conference centers, 66; dispersed, 71; mix of, 205
Fad, 177
Family recreation centers, 194
Fantasy in recreation, 8
Feasibility: of concept, 33; and planning, 42–45; RV parks, 63
Federal banking rules, 150
Fee simple, 30, 98
Filtering, of use of developments from exclusive to mass market, 22–23
Finance, future of, 222–223
Financial analysis, 44, 45; in workout, 150
Financial middleman, 48
Financial planning, 100
Financing: commercial recreation, 177; consumer, 223, contingencies, 68; creditor options in failure, 149; long-term nature, 46; resort/residential communities, 45–47; roller skating rink, 183; RV parks, 64; workouts, 68
Fire protection, second homes, 28
Fontana, Andrea, 175
Foreign travel to limited states, 5, 220
Foxcross, 137–139
Front-end costs, 132; delayed returns, 15; and low initial returns, 37
Front-end debt, reduced by land sale, 103
Front-end investment, credibility, 109
Fuel. *See* Energy.
Furniture packages, 50
Future land values, and the long-term investor, 36

Galleria, The, 215
Gambling, legalization of, 220
Ghirardellia Square, 206
Glenbrook Inn, 69
Go-cart tracks, 195. *See also* Scale grand prix tracks.
Golf, 36. *See also* Amenities, (and variety of case studies).
Golf, driving ranges, 190–191
Golf, as land consumer, 127
Golf, miniature, 192, 193
Golf course irrigation, treated effluent, 212
Government, 224–225
Government control, of land sales, 13–15
Governmental structure. *See* Home owners and community associations.
Grand Ole Opry, 155
Graphics, 52
Great America, 157
Group business, 66
Group tours, 98
Growth management, 10
Growth regulations, 224–225

Health clubs, 187
Heritage Development Group, 200
Heritage Hills, 200–201
High-amenity second-home communities, growth of, 15
High-rise hotels, primitive locations, 25
High pressure sales, 224
Hilton Hawaiian Village, 26
Home owner associations, 30, 107, 113; dues, 131; three-tiered structure, 125. *See also* Community associations.
Homestead, The, 76–79
Hotel, resort compared with commercial, 25, 26
Hotel Del Coronado, 12
Housing, and retirement communities, 62

Ice rink, in shopping mall, 215
Illustrations, in planning, 44
Image, miniature golf, 192
Image-conscious companies, and recreational setting, 212
Indoor lounge, 199
Indoor tennis, 184
Infilling, at resort/recreational projects, 222
Inflation and demand, 6
Inflation hedge, use of property as, 6
Inflation rate, 222
Inflationary effects, analysis of, 45
Innovation, and the future for recreational development, 226
Instruction, in promoting recreation, 179
Interest rates, 222
Interim land use: for agriculture, 127; as golf driving range, 191; as nursery, 213
Interstate highway system, 5
Interstate registration, 98
Interval ownership, 223. *See also* Timesharing.
Inventory, limited, 83
Inverness, 212–213
Investment, 222–223; and political environment, 220; in second homes, 27, 107
Investment risk, 47; spreading out, 41
Investor-purchaser, 127
Investor units, 74
Investors: in lots, 134; tax advantages, 75
Isolated location, need for building dwelling units, 40

Jack Frost Mountain, 120–122
Jackson Court, 226
Jitney service, 76, 90. *See also* Shuttle bus.
Joint planning, 115. *See also* Cooperative planning.
Joint venture, 41, 80, 159, 165

Kaanapali Beach Operators Association, 89, 91
Kaanapali Beach Resort, 87, 88–91
Kampgrounds of America, 64
Kapalua, 34, 54, 87, 95–97
Kennedy Space Center, 156
Kiawah Island, 82–86
Kings Island, 16, 82–86, 164–167

Lahaina, 87, 88, 91
Lake, manmade. *See* Manmade lakes.
Lake Arrowhead, 133–134
Lakeland Village, 145–146
Lakeridge, 15, 111–114
Land: converted to recreational use, 10; lease, 119; leasing, 122
Land Development Model, 86
Land sales, 13–15, 40
Land merchandisers, 15
Land use, campground feasibility, 140
Land use controls, privately administered, 80
Land values, around theme parks, 160
Landings, The, 52
Landscaping, 71; in business parks, 212; as part of recreational appeal, 202; and theme parks, 157, 162
Layout, alternative schemes, 38
Leagues, in using facilities, 179
Leasable space, making common area productive, 205
Leasehold land, 96
Leasing: arcade machines, 194; short-term for specialty shopping, 208
Legal prerogative, to execute development, 49
Leisure homes. *See* Second homes.
Leisure shopping, 207; as recreation, 8
Leisure time, 4; and hours of work, 218; and shopping, 205
Lender: and developer relationship, 150; in a workout, 69
Lenders, attitude toward single-use buildings, 185
Life cycle of a project, 218
Lifestyles, 226; marketing of, 55; role of recreation in, 218
Limited partnership, 115, 189
Litigation and public involvement, 117
Loans: short-term, 47; failure rate, 47
Location, 110, 184; of commercial recreation, 176; emerging trends in, 219–220; and prime real estate value, 91; of retirement communities, 60; of theme parks, 156–157, 174
Locational characteristics, resort/recreational communities, 32
Lodging, for project viability, 134
Lots, minimum size, 109
Lot sales, 40, 135; controlled and balanced, 20; developer financed, 133; systematic release of, 136; as threat to the environment, 20. *See also* Land sales.
Lot subdivision, 39
Low use sites, for commercial recreation, 184

Maintenance: budgets, 59; monthly assessments, 109; of recreational vehicle parks, 144; and retirement communities, 62; user fees, 59
Malibu Grand Prix, 195
Management: for commercial recreation, 178; entrepreneurial, 177; future, 222–223; to improve roller skating rinks, 182; in programming conferences, 66; and quasi-municipal organizations, 119; of rental programs in recreational community, 57–60; in workouts, 69
Management standards, theme parks, 161
Managing agent, resort condominium, 93
Manmade amenities, golf and tennis profits, 98
Manmade amenity. *See* Created amenity.
Manmade lakes, 135, 138, 140
Marina Village, 140–144
Marine parks, 155
Mariner Sands, 137, 148
Market: buyer types, 83–84; retirement, 61; in workouts, 69
Market analysis, for resort/recreational communities, 42; for theme parks, 156
Market appeal, miniature golf, 192
Market surveys, 113, 131; for appropriate products, 35; for commercial recreation, 178
Marketability, and site selection, 37
Marketing: aggressive tactics, 21; analyses, 33; communicating with buyers, 132; confidence in developer, 96; cooperative, 224; coordinated, 139; cost-to-sales effectiveness, 55; flexibility, 113; follow-up, 57; future of, 223–224; identity for industry, 213; in-house operations of, 110; off-site sales costs, 146; as merchandising, 223; and rental programs, 59; umbrella, 127
Marketing, lifestyle, 113
Marketing, resort/residential communities, 54–57
Marketing, roller skating rinks, 183
Marketing, theme parks, 160
Marketing, timesharing, 31
Marketing, using resort promotion for real estate sales, 56
Marketing statement, through environmental consciousness, 38
Marketing tools: an attractive entrance, 148; emphasis on club activities, 126; quality of facilities, 224; of supplemental recreation, 197
Markets, meetings, 65
Markups on real estate, 55
Marriott Corporation, 157
Master developer, 90, 98, 100; control, 116, 139
Master plan. See Overall plan.
Maturing population, and demand, 218
Maui, Hawaiian Island projects, 87–100
Maui Land & Pineapple Company, Inc., 95
Membership, racquetball court, 184
Merchandising, lifestyle, 224. See Marketing.
Middle-income consumer, 219
Miniature golf, 192–193; indoor course, 193
Mobile homes, in retirement communities, 62
Mobility, 220–221
Moderate income, recreational opportunities, 22
Moderate-income consumers, 57
Moderate-income market, 62
Modular design, for expansion, 169
Moss Creek Plantation, 43, 51
Mountain Bell Training and Education Center, 68
Mountains, as an attraction, 33
Move-up units, for retirees, 218

National American Corporation, 136
National Environmental Policy Act, 14
National Golf Foundation, 190, 192
National Travel Survey, 7
Natural amenities, 38; fundamental, 101
Natural resources, strained, 10
Negative cash flow, 46
Negative leverage, 18
New attractions, theme parks, 166
New concept roller skating rink, 182
Newsletters, 56, 144
Northstar at Tahoe, 18

Occupancies, and timesharing, 223
Ocean City, 15–16
Ocean cruises, 222
Office of Interstate Land Sales Registration, 13, 32
Oil embargo, effect on recreation, 15
Older city areas, resurgence of, 220
Old Country, The, 168–171
Omni International, 205
One-stop destinations, 221; and hotel chains, 220
Open space, 123, 129; and American heritage, 14; and government role, 225; as recreational amenity, 199; in planning, 39
Operations: as part of a development strategy, 40–41; profit centers, 80; profits from amenities, 36; theme parks, 171
Operating expenses, and specialty center tenants, 208
Ordinances, 125
Oregon Public Utility Commission, 105
Orlando, 33
Outdoor activities, desire for, 8
Overall plan, 45; resort/recreational community, 50–54

Overall scale, of resort/recreational development, 40
Overbuilding, 91; and commercial recreation, 177; bowling centers, 180
Ownership: recreational vehicle parks, 30, 64; timesharing, 16; types of, 30–31. *See also* Fee simple, condominium, timeshare, and clubs.

Packaged promotions, 224
Parking, 50, 111, 142; commercial recreation, 182, 187, 190, 192; theme park, 170
Participation, 22; in outdoor recreation, 6
Participatory recreation, 175; and theme parks, 158. *See also* Commercial recreation.
Partnerships, with government, 225
Passive recreation, 166; and theme parks, 155
Personal health, 9
Phasing, 46; and the community association, 59; of supplemental recreational facilities, 197; in specialty retail center, 210
Phoenix MacNab Properties, 137
Physical analysis, of site, 43
Plan of action, 48
Plan to completion, Kiawah Island, 85–86
Planned community and recreational amenities, 197
Planned unit development, 39, 123, 148
Planning: approaches to resort/recreational community, 38–40; attention to detail, 60; recreational vehicle parks, 141
Pointe, The, 129–132
Political data, use of, 49
Political process, in workout, 69
Politics, 19; sense of public investment in private project, 49
Portola Valley, 199
Post and beam construction, 130; foundations, 113
Preservation, 49; as sales tool, 79; at theme park, 170
Privacy, second homes, 29
Products: alternatives, 127; range of, 124, 131
Pro forma statement, 45; bowling center, 181; racquetball club, 186; roller skating rink, 183
Professional services, 41, 60. *See also* Development team.
Professionalism, 179
Profit centers, 41; arcade, 194; commercial recreation, 177; recreation clubs, 185
Project image, 54; quality construction, 53; supported in detailed design, 50
Project standards, maintaining through operations, 81
Project team, 208
Promotion. *See* Marketing, Advertising.
Property, desire to own, 6
Property maintenance, demand for problem-free environment, 9
Property owners' association, 136. *See also* Home owners' community associations.
Property rentals, 56
Public confidence, by spending money, 150
Public land, leased, 225
Public review, delays from, 15; Hawaii, 99, 100
Pyramid Place, 219

Qualified buyers, attracted through resort operations, 84
Quincy Market, 206

Racquetball club: management of, 186; membership fees for, 186; expenses for, 186
Racquetball courts, 184–186
Real estate investment trusts, 15, 149
Real estate values, created, 80
Real property ownership, desire for, 218
Reception centers, 55, 72, 117
Recession 1974–75, 94, 134, 149
Recreation: in commercial projects, 205, 211; as escape, 8; as necessity, 217; perceived rights of, 18; as relaxation, 8
Recreational communities, evolving character of (e.g., into retirement), 3
Recreational facility, in large resort area, 18; in isolated area, 18
Recreational land booms, 12
Recreational land subdivisions: local oversight, 14; low density, 13
Recreational land uses, as a buffer, 197
Recreational residential communities, definition of, 3
Recreational vehicle, 29
Recreational vehicle parks, 62–65; development, 63; financing, 64; ownership, 64; types, 63
Recreational vehicles: leasing of, 64; on single-family lots, 135; storage of, 142
Recreational vehicle sites: available for purchase, 30; at campgrounds, 29
Recycled building materials, savings from, 211
Redevelopment, 222
Reduced work week, 4
Register of declaration, condominium, 30
Regulation, protection of public and private, 21
Regulation, time-consuming aspects, 21
Regulations, cataloging, 48; environmental, 224; thwarting development, 127
Regulatory conditions, change in, 49
Rehabilitation costs, 69
Rental: of second homes, 27; of RV sites, 64; and workouts, 146–147
Rental pool, 67; and conferences, 65
Rental program, 59, 107; adequate rates, 81; condominiums, 93–94; management, 73, 78; SEC registration, 59
Resale market, 78
Resident mix, 127
Resort: combined attractions, 25; commercial facilities, 81; as created destination, 32; experience oriented, 25; and real estate sales, 1; self-contained (island), 88; services, 80; as setting for conferences, 65; use mixed with second homes, 73
Resort Condominiums International, 129
Resort diversification, 81
Resort programs, 126, 127
Resort/residential communities, 26; definition of, 1–3, 25; separating private homes from resort guests, 109
Restrictions, and new project sites, 224
Retail operations, as leisure time attractions, 218, 227
Retirement: custom built homes for, 28; effect on demand, 6; and second homes, 27; segment of population, 218
Retirement communities, 60–62; country club setting, 8
Return on investment, bowling center, 181
Ride parks. *See* Theme parks.
Rights-of-way, 212
Risk: commercial recreation, 176; and interest rates, 119; new resort/recreational development, 220. *See also* Investment risk.
Roads: looped, 142; along natural contours, 111; private, 104
Roller skating, 176; rinks, 182, 183
Roller Skating Rink Operators Association, 182
Rossmoor Leisure World, 61
Rotonda, The, 202–203
Rural areas, 140; approval process for, 48; lack of services, 9; lot sales, 40; weak controls in, 14

Safety, golf driving ranges, 190
Sales, by referral, 113, 143
Sales center, 55
Sales procedures, resort/recreational communities, 55
Sales staff, incentives, 55
Sales tools, resort/recreational communities, 56
Scale grand prix tracks, 194, 195
Sea islands, coastal southeast, 70
Sea Pines Company, 70, 82
Sea Pines Plantation, 32, 39, 43, 47, 53, 54, 56, 66, 222; coastal resort/recreation community, 80–81
Seasonal activity, sales, 10
Seasonal demand, 19
Seasonal homes. *See* Second homes.
Seasonal occupancy, 81
Seasonal staff, theme park, 165
Second homes: characteristics, 28, 29; costs to owner, 19; as investment, 27; location, 27; retirement, 27; seasonal, 27; U.S., 32
Second-home communities. *See* Recreational residential communities.
Securities and Exchange Commission, 59, 145
Security, 36, 50, 110, 131, 148; and retirement communities, 62; roller skating rink, 183
Services: cost of conferences, 67; food, 206; rental management, 129; retirement communities, 60; second homes, 28
Sesame Place, 159
Setbacks, from ocean, 88
Signage, 52, 91, 111
Silverado Country Club, 65, 67
Single-family units, expense, 116
Single use projects, 177
Site, bowling center development, 181
Site development: recreational parks, 63; retirement communities, 61
Site planning, 52–53
Site selection: resort/recreational communities, 36–37; theme parks, 156
Siting: determines appropriate product, 99; hierarchy of preferred, 38; second homes, 28; on steep grades, 97, 201
Ship cruises, 221
Shopping, thematic, 165
Shuttle bus, 72; mass transportation, 116
Skateboard parks, 177
Ski permit, 118
Ski rental, 121
Skiing. *See* Snowmass, Beaver Creek, Jack Frost Mountain, Lakeridge, and Wintergreen.
Small developers in larger community, 139
Small-scale theme park, 172–174
Small tenants, in specialty shopping center, 206
Snowmaking, 121
Snowmass, 115–117
Social atmosphere, 202
Softball fields, 211
Sources of money, 46
South Lake Tahoe Visitors' Bureau, 146
Specialists, theme park, 158
Specialized activities, 230. *See also* Target markets.
Specialized facilities, financing, 46
Specialized projects, 218
Specialized recreation, trend towards, 219
Specialty retail, theme, 92
Specialty shopping centers, 205–211
Spectator entertainment. *See* Passive recreation.
Speculation, land, 13
Square footage, trade-off with amenities, 204
Staffing, at retirement communities, 62
Stages of development. *See* Development phasing.
Starter product, 126
State Land Use Commission, Hawaii, 99
Staying power, 127
Streets, hammerhead, 52; double T, 53
Subdevelopers, 52, 115. *See also* Builders/developers.
Suburban locations, dinner theaters, 188
Sunbelt land forms, 53
Sunpointe, 204
Sunriver, 101–110
Sunriver Utility Company, 105
Supplemental recreation, 197–219; adding value to real estate, 197; definition, 3; commercial/retail, 205–211; industrial/business parks, 211; mixed-use development, 215; and primary residential projects, 198–204.

Taft Broadcasting Company, 162, 164
Target advertising, 56
Target, nonlocal consumer, 220
Target markets, 54; commercial recreation, 176; recreation and primary residential, 198; specialized activities, 22; theme parks, 160
Tax: abatement, 163; assessments, 208; base; 10; benefits, 41
Technology: advances in, 218; and leisure time, 175; theme park, 153
Television, as competition, 188
Tennis, 36. *See also* Amenities (and case studies).
Theater: in specialty shopping centers, 206; theme parks, 160
Theme parks, 17, 153–174; architecture of, 154; cleanliness, 167, 172; clustered attractions, 157; community impact 160; and competition, 155; construction, 158; definition, 3, 154; design, 158; educational attractions, 165; as entertainment, 154; financial aspects, 161; group rentals, 166; location, 174; mini-parks, 155; marketing, 160; sites, 156.
Themed attraction, water, 3
Timeshare conversions, 226
Timesharing, 76; concept of, 30, 31; exchange program, 30, 31, 140; financing, 30, 31; future, 223; marketing, 16, 30, 31; owners' association, 141; ownership, 16; profile of, 30, 31; recreational vehicle parks, 64, 140; reselling memberships, 144; yield, 30, 31
Tourism, 217, 225; employment, 7; and small business, 7
Tourist orientation, of specialty shopping center, 211
Town of Snowmass Village, 115
Trade-offs, quantity and quality, 54
Traditional shopping center versus specialty center, 205
Train service, 142. *See also* Shuttle bus.
Travel: auto 12, 13; reasons for, 7
Treasure Lake, 135–136
Trolley parks, 11. *See also* Theme parks.
Trolley Square, 210–211

Uncontested market, 190
Undeveloped land, use of, 167. *See also* Interim land use.
Unit clustering, 39
Unit exchange, timesharing, 30
U.S. Department of Housing and Urban Development, 13
U.S. Federal Trade Commission, 14
U.S. Forest Service, 101, 103
U.S. National Park Service, 12
U.S. tax laws, 27
Units, single-family, attached, townhouses, 29
Universal Studios Tour, 155
Upgrading older facilities, 90
Urban recreation. *See* Commercial recreation.
User conflicts, reducing with operating practices, 227
User fees, 59
Utilities, 72; availability fees, 136; public utility districts, 136; recreational vehicle parks, 63, 144

Vail Associates, 117
Value, to consumer, 218, 223
Variations in zoning, 185
Vehicle storage, recreational vehicle parks, 64
View orientations, enhanced by amenities, 198
Village center, 111
Village concept, pedestrian scale, 39
Village Resorts, Inc., 146
Villages, 74, 82; residential, 123; theme parks, 169
Visibility: and impulse demand, 179; from the street, 173

Waikiki, 25
Wailea, 87, 98–100
Walt Disney, 13, 154, 158
Walt Disney World, 5, 154, 172, 226. *See also* Disneyworld.
Water, as the major attraction, 33, 171
Wave pool, 3, 172
Weekend retreat, 27. *See also* Second homes.
Westinghouse Credit Corporation, 135
Wet' n Wild, 3, 172–174
Whaler, The, condominium project, 93–94
Whalers Village Shopping Complex, 92
Wilderness, The, 40
Wintergreen, 149–151
Workouts: definition of, 68, 69; management of, 68, 69; in resort/residential communities, 145–151; strategy, 68, 69; turnaround management program, 146–147

Year-long use, 19; occupancies, 110
Year-round destination, 76. *See also* Destination.
Yield, timesharing, 31

Zoning, 88, 99; and commercial recreation, 182, 185; overzoned land, 115

Metric Conversion Table

Meters	=	feet × 0.305
Kilometers	=	miles × 1.609
Square Meters	=	square feet × 0.093
Square Kilometers	=	square miles × 2.590
Cubic Meters	=	cubic feet × 0.028
Cubic Meters	=	cubic yards × 0.765
Hectares	=	acres × 0.405
(a hectare is 10,000 square meters)		